Plains Histories

John R. Wunder, *Series Editor*

ALSO IN PLAINS HISTORIES

America's 100th Meridian: A Plains Journey, by Monte Hartman
American Outback: The Oklahoma Panhandle in the Twentieth Century, by Richard Lowitt
As a Farm Woman Thinks: Life and Land on the Texas High Plains, 1890–1960, by Nellie Witt Spikes; edited by Geoff Cunfer
Children of the Dust: An Okie Family Story, by Betty Grant Henshaw; edited by Sandra Scofield
The Death of Raymond Yellow Thunder: And Other True Stories from the Nebraska–Pine Ridge Border Towns, by Stew Magnuson
Flood on the Tracks: Living, Dying, and the Nature of Disaster in the Elkhorn River Basin, by Todd M. Kerstetter
Food, Control, and Resistance: Rationing of Indigenous Peoples in the United States and South Australia, by Tamara Levi
Free Radical: Ernest Chambers, Black Power, and the Politics of Race, by Tekla Agbala Ali Johnson
From Syria to Seminole: Memoir of a High Plains Merchant, by Ed Aryain; edited by J'Nell Pate
"I Do Not Apologize for the Length of This Letter": The Mari Sandoz Letters on Native American Rights, 1940–1965, edited by Kimberli A. Lee
Law at Little Big Horn: Due Process Denied, by Charles E. Wright
Nikkei Farmer on the Nebraska Plains: A Memoir, by The Reverend Hisanori Kano; edited by Tai Kreidler
The Notorious Dr. Flippin: Abortion and Consequence in the Early Twentieth Century, by Jamie Q. Tallman
Oysters, Macaroni, and Beer: Thurber, Texas, and the Company Store, by Gene Rhea Tucker
Railwayman's Son: A Plains Family Memoir, by Hugh Hawkins
Rights in the Balance: Free Press, Fair Trial, and Nebraska Press Association v. Stuart, by Mark R. Scherer
Route 66: A Road to America's Landscape, History, and Culture, by Markku Henriksson
Ruling Pine Ridge: Oglala Lakota Politics from the IRA to Wounded Knee, by Akim D. Reinhardt
Trail Sisters: Freedwomen in Indian Territory, 1850–1890, by Linda Williams Reese

Urban Villages and Local Identities: Germans from Russia, Omaha Indians, and Vietnamese in Lincoln, Nebraska, by Kurt E. Kinbacher
Where the West Begins: Debating Texas Identity, by Glen Sample Ely
A Witness to History: George H. Mahon, West Texas Congressman, by Janet M. Neugebauer
Women on the North American Plains, edited by Renee M. Laegreid and Sandra K. Mathews

A Sacred People

A Sacred People

Indigenous Governance, Traditional Leadership, and the
Warriors of the Cheyenne Nation

LEO K. KILLSBACK

Texas Tech University Press

Copyright © 2020 by Leo K. Killsback

All rights reserved. No portion of this book may be reproduced in any form or by any means, including electronic storage and retrieval systems, except by explicit prior written permission of the publisher. Brief passages excerpted for review and critical purposes are excepted.

This book is typeset in Sabon MT Pro. The paper used in this book meets the minimum requirements of ANSI/NISO Z39.48-1992 (R1997). ∞

On the cover and frontis: *Woir-Oqtuimanists (Man on a Cloud) Peace Medal and Headdress; Unidentified Man Nearby*; 1892. Photograph by James Mooney (1861–1921), National Anthropological Archives, Smithsonian Museum Support Center, Suitland, Maryland (NAA INV 06109800, OPPS NEG 281 B).

Library of Congress Cataloging-in-Publication Data is on file.

ISBN: 978-1-68283-035-2

19 20 21 22 23 24 25 26 27 / 9 8 7 6 5 4 3 2 1

Texas Tech University Press
Box 41037
Lubbock, Texas 79409-1037 USA
800.832.4042
ttup@ttu.edu
www.ttupress.org

For Maela, Leon, and Tasbah

Contents

Illustrations xi
Note on Terminology: Tribe xiii
Preface xv
Acknowledgments xxiii
Introduction xxvii

Part I
Tsėhéstáno: The Cheyenne Nation

CHAPTER 1
Héstanovestôtse: A Living Nation 7

CHAPTER 2
Manahéno: The Bands 27

CHAPTER 3
Tsêhéseamanëö'o: The Cheyenne Cultural Way of Life 49

Part II
Véhoo'o: The Chiefs

CHAPTER 4
Hévese'onematsestôtse: Brotherhood 77

CHAPTER 5
The Origin of the Véhoo'o 89

CHAPTER 6
Véhooneome: The Chiefs' Lodge 109

CONTENTS

CHAPTER 7
Véhoo'o and Political Organization   121

PART III
Nótâxeo'o: The Warriors

CHAPTER 8
Before the Nótâxeo'o   143

CHAPTER 9
The Origins of the Nótâxeo'o   169

CHAPTER 10
Traditions and Customs of the Nótâxeo'o   181

CHAPTER 11
Nótâxeo'o and Political Organization   203

PART IV
Colonizing and Decolonizing the Tséhéstáno

CHAPTER 12
Vé'hó'e: The Trickster   221
Conclusion: Decolonizing "the Rez"   237

Notes   251

Bibliography   271

Index   281

Illustrations

Waatu, "Conqueror"   xix

Cheyenne perceptions of time and history   13

Anonymous Cheyenne drawing of two men performing a ceremony   31

The first four original bands of the Tsétsêhéstâhese   38

The first five bands of the United Cheyenne Nation   44

The ten bands of the United Cheyenne Nation and the two sacred covenants   46

The twenty bands of the United Cheyenne Nation   56

Cheyenne man with two children   64

Jim Frost's wife and two children, 1892   66

A young Cheyenne boy   68

The medicine wheel camp formation   97

Mary, Daisy, and two boys   99

The chiefs' lodge camp circle   110

Scalp Cane and his clan   113

Nakoimens (Bear Wings) with his wife   118

The four sacred responsibilities of the Véhoo'o   122

The balance of power and shared responsibility among the Véhoo'o   124

The balance of political power and shared authority between the Véhoo'o and the Nótâxeo'o   125

The balance of ceremonial power and shared authority among the Four Sacred Entities   126

Son of Jesse Bent   140

ILLUSTRATIONS

Yellow Nose drawing of ceremonial figures with full body paint   170

The balance of power and shared responsibility among the four original Nótåxeo'o   171

The balance of power and shared responsibility among the four merged Nótåxeo'o   176

Cheyenne and Arapaho social dance, 1903   180

The balance of power and shared responsibility among Nótâxévêhoo'o (Warrior Society Chiefs)   190

The balance of power and shared responsibility among the eight United Nótåxeo'o   193

Wife and four daughters of Man on a Cloud with ornaments, near wood frame building, 1892   197

The four sacred responsibilities of the Nótåxeo'o   204

Two women (Incl. Pauline Warren) and a child   210

Note on the Terminology: Tribe

THROUGHOUT THE BOOK, I refer to American Indian nations, not as tribes, but as nations. I did not change the terms when using direct quotes, and I understand that informants had different meanings when identifying different nations, bands, or villages and using the terms interchangeably; each, however, are different concepts among the Cheyennes. I capitalize the terms *Tribe* and *Tribal* when referencing modern offices of leadership and the entities that include the terms in their title (i.e., Northern Cheyenne Tribal President and Northern Cheyenne Tribal Council). I also use the term *tribal* to define "tribal sovereignty" and "tribal leadership" as concepts, following the principles found in tribal sovereignty, tribal law, and tribal government, which are all ideas that refer to the political relationship that Indian nations have with the US government and, more important, they are concepts that predate this relationship. I used the term *subnation* when referencing the Só'taeo'o and the Tsétsêhéstâhese. As we begin to decolonize these definitions, I believe we will begin to rely on our own indigenous languages, which unfortunately cannot easily be understood or accepted by outsiders, especially mainstreamers who may rely on the English language to define concepts.

Preface

In 1680, the political, cultural, and spiritual influence of Tsėhéstáno extended to the north to parts of modern Canada, to the southwest in modern New Mexico, and to the east along the Mississippi River. Around 1750, the Tsėhéstáno had developed into a powerful nation with the political complexity that rivaled any government of any society on earth at that time. It also had a military organization and alliances that matched their white American neighbors to the east. When the United States declared independence from British rule in 1776, the Tsėhéstáno had already developed into a nation that arguably exceeded the Americans in diplomacy, justice, peacemaking, and ecological consciousness. I intend to explore this argument in this book and its companion volume, *A Sovereign People: Indigenous Nationhood, Traditional Law, and the Covenants of the Cheyenne Nation*.

In 1804, US President Thomas Jefferson commissioned the Corps of Discovery, led by Meriwether Lewis and William Clark, to proclaim authority over lands of the Louisiana Purchase. In 1806, Clark reported the "Chyennes" as a "nation," whose citizens were the principal inhabitants of the "black mountains," later known as the Black Hills. Clark underestimated the population of this nation as well as its presence and influence among other Indians on the Plains. The Tsėhéstáno (Cheyenne Nation) had already achieved nearly five hundred years of nation building, and it could trace its roots even further into the past, nearly one thousand years. Neither the president of the United States nor his explorers could comprehend such a feat, especially since the United States was still a fledgling nation. What is the Tsėhéstáno? Who were the citizens? How did they live? I intend to answer these questions by examining the stories and the oral tradition of the Cheyennes. They are heroic and poetic and are crucial to both national and individual identities of the Tsėhéstáno.

The Indigenous people of the Great Plains were not unpredictable, unintelligent, lawless "savages" as assumed by popular perception. Long before the arrival of Europeans, guilds of spiritual leaders gained knowledge from the natural elements through careful observation. They also gained wisdom through understanding both the flaws and the magnitude of the human mind and spirit. Over hundreds of years, leaders from these guilds or societies developed ceremonies, social customs, and government systems and effective nation-building practices. These teachings were preserved in the language and oral traditions. By the time Europeans arrived to the Great Plains, the Tsėhéstáno was a nation of families that collectively lived by and employed a sophisticated way of living in balance. The Cheyenne Nation comprised ten mobile bands, which themselves comprised numerous families and were protected by the leadership of a complex political system: the Council of Forty-Four Chiefs. The Cheyenne Nation also had a well-developed military organization comprising a number of warrior societies that worked in balance to provide and protect the Cheyenne people. The Tsėhéstáno thrived under traditional foundations of governance and a philosophical belief that all humans were bound by a sense of brotherhood. Leaders lived under strict principles rooted in traditional principles, while citizens were also responsible to uphold traditional teachings for the sake of the nation's health and survival.

A Sacred People represents the new direction of the discipline of American Indian studies, as it follows a decolonized paradigm, authored by a Cheyenne person from a Cheyenne perspective. The discipline of Cheyenne studies is ever expanding in academia as scholars continue to publish books and studies on the Cheyenne people's culture, language, and history. Cheyenne society is often viewed as exotic, and in the words of John H. Moore: "The world is full of Cheyenne experts."[1] As a graduate student, I reached out to numerous, seasoned scholars of Cheyenne studies. I did not take offense when most did not respond; however, I appreciated the few who did. I established professional relationships with some of these scholars, and when I earned my PhD, I believed I was part of the guild of Cheyenne studies. Unfortunately, I came to realize that I was perceived as a threat, rather than a partner in this guild, which is more like a fraternity since it is overwhelmingly comprised of white men, historically and contemporarily. Although Moore was correct in that the world is full of "Cheyenne experts," the world is severely lacking "expert Cheyennes," especially in the field of oral tradition and history.[2] As a Cheyenne scholar, I have been ignored and at times marginalized for not adhering to the unspoken rules established by the fraternity: that Cheyennes are subjects, not investigators; that Cheyennes are studied, and do not study.[3] As an American Indian scholar, I believe time is long overdue to change these perceptions.

I am proud to represent the new school of Cheyenne studies scholars, as well as the new school of American Indian and Indigenous scholars. We are unique. I, as such a scholar, am formally educated, possessing the training and credentials to conduct publishable academic research, but I am also a proud Indigenous person to the core. I was born and raised as a Cheyenne person; I identify culturally and spiritually as a Cheyenne person, and I practice traditional ceremonies, belonging to a traditional dance society and to the ceremonial guilds that continue to practice the Sun Dance and the Fasting ceremonies. These elements of my life shape my scholarship in a manner that is unlike others working in Cheyenne studies.

I was raised on the Northern Cheyenne Indian reservation in Busby, Montana, with my three older brothers and two younger sisters. Before my sisters were born, I was the youngest child and my mother often left me in the care of my grandmother, Jesse Limpy-Long Jaw. She participated in the Massaum and other ceremonies and is remembered as the last "Contrary" of the White River Band of Northern Cheyennes. She was deaf but this did not mean much to me as I simply learned to communicate with her through the traditional Plains Indian sign language. I did not realize until I was older that my mother had "given" me to my grandmother, her aunt, in accordance with the old customs. Parents often "gave" a child to elder relatives so that they would not be lonely in their golden years. Elders could also pass on their teachings and sustain the Cheyenne cultural way of life. In the modern context, this simply meant that I spent significantly more time with my grandmother than did any of my siblings.

I spent most of my toddler days watching my grandmother bead moccasins for relatives and other residents of Busby, the White River Cheyenne people. I played outside on my family's allotment located in the center of the small town, where it seemed like a vast prairie wilderness filled with insects, birds, and snakes, and in the distance there were small packs of dogs and herds of horses, animals our people have loved throughout our existence. I realized when I was older that the land was actually quite small.

My deaf grandmother often joked and showed love, compassion, and even disappointment without words. I learned through her silence that speaking did not always make a person intelligent; neither did it always make a person correct. My time with her would be one of the last connections to the old ways of our people, and another reason for this book.

Most, if not all, modern Northern Plains Indian communities suffer from loss of culture and identity. The Northern Plains Indians of my generation share my experience: they likely have grown up on the reservation with at least one parent who was fluent in an Indigenous language and in a time when mainstream culture, television, and technology had overrun our people's storytelling traditions. Because of this shared experience, our generation is the first to confront the unseen forces of mental and spiritual colonialism without our language and traditional teachings in hand. We are certainly not the last.

Few scholars understand the dramatic cultural and spiritual losses endured by the Northern Plains Indians because they have not lived them, nor have they experienced the enduring legacy of colonialism, racism, and internal oppression. *A Sacred People* confronts this legacy. It teaches about the development of the Cheyenne spirit, as children matured into citizens, citizens into warriors, and warriors into leaders. My personal experiences helped shape my approach to reconstructing the history of my people. As a young man, I endured a brief period of insecurity and self-anguish, as I could not find purpose in life. Like many young Indian people, then and now, who feel lost in the wilderness of the adolescent world, I believed life on the reservation to be dominated by unhappiness, poverty, and the unseen and unspoken powers of grief that encapsulated all who lived there. Despite the richness of our beautiful culture and ceremonial practices, I witnessed the slow deterioration of my people through drugs, alcohol, and violence, and the ever so present division between the haves and have-nots. I was a have-not. This period of my adolescent life was full of confusion, anger, and resentment, especially toward those who were privileged, who benefited from white ways, and who could pass for white. As I had come to see the situation of our livelihood, the hidden pain and anguish, I contemplated suicide, which is unfortunately a common thought for young people in American Indian communities like mine. Two of my close relatives committed suicide not long after my own contemplation, and they completely changed my life. They are one more motivation for authoring this book. This book is needed.

My mother, Jacqueline Limpy Tang, retained her Cheyenne language and traditional teachings into adulthood, despite being a product of the Bureau of Indian Affairs (BIA) Boarding School system. She, like most Indian children before the Indian Child Welfare Act, was subject to federally controlled social service programs as an orphan. Nonetheless, she remained with her mother's side of the family in Busby and attended the Tongue River Boarding School located in the center of our hometown. Although she did not master the English language until she was thirteen years old, she completed high school and went on to college to earn a bachelor's degree in social work. She returned to her home to contribute her valuable skills and talents to serve the best interest of Indian children in our community as a trained social worker, fluent in the Cheyenne language and knowledgeable of Cheyenne traditions and customs. She eventually earned a master of social work degree and held director positions at the tribal and federal levels.

Waatu, "Conqueror," James Mooney, 1861–1921. National Anthropological Archives, Smithsonian Museum Support Center, Suitland, Maryland (NAA INV 06077100, OPPS NEG 7).

My mother has always been my model for resilience, discipline, dignity, and love. Formally and traditionally educated, strong, and dedicated to her family and people, she raised and taught my five siblings and me as a single parent. She deliberately imparted traditional values that she learned from the person to whom she was "given," Hattie Killsback, her grandmother. Hattie and her husband, Ben Limpy, are remembered as sacred people of the White River Cheyennes, since both participated in numerous Só'taeo'o ceremonies, including the Sun Dance and the Massaum.

There were numerous women of my mother's stature on the reservation; most were teachers, others served in different forums of education and in the community, but nearly all were fluent Cheyenne speakers and carried themselves in a unique manner. "Sacred" would be an appropriate term to describe these women. They never showed anger, always were the voice of reason, and consistently held fast to humility, dignity, and patience, especially when faced with adversity. These women were true leaders. Some were my blood relatives, while others I claimed as relatives because I wanted to be a part of their sacredness; they made me proud of being Indian. One of my earliest teachings from an auntie was about honor and sacrifice as she told me the emotional story of the boy hero, Stink Bat, for the first time. His story became the basis for the words you are reading now. It was also an intervention that helped me realize that the story of the Cheyenne people's struggles and triumphs began long before I was born.

Stink Bat

Stink Bat was an orphan who was adopted by an old woman, whom he accepted and loved as his grandmother. He was not yet old enough to hunt but often went into the hills to play with his friends, where they trekked on imaginary adventures fighting as warriors against mythical monsters and enemies. One day he and his friends returned home while the village was under attack by a strange people. His people were in a panic and their screams of horror sounded like thunder echoing throughout the village. Stink Bat and his friends entered his lodge, where they found his grandmother holding two young girls as bullets fell against the lodge like hail from a terrible storm. The small group wanted to make a dash for safety but they had no plan for escape.

After a brief pause, Stink Bat bravely spoke to his grandmother: "We will all run out, us boys first, then after a while you and the girls. Go to the hills and follow the creek up the draw where we always play. We will run toward these strange people and shoot at them with our bows. They will chase us and surely kill us, but by the time they do, you will make it to safety."

The grandmother looked into his eyes for the last time believing his words, realizing that this plan was better than awaiting slaughter. Without hesitation the three boys ran out into the gunfire with their toy weapons and were never seen again. Meanwhile, the girls and their grandmother ran to safety and never looked back. The girls survived into adulthood and always remembered those brave young boys who sacrificed themselves so they could live and carry on.

The girls and their grandmother were survivors of the horrific Sand Creek Massacre of 1864, while Stink Bat and so many others were victims; it is a slaughter that continues to haunt America to this day.

While the Sand Creek Massacre shows the United States at its worst, Stink Bat represents the Cheyennes at their best. His story reveals a culture of resilience and the essence of the Cheyenne indigenous identity. What compelled Stink Bat, a young boy with no family, to sacrifice his life to save his grandmother and two girls? How could he, without doubt, fear, or ego, so easily decide how he was going to die for the sake of others? What in his upbringing allowed him to be so brave and honorable? Were other children of similar character? Other adults? What kind of man would he have been had he survived? Was his personality the norm? What was in the culture that produced such people? Such citizens? Such leaders? I intend to answer these questions by revealing a way of thinking that very few people know and even fewer live today. I believe that within the stories about such leaders and events are the foundations to rebuilding and healing the Cheyenne Nation.

The world that Stink Bat grew up in was so strikingly different from mine, yet both of us clashed with an unseen force, an alien world that is relentless in attempting to predetermine the fates of Indian people. Stink Bat never let this force determine his fate, and after hearing his story, I chose that neither would I. He sacrificed his life for his kinfolk, people, and nation, and I was determined to do the same because such sacrifice—as I understood it—is what it truly means to be Indian, to be Cheyenne, to be a warrior. There comes a point in every Indian's life when one must choose to live as an Indian or not. This is the reality of being Indian in the twenty-first century. For some it is much easier to live as an Indian than others because they were born into it and taught the good Indian values of living. In my community, the choice is not always so easy because mainstream values continue to dominate and some people are ashamed to live as an Indian, let alone to be Indian.

With my choice to "live as an Indian," I realized that I was faced with a challenge that dwarfed my complaints of petty dissatisfaction. I was unable to comprehend the reality of those who lived "sacred" lives in the old times and those few who currently lived "sacred" lives. One such person was my deaf grandmother. I felt nostalgia for a way of thinking that I had come to admire but did not know much about. I longed for an upbringing that I did not have; an upbringing that belonged to those who lived generations before me in a world so close in place but so far in time. I am not the only person who felt this way, and today I know that I will not be the last. I, like so many others, am not a victim of colonization but merely a product of our people's legacy. We are survivors of colonization, not victims.

The Cheyenne world is alive. In *A Sacred People*, I endeavor to re-create this world, which goes beyond the personalities of heroes of a dying culture, beyond the details of dramatic events or battles buried in time, and beyond an Indian past clouded by idealists who search for their own identities or who try to re-create a distorted, mystified history readily and exclusively accepted by academics in ivory towers. I perceived the task of re-creating this world as a sacred task with the hope that it will reach a broader audience, especially those who are sincerely interested in the Indian voice.

Acknowledgments

FIRST, thanks to my mother, Jackie Limpy Tang, for her teachings. I am grateful for the cultural and spiritual teachings from friends and family from the community of Busby, Montana. Special thanks to my aunties Nancy Long Jaw, Barbara Maya, Cheryl Limpy, and Pat Limpy, may she rest in peace. Thanks to my uncles Eugene Limpy, Sr., Frank Long Jaw, Sr., and Ben Long Jaw, may he rest in peace. Thanks to my older twin brothers, Dion and Damion, my brother Lawrence Jace Killsback, and my two younger sisters, Zhona and Zena Tang. Thanks to my father, Eddie Tang. Thanks to my beloved wife, Dr. Cheryl Bennett. I acknowledge all those who came to live on this earth long before me, whom I never knew, but who allowed for me to exist: my grandfather Paul Killsontop; grandmother Joann Limpy; her mother, Hattie Killsback; her mother, Bessie Dull Knife; and her parents, Slow Woman and Chief Morningstar, who was also known as Dull Knife. I acknowledge Ben Limpy, husband to Hattie, and James Killsback, husband to Bessie. I acknowledge "Old Man" Limpy, father, warrior, scout, and ceremonial practitioner from Busby, who witnessed our people transition from a horse nation to a reservation lifestyle.

The social and political turmoil from the community where I was raised motivated me to write this book, nonetheless the Cheyenne spirit remains resilient. I am thankful to former Northern Cheyenne Tribal President Leroy Spang and his administration, former Vice President Joe Fox, and the former members of the 2011 Northern Cheyenne Tribal Council who unanimously approved and endorsed the publication of my research through tribal council resolution: R. D. Bailey, Donna Fisher, L. Jace Killsback, Jenny Lou LaFranier, Marlene Redneck, Tracy Robinson, Alec Sandcrane, George Scalpcane, Vernon Small, and Jule Spang, Sr. Thanks to the support and endorsement of the then tribal historic preservation officer, Conrad Fisher. Thanks to Richard Little Bear, President of Chief Dull Knife College.

Numerous people who remained relentless and loyal to their traditional teachings contributed to the manifestation of this book. I want to formally

ACKNOWLEDGMENTS

thank the traditional and spiritual leaders of the Northern and Southern Cheyenne Nations, who are too numerous to name individually. They are the chiefs, the headmen of the warrior societies, the spiritual leaders and advisors of the ceremonial guilds, the keepers of the sacred covenants, and all of the Cheyenne people who continue to participate in the ongoing traditions and cultural practices of the Cheyenne way of life. Thanks to my teachers and elders who passed away: Burton Fisher, Charles Little Old Man, Burton Seminole, John Russell, Lavern Kills On Top, Phillip Whiteman, Sr., Joe Walks Along, Sr., Donlin Many Bad Horses, Robert Shotgunn, Sr., Lee Lone Bear, Don Little Wolf, Fred Whitewolf, Sr., Perry Little Coyote, Alfred Strange Owl, Clarence Spotted Wolf, Gilbert Little Wolf, Sr., Robert Bailey, Sr., Logan Curley, Sr., Corlette Teeth, Steve Brady, Monte Little Coyote, Rock Red Cherries, Ronnie Seminole, Joe Little Coyote, Sr., Leroy Pine, Florence Whiteman, Zethel Woodenlegs, Ernestine Two Moons, Eloise Fisher, Rubie Sooktis, Alva Stands In Timber, Rose Eaglefeathers, Martha Larance, and Nancy Whitedirt. Special thanks to those who remain integral to sustaining the Cheyenne cultural way of life: Alan Jo Black Wolf, Tweetie Little Bird, Steve Little Bird, Tony Three Fingers, Silas Big Left Hand, Larry Medicine Bull, Philip Whiteman, Jr., Ronnie Bigback, Douglas Spotted Eagle, Gilbert Whitedirt, Don Shoulderblade, Conrad Fisher, Tom Rockroads, Frances Limpy, Andy Elkshoulder, Mark Elkshoulder, Tony Prairie Bear, Alan Clubfoot, Winfield Russell, Matthew Two Moons, Sr., Billford Curley, Sr., Calvin Brady, Wesley Spotted Elk, Vernon Sooktis, Otto Braided Hair, Ernest Littlemouth, Vincent Whitecrane, Michael Bear Comes Out, Sr., James Rowland, Frank Rowland, Kenny Medicine Bull, Burt Medicine Bull, Reginald Killsnight, David Roundstone, Mark Roundstone, Wallace Bearchum, Alberta Fisher, Edna Seminole, Mina Seminole, Mabel Killsnight, Rachael Carol, Betty Rogers, Florence Running Wolf, Jennie Parker, Johanna Red Neck, Rhoda Glenmore, Barbara Braided Hair, Victoria Seminole, Patricia Old Man, Elsie Wick, Marie Sanchez, Bertha Seminole, Marcelene Little Old Man, Jeannie Strange Owl, Barbara One Bear, Addie Baker, Helen Medicine, Top Yellow Robe, Rosalla Bird Woman, Lenora Wolfname, Patti Walksalong, Paulin Eaglefeathers, Elrena White Dirt, Charlen Alden, Mildred Red Cherries, Emogene Dewey, Alaina Buffalo Spirit, Charlene Evans, Farrell Evang, Ester Little Wolf, Alice Little Sun, Diane Spotted Elk, and Elaine Spotted Elk.

I formally acknowledge those of my generation, with whom I grew up, and who I continue to call friends and relatives: Abdel Russell, Rhea Russell, Roman Fisher, Erica Little Wolf, Alicia Little Wolf, Corinna Little Wolf, Robbie Limpy, Waylon, Travis, Trevor, Tasheena, Tisha, and Sven Limpy, Deanna Brady, Joanie Brady Fox, Joel Brady, Leland Pine, Mike Pine, Loren

ACKNOWLEDGMENTS

Pine (RIP), Neil Elkshoulder, Drew Elkshoulder, Jon Elkshoulder, Ben Sanders, Richard Sanders, Brian Sanders, Melvin Strange Owl, Frank Strange Owl, Rufus Strange Owl (RIP), Dayton Strange Owl, Seth and Andre Brady, Phillip Beckman, Beverly Baily, Crystal and Starla Shotgunn, Neela Bear Comes Out, Sheldon King, Jeff and J. B. King, and numerous other friends and fellow Cheyenne citizens. To my dear cousins who belong to the families of the Johnsons, the Limpys, the Long Jaws, the Mayas, the Little Wolfs, and the families of Morningstar (Dull Knife), thank you. I dedicate this book to the next generation of Cheyennes and of the generations, yet unborn.

I have much appreciation for those who have been instrumental in my development as a scholar in the academy, including professors Luci Tapahonso, Jennie Joe, Raymond D. Austin, Robert A. Williams, Jr., Robert A. Hershey, Henrietta Mann, Taiaiake Alfred, Tom Holm, and Robert Martin. Thanks to my colleagues Simon Ortiz, Rebecca Tsosie, John Tippeconnic, Laura Tohe, Tomas Sepulveda, Mary Eunice Romero-Little, James Riding In, and Leonardo E. Figueroa Helland. A special thanks goes to Saja Bex, the graphic designer I appointed to help create the book figures. Thanks to Daisy Njoku and Adam Minakowski at the Anthropology Archives & Collections of the National Museum of Natural History at the Smithsonian Institution. Last but not least, a very special thanks to Judith Keeling and Joanna Conrad at Texas Tech University Press, and to Katherine Pickett at POP Editorial Services, LLC.

Introduction

The old Cheyennes could not write things down. They had to keep everything in their heads and tell it to their children so the history of the tribe would not be forgotten.
—John Stands In Timber[1]

When Cheyennes made a decision about the future, they cared more how the future would affect their tribe as a whole, rather than how it would affect them personally. They cared about the survival of the culture and of Cheyenne as a people, sometimes more than they cared for their own lives. They held fast to their undying belief that the Northern plains was indeed their home.
—Bill Tallbull[2]

Indigenous peoples, in exercising their right to self-determination, have the right to autonomy or self-government in matters relating to their internal and local affairs, as well as ways and means for financing their autonomous functions.
—United Nations Declaration on the Rights of Indigenous Peoples, article 3, section 1, 2007

THE PURPOSE of this book is to reconstruct, reclaim, and reimagine a Cheyenne world for the sake of preserving the Cheyenne cultural way of living and thinking for the next generations of Cheyenne people. *A Sacred People* is about recovering and regaining traditional concepts of governance, leadership, and citizenship, which are interwoven in Cheyenne history, culture, and identity. This book is an epic told from an Indigenous perspective that covers more than one thousand years of antiquity and comprises numerous stories and ideas told and interpreted from a Cheyenne worldview.[3] The history of the Cheyenne people consists of several worlds and ancient ways of living that were lost in time and nearly destroyed by colonization and forced assimilation. This book represents an effort at decolonization, that is, the struggle to rekindle traditional worldviews with the fortitude to improve the current situations of Indigenous people—in this case, the Cheyenne people. Today most Indigenous peoples continue to live in unhealthy and dysfunctional situations as a result of territorial, cultural, and psychological colonization. For Indigenous people and nations to decolonize, they must first understand what their world was like before colonization. Understanding the precolonized world will allow Indigenous people to generate realistic goals and achieve positive change, reinventing themselves into the people and nations that honor their pasts and original ways of living and thinking without corrupting or disgracing them. *A Sacred People* follows this path of decolonization and comprises several teachings that reveal the true identities of the "old ones."

The identity of the Plains Indian has been repeatedly deconstructed, defined, and redefined throughout history. Today few people, even Indians, have knowledge of how Indians truly lived and thought, especially before the arrival of whites, the ravages of genocidal wars, and the destructive forces of the federal government's assimilation-based policies took their toll on once vibrant cultures. Alcoholism, drug abuse, violence, political infighting, and numerous other social and political problems plague Indian country, especially those Native nations that have a history of defying colonialism through warfare or cultural resistance and survival. As an American Indian historian, I believe it is important to link modern problems to the historical atrocities committed during the colonization of our ancestors' lands and minds. Some scholars have begun to revitalize and instill value in Indigenous identities as a means to reclaim culture, language, and religion—that which makes us human—and to improve Indian communities.[4] I believe such revitalization and reclamation are worthy pursuits.

Today, Indian communities of the Northern Plains continue to suffer from endless cycles of oppression and dysfunction. While the colonial forces of violence and domination have long vanished, the residual effects of colonialism, paternalism, and dependency continue to thrive. Meanwhile, leaders, traditional and elected, do not readily seek the teachings of their ancestors for solutions. Few leaders know the old Indian ways of thinking and even fewer find value in such thinking. Most have long abandoned traditional ways and thinking as useless relics, especially when addressing prevailing social problems on reservations and when facing the dominance of Western ways. Modern Indian leaders value white ways and mainstream culture, which only contributes to more confusion and dysfunction. *A Sacred People* is a history of the Tsėhéstáno (Cheyenne Nation) and is a deliberate effort to confront modern challenges by revitalizing and reawakening ancient values in Indian communities, in particular those of the

INTRODUCTION

Northern and Southern Cheyenne, and our relatives and fellow nations of the Great Plains.

INDIGENOUS THEORIZING

A Sacred People is meant to be a timeless piece, but by no means is it to be heralded as the complete epic of every single Cheyenne person, event, or teaching. That is impossible. As an Indian scholar, I am aware of the challenges of conducting reputable, academic research while remaining principled and loyal to my Indigenous culture. Throughout the course of my research, I had to create and re-create Cheyenne-centric paradigms of storytelling and critical analyses that fit the purpose and goals of this book.[5] In the process, I intentionally omitted numerous ideas and teachings that are strictly reserved for Cheyenne eyes and ears, even those that may have been previously recorded by anthropologists and found in archives. We as Indian people have a right to privacy and to protect our cultures. I can say without ego that I pieced together our people's antiquity with the utmost sincerity and respect for our ways. As a practitioner of Cheyenne ceremonies, I am pledged to protect the sanctity of the Cheyenne cultural way and I am responsible for any misinterpretations.

In accordance with modern protocols, I obtained approval from the sovereign entity, the Northern Cheyenne Tribe, through Tribal Council Resolution #DOI-159 (2011), to publish this history. With great humility, I apologize for any unforeseen mistakes or inaccuracies in this book. I have been diligent and sincere in research and writing, but I am considerably limited in my knowledge of Cheyenne language, culture, and traditions when compared to my traditional superiors and elders.

Although the Cheyenne people, history, and culture have been studied by numerous scholars and historians before me, my approach and perspective are unique on multiple levels. My approach to history may not fit within the conventional Western paradigm. Indigenous and Maori scholar Linda Smith describes what is at stake when rewriting the Indigenous position in history:

> Indigenous peoples want to tell our own stories, write our own versions, in our own ways, for our own purposes. It is not simply about giving an oral account or a genealogical naming of the land and the events which raged over it, but a very powerful need to give testimony to and restore a spirit, to bring back into existence a world fragmented and dying. The sense of history conveyed by these approaches is not the same thing as the discipline of history, and so our accounts collide, crash into each other.[6]

INTRODUCTION

Most of the popular studies on the Cheyenne people tend to focus on the particular era of history when the Cheyennes were engaged in war with the US military. Because of this focus, the Cheyenne people have been remembered for their exotic warlike culture, rather than valued for the elements of their ways of living that made them indigenous and human and affirmed their identity as a nation. Contrary to popular belief, the Cheyennes were a nation of families who valued the lives of their fellow humans, the Earth, living beings, nature, and the supernatural. Unlike most histories, which are written in a linear format following a chronological timeline, I organized *A Sacred People* thematically to reveal a world from a traditional Cheyenne perspective. The most challenging feat was to provide a narrative that reconstructed the Cheyenne worldview fairly and adequately enough for readers to understand and appreciate, because the Cheyenne worldview is not limited to the events and interactions with whites, which are events that are fairly recent considering the age of the Cheyenne Nation. Not surprisingly, most of Cheyenne history predates any interaction with whites.

Much has already been written about our culture and society; therefore, I will not reiterate ideas that have been explored in depth by other authors, especially in the manner that they have. Numerous scholars recorded and published, from white perspectives, Cheyenne cultural ways, oral traditions, and histories; the first scholars of Cheyenne studies include James Mooney, George Grinnell, George Dorsey, George Hyde, Truman Michelson, and Rodolphe Petter. I rely heavily on their works in reconstructing history, but I have realized that such reliance is bittersweet. The aforementioned scholars witnessed and recorded some of the oldest stories, cultural concepts, ceremonies, and ways of living that the federal government adamantly tried to annihilate through violence and warfare and then through prohibition. During the prime and pinnacle of most of these scholars, the federal government had forced Cheyennes onto reservations and imposed the most destructive laws of oppression and assimilation through the establishment of the Court of Indian Offenses in 1883, which was specifically designed to destroy Indian identity and culture as swiftly as possible. The codes of the court, known as "the rules of civilizing," prohibited "heathenish rites," including traditional dances, marriages, adoptions, rites of passage, use of medicine men, and other rituals and customs. Offenders, "Indian or mixed-blood," were punished by imprisonment and their property was confiscated or destroyed.[7] Although the 1934 Indian Reorganization Act attempted to end oppression under the "civilizing rules," a generation had already been destroyed, and the effects continue to degrade the traditional Cheyenne cultural way of life.

INTRODUCTION

Today, as we try to recover our traditional ways of governance, leadership, and citizenship, Cheyennes have come to depend on the writings of white scholars without giving thought to their ethnocentric flaws, discipline-driven methods, and theoretical approaches that do not necessarily fit within the Cheyenne worldview. Most of these first-generation scholars have been criticized for producing work from an undeveloped discipline; Grinnell in particular was criticized for being an open racist.[8] Even the work of Michelson, who should be commended for his diligence in authoring narratives in the Cheyenne language and his use of Cheyenne translators and research assistants, raises questions of ethics, since he intermittently recorded bizarre information related to sex and sexuality. Nevertheless, I like to believe that this first generation of Cheyenne studies scholars recorded our history for the sake of our cultural survival and autonomy as a nation, rather than for personal benefit or to claim expertise on our ways. But we do not know for sure what their motivations were, only that their records have endured even after they abandoned the very people they studied. Their works and records continue to be valuable to the discipline of Cheyenne studies. Recently some of their texts became available to the masses of modern Cheyennes in both print and electronic format—benefits that our impoverished and underprivileged parents and grandparents could not afford on the isolated reservation years ago.

Notable resources that I have been able to access through electronic means are the digital collections of Truman Michelson and James Mooney, stored at the National Anthropological Archives at the Smithsonian Institution, National Museum of Natural History. Both Michelson and Mooney visited the Southern Cheyenne reservation in the early 1900s to record stories and other ethnographic and linguistic data of the Cheyenne people. While Mooney tended to focus more on material culture, which cultivates the more popular subject of museum studies, Michelson expanded his work by also collecting raw narratives, oral traditions, and stories in both English and Cheyenne. With the exception of one narrative, Michelson did not publish any of his work. I first read some of Michelson's narratives in John H. Moore's *The Cheyenne Nation* (1987) and found them to be quite different from those of Grinnell and Dorsey. In fact, Michelson's oral tradition collection has proven to be impressive in both quantity and quality. His informants included some who were alive "when the stars fell" in 1833, like the Northern Cheyenne medicine man White Bull (Ice) and the Northern Cheyenne Coyote. Most were from Southern Cheyenne bands, including Wolf Chief, Bull Thigh, Harry Black, Badger, Sweet Medicine (Eugene Standing Elk), Hairy Hand, Albert Duster, White Buffalo, White Medicine, White Eagle, Iron Shirt, Handing Crow, Medicine Top, Tall Bull, Ruben Black

Horse, Mrs. High Walker, and Mrs. Black Crane. Michelson's principal Southern Cheyenne informant and interpreter was Mack Haag, and his other research assistants and interpreters were Somers and Rowland; all were Cheyennes. I have included several unpublished narratives in *A Sacred People*.

As evidenced by numerous published and archival sources, the Cheyennes were occasionally inconsistent in their storytelling and had stories that had different details, especially across distinctive bands, and, when recorded in varying eras, anachronisms—things that do not belong in a certain time.[9] The Cheyennes adopted traditions and customs from other Indian nations, and sometimes bands modified versions of the same stories according to their experiences. These differences are evident in the stories, but such changes or adaptations are not necessarily proof that the oral tradition is unreliable; instead, they expose the adaptive mechanism embedded in the traditional art of storytelling, which I call sacred historical convergence, or SHCT (sacred historical convergence theory).

SHCT is an adaptive mechanism that allows for stories from other peoples to sync with new events, peoples, or ideas to fit the needs of the band or nation. Typically SHCT occurs when uniting with a new people after a peace agreement: the unification of nations includes a unification or convergence of oral traditions across the unified nations. Among Indian people, storytellers also bare traditional knowledge, ceremonies, and philosophies, and therefore their responsibilities extend beyond the art of storytelling. In the past, the most knowledgeable became prophets, whose responsibility it was to ensure that their nation's way of living continued. SHCT occurs when traditional storytellers include new story elements to affirm, acknowledge, and preserve any significant and meaningful concepts, ideas, or stories into the existing oral tradition. The most common incidents that are preserved are those that were introduced through trade, like horses and rifles. SHCT also occurs when storytellers emphasize events that a band collectively experienced and must remember in perpetuity, like a flood, a storm, or an earthquake. SHCT also allows for stories from other cultures, sometimes the cultures of enemies, to be added to the existing, core body of knowledge. The SHCT process can lead storytellers to re-create old stories, tell them in different ways, or make subtle changes to merge old teachings with new teachings, thus ensuring the survival of both. If a new teaching is worth keeping, it is synced with existing knowledge, but it will never erase nor completely replace it. The SHCT is a process that keeps the oral tradition alive and able to adapt, however slowly, and it is evidence of a healthy people who are able to reflect upon their own experiences and preserve significant events and ideas for later generations.

The most notable stories of SHCT occurred when Tsétsêhéstâhese united with the Só'taeo'o. The amalgamation of the two subnations also led to the unification of oral traditions, which I discuss in detail in Part I. General examples of SHCT are found when several similar stories offer slightly differing details, like the process in which a culture hero performed a ritual or in what order he or she did physical feats. Some adaptations are more apparent than others, like the names of the different culture heroes. One culture hero, for example, may have been recorded as doing some of the same feats as another culture hero, when in fact the informant may have packed multiple stories into one epic. Nonetheless, the adaptive mechanism of SHCT shows that ancient traditional values and favorable traits are carried through each generation. These values and traits fit with the older, original teachings, and thus the original philosophies and principles remain intact, unaffected, and preserved into eternity.

Another example of SHCT of the Cheyenne oral tradition is found during the early reservation era, when oral traditions merged with Christianity and biblical stories. In John Stands In Timber and Margot Liberty's works, *Cheyenne Memories* (1967) and *A Cheyenne Voice* (2013), Sweet Medicine is said to have come from a "virgin birth" and that he performed a series of "miracles" and was generally perceived as a "savior" to the Cheyennes. Stands In Timber states in reference to Sweet Medicine: "Before his time they were altogether savage. They lived like animals, were killed. The white man was right calling the Indians savages then, but not after Sweet Medicine."[10] Traditional Cheyennes, including myself, disagree with Stands In Timber's description of Sweet Medicine as a savior, his assessment of the Cheyennes before Sweet Medicine's arrival, and his statement that whites were "right" in labeling Indians as "savages." Nonetheless, Stands In Timber's views were likely common during his time because the Cheyennes had to find a balance, with traditional and Christian teachings, to adapt to forced assimilation. The complete interviews, which were published in *A Cheyenne Voice*, provide better context, for which I am grateful.

Today, some Cheyennes, who know both the oral tradition and the teachings from the Holy Bible, continue to hold Sweet Medicine in the same light as Jesus Christ or a saint, a phenomenon that resulted from the dire need to keep the Cheyenne culture alive by incorporating Western concepts into traditional stories. Within one generation after Stands In Timber, the Christian teachings no longer merged with the Cheyenne oral tradition, but dominated. When the assimilation efforts overran and erased Cheyenne culture from within—that is, when the Cheyenne converts no longer passed down traditional stories—the Sweet Medicine tradition faded, much like the older traditions. Unfortunately, even as merged tradition, the Sweet Medicine tradition is largely unknown by modern Cheyennes. I have done my best to uncover those Cheyenne oral traditions that survived the ravages of forced assimilation.

Stands In Timber's narratives pose another challenge: authority. At the time of Liberty's interviews, Stands In Timber was sixty-seven years old; he was born in 1884, the same year as the establishment of the Tongue River Indian Reservation for the Northern Cheyennes.[11] He was taught in "Catholic and other churches" about remaining loyal to one's chosen religion, and he never participated in any traditional Cheyenne ceremonies.[12] Stands In Timber represents the first generation that faced the impact of forced cultural assimilation; his generation was taught two oral traditions and pressured to follow only one. His interviews reveal the people's collective efforts to remain Cheyenne, but he also remained loyal to his Christian teachings, often comparing and equating the two cultures. Some of his interviews reveal his confusion or discomfort, especially when asked why the churches of his time accused traditional Cheyennes of practicing "false beliefs" that would "send ceremonial practitioners to Hell."[13] Stands In Timber responded from a passive, yet dogmatic perspective: "God will judge them according to their works. They still have a chance."[14] Despite their Christian bent, Stands In Timber's accounts should not be devalued nor abandoned. Instead, as I have done, Stands In Timber's narratives should be examined with a careful eye and understood in context with the needs of the Cheyenne people and nation during his time.

Stands In Timber's problem with authority is not new, as this challenge is evident in the scholarship of previous Cheyenne studies scholars who also confront spiritual identity crises. Rodolphe Petter, for instance, was a devout Mennonite linguist who completed a 1,130-page Cheyenne-English dictionary. I approach his work with due diligence and bittersweet respect, since his 1915 dictionary contains a wealth of Cheyenne oral history and culture. Today the challenge of Christian loyalty is apparent with modern scholars like linguist Wayne Leman, also a devout Mennonite and a former teacher of mine. Fluent in the Cheyenne language, Leman recorded numerous narratives, in both the English and Cheyenne languages, told by Cheyenne people from my community who were knowledgeable of the oral traditions from both the Christian and Cheyenne cultures. He produced a number of valuable written resources, which I use to reconstruct Cheyenne culture and history. I believe that his works were initially for personal language acquisition, and not necessarily for cultural revitalization. I hope that my former teacher's work can be used to revive our dying language, but it is up to the Cheyennes to revive our dying culture. We cannot depend on people who are dedicated to another culture and religion to do the work we must do.

INTRODUCTION

Probably the most renowned Cheyenne studies scholar of today, Peter Powell, is also a devout Christian. Powell has published epics on Cheyenne history and recently edited a two-volume study of Mooney's ethnographic work on Cheyenne material culture. An Episcopal priest, Powell earned credentials for participating in Cheyenne Sun Dance and fasting ceremonies, even achieving formal adoption into a Cheyenne family and winning a Cheyenne name. Powell's greatest feat has been his initiation into the Council of Forty-Four Chiefs. Traditional chiefs vowed to assume responsibility for the people of the nation, and as I was told, this devotion and dedication is awakened and is never more apparent than when a man becomes a biological father, something that Powell had not achieved because his faith demands a vow of celibacy. Although Powell frequently discusses hetané'-hao'o (man power) in his texts, which is a man's power of procreation, he may not have fully appreciated its meaning and significance to the perpetuation of the Cheyenne people, culture, and nation. Some traditionalists remain doubtful of his intentions, uncertain of his loyalties and religious vows. Although my relationship with Powell has been minimal, his work contributed to my scholarship and desire to pursue Cheyenne studies. He is by far the leading scholar in the discipline, regardless of his religious affiliation and spiritual beliefs.

DECOLONIZING METHODOLOGIES

My methodological approach in *A Sacred People* is unique and unconventional compared to mainstream ones, since I take on the role of what I call a "sacred scholar," which is an adaptation of Mohawk scholar Taiaiake Alfred's idea of a "sacred protector": "those who carry the burden of peace."[15] Although "sacred scholars" follow the same principles as sacred protectors in that they are burdened with protecting and preserving territory, culture, and people, they are burdened further to learn and respect the principles and customs of the mainstream academy. This means that they must produce new knowledge using innovative research and existing scholarship, while remaining committed to their traditional, Indigenous cultural and spiritiual beliefs. The principles of sacred scholars are best expressed in an American Indian studies paradigm:

> American Indian studies faculty must view their teaching, research, and service as a "sacred" responsibility to Indian nations and peoples undertaken for the sake of cultural survival. American Indian studies faculty must play an active role in the intellectual, ethical, and social development of students so they will acquire a comprehensive and practical under-

standing of U.S. Indian law and policy, colonization/decolonization, and nation building.[16]

As a sacred scholar, I re-create and apply a Cheyenne-centered paradigm, employ Cheyenne theorizing, and rely on decolonizing research methodologies to retell and reclaim the Cheyenne reality as completely and truthfully as possible, while remaining loyal to my culture and people. I sifted through numerous published articles and books and hundreds of pages of handwritten notes, narratives, and notecards that were authored in both the English and Cheyenne languages to uncover the oldest and everlasting values of the Cheyenne Nation. The stories of the Cheyennes flow from one to the other, they are tied together, they are unified, and sometimes they become preludes or epilogues to other stories.

My mother and her sisters frequently told my siblings and me that her grandmother, Hattie Killsback, would often recount a story over the course of four days during the cold winter months. Some of the stories were sacred and were told in sporatic tellings over the course of months or years. These stories were most memorable because they included prayers, songs, and sound mimics, with sudden moments of elation and humor as well as solemn moments evoking wonder, awe, and emotion. Every story had an implicit teaching quality, even if listeners did not immediately grasp the lesson upon the conclusion of the story. The art of storytelling was a creative and elegant form of education without the dull structures of conventional schooling and exhausting lectures. I do my best to re-create the art of storytelling in this book, but I know that some creativity and elegance will not come through. *A Sacred People*, with its numerous stories, may be perceived as a body of stories for children; that is fine, because these stories helped build a one-thousand-year nation of loyal citizens and leaders. As we look to the future, Cheyennes must realize that it will be the children who will initiate and realize change, not today's adults. We remain a nation of families.

Every story in the Cheyenne tradition served a purpose, even those that may be perceived as strange, obscene, or vulgar. The early scholars, who were searching for data to complete anthropological and linguistic studies, likely perceived unfit stories as useless remnants of a dying savage society. Embedded in the oral tradition, however, are the cultural norms and the differences between acceptable and unacceptable behavior, and the differences between being Cheyenne and being something else. Most scholars, modern and past, highlight the exotic elements of Cheyenne culture that were nearly eradicated and, regrettably, would not necessarily improve the living conditions of modern Cheyennes. While these scholars chose to highlight elements of Cheyenne culture based on personal interest, they subconsciously chose to ignore parts that did not fit their agendas. These overlooked pieces complete the Cheyenne worldview and promote the continuance of the Cheyenne cultural way of life. Perhaps such marginalization was unintentional, but if it was done as a deliberate means to hide or prevent the rebirth of Cheyenne philosophy, then that is all the more reason for scholars like myself to highlight the disregarded elements.

As a child, I was often taught customs and taboos and told not to forget them in public as a way to avert humiliation. As I matured and participated in ceremonies, I was taught never to change any ceremonial or ritualistic process. I learned that the same teaching applies to oral tradition—never change them and never ignore existing stories for personal satisfaction or comfort. This teaching serves a purpose—it prevents the spread of lies and rumors. Non-Cheyenne scholars of Cheyenne studies are not bound by such principles, which is probably why entire legacies, culture heroes, and trickster stories have been discounted, ignored, or marginalized. I have done my best to extrapolate and emphasize the lesser-known stories that explain the creation and perseverance of the Cheyenne Nation and the Cheyenne cultural way of living. As a sacred scholar, I cannot simply ignore, omit, or change oral history to fit my personal interests, even if it does not match documented history. To do so would be destructive to the Cheyenne culture and way of life. If any significant differences exist, I assume that traditional Cheyenne sacred protectors and prophets created them to protect the Cheyenne cultural way of life, using SHCT as a tool for survival. Efforts to protect and preserve the Cheyenne cultural way of life continue today. There is no longer a need to converge for the sake of survival today; we simply must reveal what remains and hope that the next generation finds value in our oral traditions.

Today, the need to reclaim and protect what little knowledge remains has never been more urgent. Most Cheyenne people and their children do not speak the Cheyenne language and are not taught the traditional stories at home or in the classroom. Today, the Cheyenne traditional culture is often perceived as a novelty, commercialized, or marginalized and devalued by the unseen powers of colonial ways of thinking and greed. *A Sacred People* is an effort to revitalize, reclaim, and preserve the foundations of Cheyenne culture and in the process strengthen the Cheyenne Nation. Those who become aware of the struggle become part of the effort.

A Sacred People represents the first steps toward realizing a decolonized Cheyenne Indian world and serves as a reference to understanding the world in which Stink Bat and so many others lived. American Indian leaders from other nations may find this book to be valuable when seeking out "traditions" for aid and comfort when faced with challenges in leadership, decision making, and seeking practical solutions to problems among their own people and in Indian country. Others may find comfort and peace while searching for their Indian identity, but this book is not intended to solve people's personal problems.

I am careful not to be too ambitious in my discourse and avoid romanticizing a world that has long disappeared and that will never return in its authentic or precolonized form. As we search for our Indigenous selves, we should not try to literally reconstruct a precolonized world or its way of life, because to do so would be futile and insulting to our ancestors. But this does not mean that we should forget these ways, nor does it mean that we should ignore the teachings, nor does it mean that we should not try to revive old rituals, ceremonies, and ways of thinking. To align ourselves on a path of decolonization, we must value the past and the old ways to learn or relearn how to be Indigenous, which requires intense and insightful reexaminations of what "was." We must learn and relearn the Cheyenne language of our parents, grandparents, and ancestors. If one knows the Cheyenne language, then one will understand the culture easier, but in no way is the Cheyenne language the defining attribute of what it means to be a Cheyenne person. If we truly want to be Indigenous, then we must be reborn, and a lot of us are not ready for such dramatic change in our lives.

I have done my best to reveal a complete history by compiling and incorporating stories that alone may be contradictory, confusing, and inconsistent to linear thinkers. If told out of context and without regard to the Cheyenne methods of storytelling and philosophies, such stories would seem strange and abstruse. At times, the Cheyenne oral tradition can transition from a definite reality, composed of facts and actual events, to the metaphysical, which are adaptations that are spiritual in origin but contain embedded cultural lessons and teachings. In the Cheyenne tradition, "real" events may be closely related to abstract or spiritual events in that they may both share characteristics of carrying hidden meanings when told. In other words, there is a small gulf between how the world is supposed to work and how the world actually works. There is limited room for deception when the primary teaching or lesson of the story is more important than details, which were sometimes exaggerated to emphasize a point and are part of the art of storytelling.

I am also careful not to historicize or idealize the past. I rely on the Cheyenne language in explaining intellectual and cultural concepts that survived the ravages of colonization and assimilation. The spoken word, language and oral tradition, has proven to be an effective means in preserving concepts that have miraculously survived the tests of time. I have done my best to unpack some Cheyenne ideologies knowing that I may lose meanings in translation. Although some traditional Cheyenne ideas and concepts remain within our language and society today, most were lost, and for this reason I rely on words and concepts recorded in the 1913–15 dictionary by Petter or words drawn directly from archival documents and published accounts.[17] I depended on my Cheyenne relatives to aid in bringing these words, and more importantly these ideas and concepts, back to life; any failure to achieve this goal is completely my own.

THE CHAPTERS

The Cheyennes call all Indigenous people of North and South America xamaevo'êstaneo'o, which literally translates to "ordinary people." The core concept of this book is the "indigenousness of the Tsêhéstáno." This book answers the fundamental question of what it means to be indigenous or xamae- (ordinary or indigenous).

I have worked with several traditional Cheyenne people, including elders and spiritual leaders, since the beginning of this project. Following the oral traditions and customs of my people, I organized the chapters and their content to follow the traditional concepts that underlie the development of the human mind and spirit. I also rely on the historiography outlined by Susan Miller in "Native America Writes Back: The Origin of the Indigenous Paradigm in Historiography," which emphasizes four key principles of Indian history: indigenousness, sovereignty, colonization, and decolonization.[18]

Four is considered a sacred number among most Plains Indian cultures, including the Cheyenne. Following this traditional teaching I have divided *A Sacred People* into four parts. The first part is titled "Tsêhéstáno: The Cheyenne Nation." Chapters 1 through 3 answer the fundamental question, what is an Indigenous nation? In reconstructing how the Cheyenne people perceived their nation, I explain the traditional view of history and how the people positioned themselves on Earth and in time. I explain the significance of prophecy in history, as well as the value of the oral tradition and the interconnectedness between storytelling and indigenousness. This part sets the footing not only for the book, but also for understanding the Cheyenne worldview, which will be referenced throughout.

The second part is titled "Véhoo'o: The Chiefs," and chapters 4 through 7 answer several fundamental questions: What is Indigenous governance? What does it mean to be an Indigenous leader? What does it mean to be a leader of an Indigenous nation? What does it mean to be a leader of the Cheyenne Nation? These chapters detail the development of the Véhoo'o—

that is, the Council of Forty-Four Chiefs or the Chiefs Society—emphasizing the origins, values, and government system.

The third part is titled "Nótȧxeo'o: The Warriors," and chapters 8 through 11 answer two fundamental questions: What does it mean to be a citizen of an Indigenous nation? What does it mean to be a citizen of the Cheyenne Nation? This part focuses on the development of the complex warrior society system, emphasizing its origins, values, and function within the Tsėhéstáno. The warrior societies, which included both male and female members, were also institutions for individuals to express and develop manhood and womanhood, thus producing a healthy and sustainable nation. I also highlight women's societies, which were guilds that facilitated sisterhood, motherhood, and womanhood.

The final part, "Colonizing and Decolonizing the Tsėhéstáno," highlights the major changes that resulted from the colonization of the Cheyenne homeland from the Cheyenne perspective. Chapter 12, "Vé'hó'e: The Trickster," explores how the Cheyennes viewed themselves and their situation as they confronted new peoples from the east. They relied on traditional knowledge to make sense of new challenges. This section answers the fundamental questions: How did the Cheyennes view colonization? How did they respond to colonization? What were the major factors that led to the changes in traditional Cheyenne views of leadership and citizenship? I conclude *A Sacred People* with a discussion of decolonization and the Cheyenne Nation.

Throughout this book I cite extensively in appropriate places, especially where some cultural beliefs and practices have already been recorded, to accommodate those interested in such concepts. My role as a researcher is to find data, but my role as a sacred scholar is that of a rebuilder and organizer, to piece together previously recorded ideas and merge them with the interpretations from today's traditional keepers of knowledge. This is quite challenging. This book is an attempt to reconcile my academic scholarship demands with my responsibilities to protect the Cheyenne culture. Yet my intentions are in line with those of Richard Randolph, who in 1937 asserted that sharing the stories from Oneha, his ninety-year-old Cheyenne informant, in written format was done in an effort to help "bring about a better understanding of the Indian's nature, his ideas and his attitude toward life," and in "hopes, however, that they will retain something of the spirit which motivated their retelling to generation after generation of Cheyenne children."[19] I must assert that this book should not be used as a blueprint for hobbyists to mock, mimic, or reenact the old ways; instead, the goal is to reveal the profound sophistication and brilliance of our Indigenous past. Mindfulness of this sophistication and brilliance, rather than imitation, will lead to a more complete understanding of Indigenous identity and the world, so both Indians and non-Indians can appreciate them. This book is a guide to remain Indian, not to become Indian.

American Indian scholars must remember and retell the stories of their ancestors, which were in place long before colonization. American Indian national histories will reveal the roots of modern political unrest, economic despair, and spiritual demise, but they will also reveal stories of survival, resistance, and adaptation. Every Indian nation has a unique history from which springs wisdom to plan for the future. As with most American Indian and Indigenous peoples, the oral tradition of the Cheyenne Nation comprises heroic feats and tragic losses. By knowing such histories we can begin to heal from the intergenerational trauma that is often misunderstood and ignored by mainstream culture. We cannot continue to inflict upon ourselves unending cycles of self-destruction. In time, all vestiges of the Cheyenne culture will either be completely forgotten or, as traditional Cheyennes believe, become the narrow path for citizens to restore their hearts and minds and restore greatness to the Cheyenne Nation.

The Indigenous identity cannot easily be defined as it was in the past, and today's use of blood quantum and membership has only added confusion to the Indian identity. I, like every other Indigenous person, am connected to the legacy of my people's struggle for survival; the link is always there whether I choose to be Indian or not. To be Indian, however, means more than to merely call oneself an Indian. To be Indian today is to choose to accept the fact that we are currently at a great disadvantage as a people; that we are still fighting to keep our ways and we are losing. Today, to be Indian means to choose to struggle against the unseen forces of colonialism and assimilation, in hopes that our children and grandchildren will be Indian. The choice before us is to be warriors or not: to sacrifice as did Stink Bat, or not.

If today's Indian people knew of their Indigenous pasts and the worlds of their ancestors, then they would not accept the fear and pain that continues to dominate our communities and dictate our actions. We could help bring our people into a new consciousness where we can live healthy and happy lives and in accordance with our traditional ways. We should not so easily forget or abandon the traditional teachings of our nations, especially after we learn them. We should give these teachings a chance. My purpose is clear but it was shaped by my people's victories and defeats, especially our conscious decision to be Cheyenne. The hardships and accomplishments of the Cheyennes have inevitably led me to write these words, which are manifested throughout this book. By reading this book you also, willingly or subconsciously, become part of the Indigenous legacy and continue in the fight for survival. I welcome you on this journey, vá'öhtáma!

PART I

Tsėhéstáno: The Cheyenne Nation

They are all going to know it. It cannot be hidden. Until today it is still around. Do not hide it from the children. Tell them about this.
—Elaine Strange Owl (Northern Cheyenne)[1]

Come together, my people. Make a medicine lodge. Do honor to the sacred Arrows. Speak often of the things I have told you. Be faithful to the old ways. Remember my words. Then you will be strong.
—Motsé'eóeve[2]

TO UNDERSTAND the Indian world, we must deconstruct the language and culture that has dominated all other perceptions and embedded in our minds a negative view of Indigenous peoples.[3] We have become too accustomed to measuring human civilizations using the European, Christian civilization as the standard. Technological achievements, religion, and territorial expansion are all barometers that have allowed negative colonial views and judgments toward Indigenous people to prevail in our minds. These judgments have not only led to violence and the continued oppression of so-called primitive or "savage" peoples, but they have also led to an unfair representation of Indigenous peoples because writers do not have a complete and fair understanding of Indigenous worldviews. We must change our entire perspective of how we see history and people in history. If we sincerely want to know the Indians' story, we have to sincerely ask them: what is your story?

American Indians preserved their history in the art of storytelling and the oral tradition. Their stories can be classified into four different categories. The first is ceremonial, which comprises stories that are told only during ceremony and are not to be revealed to anyone other than a spiritual advisor or teacher and his or her pupils. No changes were to ever be made to these types of stories, for their corresponding ceremonies had to be preserved, unchanged, and this demanded that the storytellers remain pure to the original words. The second category is secular, which speaks of actual events, peoples, and facts. This category comprises war stories, adventures, and other events that were fairly recent in time. The authenticity of these stories depended entirely upon the memory and honesty of the storyteller, who recited facts and retold actual happenings. The third body of stories is philosophical and comprises moral lessons and ways of living, like trickster tales and stories of individuals' adventures. These stories may have several versions but they all convey the same moral teachings. Even if the stories differed among bands and families, their purpose was not lost. The fourth category of stories is part of a much larger body of sacred history, a collection of shared experiences and memories that reveal the national identity. These stories are the foundation of the people's way of living and describe culture heroes, prophecies, and the challenges that the people faced as a unified group or nation. These stories were often adapted to the changing ways of living and sometimes incorporated outside cultural influences that were important to the people. This body of stories contains the essence of the Cheyenne identity, where we find the story of "the Nation."

The Cheyenne oral tradition was the educational system of the Cheyenne Nation. It facilitated the intellectual and spiritual growth of its citizens and passed knowledge from generation to generation. "Stories told to children by their elders," the historian Richard W. Randolph asserts of the Cheyennes, "sought to make them fearless warriors and skillful hunters, merciless towards enemies but nonetheless kindly and considerate to their own people."[4] Because there was no written language, the history and "sacred beliefs were kept alive in the memories" of storytellers and ceremonial leaders and told around campfires and feasts.[5] Elders and family members told "sacred stories" at night while everyone was still and reverent because "it was believed that noise or moving about during the telling of sacred stories would bring misfortune to the camp."[6] The sacred stories held the knowledge and teachings that were essential to creating good citizens and good leaders, which is why storytelling was a near ceremonial affair and sometimes required a pipe-smoking ceremony or blessing of cedar before a storyteller shared his or her knowledge and wisdom.[7] The tradition of story telling had six customary laws, as articulated by Mack Haag (Southern Cheyenne) in 1932:

1. The person wishing to hear the legend related, must first of all prepare corn gravy or flour gravy, to be served at the conclusion of the legend or legends.
2. The legends are told in the nighttime only. If told in the daytime, the penalty is that the guilty one, upon old age will have curvature of the spine, causing hump back.
3. The time of the year for legends is in the winter season.
4. The one preparing the food, or furnishes the same, becomes the owner of the legend related. If it is a child, then the mother or any other relative may prepare or furnish food, and become the owner of the legend.
5. In any case, no one must interrupt the informant during the discourse of the legend. They must instead verbally approve at the end of each sentence, until the end of the story to ask a question or add a detail. If these two particular rules are broken, then the legend automatically terminates and the informant may say, "You have forced me to lapse of silence."
6. Upon conclusion of the legend, the informant may say, "Thus the length of the legend is ended," and no one is then permitted to retell the legend the same night.[8]

Today these old customs are rarely practiced in Cheyenne households, but this does not mean that they cannot be revitalized.

The Cheyenne perceptions of time and the universe were also significant in storytelling. The Cheyennes organized time as do all humans: the éše'he (sun) measured days and nights, the taa'eéše'he (moon) measured months, and aénévôtse (winters) measured years.[9] The Cheyennes were known to record historical events on their war shirts, which warriors could collect as calendric wardrobes.[10] It remains unknown if the Cheyennes kept winter counts as did their Lakota neighbors, but if they did these records likely perished in the wars against their colonizers or were pirated in the black markets, as none exist among the Cheyennes today.

Traditional Cheyennes measured large epochs of time, which were usually organized by the supernatural and unseen powers generated by the world and universe. These large epochs of time are typically determined by the change in culture and worldview and are understood best through storytelling. Cheyenne storytellers provide a frame of time of when said events occurred by identifying the transitions between these large epochs. For example, a storyteller may begin by stating "before the Cheyennes had horses" or "before the Cheyennes had bows and arrows" to place the story within a time frame.[11] There existed yet larger epochs of time that extended further into the past, which were described by even more dramatic circumstances like "when there were no buffalo" or "when the animals were giants."[12] The most notable divisions of time detailed when something was created like "this is the beginning of the workings of the mind" or "that was the beginning of using dogs."[13] With such measures of time in history, the Cheyennes had a profound sense of the oral tradition that preserved the ancient realities of their ancestors long before the people became the horse culture that is so popular in Plains history. Left Hand Bull told one of the oldest creation stories.

The Creation of the Universe

There was a time when there was no earth, only the Great-Mysterious [Ma'xema'heō'e] ruled in the wide space. It was all like fog in a dreary evening when one cannot distinguish objects. The Great-Mysterious one had four great servants, the ones whom he has set to watch the four quarters. He told these beings that he would make the earth and also human beings. "Go about and you will soon find that earth," said he to his servants. They went about for quite a time but came back and reported that they could not find anything. "Go again and look carefully," he told them. But in spite of their efforts they found nothing. Four times they were sent and came back without having seen or found anything. The fifth time the Great-Mysterious told them "now you will see something." And it happened, as they were floating about, they noticed a shapeless and dark mass looking "like one about to give birth to a child." They returned and reported what they had seen. "Go again and see what I have created, you will find a new being there, bring it to me," the Great-Mysterious told them. They went and found the earth shaped and on it a new being they had never seen before. They [brought] this being to the Great-Mysterious, who took it in his arms and said: "This being is man whom I have made to inhabit the earth, it is my child and I shall love him." After that the man was [brought] back to the earth to inhabit it and live on it.[14]

From the Cheyenne perspective, the physical Earth is a child of the Universe, which is the Supreme Being of all existence. It is remembered as a "shapeless and dark mass" that was "about to give birth to a child," therefore the Universe is female. The Great Mysterious witnesses the birth of the Earth, but he is not its father. Instead, he is the father of the humanoid being that other beings "had never seen before." The Earth is the humanoid being's mother, and this being represents the human race. But from the Cheyenne perspective, the humanoid being represents the Cheyenne people or the Cheyenne nation. Who were these people? What is this nation?

CHAPTER 1

Héstanovestôtse: A Living Nation

THE CHEYENNE people did not see themselves as a mere tribe but as beings of the universe, unified as a group belonging to a much larger, unseen, supernatural being of the universe; a sacred nation. This perception extended over the entire Cheyenne Nation and over the course of its existence. As we look into history to learn about and from the Cheyenne people, we must respect this perception and decolonize our preconceived notions of the Cheyennes and depart from defining them as a mere "tribe." *Tribe* connotes primitivism and lawlessness and although I am aware that it is appropriate to use the term in some instances, especially when describing concepts like tribal sovereignty and tribal leadership, the word *tribe* does not come close to capturing the traditional Cheyenne view that they are a nation. The history of the Cheyenne people is the history of the Cheyenne Nation, which is the story of this sacred being of the Earth and the universe.

To gain a better understanding of the Cheyenne perspective, one must view the Cheyennes as they saw themselves and other groups of people or nations. According to Cheyenne cosmology, every individual human being belongs to a nation. This nation is viewed as a humanoid being that is a child of the Earth and the Great Mysterious. All nations, according to the Cheyennes, are siblings. They are living beings, and like all living beings, possess the four necessities of life: a physical form manifested as its members; feelings and emotions expressed in the feelings and emotions of its people; intelligence and thought sustained through the minds of its thinkers and intellectuals; and a spiritual presence or a spirit, expressed through its spiritual leaders and ceremonial practices. The Cheyenne Nation is alive, and just as there are generations of people, there are also generations of nations. I use the Cheyenne term *héstanovestôtse* to describe this concept of a nation, which loosely translates to "the life of the people" but also means "the life-nation" or "the living-nation." What is the story of this living-nation?

PART I | TSÈHÉSTÁNO: THE CHEYENNE NATION

Most American Indian and other Indigenous peoples can accurately "speak of worlds or ages when they are referring to the totality of the previous world, including its humanoid creatures and their social structures as well as the physical world."[1] Throughout the history of the Cheyenne Nation, the Cheyenne people departed from old lifestyles and places to begin anew, and this phenomenon reveals much of their worldview. The journeys of the previous Cheyenne groups from world to world, like from the Great Lakes region to the Great Plains, were more than simple migrations; they were also changes in the peoples' collective reality or consciousness. Such changes were spiritual and philosophical, much like the transition of worlds endured by the Navajo and Hopi of the southwest.[2] From the Navajo and Hopi perspectives, each world represented the birth, maturity, and death of a way of life, while the people endured. Each world allowed for its people to learn, adapt, and make mistakes in the adapting process. Sometimes chaos or catastrophe, like a flood or earthquake, instigated a need for dramatic change. Other times change ensued with the introduction or the demise of objects, plants, or animals, like the arrival of corn. Likewise, in each of the Cheyenne worlds, the people gained new knowledge, wisdom, and most important, ways of living as they transitioned from one world to another. Each héstanovestôtse, evident by the group of peoples' change in culture, responded with purpose and intention, survival and prosperity, and not out of uncertainty or chance. The survival of old cultures are the evidence of this perseverance, and the people kept a record of the changes through storytelling.

The oral tradition was the means for organizing and explaining any change, from within and without. Achievements of their ancestors, culture heroes, and concepts of governance, leadership, and citizenship were thus preserved, inevitably securing the survival of a unique Cheyenne identity, while allowing for adaptations. The people depended on the héstanovestôtse for survival, and the héstanovestôtse depended on the people to sustain the original national identity, which is the first living-nation from creation.

A héstanovestôtse, like all living organisms, wants to survive and transmit its "national" qualities to its progeny, but this could only be done if its people sustained four critical elements of nationhood: ceremonial practices, sacred history, sacred geography, and sacred laws.[3] Without these four elements a héstanovestôtse would either integrate with other nations or vanish. These four elements allowed for a héstanovestôtse to persist into the future and equipped it to meet any unforeseen challenges. As each héstanovestôtse endured change, the people could thus adapt and survive. Change often came in response to violence or chaos but also in response to the introduction of new peoples, ideas, and ways of living, like the arrival of friendly or enemy peoples and the abandonment of farming. A héstanovestôtse frequently abandoned outdated customs and replaced them with new ones to secure a life for its progeny.

Cheyenne history can be viewed as the histories of several héstanovestôtse that existed in certain time periods; each had unique ceremonial practices, sacred histories, sacred geographies, and sacred laws. The Cheyenne people, who shared a common language and a common ancestry, united every héstanovestôtse, thus creating a "united national history." In each era, the Cheyenne Nation also comprised numerous bands, and these bands had their own ceremonial practices, sacred histories, sacred geographies, and sacred laws, thus creating individual "band histories." Bands are the progeny of a héstanovestôtse, and traditional Cheyennes view bands and other smaller parts of the nation—families and villages—as living beings that also endure birth, youth, maturity, and death.[4] Families are the progeny of bands, and individuals are the progeny of families; they are not merely children or parents. The Cheyenne view all Indigenous people, families, bands, and nations through this sacred kinship system.

Throughout the history of the Cheyenne nation, each héstanovestôtse of the Cheyennes had a varying number of bands depending on the population size. New bands were created when the population increased and a band split. Meanwhile, some bands may have remained throughout the existence of the nation without splitting. The presence of numerous bands throughout the history of the Cheyenne Nation resulted in numerous accounts of the same events experienced or witnessed by different groups of Cheyennes. The national history united all of the bands, meaning one body of oral traditions remained the same throughout all history and among all bands. This is what made the Cheyenne Nation a single living-nation. Meanwhile the band oral traditions may have adapted and changed.

Under a decolonized paradigm, we begin to see that the history of the Cheyenne people is much more complex than imagined. Sacred history among the Cheyenne, as with most Indigenous people, is revered and protected as holy and precious. The nation is a living reality or world, with a legacy that deserves to be treated with respect and care. Once we remove ourselves from the colonial perceptions of history, which have clouded our vision and categorized Indigenous peoples as the barbarians yet to progress to civilization, we gain a better sense of who these people were and we get a glimpse into their minds, spirits, and emotions. When we use Native thinking, we no longer see a simple "tribe" when we think of the Cheyennes.

PART I | TSÉHÉSTÁNO: THE CHEYENNE NATION

THE CHEYENNE NATIONAL HISTORY

The old Cheyennes divided their ancient history into measures of time or héstanove (a world period), which can be thought of as the complete existence (time and space) of one héstanovestôtse (living-nation). One héstanove is understood as the known universe, and one héstanovestôtse is the physical presence of the Cheyenne Nation in the universe. The Cheyenne Nation has parent, grandparent, and great-grandparent nations from which it inherited wisdom, knowledge, and life. Each héstanovestôtse lived the life span of one héstanove (regardless of calendric years) and each living-nation comprised several generations of Cheyenne people, families, and bands. As each héstanovestôtse died and another was reborn, the people abandoned outdated ways and embraced new ones. Humans did not initiate the transitions from one héstanove period to another, and they did not randomly invent new ways. Instead, the héstanovestôtse and its people drew from the environment, openly receiving the blessings and challenges the Earth provided. Such relationships to land reveal that although héstanovestôtse might die, they remained indigenous and dependent on the Earth with each rebirth. The history of the Cheyenne Nation is an epic, composed of seven héstanovestôtse, each contributing to the survival and prosperity of their descendant nations. The oldest living-nation holds the oldest teachings, so we begin there.

THE FIRST WORLD

An early origin story tells of the people's emergence into the first world, called "the land of stones." Upon emergence, they became a nation. This story took place in a measure of time called hoháovonóom (the very ancient time). From the very beginning, the Cheyenne Nation is remembered as a nation of families.

The Cheyenne people lived in an underground place where all of the human beings once lived.[5] The people resided in unknown darkness until a young person saw a distant light and decided to walk toward its glow. The rest of the people followed this person to the light until they found an opening to a new world. The families emerged from the underground, despite the sunshine that hurt their eyes, and soon became accustomed to the sunlight, and then eventually to the cycles of day and night. The families went about naked because they knew nothing of clothing and did not need it when they lived inside the Earth. They eventually made their homes in caves near the edges of cliffs. Although the climate in the new world was cold, the people managed to construct beds and keep warm during wintertime. They hunted small animals such as squirrels and birds and gathered birds' eggs, and within the next generation the people grew "large and hearty."[6] They could walk barefoot across frozen rivers and streams, climb high trees and cliffs, and run fast in groups: men, women, and children together. The country was littered with huge rocks and stones, so the people eventually came to make houses of stone; they lived in this way for some time. Large, archaic rabbits were plentiful and made for good hunting, and their hides were used for good clothing. The Cheyenne were small in population with only about five hundred, about one hundred families, but they came to reside among great magicians or prophets "who lived in mounds or stone habitations," which were beautifully decorated inside; the finest ones were guarded by lions and bears.[7] This was the first world of the first band of Cheyennes, the first héstanovestôtse on Earth, and some of the old people believed that they lived east of the Mississippi River as mound builders.[8]

In this world, some Cheyennes became astronomers and astrologers, gaining the knowledge and wisdom from the movements of the universe. The story "The Star Husband" describes the fundamental relationship between the Ho'e (Earth), Mahpe (Water), the héstanovestôtse (universe), and the Cheyennes.[9] Southern Cheyenne William Somers told the story in 1910.

The Star Husband

There was a time when this country was [inhabited] by two sisters, who lived up on this earth, when all the animals were friendly to men and could talk to each other. The names of these people were Earth and Water. They here lived in tents covered with skins of animals and for beds they used beautiful soft grass and brushes, they did not have to work for their food because they had many good friends to [supply] them. One summer night, these two sisters lay awake for a long time, looking up at the sky and talking to each other.

The Earth said, "Sister, I had a dream and I dreamed of a young man, of who it seemed that he came where the stars are." Water said that she did have a dream too, for she saw a great brave and wondered if the stars were star-men, whom they have dreamed of. Water said, if it was so that she would choose the brightest one for her husband. And Earth said, "I will choose the little twinkling star for my husband," so they did. The elder sister who chose the brightest star, found an old warrior, a very old man and [the] husband of [the] young sister was a fine looking young brave.

The star-men were very kind to their wives and lived happy with them. One day these two young women went out to dig wild turnips[;] before they started out, the old man told them to be very careful and not to hit the ground too hard, so they went out to dig. The young woman forgot and struck the ground too hard, with [a] long pointed stick which they used to dig turnips with. Soon [as] she hit the ground, the floor of the sky [dropped] or gave away and she fell into the ground below. There she was found by two very old people, who took care of her and brought [her] to their home and doctored to her troubles and [cared for] by these people. But she kept crying for her husband and wanted to go back to him some way. [In the] End [she] couldn't live without him so the old woman told her that fallen stars never returned to Heaven.

Night came on and all the stars appeared in the sky but the little twinkling star did not show[;] he was now a widower and painted his face very black. This poor wife of his waited [for a] long time [for him] to come to her. But [he] did not come. One night she dreamed she saw a tiny red star in the sky which she had not seen before. She said, "That's my son, Red Star." When in the morning she awoke she found a pretty little boy by her. Who grew to be a handsome young brave in the tribe. His cousins in the sky, the star children, always guided him by night. It is said that Red Star's children and [their] children are the Indians or red men of America.[10]

In another version, after the girls married the star-men their names were changed: Ho'e (Earth) became Ma'etohke'e (Red Star Woman) and Mahpe (Water) became Heova'ehetohke'e (Yellow Star Woman).[11] Ma'etohke'e decided to return home to Earth with her infant son and fell, but her son survived and grew up to become a great prophet and medicine man named Hotohketana'ôtse (Fallen Star).[12] The Só'taeo'o remember this prophet as Hotóhkôhma'aestse (Red Star).

The Cheyennes lived in the first world under the guidance and teachings from the celestial beings and the movements of the stars. One day those with "star knowledge" observed that a star fell from the sky and thus changed the constellations in the heavens, which was one of few constant marvels in this world. The spiritual leaders believed that a great calamity would soon destroy their nation and that the falling star was a sign for the Cheyennes to leave their stone houses and travel to a new home at the location where the star landed.[13]

THE SECOND WORLD

When the Cheyennes decided to leave, they followed Hotóhkôhma'aestse (Red Star) toward the fallen star, trusting his spiritual knowledge. The families journeyed along a large river and through a forested land. They came upon a place where unknown people had already lived, but for some reason these people abandoned their wooden structures and left only their stone

HÉSTANOVESTÔTSE: A LIVING NATION

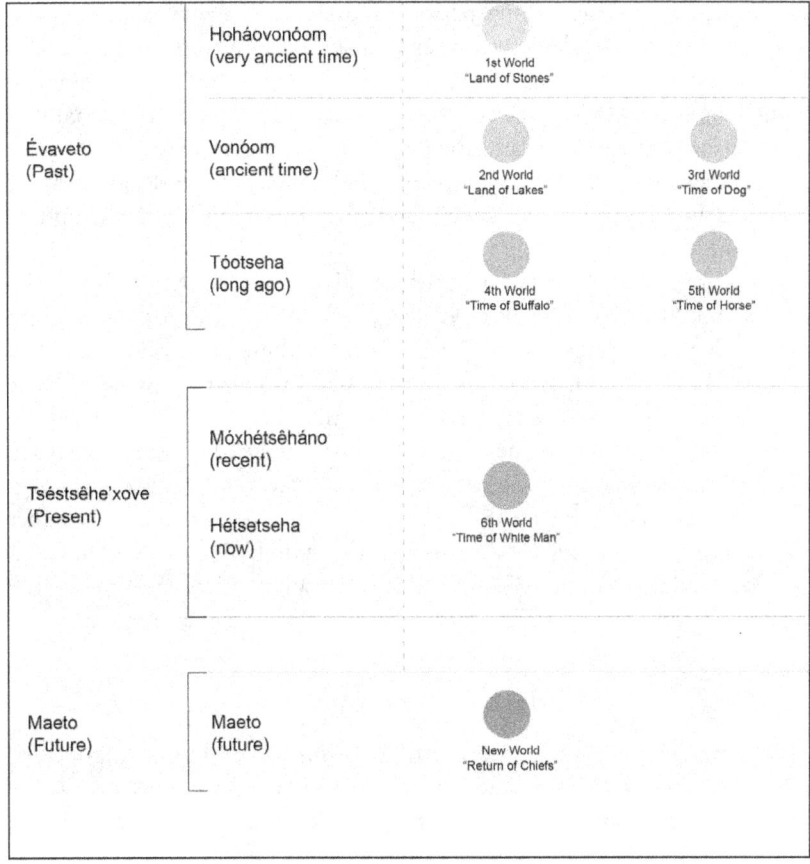

Cheyenne perceptions of time and history.

tools. The Cheyennes believed that these people must have suffered some great catastrophe, so they left and traveled farther to the shores of a great body of water, and here they decided to make their lives on a great island in the second world.[14] In this new world, known as "the land of the lakes," the people built earth lodges. Instead of using stones, the people used the bones of birds or fish for needles, knives, tools, and other sharp implements, as they were already partly made gifts from nature and much easier to carve and carry.[15] The people survived on the blessings of plentiful fish and fowl in this land of islands and their population doubled within a few generations. The woman domesticated panthers by capturing them when they were cubs, and when these panthers matured they were used to hunt deer and other game.[16] Their resilience allowed them to rebuild a new nation, the second héstanovestôtse. After a long period of time, the balance of the second world was eventually destroyed when a great flood ravaged the land.[17] This flood is known as the First Great Flood. Afterward, the people were distraught as entire families starved to death, leaving survivors "as orphans."[18] The nation was scattered and divided, but the leaders managed to come together and made a difficult decision to abandon this world and way of living. It was time for the surviving families to leave once again and enter a new world.

During this time a powerful man named Netsévôhé'so (Eagle Nest), who was born in the nest of a giant red eagle, decided to search for a new world for the people.[19] He got on the back of one of these great eagles and flew across a large body of water for four days and reached a new land.[20] The families followed him, using rafts at first, then crossed by foot when the water froze.[21] One day as they crossed, the ice broke in a thunderous roar, dividing the nation in half; some people were left forever on the other side.[22] The Cheyennes still believe their brethren reside somewhere on the other side of the Mississippi River. Meanwhile, the main body of Cheyennes continued to follow Netsévôhé'so, eventually reaching a new land to begin a new life in this new world, the third world, to re-create their nation.

THE THIRD WORLD

The third world began a measure of time in history known among the Cheyennes as vonóom (the ancient time). The Cheyennes continued to live in earth lodges, which were made of tree bark and grass and were covered in mud.[23] The Cheyennes relied on dogs as beasts of burden and for sustenance during this time. Sometimes the sacred animals were sacrificed for food. These animals, which were large and wolflike, remained a central part of Cheyenne ceremonial practices and were honored as sacred beings. This third world is known as "the time of the dog." During this time the Cheyennes befriended the Vóhkoohétaneo'o (Cree or rabbit people) in the lands of the third world. The two nations intermarried and shared customs. One custom in particular was a ceremonial Corn Dance. The Cheyennes credit the Cree for introducing this practice, which was retained among the Cheyennes until they quit farming.[24] The Cheyennes also met a people known as the Moiseyu, who were thought to be relatives of the Lakota.[25] The two nations intermarried and established a peaceful relationship.

The "Cheyennes lived on corn, wild turnips, [and] ate fish and small game" in this world "before they met the buffalo."[26] The Cheyenne Nation rebuilt itself as a corn-planting nation, the third héstanovestôtse, with a vibrant ceremonial cycle and oral tradition. White Buffalo (Northern Cheyenne) recalled the gift bestowed upon the Cheyenne people: "[My] great grandfather way back from generation to generation [said] that they had corn. The Great Mysterious One gave five kinds of corn: one red, one green, one white, one yellow, one black."[27] The Cheyennes held another major ceremony, the Green Corn Dance, which was an annual ceremony that celebrated the ripening of corn.[28] Coyote (Northern Cheyenne) described the farming days, when the people camped "indefinitely" on streams. He elaborated on the significance of corn:

> Transportation [was] by dogs. Horses were unknown [then]. They decided to camp indefinitely at the stream. They used flint implements to cultivate the ground in small spaces to plant the seed. The fall of that year they had a good crop of that corn. After putting it away in containers of hides, they decided to go on a buffalo hunt. They made some dugouts on the bank and stored the corn there. They sealed the dugouts with logs.[29]

This method of corn storage sustained the Cheyennes through harsh winters.

The third world of the corn-planting Cheyennes was beautiful, as the land was healthy and small game was plentiful, but this world was also treacherous, as giant animals and monsters inhabited their new homeland and the people struggled to prosper. The old Cheyennes believed that because times were so difficult, the old prophet Hotohketana'ôtse—Fallen Star—returned to help the people. One day he returned as an orphan boy and entered a Cheyenne village, finding the lodge of an old woman. He claimed that she was his grandmother from generations past, so she welcomed him and let him stay. He was thirsty but she had no water and the people were afraid to go near the water because the Méhne, a giant water serpent, kept eating those who were not fast enough to fetch water from the river. The young man went to collect some water, and in doing so, was swallowed by the Méhne. While inside the belly of the monster, the young man saw all of his people sitting and crying in despair. It upset him to see so many people suffering, so he cut through the side of the giant serpent and escaped long enough to cut off its head. All of his people were released and the young man returned home a hero.[30]

Later Hotohketana'ôtse was cold and asked his grandmother to start a fire. She said that the people could not gather wood because of Méstaa'e, a giant owl. It ate people when they went out to gather wood. Méstaa'e swallowed people whole or put them into his ears and kept them in his head as prisoners. The next day the young man went out to gather wood and was snatched by the giant owl and placed in his ear. He saw his people sitting with their heads down, weeping and singing sad songs in the monster's ear.

They were frightened and weak-spirited, but the young man scolded them: "Why don't you do something? Why do you sit around and let this go on? Why don't you kill this monster?" The young man gripped his hatchet, which he used for cutting wood, and shattered the spine of the giant owl monster, severing its head and killing it instantly. He rescued his people, once again, from captivity and from suffering and despair.[31]

In his third heroic feat, Hotohketana'ôtse met a giant monster that wore a necklace made of human ears.[32] His name was Ôhnešêstse'exanehe (Double Eyes) and he would bite off people's ears, especially those of mischievous children, making them deaf. Bull Thigh best articulates the story of the monster. Bull Thigh was a Southern Cheyenne Dog Soldier and Keeper of the Sacred Arrows at the time of his rendition. His band, like most, remembered the monster by the name of Méstae.

Méstae, the Big Ghost

There was a big camp of Cheyenne in the midst of a big grove of timber on the Cheyenne River. The ghost came to the camp. When he came at night he cried out. He shook the earth and frightened everyone at night. Every night he cut somebody's ear off. Three hundred and sixty-five times he got an Indian's ear. He strung them as a charm.

There was a great big lodge. One evening people came together there. There was another bunch of Cheyenne about sixty miles from the gang. A young man journeyed to the first band. He came there just before Big Ghost came there. They were all in that lodge. He asked them why they came together there. They said to him: "There's a great big ghost that comes every night and gets our ears, those of every one of us. Look at us. We all have one ear." He looked at them. They all had but one ear. They were very much afraid. He said to them: "If he comes here, I will show him a trick." The people felt glad. He said to them: "I'm going out to meet him." He went out to the forest just after the sun went down. He looked about at the bottoms of trees. He picked fungus from every tree and strung them over his shoulder. He had a buffalo robe. The hair was outside, and he watched the ghost coming. He heard the voice of a ghost. The earth was shaking as it spoke. When he heard him, he got up; walked to meet him. He went to meet him on the same path. The young man said to him: "My friend, what are you trying to do? Are you trying to come on my way and imitate my trick?" Big Ghost said to him: "My friend, I'm not trying to imitate you at all. I am coming to these people to get their ears so that I can make a charm from them." The young man said to him: "Look here; look at me." He opened his robe; he had a string of fungi. Big Ghost was terrified. "No, my friend, I'm not trying to imitate your ways." "You stay out here," the young man said to the ghost. "Let me first go to see these people." The young man insisted. He said: "What is against your ways?" "Well," Big Ghost said, "if somebody takes a hair with grease and throws it in the fire, and beats a drum, that hurts my nature." The young man went to where the people were in the big lodge. He gave them instructions. He told one of them to get buffalo hairs and grease and a drum. He went back and met the ghost. He said to him: "We are going down together; we'll go right in together. You take one half of these people's ears and I will take the other." So they came in. All were scared. There was much excitement. The one that had the buffalo hair and grease threw it right on the fire. When the smoke rose the ghost snuffed it in his nostrils. The drumming was going on. He was dead. The young man had clubbed him to death. The young man told the people next morning to make a big sweat lodge and build a big fire in front of it, and to put stones on it. He called all the people to come. He had got their ears from the ghost. This young man went in the sweat lodge with the ears. As they came he healed their ears one by one as they passed until the last. So they got their ears back. He told them to go bring wood to burn the ghost. After the fire was burning they set the ghost on the top. It was burned up, and melted into different forms of beads and hunks of ashes; and the camp moved away. So be it.[33]

By establishing a false friendship, the young Hotohketana'ôtse was able discover the monster's weakness and subdued him, but the Double Eyes was not the last demon.

The Cheyennes were threatened by yet another monster, an old medicine woman who wore a robe of human scalps.[34]

A young woman came to Hotohketana'ôtse and asked for his help. She said that this monster scalped all of her people in her village. She was the only one who was not harmed. The young hero and the young woman went to visit this old woman. The old monster invited them into her lodge and the young man offered their scalps to complete her robe. "You are missing two, and you can have ours," he said, "we are young and our hair is long and beautiful." The old monster said, "I'm glad you are here and I will take your scalps now." She approached the young man and tried to cut his scalp with her stone knife, but it broke on his head. She was frightened when she saw that the young man was made of stone. The young man hit the old monster killing her with one blow. Then he took her robe of scalps and built another large sweat lodge. He invited everyone in the village to come and participate. As before, when the ceremony was complete, everybody's scalp was reattached and everyone's health was restored. This was the last feat that the young culture hero completed. He married the young woman and lived out his life with her people for one generation.

In this third world, the Cheyenne people's population grew to nearly two thousand within a few generations. Because the nation was much larger, their way of living was eventually threatened by war from other Indian peoples who desired Cheyenne cornfields and fishing grounds. Coyote explained when the Cheyennes lost their corn and the devastation that followed: "They then went on a buffalo hunt. It was some months before they returned. Upon their return they discovered someone had been there and had stolen all their stored corn. They knew not who had done this. The Cheyennes considered this a serious loss, the same as losing a relative."[35] During the "time of the dog" the Cheyennes met different groups of peoples, some became allies while others did not. Among the enemy peoples were the Hóheehe (Assiniboine), who continually waged war against the Cheyennes. The Hóheehe harassed the Cheyennes, and the Cheyennes blamed the Hóheehe for burning and stealing their crops of corn; the Cheyennes fought back.[36] Eventually the pressure increased so much that the time came for the Cheyenne Nation to move again. After one of their villages and cornfields were burned, the leaders decided to move.

A medicine man named Ma'heo'o Ôhnee'êstse (Standing Medicine) rose as a leader to aid in the move. He possessed a unique flint-headed spear, called Ó'oxêtséme, which was attached to a wooden hoop adorned with numerous magpie feathers. This sacred object allowed Ma'heo'o Ôhnee'êstse to do phenomenal feats, like foresee future events and conceal the people from other living beings as they traveled the lands.[37] When the time came for the Cheyennes to leave, he assembled the people and led them using the power of his medicine lance. "I remember where we are supposed to go," said the prophet, "and I will show you." At nighttime he was able to summon a bright light, which showed the direction to a new land. The glowing light was the fallen star they were supposed to find from the previous world. The people followed the medicine man for several days until they eventually arrived at a large body of water, the Missouri River.[38] The light still glowed from the land on the other side, so the people had to cross. Ma'heo'o Ôhnee'êstse told the people to form a line at the edge of the water, and after performing a ceremony and singing four songs, the water parted, allowing the people to walk across to a new land.

THE FOURTH WORLD

The light from the fallen star no longer glowed at night on their new land. Here the Cheyennes began a new life in this fourth world and rebuilt a new nation once again, the fourth héstanovestôtse.[39] At this time the people crossed three major bodies of water, and they believed that when they died their spirits crossed not only these three bodies of water, but also a fourth and final lake, to reach the home of their ancestors. They remained reluctant to return to the lands of their old worlds for fear of disturbing the spirits of their dead relatives.

For several generations the Cheyennes lived in this fourth world, which became known as "the time of the buffalo" and which was also the beginning of a measure of time simply known as tóotseha (very long ago). The people camped along what is now known as the Cheyenne River and at the Black Hills. They farmed and hunted, and most continued to live in wood and earthen lodges. Collectively they acquired new spiritual ways and practices to survive in this land. As time passed they became more dependent on hunting and, initially, this resulted in many challenges. At the time the Cheyennes were unaccustomed to the colder winters on the Plains, the large birds that often harassed them, and the large carnivorous animals that also hunted big game and competed for food. A time came for a new prophet to help the people, and his name was Bow-In-Hand or Bow-Fast-to-his-Body.

Bow-In-Hand

One day when hunting became very difficult, an old medicine man asked for help from the Great Medicine. He gathered some wood and cut the best sticks and placed them into a pile. He placed a buffalo robe over the sticks and the next day Bow-In-Hand appeared in the old man's lodge. He was a young man and sat with the buffalo robe cloaked around his shoulders, and he held a strong bow and a quiver full of arrows and a fan made from the wing of a golden eagle.[40] "Grandfather, I have come to help my people," said the young man.

The first enemy that the young Bow-In-Hand faced in this new world was Hooema'hahe (Winter Man or Frost), who possessed a flute and strong medicine that kept the weather freezing cold at all times. He often chased hunters away by slapping or hitting them when they were out in the cold.[41] Bow-In-Hand found the winter spirit's lodge and challenged him to a contest of medicine. "You have caused the people to suffer for no reason," proclaimed Bow-In-Hand. "Now we must decide if you should continue to do so." The young man sang a song and waved his eagle feather fan to cause a warm breeze that melted the snow, while Hooema'hahe blew his flute to bring the cold wind and freezing snow. Bow-In-Hand was more powerful than the winter spirit, and eventually he defeated and killed him with warmth. Afterward the Cheyenne people came out and killed the spirit's offspring by pouring hot water into the crevices where they hid. They left only one, which is why there is still a winter season in the Cheyenne homeland.[42]

The second enemy of Bow-In-Hand was a giant white crow named Okohke Ôhvo'omaestse (Big White Crow). It was always scaring the game away when the Cheyennes were out on the hunt. Bow-In-Hand captured a giant white crow in the manner that the Cheyennes had since caught eagles: by hiding in a dugout and using a carcass as bait. Once he caught the crow, Bow-In-Hand scolded, "You have been causing these people to starve. I will let them decide your fate." He brought the crow to his people, and then they held him over a fire until he turned black. The crow cawed and warned, "One day I will come back and eat all of your people." The people eventually killed it and burned his body in the fire.[43]

After Bow-In-Hand defeated the Winter Man and killed the giant crow, the Cheyennes still failed in their hunts because two giant bears chased them away every time they killed an animal. Bow-In-Hand went on the next hunt and while the others ran when the bears came, the young man was able to kill them by shooting them in the one weak spot that nobody knew of, their toes. He then tracked them to their den to kill the bear cubs but decided not to since this would have led to their extinction.[44] The people then had more successful hunts. Bow-In-Hand was a great medicine man and prophet, but he was mortal and only lived among the people for one generation. He died an old man.

Despite the feats of Bow-In-Hand, the fourth world was still a dangerous place for the Cheyennes to live. There were still giant animals and monsters preying on the people. During the "time of the buffalo" another leader arose to help the Cheyennes: Mo'keheso (Little Calf).

Little Calf

Mo'keheso (Little Calf) decided one day to leave his parents and set out on an adventure when his voice started changing. Along the way he came to an old Cheyenne man who said that there were cruel giant thunderbirds from the north that caused violent storms, winds, thunder, and lightning. "I must defeat these thunderbirds," proclaimed Mo'keheso, and he set out to kill the beasts. He had to pass through a wilderness where evil spirits lived and who killed strangers, even young boys and girls. Mo'keheso met a mysterious girl spirit who was able to help him navigate through the wilderness. Mo'keheso shared his story to the girl spirit, who also wanted to kill the thunderbirds. She left Mo'keheso behind and made her way to the camp of the chief thunderbird and his family. There the female spirit was welcomed into the camp as a potential bride to the son of the chief thunderbird. This mysterious female spirit eventually killed the son of the chief thunderbird. She cut off his head and flew through the air back to Mo'keheso. Both heroes returned to the old man and presented the head to him. Mo'keheso was rewarded with a new bow and set of arrows, but the girl spirit vanished.[45]

Later the old man asked Mo'keheso to go south to kill a giant elk that had a thick hide that could not be pierced. It was a strange beast that caused massive dust storms. "I will defeat this giant elk," proclaimed the boy. So he left and along the way he traveled through the land of good spirits who all feared the great elk. The boy slept on the ground, avoiding the vengeful thunderbird spirits that still searched for him. He acquired sacred arrows from different ground-burrowing animals: a sharp-pointed arrow from a weasel chief, an agate-headed arrow from a prairie dog chief, a cactus-thorn pointed arrow from a badger chief, and an exploding arrow from a gopher chief. With each of the arrows, Mo'keheso was able to kill the monster elk. He also killed its female mate so that no offspring could create the violent storms again. The boy took the male elk's meat, hide, and giant antlers to the old man's lodge, where they feasted and revered the sacred elk antlers.[46] These antlers have since become part of the land.

Mo'keheso returned to his people still a young man. One day an eagle catcher failed to catch a giant red eagle.[47] The sacred bird scolded him and challenged him, "If he ever wanted to catch me, use your father as bait." The next day the eagle catcher's father agreed to be used as bait. The father was also a leader of the nation, and these great eagles were beautiful but often preyed upon the people, carrying them off and eating them. When these birds carried off their chief, the people were humiliated and plunged into deep despair and depression. Mo'keheso decided to help the eagle catcher retrieve his father, proclaiming, "I can defeat these eagles, but not alone. We will do this together." The two young men made a large basket, which was rigged to capture several eagles and use them to carry the boys into the sky. They arrived at a land above the earth and, after searching, they found the missing chief. All three of them then killed the giant red eagles and collected all of their feathers.[48] They returned home as heroes and just like the other large beasts, these giant birds no longer brought pain and suffering to the Cheyennes.

In the fourth world there was one beast that relentlessly tormented the Cheyennes. Momáta'évoestahe (Angry White Buffalo) or Double Teeth Bull was an oversized buffalo that frequently ate men while they hunted.[49] Mo'keheso (Little Calf) is credited with killing this giant, man-eating buffalo, but some bands recall that it was Má'kó'se (Youngest) who killed the chief animal. White Buffalo told the story, which I edited and adapted.

The Double Teeth Bull

Somebody told two young Indian boys about the Double Teeth Bull. The boys went to the place where the bull lived. As they traveled, the Double Teeth Bull met them and then galloped toward them. The boys shot at him with all of their arrows but they missed, and the bull continued to charge at the boys. The bull drove the boys back to their village, where they fled to their lodges for safety. All of the warriors of the camp tried to kill the bull, but the bull was too powerful and killed and ate them all. The bull then killed and ate the women and children. Only one child got away.

The child that got away was a boy, because he was a fast runner. The Double Teeth Bull found that he was alive and went after him. The boy ran up a hill. The bull chased him into another camp. Here the people tried to kill Double Teeth Bull, but he killed them all. Like the camp before, the bull ate all of the women and children. The boy got away again, but this time one girl also got away and ran with him; she escaped with a bow but with no arrows. Double Teeth Bull ran after the boy and girl and drove them up a hill. They fled to another camp and they hid in a lodge for safety. As before, the people of the camp tried to kill the bull. And like before, the bull killed all of the men and ate the women and children.

Once again the boy and the girl got away, because they were fast runners. This time they both escaped with bows, but they still had no arrows. The Double Teeth Bull chased them up a hill. Once again the children ran into a camp and hid in a lodge. The people tried to kill the bull, but as before, the bull killed the warriors and ate the women and children. The two children escaped again; this time they had arrows.

The bull chased the children up a hill. Here the boy, named Little One or Youngest (Má'kó'se), got tired and wanted to rest. The two children stopped, and the boy readied his bow with an arrow. He said to the girl: "I'll shoot up at the bull, but you must shut your eyes and wait." The boy moved a distance as the bull targeted and charged at the girl as she stood with her eyes closed. Má'kó'se told the girl, "Now open your eyes, sister, go on."

Unafraid, the girl watched the bull coming toward her and cried, "My little brother, do your best."

Má'kó'se replied, "I will do so. I am holy. I shoot with magic." The boy shot his arrow and it hit the Double Teeth Bull. The bull was wounded and stumbled into the trees. The trees shook as the wounded bull stumbled against the trees. Má'kó'se rejoiced, "I have shot him! I have killed him!" The bull fell dead and lay stretched on the ground. That was the end of the Double Teeth Bull, and this is the last telling.[50]

Má'kó'se is credited with killing this giant, man-eating buffalo, but again, some bands recall that it was Mo'keheso (Little Calf) who killed the chief animal, as their names sound similar. The story of the Double Teeth Bull, like most stories, implies that the youth are the ones who inevitably lead the Cheyenne Nation out of despair in turbulent times.

The fourth world is known as "the time of the buffalo" because of the large populations of both the giant and smaller types of buffalo. The giant, man-eating buffalos ruled the lands and soon the population of the giant animals began to cause an imbalance as the human population began to dwindle.[51] One group of people decided to travel to the south, where they began a new life journey.[52] After this group left, those living in the Black Hills endured a second Great Flood. The water washed away tracks of those who went south. The Cheyennes who remained in the north believed they separated from the main group forever. Meanwhile the main body endured the new world among the giant buffalo. Determined to stay, the spiritual leaders held a meeting and prayed to Ma'xema'hēō'e for an answer to the chaos caused by the giant animals.

Ma'xema'hēō'e decided that the fate of all living beings would be determined by a race. If the humans won, they could eat the buffalo, but if they lost the buffalo would continue to eat humans. The birds teamed with the humans since they shared the trait of having two legs, and most did not want to stop eating flesh, especially the eagles, hawks, and other birds of prey. The other four-legged animals, like antelope, deer, and elk, joined the buffalo herds. The dramatic Great Race around the Black Hills lasted for four days, and numerous animals died in the challenge.[53] The race concluded when a magpie won. It hid behind the horn of the fastest buffalo cow, named Swift Head, and flew out to win the race for the humans.[54] After the race, the humans and some birds were allowed to eat the buffalo, but only if they promised to maintain balance with them and with nature, a promise that giant buffalos failed to keep.

In time the era of the giant animals came to an end and the humans found their place to live in balance with the natural world. Out of the disorder and unjust world of the giants came peace and harmony. Ma'xema'hēō'e then created four sacred laws of nature to ensure that the world remained in balance. The Cheyennes were given the responsibility to uphold these laws, but also viewed them as promises to the unseen sacred beings and nature: (1) humans could not kill animals or take the plants from nature for any reason other than for survival, healing, or ceremonial practices; (2) humans could not kill or harvest more than they needed; (3) the killing of animals and plant life should be done in prayer, with respect, and not for entertainment or amusement; and (4) humans must sacrifice and pay homage to the plants, birds, and animals during an annual Medicine Lodge or Sun Dance ceremony.

When the Cheyennes first hunted buffalo, they were inexperienced because they were still planting corn and hunting small game. As White Buffalo states, the buffalo eventually revolutionized the Cheyenne cultural way of life: "Cheyennes arrived first at the top of the Black Hills. The buffalo used to eat them. A young man introduced [advanced] bows and arrows to kill buffalo. He killed the first one. They dressed the buffalo with stone knives. They found a piece of human fat near the buffalo's heart. From that the Cheyennes increased in knowledge."[55] After the Great Race, the Cheyennes began to create new ceremonies centered on hunting and gathering. Some bands remember this time as "the beginning of the workings of the mind."[56]

The Cheyennes befriended new peoples from the lands of the fourth world, including the Arapaho. Meanwhile, the Moiseyu, who were part of the Cheyennes, went back to the lands in the north because they were fond of the lifestyle among the fish and fowl on the lakes.[57] The Cheyennes believed that the Moiseyu were unaccustomed to killing buffalo, because they were haunted by the spirits of slain animals that came in dreams asking for their lives back.[58] The Cheyenne families who married into the Moiseyu also left and never returned.[59] The Cheyennes allied with the Crees, but the Crees eventually became enemies to a band of the Lakota Sioux as they competed for hunting grounds. But when the Crees allied with the Hóheehe, they also became the enemies of the Cheyennes. Meanwhile the Cheyennes and various bands of the Lakota Sioux became close allies and intermarried; their peace is everlasting. Not until the sixth world would the Crees and Cheyennes regain peace and friendship, even though the Cheyennes remembered them to be relatives from long ago.

While in the fourth world, the Cheyennes persevered in making a new life on the Plains. They acquired special medicines and ceremonies to kill buffalo in a sacred and respectful manner so their spirits could rest in peace. Soon the people began to hunt buffalo regularly, utilizing all parts of the animals: bones and horns for tools, hides for clothing, and meat for food. They also used the parts of other animals and began to honor them as gifts from the Earth. Here is where the first elk horn scrapers and porcupine combs were made and where the first earth paints were used. This is also when the Cheyennes smoked tobacco and used the front leg bones of deer and antelope as pipes.[60]

By the next generation the Cheyenne people became skilled but sacred hunters of elk, deer, and antelope, yet they relied almost exclusively on buffalo. Their way of living changed to accommodate the sacred animal, but they did not entirely abandon their corn-planting ways. In the fourth world, the "time of the buffalo," the Cheyennes eventually matured as a powerful nation, reaching prime and pinnacle, and their population increased to nearly four thousand, comprising 444 families. During this time period the Cheyennes began to divide into bands, each self-subsisting yet part of the Cheyenne Nation. Some bands remember this time as "the time they began to form camp in a circle."[61]

The nation thrived in the fourth world in balance for numerous generations, but another set of challenges had arisen. The first evil people came into existence as witches, murderers, and tyrants. The people began to prey upon one another: killing each other, stealing from and cheating their own neighbors and relatives. Lies began to dominate and some people began to lose their minds. It became so bad that children could no longer survive because parents were not fulfilling their parental duties and responsibilities. Elders became greedy braggarts and elitists. Although food, shelter, and material wealth were plentiful, as provided by the buffalo, it seemed the nation was going to crumble from within. The people remembered the sacred laws of nature, but they lacked any laws of humanity. They needed to change before they completely destroyed themselves.

A day came when a young man named Motsé'eóeve (Sweet Root Standing) brought about the much-needed change. Motsé'eóeve was intelligent and magical, and he taught the Cheyennes many things as a child, as a young man, and as an adult. While still a young man, the prophet traveled about his people's lands and learned from all that he observed. After being away from the people for four years on one of his sacred journeys, Motsé'eóeve returned, bringing with him four Medicine Arrows and four sacred laws of humanity.[62] The laws applied to all people belonging to the nation and they were, more or less, promises to the living-nation: (1) a Cheyenne must not lie or deceive another Cheyenne or the Cheyenne people as a nation; (2) a Cheyenne must not steal or cheat another Cheyenne or the Cheyenne Nation; (3) a Cheyenne must neither marry his or her own relatives nor commit incest; and (4) a Cheyenne must not kill another Cheyenne.[63] Motsé'eóeve instructed that whenever a Cheyenne killed a fellow citizen, the Medicine Arrows were to be ceremonially renewed and cleansed.

Furthermore, every year the people were to reunite as a United Cheyenne Nation to hold the Arrow Lodge or Arrow Ceremony to remind the people of the sacred laws of humanity. Motsé'eóeve was more than a prophet; he was a holy person who lived among the Cheyennes for four generations and bestowed numerous teachings.

After the arrival of the Medicine Arrows and the teachings of Motsé'eóeve, the people began to refine their way of living using the teachings and lessons from previous worlds. The Cheyenne people thrived under these sacred laws and they came to value nature and each other following the covenants set forth by the supernatural powers. The héstanovestôtse was able to renew itself in balance and harmony for generations.

THE FIFTH AND SIXTH WORLDS

After centuries of stability, the nation would endure another change with the introduction of a new animal, the Spanish-bred mustang. The arrival of the horse marked the beginning of a new world and way of life. This fifth world became known as "the time of the horse." The people did not need to abandon entirely their old ways, however. Instead they became mobile and were able to expand their presence to surrounding lands. The arrival of the horse signified the complete end of "the time of the dog," as these animals were no longer used as beasts of burden and corn was no longer a necessity of life. "The time of the horse" is the most popular era and comprises oral tradition, art, and culture of the Cheyenne horsemen of the Plains. The Cheyenne Nation rebuilt itself and thus began the life of the fifth héstanovestôtse.

The time of the horse came to an end with the arrival of alien, non-Indigenous peoples. This transition represented the start of the sixth world of Cheyenne history, known as "the time of the white man." This world has proven to be the most difficult for the Cheyenne Nation as it continues today. It has brought about the most violent and destructive assaults against the Cheyenne Nation; it is more violent and destructive than any of the monsters and beasts from the old worlds. The sixth héstanovestôtse does not live in this world, because it merely survives, as do the Cheyenne people in this time of the white man. Yet the time has come for the rebirth of a new héstanovestôtse, since the history of the Cheyenne Nation has not ended; it is still being made.

CHAPTER 2

Manáhéno: The Bands

During the time of the buffalo, in the fourth world, Cheyenne population flourished. The Cheyenne Nation émanàha'oo'o (grew in population) and expanded its territory by splitting into different manáhéno, or bands. The first split, which led to the creation of the first two bands, is remembered as a significant part of Cheyenne national history. In the Cheyenne oral tradition, three groups of Cheyennes had already separated, once while crossing the ice and twice after the First and Second Great Floods. The first formal division, however, occurred as a result of population growth and territorial expansion.

When the Cheyennes lived as one band, it began to grow in size, and this growth had an adverse effect on the people's lifestyle. The hunting and gathering way of living, which was bestowed upon the Cheyennes as they entered into the fourth world, began to take its toll near the growing camp. Game populations became scarce and the lands and waterways were polluted with human waste much sooner than before. The people did not want to violate the sacred laws of nature by taking more than they needed, so they had to change or adapt. Stands In Timber (Northern Cheyenne) explains the adaptation: "In one bunch; they learned the lesson they would starve that way, because too many would hunt over the same place. That's one reason why they cut up in groups. They say they never camped one place more than five days. They say that kept them healthy."[1] The increase in population also contributed to internal disputes, as families competed for power and resources. Some families began to leave the main village and fend for themselves. Social and political change was also imminent.

The solution for the pressing problems was for the main band to split into two equal bands, but the split had to be mutual and in a peaceful manner, since both groups were to carry on the Cheyenne cultural way of life. Rather than threatening their lives or changing their ways of living, the nation thus divided into two bands. The first split represents a survival mechanism that the Cheyenne Nation continued to follow until its last free days on the Plains. Each group, upon splitting, could continue the Cheyenne cultural way of life, each possessing and sustaining the national identity, history, and culture. Even if one were destroyed, through famine, disease, or war, the Cheyenne Nation would continue living because another group survived. Upon splitting, each band also continued to develop its local oral traditions, cultural practices, and ceremonial practices.

The band system, which is different from the colonized concept of a tribal system, of the Cheyenne Nation became the foundation of territorial expansion, sovereignty, and governance. Most, if not all, Plains Indian nations organized under the band system. A band is defined as a collective group of families that share similar experiences, cultures, customs, and beliefs; that camped, hunted, and traveled together; a smaller community belonging to a larger nation. The size of bands varied from thirty to forty families for a smaller band, with larger bands comprising one hundred or more families. Band camps were organized as mobile communities. Each family resided in the same location of the camp circle regardless of where the large camp was located. Family camp locations were determined when the band was originally founded. The first families of the band were located on the west side, and as the families grew and expanded, their camps expanded on either the north or south sides. As the band grew, so did the camp circle.

The band camp had a "door" that opened to the east where nobody was allowed to camp. At any given time or for any event, it was common for several bands to camp together. Standing Bear (Oglala) describes the band system of the Lakota:

> It was the rule for several bands to erect their villages close together. This allowed for social activities of which the Lakotas were very fond and, in early days, it added protection and strength to the bands. The common arrangement, in olden times, was the *dopa* village, or the village of four circles or bands. These four circles of tipis were set in a square, in the center of which was the *hocoka*, meaning middle or center. This inner or middle space was the social meeting ground for the four villages, where games, ceremonies, and festivities of all sorts were held. The *hocoka* was used much like the squares and plazas in the Pueblo villages.[2]

The four camp circle arrangements were considered a sacred village since it represented the four sacred directions. Larger camp circles included as many as ten bands, as in the case of the United Cheyenne Nation, and even included bands from other nations.

MANÁHÉNO: THE BANDS

The Cheyenne band system also established a sociopolitical system that fit the Plains environment and buffalo-dependent, mobile lifestyle. As the population increased with the introduction of the horse, the original five bands grew and split, creating the ten bands of a united nation. According to Cheyenne traditions, the entire Cheyenne Nation accounted for 444 families across ten major manáhéno. Each band comprised approximately forty-four families and had a population of approximately three hundred people.[3] Approximately sixty to seventy lodges made up a typical band.[4] Smaller villages may have been thirty to forty lodges, half the size of a major band, but still part of the Cheyenne Nation. Before the reservation era, the Cheyenne population fluctuated around four thousand souls, but this did not mean that the Cheyenne Nation was unorganized over a large area of land. The bands were key to Cheyenne survival and prosperity.

The band system is the closest the Cheyennes had to a clan system, since members of the Cheyenne Nation primarily identified themselves based on their respective manáhéno. Every citizen belonged to a band, as band membership was equivalent to citizenship of the Cheyenne Nation. The bands were made up of tight-knit family groups with extended kinship relationships, meaning that band members also carried a set of responsibilities to their respective band, such as loyalty, service, and dedication. Outsiders, who did not belong to a band, were not considered part of the Cheyenne Nation in that they did not have the responsibilities or rights provided by the bands. If a person had a single Cheyenne parent, whether mother or father, they automatically belonged to the band of that parent. If that person did not grow up in their Cheyenne parent's band, but rather with a band of Sioux or Arapaho, that person was not a member of the Cheyenne band and therefore not a citizen of the Cheyenne Nation. This person could choose to belong to their Cheyenne parent's band so long as he or she decided to live with their kinfolk. Band membership was typically matrilineal, since families customarily lived with the mother's family and band, but it was not a strict rule. A person whose parents were from different bands could choose to belong to either band, but could identify with both depending on where he or she decided to live.

Non-band-member Cheyennes—individuals who belonged to a different band and who were not married or settled into another band—often found themselves as outsiders, even if they were full-blooded Cheyennes. Coyote (Northern Cheyenne), as a young man, experienced this when he decided to follow the band of a young woman he wanted to court. The warrior leaders of the woman's band told him to return to his own band because he had "no relatives"—no one to feed, shelter, or protect him. Coyote had no choice but to return to his band.[5] Unlike the clanship systems of many

Indigenous peoples, the Cheyennes had no formal marriage restrictions between the bands. Cheyennes could marry within their own band and with members of other bands, "so long as they are not blood relatives."[6] Nonetheless, the Cheyenne incest law encouraged marriage with members of other bands, since bands largely were composed of blood relatives. Intermarriage with other Indian nations also led to an increase in population and the creation of new, smaller manåhéno.

THE HOOP AND SPEAR GAMES

From the traditional Cheyenne perspective, the splitting of bands was a ceremonial affair, an event involving elements of spiritualism and celebration. To understand how the Cheyennes perceived the creation of new bands, we must relearn the traditional game called the hoop and spear game, which was introduced by a prophet named Cherry Eater.[7] The hoop and spear game, like the wheel game, has ancient origins. Evidence of rawhide-netted hoops has been found in the cliff-dwelling ruins of Colorado, and the game was played by other peoples.[8] The hoop and spear game trained young people how to hunt with spears, but it was also a competitive, challenging, and athletically demanding sport. Much like lacrosse for the Iroquoian (Haudenosaunee), Great Lakes, and southeastern peoples, the game was legendary, with numerous rituals and rules of play.[9] For the Haudenosaunee, the game of lacrosse has deep spiritual meaning, as evidenced by a statement issued by the Grand Council of the Haudenosaunee Confederacy. Lacrosse is described as "one of our most revered traditions, spiritually and as a celebration of health, strength, courage, and fair play."[10] Like lacrosse for the Haudenosaunee, the hoop and spear game of the Cheyennes was a fiercely competitive game that fostered skilled and talented players.

The origin of the game comes from the story "Cherry Eater's Magic Hoops."[11] The boy, Cherry Eater, introduced the hoop and spear game to feed his starving family and village. As he speared four hoops, the hoops changed into slain buffalo. His starving people feasted on the animals and were thus saved from famine. The game of hoops requires three players, although more players could be divided into two teams. The target was either a simple hoop, called an axkôo, ä'ko'yo, or äkwi'u, that measured about eighteen inches in diameter, or an oxzevonistoz, which was a hoop that was netted with a "network of rawhide." The players used spears, called hooeseonoz or hoo'isi'yonots, which measured about thirty inches in length, and the players threw them at the hoop while it rolled.[12]

There are several methods to playing the game; the most common is for two teams to toss a number of wheels or hoops back and forth across a field

Anonymous Cheyenne drawing of two men performing a ceremony, before 1879. National Anthropological Archives, Smithsonian Museum Support Center, Suitland, Maryland (NAA MS 7463).

as each team attempts to spear them. A speared wheel or hoop is "won" by the team and scored. They toss the others back. This continues for several games and several hours. Another method requires running. On a flat field, two opposing players meet and one thrower stands between them. The thrower tosses the wheel in either direction as the players anticipate the throw. As soon as the wheel is released, the players must run along parallel to it and spear it. The one who spears, hoops, or nets it scores a point. The thrower follows the players and referees if any player gets too close or crosses the path of the hoop. If one does, the foul ends the match. The thrower resets the players and tosses the wheel in the other direction for the second match. The thrower tosses the wheel back and forth, while the players run back and forth across the field competing to spear the hoop and score. Games can be played up to 100 points by scores of 5, or to 1,000 by scores of 10. Teams would often alternate throwers and would sometimes have several wheels going at once. Points were kept using score sticks, and sometimes games would involve as many as twenty players with hundreds of matches, as competition was fierce. Each player wanted to be the best.

On a formal level, the spear and hoop game was played during the large encampments when multiple bands united. The competition was at the professional level between the best players and warriors from each of the bands. Before such a grand event, however, warrior society headmen and spiritual leaders held rituals and a formal event known as the Wheel Ceremony.[13] This ceremony has been long extinct, but its origins are traced back to the third world where Ma'heo'o Ôhnee'êstse (Standing Medicine) possessed the Ó'oxêtséme, a sacred wheel lance that helped the people traverse through the wilderness. The Wheel Ceremony represented elements of the feats of Ma'heo'o Ôhnee'êstse, as well as elements related to hunting, the warrior culture, and the male physique and athleticism.

The hoop and spear game eventually came to represent the formal division as well as the formal unification of different Cheyenne bands. It was a form of nonviolent warfare, and it relieved conflict and tension between two opposing sides. The Cheyennes have numerous stories that highlight the hoop and spear game as part of the intratribal and intertribal unification process, known as "Old Woman's Spring" stories.[14] Despite the differences in the stories, there are significant constants. The first is that each story highlights a single, large camp circle; the second, the presence of the hoop and spear game; third are two leaders, who represent two different bands but who are dressed exactly the same; and finally, that the two leaders befriend each other and bring their peoples together in a peaceful and celebratory amalgamation. While the story is about a unification of two different Cheyenne bands, it actually represents how the original band of the Cheyennes split into two identical groups.[15]

The following story takes place in the fourth world, in an era known as "the beginning of showing miracles to the starving people" and during "the time the Cheyennes camped in a circle."[16] In a big camp, as the story goes, the people gathered to watch a contest of the hoop and spear game. The two competing teams represented two bands camped in one big circle: one band camped on the north side, while the other camped on the south. The story of the first split occurred as told by White Buffalo. During this time, the Cheyennes were one large group and "were so numerous that they were starving." The Cheyennes were likely on the verge of imploding, but the events that unfolded led to the first split.

The Two Young Men

In the center of the camp, they used to play the wheel game. The people were so numerous that they were starving. While the wheel game was being played one afternoon there was a big hill due east. A young man started from the right-hand corner of the circle and to the middle of the opening. He had on a buffalo robe with the hair out. His face was painted like the circle. The center of his forehead was black. While he stood there, another fellow came from the left end of the circle; he started toward the middle of the entrance. He was dressed almost like the other fellow. The first said: "Why are you dressed just like me?" He said to him, "I guess you've come to imitate me. I dress this way for my own purpose." [According to Cheyenne custom, it is rude to copy another person's ceremonial paint, dress, appearance, or behavior without permission or rite.]

The other said: "If you have a purpose, I think I have one."

[The first responded,] "What one?"

He pointed to a spring. "I have one from that spring."

"So have I," said the other.

The people playing the wheel game came out to see them. They went into the spring. They came out. They brought corn and five pieces of meat, and red paint. The people left the wheel game and came near them. This corn [that they brought] was to raise corn hereafter. The five pieces of meat was multiplied. There always remained five pieces. Everyone had enough. The corn was given away for the people to plant. When this was done, then the buffalo hunt began. Although there were no buffaloes, every young man went hunting. They would stand in a circle at a great interval apart. On each end one was sent off to head the buffalo towards the circle. When they began to come in, the people closed the circle. They narrowed it, [then] shot the buffalo with bows and arrows and axes.[17]

The two young men who entered the spring met an old woman who gave them different ceremonial and sacred gifts to make them powerful leaders. Traditional storytellers describe the men as being the same height; they braided their hair in the same fashion, and both wore buffalo robes with the fur turned inside, as warriors, and were painted with red and yellow earth paints. They returned with clay jars, one filled with meat and the other with cornmeal. The Cheyennes continued to use clay pots until the wars with the whites.[18] A formal Wheel Ceremony, which has long disappeared, and the hoop and spear game came to represent the traditional Cheyenne cultural ways of remembering and reenacting the unification.

Although White Buffalo does not name the two young men, the historian George Bird Grinnell provides five similar stories about "The Buffalo and the Corn," each story containing differently named men but the same teacher, Mā-tā-ma' (Old Woman), and the same location of the camp, Mā-tā-ma' Hĕh'k-ā-ĭt (Old Woman's Water), which is located "at the mouth of the Cheyenne river where it empties into the Missouri."[19] The event, which is always introduced with an intense communal "wheel game," is so significant to the Cheyenne national history that it is remembered in different band histories. The old woman, Mâhtamâhááhe (modern spelling), is remembered as a woman prophet who taught the young men, among other philosophies, the importance of brotherhood and how to establish peaceful relations by hosting a feast with ceremonial food.[20] She also taught the young men how to paint themselves and how to behave as warriors, laying the foundation for proper Cheyenne warrior etiquette.[21] Her teachings became essential to the building of the Cheyenne Nation as it expanded throughout the years and as the Cheyennes befriended other Indian nations. Stands In Timber (Northern Cheyenne) tells the same story to explain the peace alliance between the Cheyenne and Lakota, using different names.[22]

When examined in its entirety, the main story reveals that the two young men represent two Cheyenne bands that decided to live apart from one another and that operated two different economies. The two bands united in one large camp circle to feast as one nation, and the story shows how the original camp now comprised two. The story preserves a unified Cheyenne identity, emphasizing that both bands were equal in all ways by highlighting the hoop and spear game, which all Cheyennes played, and that the two leaders were of equal stature, appearance, and dress.

In the story, the young man who represented the corn-planting band was identified by several names: Mâháeme (Corn Kernel), Cornleaf, Corn Tassel, Red Tassel, Red Tassel of Corn, and Corn Tassel on the Head, as well as Standing on the Ground. The young man who represented the buffalo-hunting band also had several names: Mai-tŭm' (Red, red, red, red), Rustling Leaf, Rustling Corn Leaf, and Sweet Medicine. The names Standing on the Ground and Sweet Medicine were converged with the Great Unification of the Tsétsêstâhese and Só'taeo'o, which is a completely different event that occurs after the story of the two young men and which I discuss in depth later in this chapter.

In the story of the two young men, after the old woman, Mâhtamâhááhe, imparted wondrous teachings upon the two young men, she painted them and dressed them in different clothing. As part of the ceremony, she also gave them new names: Corn Kernel was renamed It Goes In (his proxy Rustling Corn Leaf was renamed Beautiful Bird Wing); meanwhile, Rustling Leaf was renamed Red Paint (his proxy Corn Tassel on the Head was renamed Red Feather on the Head).[23] The new names represented the rebirth of the two young men, meaning they formally and spiritually changed from their previous character to follow a new promise or new way of life. According to Cheyenne custom, individuals are renamed at the first sign of puberty; young men and women thus acquire new responsibilities and duties as adults. The renaming element in the story is consistent with Cheyenne naming ceremonies.

At the conclusion of the story, the two "new" men invite all of their people to enjoy a grand feast. Afterward the two bands depart on friendly terms and frequently return to the same location—it is sacred ground—to hunt buffalo and plant corn. This is how the Cheyenne Nation divided into two bands but remained as one people.

Máháeme (Corn Kernel) or It Goes In was the young man who represented the corn-planting band, which became known as the Ohmésêhese (Eaters), while Mai-tŭm' (Red, red, red, red) or Red Paint represented the buffalo-hunting band, which became known as the Heveškėsenêhpåhese (Aortas). These were the first two bands of the Cheyenne people, who collectively called themselves Né'ohma'ehėtaneo'o (Sand Hill People).[24] Upon separating, each band created its own oral traditions or band histories, including origin stories of how their band came into existence. While the Ohmésêhese (Eaters) continued to rely on corn, the Heveškėsenêhpåhese (Aortas) were the band that began to rely more on hunting buffalo, as emphasized in their band history.

THE HEVEŠKĖSENÊHPÅHESE

The Heveškėsenêhpåhese (Aortas), according to White Buffalo, originated from the first man and first woman of Earth, created by the Great Medicine. They became conscious of living and procreating by understanding that babies are born ten moons after conception because humans have ten fingers, and that humans live for one hundred years. They also invented numerous creations, like fire, flint knives, arrowheads, bows and arrows, elk horn scrapers, buffalo horn spoons, wooden buckets, and how to domesticate dogs. They put their children on travois and used a porcupine tail comb and red paint to groom themselves. They also made clothes from deer hides and eventually came to killing buffalo to make robes, as elaborated by White Buffalo:

> After this was done the man thought he would smoke. He cut a piece of the buffalo's aorta and dried it hard like a rock. Then the woman said to him, "What are you going to smoke in that pipe?" He said, "I know, there's a weed that grows on sand hills which I am going to get, and mix it with Cree tobacco." That shows that Indians were the first people to introduce tobacco. After he used the aorta pipe he used one of deer bone. The aorta pipe is the origin of the Aorta clan. Up to this time there was but one family.[25]

The Heveškėsenêhpåhese earned reputations for smoking from their buffalo-aorta pipes and were remembered by the other Cheyenne bands as the first band to part from the main group. The culture hero who represented the hunting lifestyle, Mai-tŭm' (Red, red, red, red), is also remembered in Cheyenne national history as Wōtsitsí ōwō'a (Blood Bachelor), who did similar feats as Cherry Eater. All three personas and names represent the buffalo-hunting culture.

THE OHMÉSÊHESE

The larger band of Cheyennes were the Ohmésêhese (Eaters). According to modern oral traditions, these Cheyennes were called Eaters because they "ate good," as they enjoyed the nutrition of both corn and buffalo meat. The Ohmésêhese kept the bundle of the first five colors of corn that was bestowed upon them when they arrived to the world of corn. The people from the other bands respected its power to help the growth of plant life. The Ohmésêhese also developed local stories to explain the origins of their band. Wolf Chief, a Northern Cheyenne chief and member of the Ohmésêhese who was born in 1851, provided a narrative in the "Story of the Holy Head of Eaters."

Story of the Holy Head of Eaters

A great many years ago, this story was told by my then very old great-great-fathers who lived on the east of the Mississippi. There was a man [who] came from the forests to this band. It was not known where he came from; he was lost in the tribe. About 40 years after there was another boy who came to the same clan. He also never knew where he was from. The people thought he was only a medicine-man. They told him, "You're too young to be holy. This clan has got its own holy man." He disappeared again [away from] this clan. About 40 years after this second one, another came about. He was so small to teach the people about his tricks that should hereafter come to pass. The people said: "you are too small, and you will not live long enough to teach these people. You will have to go on." And he disappeared into the tribe again. About 40 [years] after this third time there appeared a young man [at the] age of 30, with [a] wife of [the] same age. He came to this clan. The people were glad to see them both, asking them where they came from. The young man told them that they had come from the big forest east of the Great River [i.e., Mississippi]; that they once were wild beasts from that forest, and had come down to tell what they knew for the good of the people. When these two people both slept at any time, they used to have a buffalo-child in their midst. It was a boy-child. As he was growing up to be a boy, the horns grew upon his head.[26]

This buffalo-child was a shape-shifter who could change into a buffalo calf and back into a child. He matured and became a prophet who did wondrous things to help his people, especially when they were starving. The unnamed child had done feats similar to those of the famous prophet Sweet Medicine, suggesting that this early story is the foundation for the Sweet Medicine legacy that eventually became a significant part of the Cheyenne national history.

For generations, the two original bands reunited at the sacred site Mā-tā-mā' Hĕh'k-ā-ĭt (Old Woman's Water), at the confluence of the Cheyenne and Missouri Rivers. When the Cheyennes found that their cornfields were either destroyed or robbed by enemy Indian nations (Crees, Rees, Arikaras, Pawnees, and/or Assiniboines), they were forced to abandon the corn-planting lifestyle, which in turn influenced their decision to visit the fertile land at Mā-tā-mā' Hĕh'k-ā-ĭt less frequently. Eventually the land was settled by whites, severing the Cheyennes from the site completely.[27] After the Cheyennes abandoned their corn-planting ways, but before the arrival of whites, they relied exclusively on hunting and gathering. They were very successful as they continued to expand to eventually become four bands: Heveškėsenêhpåhese (Aortas), Heévâhetaneo'o (Rope People), Mahéško'ta (Crickets), and Ôhméseheso (Eaters). These first four bands of the Cheyenne Nation resided and traveled throughout their homelands around the Black Hills and in the Cheyenne River basin, frequently interacting with other nations. United under the principles of the national history and the annual ceremonies, the Cheyenne Nation persevered.

As the Cheyenne population grew, the Cheyenne Nation continued to expand through "the time of the horse," eventually becoming ten bands, with several sub-branches or pseudo-bands. The principles of the Wheel Ceremony played a crucial role in preserving the sanctity of bands that parted from larger groups. Today the tradition of the hoop and spear game remains as part of the Northern Cheyenne culture as found in the sport of basketball. Not only do young Cheyennes play basketball to engage in a disciplined and competitive sport, but they also strive to demonstrate their athletic skills and talents while representing their respective manåhéno. One need only watch the epic Class C, Montana High School basketball games between the Northern Cheyenne Eagles of Busby (White River Band) and their rivals, the Morning Stars of Lame Deer (Black Lodge Band), to understand that the tradition lives on.

PART I | TSÈHÉSTÁNO: THE CHEYENNE NATION

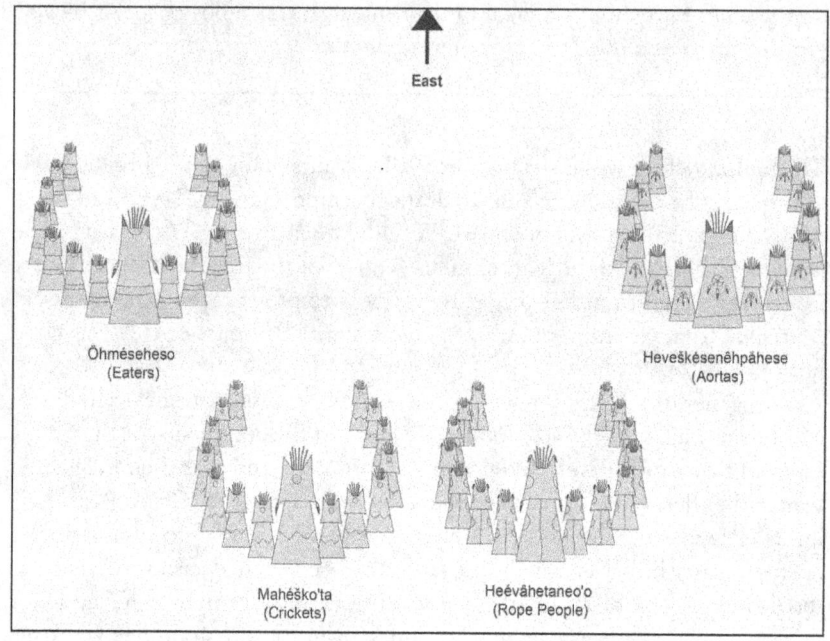

The first four original bands of the Tsétsêhéstâhese.

THE SÓ'TAEO'O

The story of the Só'taeo'o begins in the second world, "the land of the lakes." During this time the Cheyennes endured the First Great Flood and a group of people were separated. These people are thought to have become the Só'taeo'o, while the rest of the Cheyennes made it to the Black Hills. Ice, a renowned Northern Cheyenne medicine man, states that the "Sutaio came from [the] North East, across the Mississippi," when a "big flood" ravaged the land. The extent of time that the two nations spent apart is not known for certain but Ice indicated that it was long enough for their languages to change: "Their language was slightly different from the Cheyenne."[28]

Before reunification, after the first flood, the Só'taeo'o thrived and lived independently along the northern part of the Mississippi River valley next to "a great big lake" and rebuilt their nation.[29] Like the Cheyennes, they also developed a lifestyle of corn planting in a new world or era, known among the Só'taeo'o simply as "before the Só'taeo'o and Cheyenne came to live together." Badger, a Só'taa'e born in 1846, recalled his ancestors' experience: "The Sutaiu used to live East of the Mississippi. No buffalo [existed] across the Mississippi. [They] lived on birds, fishes, [and] other small animals. [They] planted corn. Reed grass and barks of trees [were] used to make lodges before crossing [the] Mississippi."[30] Not much more is known about the Só'taeo'o lifestyle during this era, only that it was similar to that of the Cheyennes.

A generation or two after the First Great Flood, the original band of Só'taeo'o experienced the Second Great Flood. The water split the Só'taeo'o into two groups; one was swept south and did not rejoin the Cheyenne Nation, while the other managed to move west and eventually met the Cheyennes. The consecutive natural disasters forced the Só'taeo'o band to search for a new home across the Mississippi. As they traveled across the land, they eventually crossed the Mississippi River and faced another tragedy: some of the families could not cross and were completely "lost."[31] The loss put much pressure on the small remaining Só'taeo'o population, but the people were determined. As Badger explained, the main Só'taeo'o band persevered and frequently camped with larger Lakota and Dakota band circles: the "No Colds" to the north; the Santees, led by Chief Medicine Lodge, to the east; and the "Burning Thighs" to the west.[32]

Eventually the band of Só'taeo'o traveled to a place called Ma'ōhōnaiíva, which means Red Rocks.[33] They found the pipestone quarry in present-day Minnesota; they were the first people to settle there. They rebuilt their nation and made four straight ceremonial pipes, the first red pipes of the Great Plains.[34] They hunted small game but continued to plant corn. A person known as Otter Man helped the Só'taeo'o by bestowing upon them tobacco, red paint, and a round plate of pipestone, which had the power to tame buffalo when a spiritual leader ceremonially burned certain herbs on its glossy surface. During this time, the Só'taeo'o lived in small lodges made of grass and wood and camped in a circle with an opening facing the sun; they weaved their clothing from tall grass and wore bark-soled shoes.[35] Só'taeo'o custom dictated that they speak only during the daytime and remain quiet at night, especially when young men courted young women. They did not yet have the Buffalo Hat and Sun Dance, but a prophet named Vóetséna'e (White Clay or Lime) came to lead them. He taught the Só'taeo'o how to dress in buckskin and paint themselves, and he showed the people how to have dances, which brought joy.

In a generation the Só'taeo'o increased their population, replenishing their band, thanks to the blessings of the buffalo, the "medicine" of the four straight pipes, and the round stone that tamed the buffalo. As a single band, the Só'taeo'o began to find an increasing value in the sacred buffalo, so they crossed the Missouri River following the herds away from the land of the red rocks. The move west across the Missouri River was also tragic for the Só'taeo'o, as Bull Thigh recalled how the Só'taeo'o arrived to the Black Hills, stating that they made rafts to cross the Missouri River. While they crossed, some of the Só'taeo'o families drifted down and were never seen or heard of again. Once the rest of them made it across, they traveled for about a month until they reached the Black Hills, where they met the Cheyennes and were united.[36]

The Só'taeo'o oral tradition details two major floods and two major river crossings; each were bittersweet victories. Friends, relatives, and entire families were lost, yet the Só'taeo'o were able to prevail. Once they united with the Cheyennes, their history converged and their triumphant legacy became part of the Cheyenne national history.

Before the Só'taeo'o met the Cheyennes, the Só'taeo'o built their band-nation under the leadership of several women prophets, since the culture was traditionally matriarchal. Voestaehneva'e (White Buffalo Woman) is credited with creating the chiefs, and Heovèsta'e'e (Yellow Top-to-Head Woman) is credited with bringing two major ceremonies that centered on hunting and earthly renewal. Vóetséna'e (White Clay or Lime) lived for one generation and named his successor Hō-īv'-nĭ-ĕsts (Standing on the Ground).[37] Hō-īv'-nĭ-ĕsts (also called Ho'ehêvêsénóó'e) received the gift of the power of prophecy and acquired the Ésevone (Buffalo Hat) and the ceremony associated with the hat, the Sun Dance. Afterward, he chose two old women to be the keepers of the Sacred Corn Covenant, which was secondary to the Ésevone.[38] Under the principles of the Ésevone and the teachings bestowed upon them from other prophets, the Só'taeo'o became successful buffalo hunters. The time came when they met the Cheyennes.

THE GREAT UNIFICATION

Although there are varying accounts of the unification of the Só'taeo'o and the Cheyennes, the following account is pieced together from documented sources, the oral traditions and perspectives of the White River Band of Northern Cheyennes in Montana, as well as versions from other bands. In every case, the Great Unification is remembered as a significant spiritual and political event in the Cheyenne national history. The event is known as móstamámòhevéstanovèhevóhe, "When they came to live together." This single event is the foundation for Cheyenne peacemaking, nation building, and sovereignty, as it embodies traditional Cheyenne principles of governance, leadership, and diplomacy. Traditional Cheyennes believe that the complete reunification was a blessing, since their lost relatives returned and rejoined the nation, thus healing the héstanovestôtse from traumatic loss. But as history reveals, the unification was not an easy feat to accomplish. In fact, it took two attempts for the Só'taeo'o and Cheyennes to finally unite and establish lasting peace.

White Eagle (Southern Cheyenne) asserted, "The Cheyennes [were] first found at the Black Hills at South Dakota" and "his grandfather's grandfather told that this was the place where they had their origin about 3–4 hundred years ago."[39] Ice (Northern Cheyenne) and Grasshopper (Southern Cheyenne) also assert that the Cheyennes had been in the Black Hills at least one hundred years before meeting the Só'taeo'o.[40] From the Cheyenne perspective they "originated" in the Black Hills, meaning they had been there for a number of generations.[41] Both the Cheyennes and the Só'taeo'o claim the Black Hills as their original homelands, even though they can trace their presence and history farther east. Nonetheless, their claim is legitimate because the Cheyennes lived in the Black Hills for hundreds of years and since the Só'taeo'o united with the Cheyennes, and adopted their lifestyle, they also share the claim to have originated in the Black Hills.

According to Ice, the Só'taeo'o met the Cheyennes on two different occasions at two different places. His account is consistent with those of other Cheyennes as well as the modern oral tradition.[42] The first meeting, Ice says, took place at the mouth of the Yellowstone River, at the confluence with the Missouri River. The location is somewhere between the present-day Fort Peck (Montana) and Fort Berthold (North Dakota) Indian Reservations. Accordingly, Ice states that the second meeting, which led to the Great Unification, occurred at the mouth of the Cheyenne River, "where the Standing Rocks [Sioux live]," which is the present-day location of Lake Oahe.[43] The meeting site is located somewhere on the present-day Standing Rock Sioux and Cheyenne River Sioux Indian Reservations in North and South Dakota, at the confluence of the Cheyenne and Missouri Rivers. Ice emphasized that here "is where the Cheyenne met the Sutaio, over 200 years ago," which would be around 1700.[44]

Bull Thigh also affirms the second meeting on the Missouri River: "Near where Pipestone is, on the Missouri River, is where the Sutaio came from, [they] met Chey[ennes] at Missouri River."[45] Wrapped Hair (Northern Cheyenne) confirms that the unification took place on the present-day Standing Rock Sioux Indian Reservation. He states, "It was on the east side of the Missouri River near the Ree country where the Ch[eyennes] and S[ó'taeo'o] met. The S[ó'taeo'o] had crossed the Missouri and went towards [where the] Standing Rock Agency now is and met the Ch[eyennes] there."[46]

It is clear that Lake Oahe and surrounding lands are significant to the Cheyennes and Só'taeo'o as much as they are to the Lakota and Dakota peoples who continue to reside there.

THE SÓ'TAEO'O AND THE HEVEŠKÈSENÊHPÅHESE

The first meeting of the two subnations did not lead to any peace. Wolf Chief (Northern Cheyenne) was a chief of the Ôhméseheso Band and recalled that this first encounter between the two nations was unpleasant. He remembers it as a fight between the two peoples.[47] Bull Thigh simply states that "during the fight, they all fell, but rose, surrendered to each other, proclaimed peace, and went to the Black Hills."[48]

As the population of the Cheyennes grew, more bands expanded deeper into the Plains. It was inevitable that the Cheyenne Nation met and interacted with other Indian nations. One day members of the Heveškèsenêhpåhese Band of Cheyennes met another group of people. They feared that these aliens were hostile, so the leaders sent some men to observe these new people. When the Cheyenne hunters arrived, they came to the confluence of the Yellowstone and Missouri Rivers and on the other side they saw a camp of people living in white conical skin lodges, similar to their own conical wooden lodges. The men and leaders from the strange village spotted the Cheyennes. The alien people, who were dressed in white buckskin clothes, then quickly gathered to defend their people, for they feared attack from the Cheyennes. Meanwhile, the Cheyennes were still on the other side of the river and did not yet cross, but they could see the people in a panic and the men preparing their weapons for a fight. The Cheyennes returned home.

A council was held because the Heveškèsenêhpåhese did not want to deal with another threatening nation in their world, so their leaders deliberated on what to do. They concluded that rather than live in fear of attack, they would coax the warriors of the strange people to chase them. While they crossed the river, the Cheyennes would kill them all. Afterward, the Cheyennes would cross the river, enter their camp, and adopt all the women and children into their band. Meanwhile, the leaders from the new group of people also deliberated on what to do. They decided to wait until the Cheyennes were crossing the river and then they would annihilate the trespassers as they waded through the water. They would then follow their tracks to find their village and adopt all of the Cheyenne women and children.

When the Cheyennes returned to the river, the two groups came to a standstill, since neither would cross, fearing attack while they were occupied. Instead, they began insulting one another. Much to their surprise, they realized they easily understood each other's speech. Astounded and confused, the Só'taeo'o leader invited the Cheyenne leader to a meeting. As White Buffalo recalled, White Buffalo Tail was the head chief of the "Sutaio," and Red Paint was the head chief of the Heveškėsenêhpåhese. They decided to meet on a high butte, where they smoked from their own pipes and discussed a resolution to their territorial dispute. A spirit arrived from the unknown to aid in the decision-making process. White Buffalo Tail and Red Paint began to quarrel, accusing each other's people of trespassing. In the end "Red Paint's feelings were hurt and angry." The Cheyenne chief of the Heveškėsenêhpåhese was found in the wrong: "He bowed his head down and sat still," and his people left without him. When his band of Heveškėsenêhpåhese camped in the distance, he could be seen still sitting on top of the hill alone. His people missed him and they told his son to go back and rescue the chief, but by the time he arrived, Red Paint was gone. The boy could not find his father. Red Paint never was found.[49]

The significance of the story reveals that the Cheyenne leader of the Heveškėsenêhpåhese, Red Paint, was shamed for attempting to attack and kill the Só'taeo'o, who were also considered to be Cheyennes. The spirit who aided in the negotiation likely enforced the Cheyenne law that prohibited murder. Red Paint exiled himself, even though he was not a proven murderer. For the Cheyennes this first meeting ended in utter failure, diplomatically and spiritually.

THE SÓ'TAEO'O AND THE ÔHMÉSEHESO

Not long after the first encounter, the time came for the two subnations to formally make a peace agreement. The next meeting took place near the Black Hills on the Cheyenne River. A Cheyenne leader of the Ôhméseheso named Wise Buffalo sent four of his chiefs to meet four chiefs of the Só'taeo'o.[50] This was a formal act that proved to be successful in diplomacy. The Cheyennes adopted this practice of sending four representatives when meeting with other nations from then on.

At the meeting, the Só'taeo'o conducted a very formal welcoming ceremony and invited the Cheyennes into their most sacred lodge, which housed the Ésevone (Buffalo Hat) and which was described by Wolf Chief as beautifully decorated and painted. Wolf Chief described this meeting to be full of material splendor, as the Só'taeo'o possessed exquisite material culture, ritual, and ceremonial practices. All the people dressed nicely and groomed their hair, wrapping themselves in buckskin and furs. Wolf Chief states: "At the time when the Cheyennes and Sutaio met both wore moccasins without

PART I | TSÈHÉSTÁNO: THE CHEYENNE NATION

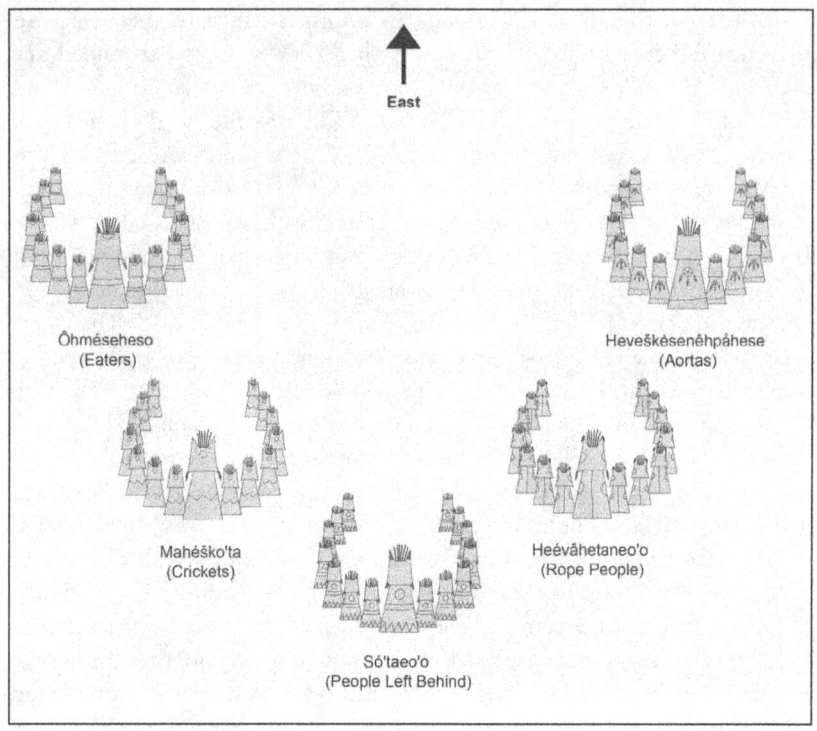

The first five bands of the United Cheyenne Nation.

the double sole. The Sutaio wore hides which suspended over their shoulders." Evidently the Só'taeo'o were ceremonially prepared to formally "give" the Ôhméseheso their sacred Sun Dance. The Só'taeo'o prophet, the spiritual leader who had the authority to do so, was described by Wolf Chief: "[The] Sundance [came] from Sutaio, at [the] presentation the culture hero dressed up in proper attire and paints for the lodges to follow. At the meeting, the tipi [was] in vogue on both sides. The painted lodges originated with the Sutaio."[51] At the first meeting, the leaders from both nations also discussed their origins and shared oral traditions. Based on these ideologies and a shared history and culture, the two groups decided to make a peace agreement.[52]

The peace alliance was formalized with the unification of the two nations in a large camp. The four large bands of the Cheyennes met with the four smaller bands of the Só'taeo'o, who were camped on the western end of the circle.[53] The western part of a ceremonial encampment is considered the place of honor, as individuals who sit on the west side of the lodge face the rising sun. The people held a grand feast and celebration, where they shared stories, danced, and played games, including the sacred hoop and spear game. The young people also held a social dance in the evening, and over the course of several days, some of them were married. The Só'taeo'o children, whether mixed with Cheyenne blood or not, were considered part of the Cheyenne Nation.[54] From then on the Só'taeo'o bands became part of the Cheyenne Nation as one band, with four chiefs.

THE SÓ'TAEO'O AND THE TSÉTSÊHÉSTÂHESE

After the union, the two peoples no longer perceived each other as strangers. As a formality, they gave each other new names, symbolically welcoming each other into a new way of life as relatives; this is when "new names appeared."[55] The Cheyennes believed these new people they met were those who were separated from the living-nation long ago, when the Cheyennes crossed the ice, so they called them Só'taeo'o, "the people left behind" or "the people descended."[56] This name also translated to "Desert People," since the Cheyennes believed that Só'taeo'o lived in the desert south while they were separated.[57] Só'taeo'o also translates to "Buffalo People," since they ate buffalo and possessed the Sacred Hat. The Só'taeo'o, on the other hand, believed that these Cheyennes were no different and were related in some way, so they named them Tsétsêhéstâhese, "the people with hearts like ours." From then on, only during ceremonies did the Cheyennes refer to themselves by their old name, Né'ohma'ehétaneo'o (Prairie People).

When the two peoples joined during the Great Unification, they shared spiritual and cultural teachings. The Só'taeo'o possessed the four original straight pipes made of red Catlinite and the Ésevone (Buffalo Hat) covenant, which could summon animals, bring plants to life, and renew the entire earth. The prophet Ho'ehêvêsénóó'e brought this to the Só'taeo'o long before the unification. After bringing this covenant, his name was changed to Tomôsévêséhe (Erect or Straight Horns), which is the name he is remembered by today. The Tsétsêhéstâhese possessed a covenant called Maahótse (Medicine Arrows), which was brought by the prophet Motsé'eóeve. This covenant had a duality: it could be used for peace and justice by restoring balance through renewal, but it also could be used for war and hunting by initiating controlled and deliberate imbalance for short periods of time. With these two covenants, the United Cheyenne Nation would become one of the most powerful of the Great Plains. It should be noted that various bands of the United Cheyenne Nation frequently returned to the Só'taeo'o homeland, Ma'ōhōnaiíva (Red Rocks), to hunt, plant, and harvest the sacred red stone for ceremonial use.[58]

PART I | TSÈHÉSTÁNO: THE CHEYENNE NATION

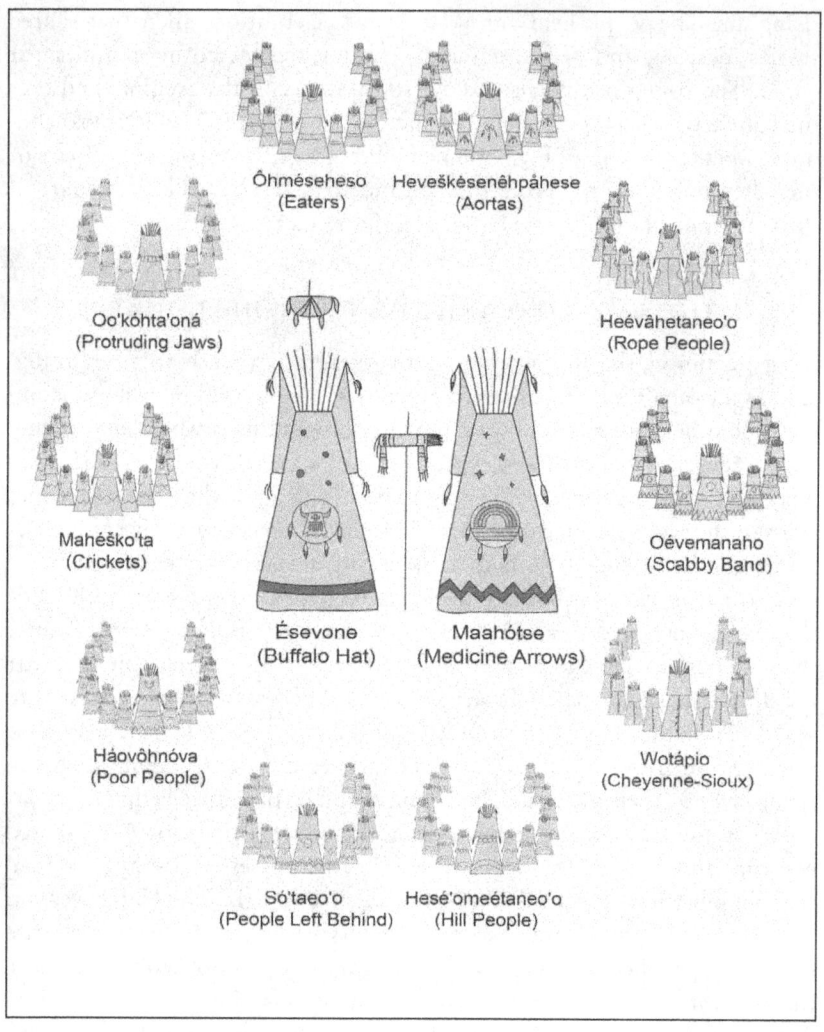

The ten bands of the United Cheyenne Nation and the two sacred covenants.

As the Cheyenne Nation expanded to ten bands, the people's warriors began to trek into other lands and this led to trade and warfare with warriors of other nations. The Great Unification became a model for peacemaking with other Indian nations, and the practices of celebrating, feasting, and sharing spiritual beliefs became the method for the Cheyenne Nation's future diplomatic relations with several other nations. The unifications with nations like the Arapaho and Lakota were not limited to political and military alliances but extended into the cultural and ceremonial practices.

Since the peacemaking process was more than a political act, the Cheyenne Nation was able to ally with other nations regardless of whether they spoke the same language, and even befriended nations that had been long-standing enemies. As part of the unification process, the Cheyennes also allowed their new allies to name them, or at least the two parties accepted the names given to them in the spirit of brotherhood.

Marriage across unifying nations was also part of maintaining and securing peace in perpetuity. During the Great Unification, when numerous individual couples married, families also merged, thus transcending the peacemaking to the amalgamation of villages and bands. Upon amalgamation, however, the Cheyenne bands retained the Cheyenne national history, while adopting individual family histories, cultures, and customs. This is evident, among other aspects, in the preservation of the traditional names of individuals. Those from the Tsétsêhéstâhese were typically identified by names passed down from ancestors that were descriptive of bears, corn, or stars (for example, Bear Robe, Corn Woman, Star Man). Só'taeo'o families, on the other hand, commonly named their children after ancestors whose names were descriptive of buffalo, birds, or the earth (such as White Buffalo, Bird Woman, or Red Earth). Upon unification and with intermarriage, the custom of inheriting names from older relatives remained, diversifying the blood and names, but preserving the names and stories of relatives.

Probably the most significant unifying attribute is the combination of oral traditions. After the actual unification, old stories were merged and the names of old culture heroes and leaders from both nations also merged. From within the lodges of sacred storytellers came stories that also highlighted the Great Unification, to symbolically show that the union was mutual and the nations were truly equal. The unification or adaptations of stories was significant to the future of the Cheyenne Nation as its leaders continue to create peaceful relationships with other peoples. The convergence of oral histories will appear in later chapters.

CHAPTER 3

Tsėhéseamanēō'o: The Cheyenne Cultural Way of Life

TSĖHÉSEAMANĒŌ'O, the Cheyenne culture, encompasses every facet of Cheyenne peoplehood: language, sacred history, ceremonial cycle, and land.[1] The foundation of Cheyenne sovereignty is deeply embedded in the Tsėhéseamanēō'o and vice versa. Without the Cheyenne culture, the Cheyenne people would cease to exist as a distinct people, and the Cheyenne Nation would cease to exist as well. Families of the Cheyenne Nation hold fast to tradition and customs.

The Cheyenne people lived by strict rules to sustain a Cheyenne cultural way of living. These teachings were acquired throughout the previous worlds and survived as fundamental beliefs and values. Other Plains Indian nations may have shared similar cultural and spiritual beliefs, for example, the significance of the buffalo. Each Indian nation, however, also developed its own philosophies that made it unique. American Indian and Indigenous people rely on these philosophies for prosperity, survival, and healing. For the Cheyenne people, traditional beliefs and values helped sustain the héstanovestôtse through hardship, as these beliefs and values adapted to whatever challenges arose, like a flood or famine. The Cheyenne people were also able to adapt, while retaining the foundational concepts of Tsėhéseamanēō'o. I present some of these concepts below with respect to the extant practice of the Tsėhéseamanēō'o and without violating any cultural, spiritual, or traditional restrictions.

OVANHESTÔSTSE

Prophecy in American Indian cultures is more than fragments of a primitive mythology. Prophecy is testimony of thriving cultures that join historical fact with spiritual divinations to explain inevitable and difficult cultural and social changes. The Cheyennes, like most American Indians, recognized that their living-nation's existence was limited by its own growth and decay, its birth, rebirth, and inevitable death, which is understood as its transition to another reality or world. Because of this recognition, they could organize their pasts as worlds and explain their own history as a series of gains and losses, like the catastrophic floods and the Great Unification.[2] Although oral traditions can reveal an individual's actual experiences, these experiences are insignificant when compared to how the people collectively responded to the life-altering gains and losses.[3] This is why it is appropriate to view the Cheyenne Nation as a living organism, with parents and progeny. The Cheyenne people preserved their history through stories that included dramatic change and catastrophic events, and throughout this history they also tell of prophets who predicted these changes and who participated in the changing events. Ovanhestôstse, prophecy, reveals the values of the people who lived during these changing events, as well as how they interpreted their changing world. When a change was upon them, prophecy also revealed what new changes in lifestyle were significant and should pass on to future generations. We gain a better understanding of older ways of living since the people's values and experiences are preserved in the stories as prophecies.

The Cheyenne national history can be understood through (1) prophecies and (2) their fulfillment. The most notable are those that describe the "end" of something, like "the Cheyennes will no longer grow corn." Prophecies like these provide another framework of Cheyenne history. Not only is the Cheyenne concept of time organized "before" something existed (e.g., "before the Cheyennes had horses"), but it is also organized by the anticipated cultural changes. Some stories state prophecies that explicitly describe the arrival of something different, like "the Cheyennes would begin to eat a new animal." There are also numerous stories that have prophecies embedded in hidden codes or in adventures. These stories usually reveal prophecy as after something was lost, like "the Cheyennes forgot how to use this medicine." Each of these storytelling methods reveals not only the approximate time frame of when a story was taking place, but also the juncture in time when a prophecy was fulfilled. By knowing when something occurred as it relates to prophecy, we gain a better understanding of what life was like before, during, and after the story. Prophecies relate worlds that are beyond the comprehension of those present during recitation. How awesome and frightening would it have been to hear stories of a new animal like the horse, or the existence of flying objects? We can examine prophecies to see how the Cheyennes perceived their own existence within particular time frames and in the process also demonstrate the importance of storytelling.

MA'HEÓNĖHÓO'XEVÁHEO'O

In the previous stories I shared, leaders came into existence and reveal themselves during the transitional periods from one world to the next. These leaders are remembered simply as prophets, oracles, or magicians as there is no separation of their talents within the Cheyenne culture. Sometimes they were defined as chiefs, which is a different concept and I explore that in Part II. Ma'heónėhóo'xeváheo'o, or prophets, in Cheyenne history are often remembered as culture heroes who tell of future events and, more important, future worlds. Several prophets appear throughout Cheyenne history to contribute to the well-being of the people. These prophets were essential to the survival of the nation as they instructed leaders, contributed spiritual wisdom, and allowed for generations to carry out a way of living that honors ancestors and allows the people to remain indigenous.

Each ma'heónėhóo'xeváhe maintains a reverent status in Cheyenne culture because of his or her effort to discover the future and make decisions based on these discoveries.[4] The modern idea of a prophet could simply be medicine men or women, priests or priestesses, but because of the loss of traditional ways, a prophet in the traditional Cheyenne sense does not exist in the modern world. Ma'heónėhóo'xeváheo'o stand apart in traditional Cheyenne culture because they are often perceived as awkward or mysterious. They separated themselves from the general public because of their spiritual power and uncanny knowledge, yet they remained within the realm of humanity. Most prophets, if not all, were actual people but their names and personalities are moved into a mythical realm and memorialized in the oral tradition. After they die, they are remembered as those who possessed extraordinary powers. Prophets within the Cheyenne culture are typically those who aided in securing, strengthening, and preserving the sanctity of the Cheyenne Nation. Some prophets were not spiritually or intellectually gifted to have grand predictions, but most were observant, disciplined, patient, and knowledgeable of the ways in which the earth and the universe functioned.[5] Prophets gained knowledge from nature and the supernatural and, because of their genius, were generally "more feared than trusted."[6] Prophets were potentially burdened with securing the survival of the nation because they held the knowledge of the oldest stories to remind the people that nature, not humans, was in control of the universe. Such burdens were particularly significant should the living-nation die and the people be forced to endure transition to another world.

The beginning of the universe and its end are inextricable and inseparable according to the Cheyenne worldview. Hováhneo'o (animals) helped create the surface of the earth, one of which was pompous and jealous because he was also a builder.⁷ The beaver was the best builder but also the most egotistical.⁸ The earth was created similar to the house of the beaver atop a turtle's back, which is why the earth is hemispherical and rounded.⁹ According to the Cheyenne worldview, a pole balances the earth, like a turtle balancing on the point of a stick. The pole is grounded to the end of the universe, far below the water world. The pole points directly at the North Star, and the earth rotates this axis. At the base of this pole, in the water world, is the angry beaver whose job is to destroy the entire world. Human wickedness motivates the beaver to chew at the pole; the more humans become wicked, the more the beaver chews.¹⁰ He wishes to return things to the time before humans so he can build a better world. Meanwhile, the few righteous humans keep the earth in balance by continually offering prayers to the four sacred directions, thus ensuring that grandmother earth does not tip over in any one direction. Every earthquake is a sign of the imbalance of the world and one of these days the beaver will have his way. The beaver is respected for his connection to the supernatural as well as his ability to build. Cheyennes believed that one could obtain medicine from animals like the beaver and become doctors.¹¹

Another hōva of power is the badger, who represents honor, strength, and wisdom. The badger is credited with being a wise and sacred animal; he predicted the outcome of the Great Race. Upon predicting the outcome, the badger decided not to take sides and convinced other animals like the bears, raccoons, and other small rodents to not get involved. This is why these animals go underground, hibernate, and are omnivorous. The wise badger is closest to grandmother earth and was occasionally sacrificed by spiritual leaders to tell the future.¹² Prophets prized the hide of a badger, wrapping their ceremonial objects and covenants in these sacred animal skins. Should an unworthy person use the badger's skin or flesh, he or she could become ill and die due to his sacrilege.

Other than using animals, the ancient prophets could also read the stars and gain knowledge from constellations and the movements in the heavens.¹³ One of the most significant events occurred in 1833, known as "when the stars fell." The event is used as a reference point in Cheyenne secular history because of subsequent events that are linked to the Leonid meteor shower.¹⁴ The "star" prophets and their ways have long disappeared, but their legacies remain evident in the Cheyenne national history. Flathead, an old Cheyenne informant to the linguist Rodolphe Petter, reported having known priests who classified stars into several groups and who used them to recall and predict certain foreseeable and cyclical events. Much of the star knowledge of the Cheyennes has been lost over the course of colonization, although some remnants are embedded in sacred stories and among the practitioners of the old ceremonies.

The most notable prophets were those who could "foretell future events by the form of certain clouds, called ehōstonevoeoxz, telling clouds."[15] Flathead described that these prophets derived their predictions primarily from the clouds during sunrise and sunset. The most telling readings came in observing a cloud's shape, color, and formation.[16] Laura Rockroads (Northern Cheyenne) was one of the last to know of such sacred ways, as she explains:

> I know of how the Indians used to know things such as looking at the stars and the moon, of what kind of day it's going to be, and a little bit is still known today. Just like at this time the beaver (constellation), they say, shows up at this time at the beginning of spring when they appear, there's four stars and some distance away there's three (more) stars hanging, like there's seven of them that they talk about, it is also called "den." When there they appear at daybreak it is springtime again. That's when everything melts, when the old people knew this they would be very happy. Whenever the beaver appeared these people would say, "We made it to another spring."[17]

The old Cheyennes were also aware of the changes in the seasons, in particular weather and temperature patterns. Some of these prophets or seers could sense the energy from the fog, mists, or even the steam from a large body of water. These prophets were also known to use incense or steam from a cooking fire. Because of colonization, the old Cheyenne astronomer-astrologists and nephololognists became extinct. Today only a few teachings and ceremonies remain but are not known and respected as much as are Christian priests.

Cheyenne prophets and medicine people were active even through the colonization of the lands and the introduction of new ways from the white world. The era known as the "time of the horse" proved to be both prosperous and disastrous for the Cheyennes, although this fifth world is considered the pinnacle of the Cheyenne Nation. Spiritual leaders during this era had to refine their skills to consciously preserve the old ways, oral traditions, and ceremonial practices, while producing new knowledge since the old prophecies told of a time when the Cheyenne culture of living would change. With the arrival of the white man, these prophets often blamed imbalances in nature and strange supernatural changes on the alien ways of these newcomers. One claimed that the constant tornado destruction upon early white townships resulted from the spirits of dead Cheyennes who were unwelcoming to the white man's strange antics and contradictory behavior.[18] Another prophesized that Halley's Comet or another of the sort, which frightens white men so much, would likely collide with the earth as punishment for their crimes.[19] The traditions of prophets and prophecy continue to remind the Cheyennes of their responsibilities to the earth, nature, and each other.

MOTSÉ'EÓEVE

The most popular prophet of the Cheyennes is Motsé'eóeve (Sweet Medicine), who was also known as Sweet Root Standing. Upon his departure, Motsé'eóeve foretold a number of dramatic changes to the fourth world.[20] "The time of the buffalo" was going to end and the people forever changed, with the arrival of a new sacred animal, the horse. This animal would change the way the people lived, hunted, and traveled. But not long after the arrival of the horse, an "Earth man" was to arrive, seeking to accumulate and devour all of the earth for himself and his people.[21] He was going to be in constant search of a shiny stone and would not stop even after he found it.[22] This man was to bring with him disease and sickness unlike any known to the Cheyennes. He was to bring a new weapon that could kill people by shooting a hard stone as well as new potions that could kill numerous animals all at once. Motsé'eóeve also described the loss of the Cheyenne cultural way of life, beginning with the dramatic decline of the buffalo that were so vast and plentiful on the Plains. At the time, even the wisest Cheyennes could not believe in what Motsé'eóeve was saying about the massive buffalo herds. A new animal would replace the buffalo, but this animal would also carry disease and sickness. The Cheyennes would begin losing their spiritual ways and forget the laws of humanity. Their children would be taken by this "Earth man" and forced to learn his ways, and the people would leave their religion for something else that they would "love and respect more." The Cheyennes will become helpless, act foolish, and lose respect for themselves and their leaders. Soon they will start quarreling and fighting each other and become "worse than crazy."[23]

Old She Bear, a member of the Eater Band born in 1842, narrated part of the Sweet Medicine prophecy in 1910:

> He told them he was next to the god who made all. He told them [about the] god [who] is a white man. He set the Indians in one place, the whites [in another]. He told them white men lived by gold. He told them gold was hidden in the Black Hills. He told them the white men were crazy in what they had done to God: "After a while the whites are coming

across North America to take the lands away from the Indians." The Indians didn't know they had any relations (i.e. whitemen) [that there were other peoples in the world]. He knew the white men were coming here to destroy everything for the Indians. He knew the Indians would still live on the land, and that the whites would not take all the land. Matsíoyōiv [Motsé'eóeve] gave the Indians the land so they could make their own living. You know what the whites are doing now, so it's time about this medicine man [his prophecy is true]. Matsíoyōiv got to be an old man [and] died.[24]

The legacy of Motsé'eóeve is not his apocalyptic prophecies, but the life of the people he represented and served. Ovanhestôstse (prophecy), as in the case of Motsé'eóeve, is an invaluable mechanism for the survival of the Cheyenne people. At the juncture of change, as an old world ended and a new one began, prophecy brought understanding, acceptance, and eventual adaptation to sometimes threatening circumstances. Ovanhestôstse cannot be prevented; if it could, it would cease to be prophecy and simply be a hypothetical conjecture of future events. Prophets and prophecies are significant to how the Cheyennes perceived their cultural history. The Sweet Medicine prophecy reveals, among other things, the Cheyenne people's forthcoming relationship with white people and the eventual decline of the buffalo-dependent nation. The Great Cheyenne and Sioux War of 1876 began with the discovery of gold in the Black Hills, just as Motsé'eóeve foretold "the coming of white men" and their search for a "shiny stone." To the Cheyennes, the cause of the war, its end, and the subsequent events all fulfill the Sweet Medicine prophecies. Motsé'eóeve emphasized: "He will destroy for you everything that you used to depend on. He is going to destroy it all."[25]

While Motsé'eóeve predicted the end of "the time of the buffalo," he also issued warnings to survive and sustain the sacred way of life of the Cheyennes, emphasizing not to "take up" any of the white man's ways and to remain true to traditional teachings.[26] He instructed the people to never forget what he taught, to continue to practice the major ceremonies, and most important, to remember the sacred laws of humanity and nature, as retold by Rachel Strange Owl and members of her family on the Northern Cheyenne Reservation in 1967:

> They will try to make you forget Maheo, the Creator, and the things I taught you, and will impose their own alien, evil ways. They will take your land little by little, until there is nothing left for you. I do not like to tell you this, but you must know. You must be strong when that bad time

comes, you men, and particularly you women, because much depends on you, because you are the perpetuators of life and if you weaken, the Cheyenne will cease to be. Now I have said all there is to say.[27]

After the Cheyennes were forced onto reservations (the Northern Cheyenne Reservation was established in 1884), the warnings of Motsé'eóeve came to full fruition. The old ceremonial practices were outlawed by the United States, and the entire sociopolitical structure of the nation began to collapse as leaders were stripped of their power and authority. Government-assigned "Indian agents" wielded political power and were backed by a police force, depriving the warrior guilds of their sacred roles. Children were forced to attend boarding school, and disease and sickness plagued the frail communities. Starving families struggled as they became dependent on government rations. Cheyenne men were thrown into jail if they killed the cattle of white ranchers in their effort to feed their kin. Alcoholism and depression dominated, while cooperation and principles of humanity were replaced with individualism and corruption.

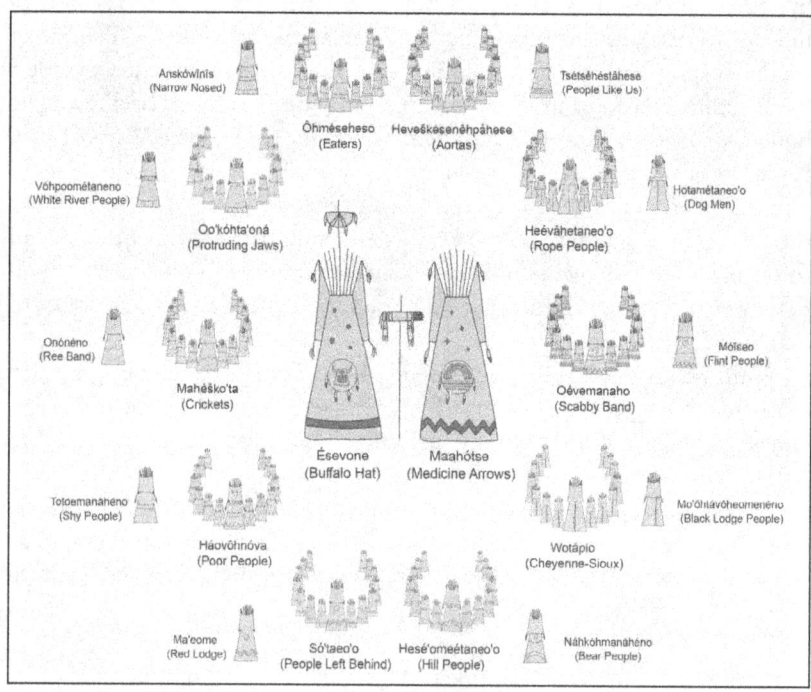

The twenty bands of the United Cheyenne Nation.

The end of the time of the horse was complete when the Bureau of Indian Affairs planned a full-scale reduction of Cheyenne horses in 1919, which decreed that one hundred horses were to be killed each month for ten years. BIA officials killed approximately twelve thousand mustangs; their hides were sold for short-lived income, and their meat was substituted for beef rations to wean dependence on government rations and to save money.[28] Many Cheyennes refused to allow their animals to meet such a disgraceful fate, so they released them into the reservation hills to continue as a free herd. By 1929 there were only three thousand horses reservation-wide and the US government treacherously reported that the Cheyennes were "glad" to eat their own horses.[29] From then on the Cheyennes would be forced to live in a strange world where everything seemed backward and made no sense: "the time of the white man." It was in this world that the Cheyennes endured the most damage to their way of life, but also when a new hope was born.

The Cheyennes had already held in their oral traditions that the most powerful prophet, Motsé'eóeve, would return one day, after a cycle of four hundred years.[30] His return would manifest not in human form, but in the peoples' collective return to Indigenous ideologies and values, rooted in the spiritual ways of living. The "prophecy of chiefs" tells of the return of all the past leaders; their spirits will be in children who will mature to lead the Cheyenne people away from the vices and entrapments of the white world. Like the previous worlds, the time of the white man will inevitably come to an end, either through catastrophe, environmental change, or human-caused change. The Cheyennes believe that a new world is on the horizon. The prophecy of chiefs was revealed during the initial stages of the reservation era by the Chiefs' Society, a group of leaders, not one specific prophet or seer. It survives in modern oral traditions as the Chiefs' Prophecy and is commonly referenced as the "Return of the Chiefs" or "the return to greatness."[31] At one point the vision statement of the modern tribal government spoke directly to the prophecy: "In the name of our children and future our sacred responsibility before Maheo is to intelligently lead the Cheyennes out of despair into a new era of history through a reconciled tribal spirit to fulfill our self-determined destiny of self-sufficiency, sustainability and economic independence."[32] This "return to greatness" could simply mean the return to a healthy and balanced way of living: a decolonized way of living that heals the colonized and damaged héstanovestôtse to re-create a healthier living-nation.

TSÉHÉSEAMANĒŌ'O

To gain a better understanding of the Cheyenne worldview, I provide several ideologies that have remained constant in Cheyenne culture and philosophy through the ages. Most of these concepts are embedded in the Cheyenne national history; they are certainly fundamental concepts to the Tséhéseamanēō'o, the Cheyenne cultural way of life. While oral traditions and interpretations of history can change and adapt, these concepts correspond directly with what the Cheyennes believe to be the soul of a human and the spirit of their way of living. In other words, the essence of being Cheyenne comes from core concepts that transcend the modern ideas of "Indian," "Native," or "tribal." These principles go deeper than the so-called Indian identity. By comparison, enrollment, blood quantum, tribalism, and traditionalism are shallow, mere glimpses of foreign ideas that explain nothing of what it means to be a people that compose a life-nation. To learn of and appreciate the following principles is to see beyond the foreign ways of thinking that have been forced upon the Cheyennes through assimilation and colonization. To believe and live by these principles is to contribute to renewing and maintaining the life of an indigenous nation that was first born out of the first being from an empty universe, five worlds ago.

1. *Éškemane (Earth/Grandmother)*

The earth is perceived as a living being. Because of its characteristics as the oldest being, it is respected and revered the same way as a grandmother. A woman goes through four changes in life, and at each stage she must learn different responsibilities of life. These four changes are puberty, motherhood, menopause, and death. Unlike men, who only go through two changes, puberty and death, women carry the gift and responsibilities of life, while men must search for other means of growing throughout their time on earth. Men can achieve growth through ceremony or facing death in warfare. Women go through changes naturally and only need guidance from older women and relatives to ease the transition from one phase of life to another. Grandmothers are at their summit in life. Likewise, grandmother earth is wise, patient, generous, and honest and always provides people what they need and rarely what they want. Cheyennes have a kinship system that teaches children to respect their elders, and this respect is carried into adulthood. Teachings related to the grandmother are especially important for the family unit, for the community, and for a worldview that honors and respects the earth. Grandmothers were not to use coarse language, for they can cause much pain toward their grandchildren.[33]

Until colonization, it was quite easy for the Cheyennes to perceive the Earth as a grandmother. Modern Cheyennes who practice ceremonies or who have relearned their spiritual ways think of the Earth as grandmother. We have already reviewed some stories that involve an old woman or women who embody the image of a grandmother. These older women are teachers and always bring about a teaching or philosophy that highlights the special relationship between humans and the earth through hunting, planting, and living in harmony. Éškemane appears in later stories as well.

II. *Ma'heo'e/Ma'hēō'e/Ma'hëö'o/Maheo (Sacred Medicine)*

This concept is difficult to translate from Cheyenne to English. Ma'heo'e has been translated to mean "God," or literally "All Father."[34] It was also translated to "Great Spiritual Power."[35] A more accurate translation would be sacred power or medicine using the Cheyenne cultural way of thinking. It is a philosophical concept that refers to a spiritual state of being; it can be applied to objects or a way of doing things; it means without discomfort or imbalance; it refers to purity and peace; it can be in anything, and anything can be it.[36] Ma'heo'e is significant to the Cheyennes because, like most Indigenous peoples, they believe that sacredness is in all things in nature and in people. Traditionally, spiritual leaders were observant and patient to see if someone was sacred or if they possessed anything sacred. For example, when the chiefs refused the peace medals of Lewis and Clark, they believed these objects to be a form of medicine. The Cheyennes respect the sacred medicine of other Indigenous peoples and other peoples. Sacred medicine that is used for evil is no longer associated with Ma'heo'e.

III. *Ma'xema'hēō'e (Great Medicine)*

This is the most powerful and holy supernatural being. The Lakota have a similar concept called Wanka Tanka (Great Mystery). It is a formless, unseen, omnipresent being; it is best understood as a being of the universe; it is the feeling that all living beings have at the moment before their birth and after their death. Living beings cannot understand it, but they can feel it and ask for its help. Ma'xema'hēō'e is a supreme being of life: the grandfather of all life on Earth. Its presence is especially significant when the Cheyennes collectively face challenges, like when the nation endures pain and suffering. Participants in the most challenging ceremonies, like the Sun Dance, pray to Ma'xema'hēō'e for compassion as they make sacrifices through their tears, flesh, and blood. Sometimes the Great Medicine listens and blesses a worthy person, which may be in the simple form of happiness and health. Maintains a sacred relationship of balance with Éškemane, the universe, and all living things on Earth. Cheyennes are careful of what they say and do, for it could come back to inflict harm or pain on them or their family members. Ma'xema'hēō'e is also the supreme dispenser of justice.[37]

IV. *Hoháatamaahestôtse (Power)*

In the Cheyenne culture, power is understood as a product of nature, but it can be harnessed by humans. Power is not a possession that people can hold and wield through a position or title. It is understood as spiritual, something that can be given or earned and is influenced by people's actions and prayers. Power is a mystery, an unseen force of energy that can never be abused or misused. The éše'he (sun) is the source of all physical power on earth, since the sun's power is used to create and sustain everything living on the planet. It rises and sets every day; too much sunlight would cause calamity; just enough light allows for life to exist on earth. By shining its light upon the earth for centuries, the sun gives its energy to rocks and mountains, which will always exist. Plants and trees are nurtured by the sun and hold within them strength and life. The sun's power is released when wood branches, brush, and leaves are burned; some release special fragrances and incense, which can benefit other living beings especially when humans use the smoke as medicine. Others provide the necessary heat to warm their bodies. Cheyenne children were taught to always rise before the sun touches their bodies, that the sun should never wake them up, and that they should be the ones who "help" the sun rise in the morning, because the sun does so much work every day to keep things alive. Before colonization, adults would step outside to meet the rising sun, raise their arms as if they were flowers and plants in bloom, and take in the power of the sun.[38] Modern Cheyennes continue to respect the sun's power in ceremony.

Fire is also a source of power and every component has significance: the coals, the flames, the smoke, and the ash all represent life. The hot coals are no different than a living being, emitting heat and the life color yellow, relying on both air and earth to burn, and gleaming with an aura. The flames represent the release of energy, positive or negative. Whether manifested in a storm or in the heat of battle, the flame and the color red represent life at its fullest. Smoke is no different from breath, what all living things take from air and return with each breath of life; the color white represents breath. Ashes are no different from the afterlife, peace after war, balance after conflict, and the ultimate event of life: death. The color black represents death and the ashes represent the remains of sacrifices. The greatest sacrifice a human can make is giving up his or her life, as it is for all living beings.

Two of the most powerful elements of nature are nonóma'e (thunder) and ho'ota (lightning). Both are feared living beings that possess power and from which humans can obtain power through prayer and sacrifice. Such power is personified as rain, which is a being called Nemevota, who controls the weather and often helps humans in time of need. When the powers of fire, the sun, and water are combined, steam is released. Symbolic of a powerful buffalo bull, this process is ritualized in a sweat lodge ceremony.[39]

v. Héstanėheo'o (Humankind)

This concept refers to the energy that all humans possess, male and female, young and old. It is the collective energy of a group of humans. There are differing degrees of human energy, since some groups of humans can choose to develop their humanity and relationships with the earth and the supernatural. This energy can sometimes cause pain and suffering but can also create peace and happiness. "Humankind" among the Cheyenne is often associated with spiritual and ceremonial actions or inactions, which radiate the power of life and can deflect the power of hate and evil. Sometimes inaction can influence humankind. Although the Cheyennes' concept of human energy can be used to describe might and force, it also refers to talents and skills, which are more telling of a person's character and discipline, rather than form or status.

All humans have talents in whatever craft, skill, or art they enjoy. Humankind benefits from these talents. The true essence of humanity is revealed during a person's exhibition of these talents, since these skills can be used to directly contribute to the needs of the people, like horseracing, making clothing, doctoring the sick, conducting ceremonies, organizing warfare, hunting, or navigating the land. Other old talents included storytelling, public speaking, and creating art. Modern Cheyenne traditionalists depend on the youth who exhibit athletic, intellectual, cultural, and ceremonial talents to energize humans.

Like all living beings, humans also possess a simple power known as ómótóme, which is the "breath" that keeps people alive. A person's breath is a powerful medium in ceremony because it represents his or her meditation. When humans practice breathing or simply breathe, they are practicing the art of living. Breathing either lifts a person to a higher spiritual life or slows the person down to a balance. In either case, achieving and living a simple life is more powerful than gaining any other form, title, or status.

vi. Máhta'sóoma (Spirit/Soul/Aura)

All living things have a spirit, which reveals the true nature and character of that being. In the Cheyenne culture, a person's spirit is equal to his or her shadow, but the spirit is the witness to a person's true identity. Humans have spirits that can be best understood as the silent, unspoken, unwritten biography that each carries throughout daily life. The spirit cannot be seen, as it is completely abstract, but it can be felt; it is where the true essence of the living being resides. This philosophical concept exists in other cultures but is paramount to the Cheyenne identity.[40] The Cheyennes believe that a person's spirit reveals that person's character; therefore, people should be conscious of their spirits. Southern Cheyenne Mike Haag explained in 1930: "Cheyenne believe sickness is due to 'soul-stealing' and the penetration of foreign objects [to the soul]."[41] Witches are believed to use manipulation of emotions and feelings to "steal the souls" of others, or they use medicines or objects to penetrate the soul.

The umbilical cord represents a person's path or route to their måhta'sóoma. When a child is born, the mother or an aunt sews the dried portion of the umbilical cord into an effigy: lizards for girls and turtles for boys. Parents attach these ornaments to the child's cradleboard until the child matures and then it is fastened to his or her clothing. The charm represents the eternal connection that all children have with their mothers and that all Cheyennes have with their homeland. The Southern Cheyenne ceremonial leader and sacred scholar Henrietta Mann states: "This object symbolized the essence of a whole person; if it should be lost, the individual would never be content, continually searching for a meaning to life."[42] Wrapped Hair explained the old Só'taeo'o customs for children: when a girl was born, a certain medicine was put on the knife and used to cut the umbilical cord; if it was a boy, a mixture of charcoal and the same medicine was used on the knife. Then "buffalo chips were pounded into dust for a bed for the child, and the child was painted red all over. The belief was then that child would grow up ok. The severed umbilical cord was wrapped in a raw hide, and after some kind of a ceremony, was put up in the forks of a tree."[43] The custom was to "attach" the child to a physical and spiritual homeland.

Children are taught that if they play outside long after dark or too far away from home, they can lose their spirits; thus, they are instructed to "call their names back." Such a practice instills internal harmony, restores a person's mental health, and contributes to a person's physical and spiritual health. Some believe that a person's spirit can be lost if he is exposed to something he is not supposed to experience or see, such as being a victim of violence or perpetrating a heinous crime. People who have "lost" their spirits must undergo numerous healing ceremonies, while others may be banished since the pain they created is too much to forgive. In the modern world, those who "lost" their spirits would likely be diagnosed with post-traumatic stress disorder or another mental illness.

Individuals strengthen their spirits through ceremonial practices that demand physical and mental stamina and discipline, like piercing the flesh, fasting, and the sweat lodge ceremony. Community ceremonies, like the Sun Dance, allow the entire nation to participate in strengthening of individual spirits and the entire nation's spirit. Healthy individuals create and sustain a healthy nation, and it is from this culture that the best leaders were selected. People who live in harmony with their spirits are pleasant to be around as they express the best qualities of humanity. They are good parents, firm but fair, determined but gentle, orderly but humorous, and these qualities were highly valued by the Cheyenne people.

VII. *Oestóonôtse (Sacrifices)*

Sacrifice in Cheyenne culture means submitting to duty while ignoring desire. The life of a Cheyenne—and of all humans, it is believed—is composed of sacrifices. Life is not a series of games to be won; it is not measured in wins or losses, or status or ego. Life does not end with rewards and recognition but continues to face more challenges. The more a person achieves, the harder the challenges become. The Cheyenne people believe that one fundamental law of nature—balance—governs all life. Happiness, joy, and elation will all eventually fade and pass in time, just like sadness, misery, and pain. Although these emotions are a part of life, none equate to life itself. Cheyennes believe that they do not control nature, but they can use the supernatural powers and the law of balance to their advantage in times of need. Power is summoned by making sacrifices. However small or grand the sacrifice, the Cheyenne people are determined to respect the inevitability of balance. The historian Grinnell writes:

> On the spiritual side, the Cheyenne's life was hedged about by a multitude of barriers of ritual and custom. If his beliefs demanded that he should do things that were worthy, it seemed quite as important that he should abstain from things forbidden and believed to bring bad fortune. The Cheyenne prayed constantly and offered many sacrifices to propitiate the unseen powers and to enlist their help. He practiced charity, for from earliest youth he had been taught to be kind to his fellow men, to feel sympathy for the unfortunate and to make efforts to assist them. It often costs civilized man a struggle to carry out the precept to love his neighbor, but the Cheyenne did kindly, friendly, or charitable acts of his own free will, and took no credit for them. Yet he lived in constant fear of doing some forbidden thing which would bring him bad luck.[44]

Practitioners of the big ceremonies endured hardships through fasting for a number of days and sacrificing bits of flesh and blood. All forms of sacrifice strengthened a person's spirit to give without reward, withstand criticism, and maintain honor and humility. The Cheyenne people lived with one another and managed to survive as a nation by continually making sacrifices, small and large.

Cheyenne man with two children, ca. 1890–1907, C. C. Stotz. National Anthropological Archives, Smithsonian Museum Support Center, Suitland, Maryland (OPPS NEG 56122).

VIII. *Héhe'estovestôtse (Fatherhood)*

Traditional Cheyenne customs dictated that fathers teach their children the Cheyenne cultural ways.[45] In order to perpetuate the survival of the nation, each generation needs to be healthy in mind, body, and spirit. Parents teach all the values of the Cheyenne cultural way of living to each generation.

While younger men were allowed and encouraged to live a carefree life, they were expected to have families when they reached their thirties. At this age, they were much better prepared to be effective fathers than those in their twenties. Once a man became a father, he spiritually and emotionally entered into the realm of fatherhood, which was often ritualized on a personal level, through one day of prayer and solitude. No longer do the petty wants and desires of youth dominate his life. A father's goals and responsibilities change for the better, as he now must build a safe and secure life for his children. Should a man fail to spiritually enter into fatherhood, he could cause an imbalance in his family, which could affect his child. A father's role is not status, fame, or privilege. Simply put, fatherhood is sacred and is not something that any man can aspire to. In fact, among the Cheyennes, one of the greatest attributes of a man is to take responsibility for his children. Should he abandon them, he makes them orphans and this is known as "throwing them away." Some fathers, in traditional Cheyenne culture, took on multiple wives and continued to care for their children from multiple mothers. The Cheyenne Nation remained stable because of the presence of fathers, who were first warriors, later spiritual or political leaders, and then teachers to the next generation. Fathers were the first line of defense and were the ones to sacrifice their lives for their families and people.

IX. *Heške'estovestôtse (Motherhood)*

A popular Cheyenne proverb states: "A nation is not conquered until the hearts of its women are on the ground. Then it is finished, no matter how brave its warriors or how strong their weapons." Mothers of the Cheyenne Nation are unfortunately burdened with more responsibility than that of fathers because mothers are the first caretakers of the children and they impart knowledge to children before other family members do. The warning of Motsé'eóeve, mentioned earlier, emphasizes the importance of women: "particularly you women, because much depends on you, because you are the perpetuators of life and if you weaken, the Cheyenne will cease to be." Mothers are the first to teach language, songs, morals and values, and most important, love and humanity. Mothers are the caretakers of the next generation of the entire nation, so their discipline and dedication to the Cheyenne cultural way of living were greater than those of fathers. The Cheyenne cultural way elevated the roles of mothers to a sacred level: motherhood equates to godliness. The mother was the person who taught girls to carry on the sacred responsibilities of women of the nation. Mothers also taught boys how to behave well and to "behave as chiefs did." These tasks were not easy, which is why mothers often assisted fellow mothers on childrearing and for emotional and spiritual support.

Jim Frost's Wife and Two Children, 1892, James Mooney, 1861–1921. National Anthropological Archives, Smithsonian Museum Support Center, Suitland, Maryland (NAA INV 06119700, OPPS NEG 351 A).

The bond between a mother and her child is like no other. The Cheyennes believe that adults, men and women, are spiritually and eternally connected to their mothers through their navel. During times of war, when a father was killed in battle or on the hunt, the mother became the primary caretaker. Motherhood is a life-changing, spiritual event that brings a woman from her previous life of wants and desires to a life of sacrifice for her children and grandchildren. Her spirit changes, as she becomes a new sacred being, responsible for the next generation. Her transition into motherhood was ritualized through a formal ceremony, which all the female relatives attended and gave gifts and advice, much like a modern baby shower, only that the meetings continue after the child is born. Should a woman transition into motherhood without the help of other mothers, she may have a difficult time parting with her previous lifestyle, which could have residual effects on the child. Just like fatherhood, motherhood is a spiritual reawakening that is respected as part of humanity.

x. *Ka'ėškónevestôtse (Childhood)*

Probably the most underestimated and least respected stage of life is childhood. All humans live a period of childhood, and from this rather short period of time, they learn the joy of play and freedom as well as the simple ways of living. From the time a child learns to run to adulthood is the freest and most liberating. Babyhood is considered a sacred time, as explained by an unknown Southern Cheyenne in 1929: "Cheyennes have 'doctors' who understand babies before they talk. The claim is made that babies are more intelligent than grown persons. One man understood a baby to say men were nearby to steal horses. They did. Probably Pawnees. How did the baby know?"[46]

Childhood is a sacred time when we learn what it means to have friends and respect elders, as well as the beauty of life itself. This is the time when a child learns from the behaviors of adults. A child can take on the best qualities of relatives, in particular their parents, which is why adults need to be conscious of their behavior around children. Historically, parents often "gave" one of their children to a grandparent so that the child could take on the character of an elder and learn their good habits. This custom continues today but is less formal and ritualistic. The Cheyennes believe that children possess the sacred ability to learn and develop beyond the boundaries set by nature. In other words, with proper teaching and training, children have the ability to advance physically, mentally, emotionally, and spiritually to potentially become as powerful as any one of the prophets or heroes who are remembered in the oral tradition. Conversely, if a child learns bad habits from adults, he or she would likely maintain these bad habits in adulthood. It is normal for children to be jealous, selfish, and resentful toward other children, but among the Cheyennes, these feelings must be overcome because they can lead to a self-destructive adulthood. Children are allowed to express such feelings, but parents and relatives guide their children through them by emphasizing Cheyenne values. Adults must teach and consistently show compassion, sharing, fairness, and love for others to foster spiritual and emotional growth. Traditional Cheyennes believe that jealousy, selfishness, and resentment are behaviors that are acceptable for children, but these should not be carried into adulthood. Traditional Cheyennes believe that adults who behave in such manners become pathological liars and cheaters and possess other unfavorable qualities that make them unpleasant company; they are labeled as people "without parents" or "who did not have a fulfilling childhood."

A young Cheyenne boy. Anonymous. National Anthropological Archives, Smithsonian Museum Support Center, Suitland, Maryland (OPPS NEG 239 A).

CONCLUSION

The Cheyennes believe that their ideologies of life depend on one another, thus creating a complete worldview. One ideology cannot be separated and used without the others; all parts must be understood together. Without that, the identity of the Cheyenne Nation will weaken. I have provided the Cheyenne paradigm and will refer to these ideologies throughout the book in my effort to reveal a Cheyenne perspective of the Cheyenne national history. As with a living organism, the nation's blood cannot be drained, its heart cannot be removed, its brain cannot suffer damage; otherwise, the entire being will be destroyed. I have done my best to provide a complete piece, without exploiting my own people's beliefs and disrespecting my own culture. Providing a more complete picture of our culture is a challenge for modern scholars who study mere components of an Indian nation's culture, like law or ceremony. Sometimes cultural ideologies are lost, ignored, missed, or presented incompletely. Likewise, to provide a more complete picture of an Indigenous culture is also a challenge for proponents of the decolonization movement, who may desire to initiate change to specific areas, like the decolonization of tribal governance or the decolonization of tribal enrollment. A holistic approach to decolonization, by initiating a full-scale evaluation and understanding of an Indigenous people's culture and history, as I continue to reveal of the Cheyenne Nation, will yield much more promising, long-term results of positive change than mere immediate remedies. One component cannot be isolated for commercial purposes or cloned for personal gain; it will only pollute or deform a system of beliefs that developed over hundreds of years through growth and adaptation. This framework and the following narrative is part of the héstanovestôtse, which continues today among Northern and Southern Cheyenne people. In the rest of the book we will see how the Cheyenne cultural way of life and the living-nation adapted and changed throughout time.

PART II

Véhoo'o: The Chiefs

They taught him the wise laws of the forty-four chiefs. They taught him how to set up rules for the warrior societies. They taught him how women should be honored. They taught him the many useful things by which people could live, survive, and prosper, things people had not yet learned at that time. Finally they taught him how to make a special tipi in which the sacred arrows were to be kept. Sweet Medicine listened respectfully and learned well.
—Unknown[1]

Listen to me carefully, and truthfully follow up my instructions. You chiefs are peacemakers. Though your son might be killed in front of your tepee, you should take a peace pipe and smoke. Then you would be called an honest chief.
—Motsé'eóeve[2]

You will have to swear. You will have to take an oath that you will be honest and care for all the tribe.
—Mukije[3]

THE COUNCIL of Forty-Four Chiefs was known as the Véhoo'o (Chiefs) or the Véhone Nótâxeo'o (Chief Soldiers or Chiefs Society) and is considered one of the most elaborate institutions of Native North America. The emblem of the Véhoo'o was the golden eagle; it represented a council comprising the finest leaders known to exist among the Cheyennes and all Plains Indians.[4] The system remains in history as an example of Indigenous ingenuity and American Indian political genius. Northern Cheyenne tribal historian and leader Conrad Fisher states: "The system involved everything from the military structure, to the kinship system, and the ceremonial realm."[5] Before the Cheyennes were colonized, the chiefs system persevered independently for nearly two hundred years, maybe longer. Today it continues to function and remains in the ceremonial realm of both the Northern and Southern Cheyenne nations, but it does not have the political power that it did in the past.

The authority of the Véhoo'o depended on two factors: (1) the governing structure, which rested in the balance of power and responsibility, and (2) the integrity of the chiefs, which came from the culture from which leaders were raised and selected. The Cheyenne culture of leadership was sacred and developed over the course of hundreds of years and preserved in the sacred national history. This culture of "sacred leadership," however, was not always the standard, since the Cheyennes collectively remember the time before there were chiefs. As I reveal in this section, the Cheyennes were quite familiar with and experienced in dealing with unfair, unjust, and petty tyrants. Their selfish ways were preserved in the oral tradition to remind the future generations of Cheyenne people of the chaos and hardship that previous leaders inflicted upon their own people. By remembering these previous leaders and their behavior, the people and their descendants would remember why the Cheyenne culture of sacred leadership had to be protected and honored.

In theory, the Cheyenne culture of sacred leadership positioned every male as an eligible candidate to be selected to sit on the Council of Forty-Four Chiefs if they behaved "chiefly" and proved to be worthy, virtuous, and righteous adults. The culture of sacred leadership, along with the ongoing practices of ceremonies and the reinforcement of traditional values, were known, encouraged, and expected of every citizen. Males, however, were held to a higher standard and deliberately trained and groomed to be military leaders, which was generally the path for them to become chiefs. Young men were to constantly and consistently demonstrate the best behaviors, morals, and values because each had a fair chance to earn a reputation to lead, regardless of the rank or position of his father. There was no class of individuals or families that determined the leadership or who sat on the council. There was no hereditary chieftainship. In this environment any child, like Stink Bat, could grow up to lead; thus the Cheyennes were truly a nation of chiefs.

The Cheyenne concept of a chief was exceptional in comparison to non-Indian and non-Cheyenne concepts, since the Cheyenne perception of leadership was defined by the unwritten set of principles and values rooted in the oral traditions, philosophy, and way of living. The demands of the Véhoo'o, in fact, are best understood by these values, which I outline as ten "principles of sacred leadership." The structure of the Véhoo'o was also exceptional, since it was based on the band system. Chiefs were selected to lead for a set, ten-year term. They made decisions of local concern and addressed immediate matters related to the needs of the nation.

Chiefs were not prophets, which have been identified and discussed in the previous pages. Prophets are those individuals who were, first and foremost, spiritual leaders who possessed spiritual leadership. Although they were sometimes burdened with the duties and responsibilities to lead the people, they were not necessarily chiefs in the Cheyenne sense. They did not sit in positions of higher authority to make decisions on the future of the nation, nor did they belong to a council or the formal government as chiefs did. Prophets were unselected and typically individuals who ascended to spiritual distinction and prominence. They were the ones who introduced new ways of living and teachings for the benefit of the people. By comparison, chiefs typically possessed sacred leadership qualities; their decisions protected the nation and maintained stability to ensure the nation moved into the next generation. Who were these sacred leaders? Where did the Council of Forty-Four come from? How did it function?

The two major bodies of authority of the Cheyenne Nation were the Council of Forty-Four Chiefs and the warrior societies. Most scholars of Cheyenne studies see the Cheyenne national government as a dual system, where the two institutions were in constant competition for power and authority: one represented a "peace faction," while the other represented a "war faction."[6] Scholars also divide the Cheyenne leadership into factions of "peace chiefs" or "war chiefs" depending on a particular chief's view toward white invasion. Under this theory, the actions, "behaviors," and policies of "war chiefs" may be perceived as "unfavorable" to white invasion, but from a Cheyenne perspective, such "behaviors" of "war chiefs" are more complex, and I will discuss that in Part III.

To mainstream historians, the polarization of unfavorable behavior justifies the labeling and stereotyping of some Cheyenne chiefs as "intransigents," "criminals," and "war chiefs," while labeling others as "collaborators," "progressive," and "peaceful" to white invasion. Although such divisions existed during the early reservation period, I do not think the theory applies to the Cheyennes: it is too simplistic and unfair to the Cheyenne responses to invasion.[7] By applying political theories from the colonial point of view and relying on the governing systems of other Indian nations to explain the Cheyenne experience, mainstream historians falter when they mislabel chiefs, warriors, and other leaders as warlike. Unlike mainstream anthropologists and historians, I assert that all Cheyenne chiefs valued peace for their people, and by reevaluating the situations that these chiefs were forced into, rather than merely labeling factions, we can gain a better understanding of the history of the west; this is a study for another time and another book. The goal for this section, however, is to highlight the culture that created sacred leaders, the structure of the Cheyenne chiefs system, and the values and principles of sacred leadership embedded within the Cheyenne culture.

There is some merit in highlighting the duality of the chiefs and warrior societies, especially during the wars with the United States, which led to the polarization of the Dog Soldiers in the south. However, I believe that the two institutions, the chiefs and the warriors, were not at odds with one another. It was not accepted practice for them to be at odds. The chiefs and warrior societies could not have dueling interests or agendas and effectively function to serve the people. Instead, the Council of Forty-Four Chiefs and the warrior societies cooperated with one another under a strict principle of balance. The Cheyenne concepts of balance and harmony are central to persistence in the Cheyenne cultural way of life, since the Cheyenne worldview depended heavily on their relationships and the balance they maintained with Éškemane, Ma'xema'heō'e, and the Universe. This balance is also represented and demonstrated through the ceremonial practices.

The best evidence of the Cheyenne concept of balance in government is found in the oral traditions of both the Tsétsêhéstâhese and the Só'taeo'o, as well as in the United Cheyenne national history. The Tsétsêhéstâhese story of the two young men and the hoop and spear game emphasizes balance as the Aorta and Eater bands split on equal footing. Balance and equality are also emphasized, since both young men were of similar stature, appearance, physique, intelligence, and consciousness, and both represented their bands, which were also similar. The Cheyenne concept of balance is preserved in the story and in reality, since the two bands remained in balance and did not compete or try to subdue one another. The philosophy of balance went beyond surface culture; it went deeper, reaching the core of the Cheyenne identity—politically, ideologically, and spiritually.

CHAPTER 4

Hévese'onematsestôtse: Brotherhood

I N THE CHEYENNE culture, balance is understood best as hévese'onematsestôtse (brotherhood).[1] Hévese'onematsestôtse refers to the "buddy" relationship that two young men establish as a result of living in the same band and growing up in the same environment. Sometimes these "buddy" relationships are with blood relatives—first or second cousins—but not always. For the Cheyenne people, these "buddy" relationships commonly begin when two parents of either gender become "buddies" and their children, who are close in age, frequently meet, play, and interact with one another. For this reason, a better translation for hévese'onematsestôtse may be "siblinghood," since it also includes the relationships between two girls or two young women. Nonetheless, these relationships are special, since most families were not large and siblings were likely to be separated by several years. Brotherhood, sisterhood, or siblinghood is the foundation of Cheyenne governance. Leadership skills like cooperation and the fair distribution of power are built from the foundation of hévese'onematsestôtse. To best understand Cheyenne Indigenous governance, we must first explore and examine hévese'onematsestôtse.

The Cheyenne Nation, comprising several united bands, was established under the principle of hévese'onematsestôtse, but this concept predates the nation. Balance, fairness, and the sharing of power and responsibility are all traced to both the Só'taeo'o and the Tsétsêhéstâhese. While the Tsétsêhéstâhese highlight and preserve hévese'onematsestôtse in the stories of the two young men, the Só'taeo'o concept of hévese'onematsestôtse is preserved in the epic stories of sacred hero twins. What are these stories?

As children, my mother and her siblings were told stories about the "sacred twins" from their grandmother Hattie. My mother told us the same stories and remembered the teachings of her grandmother because my two older brothers, Dion and Damion, are twins. The story of the "sacred twins" is an epic and told over the course of several nights; the last night of stories was only told during ceremonies and reserved for traditional Cheyennes. The story teaches about cooperation and balance as a way to avert competition among siblings. The following stories are embedded with cultural teachings and principles—cooperation, leadership, and collegiality—which are all important values and principles for chiefs and the Cheyenne system of governance. I have left out the last section, as these are to remain unwritten stories.

In 1963, Mrs. Yellow Eagle (Southern Cheyenne) of Oklahoma shared the story about the twins in her narrative "Hesta'heso" (Little Afterbirth).[2] Her story, as opposed to others, most resembles the story my mother told my brothers and me as children. In the first part of the story, a pregnant woman died giving birth to a child and the father threw the afterbirth into a nearby lake. Another baby was among the afterbirth and grew into a boy while in the water. He frequently reemerged from the lake to play with his twin while the father was away hunting, and then returned to his water home. The boys did not know they were brothers. One day the father caught the boy using a water bag full of air, by tying it around his hair, which prevented the boy from diving back into the water. Hesta'heso eventually came to live with the boy and the father, who told the boys they were twins and recounted the fate of their mother. From this point, the twins embark on several adventures, highlighting the concept of Só'taeo'o brotherhood. In his collection of handwritten narratives, historian Truman Michelson recorded similar stories from Southern Cheyenne informants and also did not record the last body of ceremonial stories. In 1910, Bull Thigh recalled the story as part of a much larger epic of a woman who was pregnant by a man who saved her from an evil spirit. I divided the story according to the nights the story should be told. My additions to the story are in brackets only.

Hestáhkeho (Twins), Version I

First night: The man said to her [his wife]: "I'm going out a little way. You mustn't come to the door when I am gone, or look out from the door. There might be a person at the door."

While she was alone at the lodge, somebody came to the door. He threw it open. He saw a girl inside. He said to her: "Please look at me." The girl never looked. When the person walked off, she thought she would look out. She got her arrow and made a small hole with it in the tipi. She looked through it. Somebody was right at her back, pushed her outside the door, and pounded her to death. He cut her body open. He found a baby inside. When he was doing that, the human being [the husband] came. The person got away.

The human cut a stick and made a bow and arrows. He spoke to his wife:

"Look out, the arrow is coming down." Just as the arrow nearly reached her, she moved. It struck a foot from where she lay. He shot a second time, and said: "Look out; the arrow is coming." They both moved. The third time he shot: "Look out; the arrow is coming." The fourth time he shot, he himself got up and shot square up in the air; and the arrow struck near them. They got up. They were healed. They went back into the lodge and lived there again with the child. This child was called Twin.

Second night: There was another child at the river. When their son went out to play, this boy came out of the water, and they played together. When their son went home, the other boy went toward the river. One day the man said to the boy: "While you are playing with that boy, you must catch him and wrestle with him, and throw him down." The man made a jump at him, caught him. He became one of his sons, and was raised up with his child. When grown up, the father said: "You must not go down there; there are great birds there; they might kill you." So one of the boys said: "Let us go over there where our father doesn't want us to go, and find out what's there." They went over there. They found a great big nest. In this nest were four young birds who as yet had no wings. They killed them all. They came home. They told their father that they had been over there and found the young birds in the nest, and they had killed them.

He said to them: "Oh my, these birds are thunderbirds. You mustn't go over this way [pointing in another direction]. There are animals there. They might hurt you." So they thought they would go over there and find out what was there. They came to the place. They found great serpents. The snakes crawled to meet them. They both had clubs with them. As they came to them, they beat them down as fast as they could, and killed every one of the snakes. After they killed them all, they cut every rattle off the snakes. They strung them. They both made a hole in the center of their heads. They took out their brains. They placed the rattles inside and pulled their hair over again. They said to each other: "When we are going to eat, we will use our hands, and hold the meat in our teeth, and jerk it so our heads will rattle." Just before they started they put their brains in a small place where they had killed the snakes. They went home. They both sat down together near their father and mother. Their mother gave them slices of meat at the same time. They grabbed it the same time, placed it in their mouths the same time, and jerked it. There was a terrible noise over their heads. They frightened their father and their mother.

They said to them: "Take those rattles back to where you got them, for they are holy, medicine." So they got up, went back. They took the rattles out of their skulls and got their own brains and placed them back in their own heads.

Third night: "In another direction there's a big stooping tree; if anybody passes under there, the tree drops down and kills the people," their father told them. They came to that tree. They stood right near the tree. Every time they ranted at it, the tree moved as if it was going to come down. They stood back. They stood as if they were going to run under the tree; they started to run as fast as they could. As they got close the tree went down and they jumped over it. They killed the tree. So be it.[3]

In 1932 Harry Black (Southern Cheyenne) also told the Só'taeo'o story of brotherhood. I also divided the story according to the nights it should be told.

Hestáhkeho (Twins), Version II

First night: There was a lone tipi, a man and his wife lived together. The man was always out hunting game during the day. The woman was pregnant. An old woman came to visit her. "I come to warn you, you are going to have a visitor. This person is a witch. You must not even as much as to glance at this person. If you do, it will be hard for you," said she. Then the old woman left just as suddenly as she had come.

The visitor came, but stood outside. "What is my grandchild doing?" said she. The wife made no reply. The witch then peeped in. "Ah!-Ho! What is my grandchild doing?" said she. The wife made no reply. The witch then came into the tipi. "Ah-Ho! What is my grandchild doing?" said she, but the wife did not look at her or say anything, but kept on sewing the moccasins. The witch uttered a cry like a baby in distress. The wife looked up as if scared. "I know you would look at me," said she. Then the witch grabbed her, slashed off her head and cut her abdomen open, threw all the inside of the woman including the unborn twin babies on the ground and took the body with her.

The old woman came to visit the wife again, she was gone, but she found the twin babies living on the ground still alive. "I warned her not to even as much as to glance at her," said she. She took the twins to raise and they grew up. [The twins] carried water and gathered fire wood for her. The twins made a sweat lodge, they gathered up human skulls and bones [of their family]. They arranged the cactus and sage for seats in the sweat lodge. They carried the human skulls and bones into the sweat lodge and arranged them as if they were live persons sitting on the cactus and sage, covered the lodge and had a sweat bath. [The] skulls and bones returned to human beings, some were moaning and others whispering. This was because they were sitting on the cactus. When the door flap was raised they all came out good and alive. The twins and their mother went back to their father. The twins grew up to be powerful and knew the art of witchery, and were afraid of no danger.

Second night: The father warned them not to go near a large tall tree. "There is a nest upon the foremost top of the tree," said he. But the twins said to one another, "let us go and see what our father has forbidden us," so they went and found a large tree, so straight and tall with no limbs, only near the top, and they saw a nest upon the foremost top of the tree. They found little birds in the nest covered with white downy fuzz. When the little birds blinked their eyes, streaks of lightning flashed.

"Little birds, what kind of voice have you?" said they. The little birds made a roaring sound, as of distant thunder. The twins took the birds to their father and mother, who were greatly alarmed.

"They are Thunder Birds. Return them to their nest," said they.

The father told his sons not to go near a certain tipi. "There lives an old woman that kills people and devours them," said him. But the twins were curious and wanted to see the old woman. They found her living alone. She invited them to come in.

"My grandchildren are hungry," said she. She searched in her bundle and brought out something, poured it into a pot which was hanging over the fire. "My grandchildren are going to fill up on something good to eat," said she. She was cooking human brains. The twins noticed the human skulls and bones lying about. They also saw human ears strung on the string hanging in the tipi, while the old woman was stirring the contents of the pot. "My grandchildren, scratch my leg," said she. As this was the way she killed her visitors. Her leg would sharpen and kick them with the sharp leg. But the twins attacked and killed her. They took the ears strung on the string and wore them for a necklace. When their father and mother saw what they had around their necks, they were greatly alarmed.

"They are human ears, return them to the old woman's tipi, surely the old woman's witchery and vengeance will be upon us," said they.

"But we have killed her," said the twins.

Third night: The father warned his sons not to go near the river. "There is a large serpent that dwells there," said he. But the twins were curious and wanted to see the serpent. The serpent saw them coming, it jumped into the river to hide. The senior twin brother tied the bladder [a water container for travel] on his junior twin brother's head of hair, and told him to dive into the water after the great serpent. This bladder contained the life [a breathing device] of the junior twin brother. The bladder floated on the top of the water, so they killed the great serpent. This serpent was [the one] that killed their mother. Thus the length of the legend is ended.[4]

Mrs. Yellow Eagle's story completes the third night's events:

> *Third night conclusion:* And the next morning he told them, "Don't go over there! The owls (spooks) are powerful," he told them.
> "Let's go see those owls," said Little Afterbirth. So they went over there. They killed big owls, there were two of them. He [Little Afterbirth] skinned them. He put the skin on himself. Then they went home. It was getting toward evening. They climbed a tree, they perched (in it). They would make sounds like an owl. And their father would come out, he would stand and look all around. Then he brought out his bow. He was going to shoot them.
> "Hey father, don't shoot us. It is us," he [Little Afterbirth] said. "It is us, we're just dressed like owls."
> "Oh, take them back!" he told them. They went back over there. They took off their outfits. They let go of the owls. Then they went back home. "You do not listen. You go everywhere," [their father] told them. The end.[5]

The epic of the sacred twins reveals the traditional concept of balance on a level that encourages young people to appreciate, since children are often at odds with their parents' warnings. As evidenced in the varying versions of the epic, each miniadventure can be told on differing nights and still carry the same message. Like the epic of the Navajo Hero Twins, Monster Slayer and Born for Water, the story of the Cheyenne sacred twins (Little Afterbirth and Oldest) are the foundation of sacred leadership and the traditional governing system.[6] Without such stories, young people would not understand cooperation, responsibility, reciprocity, and the sharing of power, duties, and responsibilities. The story of the sacred twins was not limited to the Só'taeo'o. Upon unification, the Tsétsêhéstâhese adapted the oral tradition of twins from one of their old prophets, Cherry Eater, who came to share the names of other prophets of his time: Youngest, Red Buck, Red Hair, Blood Bachelor, Red-red-red-red, or Mai-tŭm'. The emergence of the Tsétsêhéstâhese twins is told by Somers (Southern Cheyenne) in 1910:

> The old woman kept the child as her grandson and when he was old enough to walk, she made a wheel for him. And she told him, "you mustn't throw this over the [lodge] for fear you [will] get hurt." And once the child thought he would throw it over the [lodge]. He threw it over, when it came down it hit him in the head and split him into two; two boys appeared. This was the beginning of showing miracles to the starving people.[7]

BEFORE THE VÉHOO'O

In the Cheyenne national history, there are varying accounts of how the Véhoo'o came into existence; most can be linked to the matrilineal Só'taeo'o stories, which emphasize the significance of women, marriage, and family. After the Great Unification, of course, much of the stories from both the Só'taeo'o and Tsétsêhéstâhese merged, thus converging the names and actions of cultural heroes. As with almost every origin story of the Cheyennes, there is not a single version that supersedes others, nor is there a single authority, living and in the past, whose words are superior to others. The oral tradition of the Cheyennes is still alive, and there are significant consistencies in the varying accounts of the origin of the chiefs. These consistencies should not overshadow the primary teachings. When tracing the origin of the Véhoo'o, one consistency across numerous stories is the dire need to protect the people from cruelty or inhumanity. From chaos, the Véhoo'o were created to bring an end to outdated ways and to introduce new ways of living, laws, and ceremonial practices. To set the stage of when and why the Council of Forty-Four was created, we must gain a sense of what Cheyenne life was like without the Véhoo'o, and this is best demonstrated in the legacy of Mo'keheso (Little Calf).

Before the creation of the Council of Forty-Four Chiefs, leaders were free to lead as they wished, and there are accounts of them abusing their power and authority. One in particular was named Havevs (Many Horns), and they could rule without boundaries and without restriction. Randolf provided the story of Mo'keheso defeating the tyrant chief Havevs in "The Magic Arrows," while Krober provides the same story as an unnamed "tale."[8] In 1910, Wolf Chief (Northern Cheyenne) recited the story of Havívsts (Buffalo Horns), who represented corruption and poor leadership, and the hero Mahōtsts (Red Buck), who represented diligence and righteousness.[9] Traditional storytellers told me that this story was also an epic to be told over the course of several nights. The original text is authored by Somers and is an "interlinear" transcription, alternating from Cheyenne to English. I summarize the story based on my understanding of the story and consulting with knowledgeable people, elders, and storytellers. The setting of the story is at a camp located near a geyser.

Havívsts

First night: During the time of the buffalo, after Mo'keheso defeated the monsters and after the Great Race, a cruel man came to be the leader of one of the Só'taeo'o bands. Havevs (Many Horns) was greedy and selfish, he was named after a mythical creature that had horns all about its body.[10] Some believed that he was the actual monster. He rose to power and authority by claiming it because he possessed an old relic that held ancient medicine; it was a stone, likely from the world of stones. He used the medicine and power from this stone to influence and manipulate others. He became so influential and intimidating that nobody opposed him. He disbanded the only existing warrior society and required that warriors give him part of their kill after each hunt as tax. "Because of this law, Many Horns had more food than any other Indian in the camp. He would not permit anyone to hunt until his own meat was all eaten. In this way he caused much suffering among his people, while he himself remained well fed."[11]

The chief often used the beauty of his daughter to manipulate others, especially the young men who wanted to marry her. Her name was Voestaa'e (Pearl or White Buffalo Calf Woman) and she was very beautiful.[12] Havevs would ask for suitors to provide him with the best clothing and material wealth as dowry for his daughter's hand. Once they provided the gifts, he stopped the agreement and refused to offer his daughter, but kept the gifts. This created much dysfunction among the people, since suitors often gave the entire wealth of their family and relatives. Soon families became divided and spiteful of each other. Havevs was a true tyrant who was intelligent, manipulative, and cruel.

Second night: The time came when the people demanded that Havevs marry-off his daughter. On three occasions a suitor was selected, but met an unfortunate and accidental death by mysteriously falling into the geyser. The reality was that Havevs had become a full-blown murderer and was killing the young suitors by throwing them in the boiling water. The time came when Havevs accepted the fourth petition for marriage, which came from Mo'keheso. In Wolf Chief's account the boy's name is Mahōtsts (Red Buck).

Third night: During the first day of formal courtship, Havevs took the young man to the geyser and threw him in, but Mahōtsts was not hurt. He returned later that night to the lodge of Voestaa'e. Havevs did not allow the boy to sleep next to her. In the morning Havevs asked the boy to pick some cherries, which were not in season. Mahōtsts left and prayed for help. A voice said, "I will show you where to get what you need." The boy found the berries, picked them, and returned to the camp. His wife met him part of the way. Havevs was angered and claimed that he did not want cherries. That night Havevs did not allow the young couple to sleep together.

In the morning, Havevs asked Mahōtsts to pick some plums, which were also not in season. Again Mahōtsts left the camp, prayed, and eventually found and picked plums. He returned to camp and his wife met him part of the way. Voestaa'e said to Mahōtsts, "I think it is time for you to kill him." Havevs was angered and proclaimed that he did not want plums. That night Havevs asked his daughter what they were talking about, but she did not say anything.

Fourth night: In the morning, Havevs asked Mahōtsts to find some good sticks for arrows. Once again Mahōtsts left camp, prayed for help, and was helped by [a] spirit. The boy was led to a lake where he harvested a number of good sticks. He returned to camp and his wife met him as he came close. Havevs was angered and said, "This is not what I wanted." He also asked his daughter if they were up to a scheme, but she did not reply.

In the morning Havevs asked Mahōtsts for good feathers for his arrows. Once again Mahōtsts left, prayed, and was helped by a spirit, who was able to summon eagles from the air. The eagles flew above Mahōtsts and shook their tail feathers out. Mahōtsts retrieved the feathers and once again returned to camp. His wife met him as he returned. Havevs was disappointed and proclaimed the feathers were not good, yet he still took them. They went to bed, but followed the same rules and repeated the same actions as the previous nights.

In the morning Havevs asked Mahōtsts for some good sinew, and the next morning Havevs asked for good arrowheads. Each time Mahōtsts met the needs of the tyrant and each time Havevs was disappointed, but still accepted the gifts.

Fifth night: In the morning Havevs completed making his arrows; he had five quivers, each with ten arrows. He then asked Mahōtsts to "call in" the buffalo so the tyrant could shoot them. Mahōtsts asked the spirits for help and four buffalo bulls appeared. Mahōtsts told his situation, upon which the four bulls decided to test their strength on who would challenge Havevs. Each one tried to crack a large boulder, and three failed. The last bull was the strongest and decided to help the boy. As the boy returned to camp, he ran while the bull followed. Havevs ordered the boy to lead the bull to the chief's lodge so he could have an easy shot. The bull ran around the lodge as Havevs shot at him. Havevs could not hit the buffalo bull after shooting all the arrows from the five quivers. After Havevs ran out of arrows, the bull charged at Havevs and threw him into the air killing him. But Havevs had the power to regenerate himself. Each time the bull charged and tossed him, Havevs returned to life. After a number of times, the bull finally started to chip away at Havevs as if he was made of stone. Soon the bull was able to destroy Havevs.

The anthropologist Richard Randolph's informant, Oneha, best concludes the story:

When the duel was ended, the people came out of their hiding places to see what was left of their chief. They could find only one leg. Many Horns' widow carried this away and buried it. The other people did not mourn for him.

"He got just what he wanted," the chief's daughter said.

So Vosta and Moksaess [Mahōtsts] were married. The orphan boy became ruler of the village and was a much kinder chief than old Many Horns had been.[13]

The defeat and overthrow of Havívsts represents a milestone in Cheyenne national history because the story reveals how power can corrupt leaders and threaten the survival of the nation. The problem with having one chief is that a band or village was susceptible to corruption, since too much power rested in the hands of one leader. In such a case, the fate of a band or village depended on the integrity of the chief: if he was good, then the people would thrive, but if he was corrupt, then the people would suffer. Such social insecurity and political inconsistency in leadership was doomed to fail the people; a band would never be able to grow and flourish under such instability. The Só'taeo'o understood the problems resulting from an underdeveloped leadership system, and it was preserved in another story, this time about a "good" chief's children.[14]

Hovesenehev (Heron)

About the same time when Mahōtsts defeated Havívsts, in another band of the Só'taeo'o, a righteous chief rose to be the leader. He was kind and generous, and he dedicated his life to the prosperity of the nation. The chief had two sons, Hovesenehev (Heron) and Nakooss (Little Bear), and a daughter named Vosta (White Buffalo Woman). The chief was earnest and the younger son, Hovesenehev, followed his example of kindness, generosity, and discipline. The older son, Nakooss, on the other hand, was spoiled and did not care for others as his brother did. He grew to become a jealous man who always wanted what others had. Despite his unfavorable personality, Nakooss married a beautiful woman, but she was secretly in love with Hovesenehev, even though the young man never looked at her. Hovesenehev was still a young man and the people enjoyed his presence and loved his personality. One day when he wounded a bird hunting, it scratched the face of his sister-in-law. This made Nakooss angry.

The time finally came when Nakooss became exceedingly jealous of his brother, enough to get rid of him. Nakooss gathered some hunters and convinced his brother to go with them to hunt deer on an island in a large lake. Once they arrived by canoe, they set up camp and hunted for the next few days. One day, the hunters and Nakooss returned to the shore while Hovesenehev was still out alone on his hunt. They left him stranded on the island; when the young man saw them leave, he ran and yelled at them to return, but they yelled back that he was always causing trouble. "Heron was surprised and angry to hear this accusation. He had done no wrong and had never suspected his brother's jealousy."[15] They left him alone with only his bow and arrows and a hunting knife.

Hovesenehev was stranded for several days, crying and praying for help. Finally a group of eagles called a council to help the young man who had done no wrong. They felt sorry for him because they had witnessed the entire incident, starting with the foolishness of his sister-in-law. It was settled that the eagle father would carry him across the lake. Once they made it across, the eagle father instructed the boy on how to defeat a giant mosquito en route home. The boy killed the mosquito and took its head and stinger as a trophy, but it was also in the shape of a good weapon.

Hovesenehev traveled for days thinking about his younger sister and how he would punish his older brother. It was wintertime when he arrived to the old camp of his people. The lodges were scattered and it seemed that a lot of families had either left or perished. The young man noticed a bear sitting in the middle of the stream, so he prepared his bow to kill it. After he watched, he noticed that it was a person covered in a robe. It was a woman who was crying. He approached closer and found that it was his younger sister, Vosta. The siblings cried and embraced one another. Vosta rejoiced but then explained how Nakooss enslaved her by making her sit and stir the water hole so it wouldn't freeze. He made her carry water to the lodge without spilling it. She explained how their parents moved to another camp and did not know what had become of their family. She continued: "When Little Bear returned from the war he said that you had been killed. He told of many brave deeds he had performed. Father was so proud of him that he made him chief of this band. He is cruel, though, and the people do not like him."[16] She explained how Nakooss always taunted her about her brother, and how he made her carry red-hot coals in her hands. Hovesenehev was angry and decided to bring Nakooss to justice.

Vosta and Hovesenehev brought water to the tyrant, but the young man purposefully splashed it around to provoke a reaction from Nakooss. "You act as if your brother is here," said the tyrant.

"I am here," proclaimed Hovesenehev. He then splashed the cold water in his face. Nakooss was frightened and a true coward, but he did not want to show fear. He cooperated with his younger brother in hopes that he might be spared from any more punishment. Hovesenehev then asked his older brother to bring hot coals with his bare hands so that they could smoke together. Nakooss did so and burned his hands but pretended not to be hurt. Hovesenehev then asked his sister to bring their parents back because he wanted to perform a ceremony. When Vosta left, Hovesenehev went throughout the village looking for those other hunters who left him on the island. He found each of their lodges and lit them on fire by simply touching them with his new weapon, the mosquito head club. When some of the men ran out on fire, they ran into the freezing lake to cool off. Then Hovesenehev touched the ground with his weapon and said, "Boil them." Then the freezing water turned to boiling water, killing the men.

Hovesenehev returned to the lodge of his brother and sister-in-law. He made them carry fifteen large branches to construct his medicine lodge, which cut their backs. He then made them carry fifteen heavy rocks on their backs, which bruised their backs, arms, and legs. Hovesenehev whipped them while they worked. Soon Vosta returned with their parents and Hovesenehev explained truthfully what had happened and why he was treating his brother and sister-in-law so badly. Hovesenehev built a dome-shaped lodge and covered it with buffalo robes. He started a fire and began heating the fifteen rocks. His mother was crying and his father turned away; they both knew that justice had to be served. Hovesenehev gave his final order to his brother: "Now carry these hot rocks into the lodge with your bare hands." Nakooss picked up a rock and was incinerated. Hovesenehev then ordered his sister-in-law to do the same. "All this happened because of you. You deserve no better treatment than your husband."[17] When she picked up a red-hot rock, she was also incinerated. There were no more cruel people in the camp and Hovesenehev gave himself a sweat bath. Meanwhile all of the eagles, hawks, crows, and other birds from the island flew around and into the camp, signifying the return of a righteous leader. Hovesenehev lived a full and happy life for a generation with his people, and he is remembered in the Cheyenne oral tradition as the young man who punished the cruel people.

Embedded in the preceding stories are the values of good and bad leadership: righteous and cruel chiefs, as well as the major problems that arise in any society when power is unchecked. The people who lived in the old single-chief bands were often faced with dysfunction, as captured in these stories. The population was still small enough where every citizen depended on one another, so the small bands frequently restored themselves to balance. Nonetheless, disorder was common, since there was no organized system in place. Most of the problems arose with the leadership, typically when chiefs like Havevs and Nakooss oppressed the people. The corruption often led to complete disorder and tyranny when bands of men organized to control the people. These early bands or societies of men overthrew dictators, but the latter retained power by enforcing oppressive laws and even resorted to killing people who did not follow their orders.[18] The nation was undeveloped.

CHAPTER 5

The Origin of the Véhoo'o

IN THE Cheyenne oral tradition, there are multiple stories that tell of the origins of the Véhoo'o (Council of Forty-Four Chiefs). The most popular is the Sweet Medicine oral tradition of the Tsétsêhéstâhese, which places the origin of the "Chiefs Society" at the same time and place as the origin of the Nótâxeo'o, the warrior societies. The Só'taeo'o oral tradition tells of a different story of the origin of the Véhoo'o. As the Cheyenne Nation continued to grow and prosper, the oral traditions of both the Só'taeo'o and Tsétsêhéstâhese merged. I present both subnations' oral traditions as well as the synced one in the following pages.

ORIGIN OF THE VÉHOO'O: SÓ'TAEO'O VERSION

Before the creation of the Véhoo'o, or Council of Forty-Four Chiefs, and before the Great Unification, one chief governed each of the four bands of the Só'taeo'o and the four bands of the Tsétsêhéstâhese. If we recall the meeting before the Great Unification, when the first bands of Só'taeo'o and Tsétsêhéstâhese met on the Yellowstone River, one chief from each side could not reach an agreement: White Buffalo Tail of the Só'taeo'o and Red Paint of the Tsétsêhéstâhese were at the center of the intertribal dispute and could not reach a peaceful resolution.[1] The "single-chief" system was a proven failure for both internal affairs and external diplomatic relations with other Indian nations. By the time the two "tribes" met the second time, however, they had already begun reshaping their political theory. Each sent four representatives to meet, which led to the successful union on the Cheyenne River (see Part I). The Cheyenne trace the custom of selecting and sending four representatives for any diplomatic meeting to the Great Unification.

Logically, the Véhoo'o were created when the time eventually came for the sacred leaders to organize themselves to share responsibility, authority, and power to avert any corruption, greed, and tyranny. Instead of one leader, each band began selecting four sacred leaders to represent all of the families of the band. The original Só'taeo'o bands were made up of several families, and each family already established one matriarch or patriarch who was informally selected as a sacred leader: the most intelligent, reasonable, and wise person, to represent the family and its interests. This person was likely the one who acted as a mediator when disputes arose "across the door" (between family members) and "across the camp" (with other families). Before the establishment of the Véhoo'o, before the people hunted buffalo, all the family matriarchs and patriarchs of the band selected four among themselves to represent the entire band. These four sacred leaders were responsible for making crucial decisions during dire circumstances, like when and where to move camp. Their seats were temporary since they knew that another matriarch or patriarch of equal or greater stature could take their place for the next critical decision. It was not until after the establishment of the Véhoo'o that the leaders become exclusively males, and they ceremoniously and spiritually accepted and committed themselves to the duty and service to lead for ten-year terms. The role of the band leaders was first and foremost peacemaking and resolving conflict.

In time, the four band chiefs of the first bands of the United Cheyenne Nation became the first "Big Chiefs" of what would become the formalized Council of Forty-Four Chiefs. Before the Great Unification, the Só'taeo'o had four bands, which were named after the one chief that governed each.[2] The Só'taeo'o practice of naming bands after their head chiefs continued until the decline of the band system. The practice became necessary when the Cheyenne Nation was destabilized when the United States invaded Cheyenne lands. For example, the Two Moons Band, Little Wolf Band, and Morning Star People were all part of the Ôhméseheso (Eaters). At the time of the Great Unification, the Só'taeo'o population was smaller than that of the Tsétsêhéstâhese, so their four bands equated to one band in the United Cheyenne Nation. The four chiefs retained power as band chiefs. As the United Cheyenne Nation grew and the bands increased to ten, this Só'taeo'o practice of naming four band chiefs eventually led to the creation of the Council of Forty-Four Chiefs, affirming that the system is of Só'taeo'o origin.

While the custom of selecting four Big Chiefs (band chiefs) led to the creation of forty-four Big Chiefs, the first forty Véhoo'o later selected the first four "Principal Chiefs" or "Old Man Chiefs" to lead the entire United Cheyenne Nation—that is, all of the bands. The Principal Chiefs were also created under the traditional principles of balance, since they made the decisions that were "passed" to them when the forty band chiefs could not reach a consensus or they did not have the authority. This is how the chief system developed concurrently with the ten bands of the Cheyenne Nation.

The United Cheyenne Nation expanded into as many as twenty bands, but not every band was represented in the Council of Forty-Four, either because they were fairly new and small, or because they were birthed from outcasts. The system did allow for smaller bands to earn the right to be represented at the grand council, especially when some of the original bands were annihilated or destroyed by disease and war with whites; their survivors thus joined existing bands.

Each subnation, the Só'taeo'o and Tsétsêhéstâhese, has different origin stories of the Véhoo'o. There are several different versions, which resulted when the sacred histories converged after the Great Unification. Nonetheless, the creation of the chiefs system is rooted in the sacred history, the ceremonial cycle, and founded on the sacred laws and teachings of both the Só'taeo'o and Tsétsêhéstâhese ways of living. Without this foundation, there would be no unity across the bands, for none would have ownership and respect over the system. The oldest story of the creation of the Véhoo'o, however, is a matrilineal Só'taeo'o tradition. Later the origin story converged and synced with the Sweet Medicine oral tradition of the patrilineal Tsétsêhéstâhese. The epic of the creation of the Véhoo'o reinforces values found in Cheyenne concepts of parenthood, justice, and responsibility. In 1987, Laura Rockroads (Northern Cheyenne) asserted that the following epic teaches how women, men, and children should be taken care of, and how they should care for one another.[3] As before, I have divided the story into chapters based on each night a section was recited. Wolf Chief, a Northern Cheyenne chief, begins the story.[4]

The Rolling Head, Part I

First night: There was a lodge nearby a pond. In the lodge was a man with a wife and two children. Every morning the man dressed his wife in very good shape. After he did this he went out to hunt game. Another morning he dressed up his wife again and went out to hunt again. When he came back the same day, he looked at his wife; she was turned very white. He wondered what was the matter with his wife. Three times he dressed her, he wondered what was the matter. She always turned white. One early morning he went to the pond and lay down in the brush to find out what seemed to be the matter with his wife. While he was there he saw his wife come, run down to the pond. As soon as she got near the bank, the waves of the pond came rolling towards her, and there he saw a big serpent licking his wife. As soon as he saw the snake he ran down to his wife, cut her head off and cut the snake in two, and dressed his wife, took one part of a rib off, took it to his children to cook. After it was cooked, then put it in a wooden pan, and gave it to his children to eat. The little boy said, "My mother tastes just like it." The man said, "No, it is a young moose. I just killed it." When they were through eating, the man took the head off and took it before the children and asked them [in a wicked manner], "What does your mother taste [like]?" He left his children. The children cried because their father had left them, expecting never to see them again.

These children were terrified[;] they thought [they] would go some place [else]. When gone a far distance, they looked back. They saw a head rolling down towards them, asking them to wait. [It was their mother's head.] They were so frightened that they did not wait. While running the boy said to his sister, "Sister I am tired out." The sister had a staff with her. She said to him: "When I used to play, I could not go through the sticky pears." She hit the earth and they were so thick [bushes of sticky pears]. So they ran on. The head came to the pears and could not get through for a long time. They both looked back. They ran, the head [was] coming again, way off.

At the same time the boy was tired out again and [his sister] said, when the head was [close] at hand, "When I used to play, I sometimes could not get over a high bluff." She struck the earth and there became a high bluff behind them. So the head was on the other side. The head said, "My children, I love you both. Why don't you lay down the stick so I can crawl over it?" So the sister put her staff over the bluff. When the head was right on the center, the girl turned the stick over and the head fell in a hallow, and the earth closed. When it was closed in, they never expected to see it anymore.

Here the story ends for the first night. There are different versions of the story of "The Rolling Head." Somers, a Southern Cheyenne, stated that the family was "from the tribe of certain clan of Indians, they were lost family" [*sic*], which explains why some believe that their isolated and solitary lifestyle led to dysfunction.[5]

Somers' story includes some additional major points worthy of note:

- The man painted his wife with red paint, dressed her in fine clothing, and braided her hair before he left; when he returned, the paint was removed and she was not as fine as when he left her. According to Cheyenne custom, a woman who is not dressed and painted nicely is perceived as widowed.
- The boy tasted his mother because he was still nursing. According to Cheyenne custom, children self-wean, typically around the age that they begin to speak. This point also indicates that the only way the children

knew something was odd was because the boy found a familiar taste in an odd place.
- The mother accuses the children of violating a taboo (eating human flesh). The Cheyennes, like the majority of human cultures, viewed cannibalism as an inhumane grotesquery.
- The girl creates four obstacles for the rolling head: thorns from prickly pear bushes, thorns from plum bushes, thorns of rosebud bushes, and finally the high bluffs.[6] The plants are significant to the Cheyenne lifestyle but are particularly difficult to gather. Gathering and preparing such plants were primarily a woman's responsibility: prickly pear fruits and roses are made into tea, and plums are a common fruit. According to Cheyenne custom, high bluffs are known to be the burial locations of the oldest of humans on earth.

Wolf Chief continued the story:

The Rolling Head, Part II

Second night: They came upon a hill. They saw a great big camp. As soon as they came up the people saw them. Their father was already there, and told the people to move away from his children, who were human-flesh-eaters. A society got hold of these two children, tied them hand and foot and pitched them to the ground so they could not come out. The camp moved but these two children were left tied to the ground. But a very old dog was left hid in the brushes. When the people were gone, he came up where these children were tied and untied the oldest one with his mouth. After he untied her, the girl untied her brother. The old dog was with them. He said to them, "I got a piece of firewood, a piece of fire-stone, a piece of sinew, and one awl." He gave them to them that they might use these things.

They moved away and went to timber. While siting there, the boy saw a bunch of deer coming nearby. He asked his sister to look at them. She said, "If I look at them it won't do any good to me." Bye and bye she looked at them. The bunch of deer were dead at once. They both went to where the deer were lying dead and dressed them all, and brought the meat down to where they were. She sliced it, dried it on the branches of trees, and kept good care of the old dog.

Third night: The old dog went around to a distant place where the Indians were camped and came back to tell them about the Indians. When they were at the place where they had sliced beef [meat], a crow flew about the place. The girl asked the crow to come. The crow came. The girl gave the crow a piece of fat. He took it in his mouth and took it into the circle of a big camp where the people were starving. So he flew there and dropped the fat where some men were playing the wheel-game. The people said, "The crow has fat in his bill and drops it for us. The children are somewhere you left, are having plenty to eat."

In due time there were great herds of buffalo [that] came near the place the children were. "Sister," said the boy, "look at the herds of buffalo that have come."

"Oh no," she said, "If I should look at them, it would not be of any benefit to us. They are so many." Bye and bye she looked at them. They were all dead at once. They dressed them. While sitting together, his sister asked, "I wish we could have mountain bears and wild panthers with us so we could scare anything away from us." So they came.

At this time the people were moving back to where they were. The people came to their house for a feast. While they were present in the home, the bears and wild panthers looked out for the children's father. After many were in the house he came about the last man. Their bears and wild panthers recognized him and dashed upon him. And there he was torn into pieces while the people kept eating. And that's the end.[7]

Here the story concludes for listeners who are of younger ages. Other recorded versions of the epic comprise varying details that are worthy of note:

- The old dog was toothless, meaning it was harmless and likely abandoned.
- A big lodge appeared when the girl looked, following her brother's plea to do so. A replica of the big lodge is used when conducting the formal chiefs' seating ceremony.
- The animals that were killed "by looking" vary from deer and antelope to buffalo. This method of killing—by looking at animals—is significant to the communal and ceremonial hunts.
- The number of times the girl killed the animals "by looking" is assumed to be four. According to Cheyenne custom, the number four is sacred when conducting or enacting rituals.
- The presence of a crow, and no other bird, is consistent in every story. According to Cheyenne custom, the crow cannot be eaten because it scavenges on human flesh. Consuming crow meat is equivalent to cannibalism.
- The presence of the hoop or wheel game is consistent in most stories. As discussed in previous pages, the hoop or wheel game is the founda-

tion of Cheyenne sovereignty and governance because of its unifying properties and philosophies.
- The presence of pet bears and lions is consistent in every story.[8] These animals are reminiscent of when the Cheyennes lived in the "time of the stones," when they domesticated bears and lions.

According to Somers, the wild animals ate the father to "repent to the law" he broke (killing his wife, lying to his children, and accusing them of being cannibals).[9] This is the only Cheyenne story that has any instance of cannibalism, and it was done as a result of deceit and cruelty when the children were misled by their father.

The fourth night or chapter of the origin of the Véhoo'o emphasizes the actual creation of the system, yet most recorded versions do not include it as part of "The Rolling Head." In 1936, E. Adamson Hoebel recorded the fourth night, told by Elk River to Black Wolf.[10] The girl prophet is identified as Mukije (Short Woman) and her father is Bull Looks Back. Black Wolf narrates the story as if he were Elk River, who was born in 1810 and died in 1908:

The Rolling Head, Part III

Fourth night: Now she sent for the men, and the women too, because she had cooked up a lot of food. When they had eaten she spoke to the men.

"Tomorrow you move down on this flat and put yourselves in a nice circle. We are going to make chiefs. You people know I have been accused of killing my mother. That is not true. Now, however, I have killed my father through animals. We shall make chiefs, and here after we shall make a rule that if anyone kills a fellow tribesman he shall be ordered out of the camp for from one to five years. Whatever the people decide."

When they had arranged the camp circle they took two big lodges and made one in the center. She asked them to move five other tipis into the space within the circle. These were put in the medicine wheel arrangement. When everything was finished she packed a large bundle and walked around the circle to enter it before the big lodge. First, she took some dirt from the north side of the lodge. Carefully patting it, she arranged it in a mound in the center of a cleared space. It represented the world. Next she set up five sticks representing the men she would choose as head chiefs. She filled her pipe. She held it to each stick, showing the people what would be expected of them.

"You will have to swear," she said. "You will have to take an oath that you will be honest and care for all the tribe."

Following the instructions she gave out, her brother purified himself in the smudge of the sweet medicine grass. Now she told him to go out to walk four times around the camp.

"When you go out you have a starting place. Go around until you come back to it. Do this four times," she ordered.

He had already been told what men to select. After the four circumambulations he sought out the first man, leading him into the lodge. Then the other four were brought in like manner.

They were seated, the sister told them everything. She had all she needed in that bundle. She told them she was going to make them chiefs to rule the camp. And this is what she said.

"You have seen me put up five sticks here. You shall have to do this to the others who come after you. Now you five men are to be the chiefs of the entire tribe. You must rule the people. When the tribe comes to renew the chiefs you must put up these five sticks again. If any one of you still lives, and the people want him again, then you must call him in to take his old place."

Now she finished telling them. (Reverts to voice of himself, Black Wolf) She is going to swear them in. She is holding the pipe herself, in both hands with the stem out. They smoked. The pipe is smoked for peace. That was done so that if some persons ever used strong words to the chiefs, they would have strong hearts and not get angry. The sweet grass was used on all of them.

Then the big crowd came in. Enough more were in the lodge to make forty-four men. She did the same to each of the rest of them. When this was done she told them to pick two men and sit on each side of the entrance.

"Some day you will have a lodge of your own," she informed them. "Then you can use these two. They can cook for you, or you can send them out on errands. They shall be your servants and messengers."

These two could not be of the five.

"Every ten years you must renew the chiefs. But each time keep five of the old ones," the maid continued.

She had a parfleche for the stuff they used in the ritual.

"When you move camp," she exhorted them in closing, "keep out in front of the people. Stop and rest four times with it [the Chiefs' Bundle] on the way."

After she made the chiefs, she took out five bones, just as many as these five chiefs. "Now you can make soldiers troops. You may call them what you want. You could call them Elks." Later on, Sweet Medicine made the dress of these soldiers.

"When you people move camp, leave me here. Every four years, you come back to this place where I shall be."

Although this is a good ending for the epic, the story actually continues and branches off into stories that are tied to other teachings. Some stories explain the origin of various ceremonies, ritualistic guilds, and other cultural teachings.

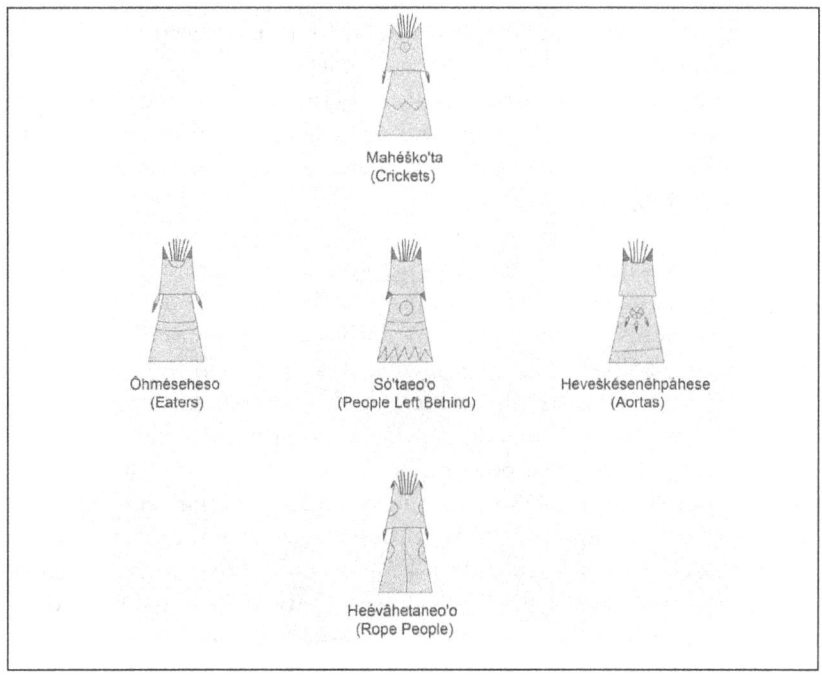

The medicine wheel camp formation.

The epic of "The Rolling Head," Mukije, and the creation of the Véhoo'o is unconventional to Sweet Medicine oral traditions because he is not identified as the principal founder of the Véhoo'o. They can be best explained because of the common adaptations in stories that resulted after the Great Unification, when the Só'taeo'o and Tsétsêhéstâhese began converging oral traditions to preserve the legitimacy of the Véhoo'o and to sustain balance with the warriors. Evidence of sacred history convergence is easily found in the details of the story. For example, according to Black Wolf, Mukije placed the five tepees in a "medicine wheel" arrangement, with one in the center and one lodge at each of the Cheyenne cardinal directions. The center lodge represents the first chief's lodge, while the four outer lodges represent the first four bands of the Só'taeo'o. One chief from each band became the first Big Chiefs and eventually became the first Old Man Chiefs. The four outer lodges could also represent the first four bands of the Tsétsêhéstâhese, since they also had four original bands. In another interpretation, the four outer lodges could represent the first bands of the Tsétsêhéstâhese and the large center lodge could represent a single Só'taeo'o band: the arrangement thus representing the Great Unification. Whatever the case, the Só'taeo'o origin story (with Mukije) fits both the Tsétsêhéstâhese and Só'taeo'o traditional histories, as well as the United Cheyenne national history. One certainty is that there were five original chiefs who are remembered as the first five Old Man Chiefs, even though their specific bands remain unidentified.

Other evidence that Véhoo'o are of Só'taeo'o origin is that embedded in the epic of Mukije lay the traditional Só'taeo'o teachings and values that centered on the power of the female gender. The Só'taeo'o are a matrilineal society. Mukije, as a young female virgin who cares for her younger brother and who eventually feeds the entire village, saving them from starvation, represents the finest of traditional female characteristics and personality: she is caring, compassionate, motherly, determined, and nurturing. Because she possesses the power to summon and kill animals with her "look," as well as summon the protection of fierce lions and bears, she also represents the supernatural forces of Éškemane (Grandmother Earth). She eventually comes to embody Éškemane and by the end of the story, Mukije becomes part of the Earth, never departing from the land where she made the Véhoo'o. She makes the land holy. She also instructs the people to return every four years, as if they are returning to their place of origin or birth.

Because the Véhoo'o are of Só'ta'eo'o origin and the woman prophet Mukije represents motherhood and womanhood, these values became central to the United Cheyenne national culture and identity. The persistence of the Cheyenne Nation depended on the strength of women because they were responsible for teaching principles and values of leadership and citizenship to the children. Women may not have been able to become military or political leaders, but their roles as mothers of the nation are recognized throughout Cheyenne ceremonial practices and the oral traditions. Most notable is women's roles in every major ceremony. The legacy of the woman prophet also established the identities as ideal Cheyenne women, something young women aspired to follow, who inevitably led the Cheyenne Nation to prime and pinnacle.

THE ORIGIN OF THE VÉHOO'O

Mary, Daisy, and Two Boys, Children of George Bent Native Dress with Ornaments, Boys with Breastplates, 1891. National Anthropological Archives, Smithsonian Museum Support Center, Suitland, Maryland (NAA INV 06119300, OPPS NEG 346 A).

PART II | VÉHOO'O: THE CHIEFS

ORIGIN OF THE VÉHOO'O: CHEYENNE NATIONAL VERSION

The epic origin of the Véhoo'o highlights several attributes significant to the Cheyenne national history. In the previous story the father was a murderer and liar and tried to cheat his own people, and in the end he was punished. The mother, who was presumably unfaithful to her husband, destroyed her family. The presence of the bear and mountain lion indicates that the way of life from a previous world continued to have an influence. The preceding epic also involves a young woman and a boy, which is common in Cheyenne storytelling and is representative of the significance of children in maintaining the nation's existence. The children also took on roles as executers of justice and peace, and the young woman selected and taught the first five chiefs the values and principles of sacred leadership. It is well known today that the primary duty of chiefs is that they adhere to the wishes of women and children to protect future generations of the nation. The origin story reinforced new traditional teachings, while bridging old ones, and highlighted sacred laws and cultural beliefs. These philosophies were worthy of keeping in perpetuity.

Upon the Great Unification, the origin epic of the Véhoo'o began to incorporate traditions and values of the Tsétsêhéstâhese, including those of the prophet Motsé'eóeve, which I discuss later. George Grinnell and James Mooney have both recorded Tsétsêhéstâhese-influenced accounts of the origin of the Véhoo'o.[11] Their informants emphasized that the Véhoo'o were created out of the wars between the traditional enemies of the United Cheyenne Nation, the Hóheehe (Assiniboine). In a time before they had guns and horses, the Cheyennes frequently fell victim to enemies, and their children were often absorbed into other nations like the Hóheehe. The biggest threats to the Cheyenne Nation were such enemy tribes who often attacked Cheyenne villages, and some believed that the entire Cheyenne national identity would disappear. According to Tangle Hair, one of Grinnell's informants, the Cheyenne national version of the origin of the Véhoo'o resulted from conflict with the Hóheehe. In the following pages, I summarize the story based on unwritten accounts I heard and my understanding of our oral tradition.

Voestaehneva'e (White Buffalo Woman)

First night: One day, while the men were out hunting, a band of Hóheehe attacked a village. The daughter of the chief assumed the role of village

THE ORIGIN OF THE VÉHOO'O

leader since her father was away. The Cheyenne woman was young and beautiful and named Voestaehneva'e (White Buffalo Woman or Pearl, not the wife of Mo'keheso). As the enemy attacked, she was able to send the women and children away to avoid capture, but she realized that she was about to be captured herself. Once she realized her fate, she walked toward the pursuing warriors and bravely stood awaiting capture. Her actions shocked the Hóheehe, but she was effective in distracting the warriors long enough to allow for her people to escape unharmed. The leader of the Hóheehe claimed Voestaehneva'e while his warriors looted the empty village. She was the only captive.

After the next few days, the head warrior took the Só'taeo'o woman and led his warriors across the country to the Hóheehe village. What nobody knew at the time was that she was already pregnant from her Cheyenne husband, Ma'êhoomahe (Red Painted Robe). Not long after she was taken, she gave birth to a boy. Her Hóheehe captor grew fond of her and the child and he wanted her to be his wife, even though he was already married. The man was a principal chief of his nation and was already married to the daughter of an older chief who was equally as beautiful as Voestaehneva'e. When the husband left to hunt and hold council, the two women did not get along, especially since the Cheyenne woman remained resentful because she and her son were captives. She believed that one day the Hóheehe would try to kill him.

Over the next months, Voestaehneva'e noticed that her captor frequently attended council meetings with other prominent men, chiefs, and headmen of the village. One time he hosted such a meeting and Voestaehneva'e helped prepare food. She noticed that the chief carried a beautifully decorated, redstone pipe and stem, and the leaders smoked from it before they held councils. Voestaehneva'e came to trust the chief and no longer feared for her son. Unfortunately, she became sad and depressed because she missed her Cheyenne home and family. This caught the attention of the Hóheehe wife, who began to feel sorry for the Cheyenne woman. She decided to help the Cheyenne woman return home.[12]

The Hóheehe wife began to show compassion and communicated with Voestaehneva'e using sign language. Once she believed that Voestaehneva'e trusted her, the Hóheehe wife began telling her about the surrounding landscape and where she could find the Cheyenne people. "It is wintertime now, the best time for you to escape with your son," said the Hóheehe wife. Voestaehneva'e planned to escape with her son. The Hóheehe wife made extra pairs of moccasins and the best winter clothes, including a buffalo robe, so the Cheyenne wife and child would not freeze. She also packed dried meat and pemmican for her long journey. The two women embraced one last time, for they became like sisters. "I won't forget how you helped my son and me," said Voestaehneva'e. Then the Cheyennes departed in the night when the whole village bedded down during an evening snowfall. The next morning her tracks were covered. Voestaehneva'e traveled for several days and was careful not to be seen by returning hunters. She crossed a large frozen river following a path or bridge made of wood, just as the Hóheehe woman described. After several days of traveling, Voestaehneva'e depleted her food and resorted to scavenging the carcasses of slain animals. Her journey was difficult and her child almost perished, but she was able to make it back to a Cheyenne village that was not her own. Later that winter, she was reunited with her father, husband, and relatives in her home village.

Second night: Voestaehneva'e shared her story with her family and told of how the Hóheehe woman helped her. She proclaimed, "If enemies can become like sisters, then the women of the village could also become like sisters and work together." She told her husband and father how they selected leaders and they smoked from a pipe during council meetings. She declared, "If the bravest and most headstrong men of the Hóheehe could sit together to talk, then so could those of the Cheyenne." She believed that she witnessed these events for good reason, and it was her duty to share what she learned. When springtime arrived she asked her father to hold a special hunt, unlike any before. This was going to be a new way of living. She wanted him, as chief, to order that the hunters kill forty-four buffalo bulls. "Do not let them kill any more or any less, and they must be bulls," she ordered. All of the families had to participate in preparing the meat for a grand feast, which was going to signify the start of the spring hunting season. "Cut and dry all of the best pieces of meat for our feast, and feed your family any leftovers," she announced. The best women and their families were to tan and dress the hides. "You must do your best to represent your family by creating your best work," she ordered. "Decorate them with quills, feathers, and other ornaments, and paint them with beautiful designs." The best men were chosen to make forty-four plain pipes with no decorations. "These must be the finest pipes that you ever made, they must be perfect," she proclaimed. Meanwhile the father, who was the only chief, was to find and cut forty-four arrow shafts, but not to make arrows. Instead Voestaehneva'e straightened them, painted them red, and cut them to be of equal length. These sticks represented the "straight" lifestyle and behavior of the best leaders.

After a few days, everything was prepared and everyone was ready for the grand meeting and feast. The families finished drying the buffalo meat, the best women finished decorating forty-four robes, the best men finished making their best pipes, and Voestaehneva'e finished making forty-four ceremonial sticks. Each stick was painted red, a sacred color. Voestaehneva'e and the women set up a double lodge, with forty-four poles and two large lodge skins. She asked her father to invite the best men to bring their families to eat, but she intended on holding a ceremony so everyone was invited to feast and look on.

THE ORIGIN OF THE VÉHOO'O

After the meal, the center of the lodge was cleared and Voestaehneva'e and her father began selecting certain men from the crowd to sit in a circle. These men were selected based on their "bravery, wisdom, and fine physical appearance."[13] In a short time, forty-four of the finest men of all different ages were sitting in a perfect circle in the lodge and the rest of the people sat on the outside looking in. Voestaehneva'e left for a brief moment and returned with the forty-four buffalo robes. She placed each in front of the men. Then her father returned with the forty-four pipes and placed one on top of the buffalo robe so each man received one. Voestaehneva'e left and returned with a bundle of forty-four sticks. These chiefs were to remember that each stick represents the necessary number of poles to construct the Chiefs' Lodge, and that alone, each stick can be broken, but together the bundle will never break. As long as the Chiefs' Bundle is never lost or broken, the nation will remain strong. She stuck one stick in the ground in front of each man.

Voestaehneva'e bestowed teachings and responsibilities to the chiefs, asserting that they hold council whenever there was any major conflict that needed resolving or when there was a need to make a major decision. She stood and explained to the men, outlining their responsibilities to the nation: "You were chosen to protect the Cheyenne people and to protect them from all danger. You are responsible for the land and the people; protect them. Especially protect the women and children, for they are the future. Take care of them when they need help, especially if they are sick, starving, or abandoned." The council was to hold the Chiefs' Lodge ceremony after ten years and select new sacred leaders. The ceremony concluded after each of the forty-four men accepted the responsibilities and consented to serve for ten years.

The story of Voestaehneva'e positions the Hóheehe at the center of the origin of the Cheyenne Council of Forty-Four, while honoring the enemy tribe as worthy adversaries to the nation. This is evidence that Cheyenne sacred protectors, while converging oral histories, fortified Cheyenne ownership over a governing system that came from the Hóheehe. Without the new story, the governing structure would be prone to failure because the people would not believe in an enemy's way of governing. If the system failed, then the people would suffer the consequences of the failed government.

In another origin story told by the Southern Cheyenne chief Lone Wolf, one of Mooney's informants, the Cheyennes are remembered as the aggressors against an enemy people called the Ówū'qeo, who likely were the Hóheehe. One winter the Cheyennes attacked the Ówū'qeo and drove them to the ice in a surprise attack, eventually massacring all except for one woman.¹⁴ The captured Ówū'qeo woman invented the Cheyenne Council of Forty-Four Chiefs, which is quite different from previous accounts. Petter described a similar story in which the Cheyennes were the aggressors:

> Cheyenne say that this system of having a council of forty-four chiefs was adopted from another tribe, which the Ch. had practically annihilated. A woman prisoner told her captor (a chief) of the ways of her own people in selecting chiefs. The method pleased the Ch., who under the woman's instruction set up the "vehoneom" [chiefs' lodge], fixed the forty four sticks and elected their chiefs on the new plan" [sic].¹⁵

Most scholars agree that there is no evidence that the Hóheehe had a Council of Forty-Four Chiefs before the Cheyennes, or that another Indian nation was involved in the creation of the Cheyenne council. The system of the Council of Forty-Four Chiefs is unique among all Plains Indian nations, but similar to the principles of the Haudenosaunee Confederacy. The confederacy united different tribes under a charter of peace, was also created out of chaos, and involved a prophet, who established a system of chiefs, laws, and governance to protect future generations.¹⁶ Traditional Cheyennes, however, believe that the Véhoo'o was created out of a combination of the people's unstable political situation, circumstances of innovation and luck, and the unseen forces of the universe and nature. The differing origin accounts may vary in which nation was the aggressor and to which nation the founder belonged, Cheyenne or Hóheehe. Nonetheless, the Cheyenne national history reaffirms that the creation of the chiefs resulted from violence and aggression with an enemy nation. There is a possibility that this enemy nation was the Só'taeo'o, but the Cheyenne identified them as Hóheehe after unification to preserve the origin story and unity. Inconsistencies in story are unimportant to the main theme preserved in the story: that a woman created the governing system. From the Cheyenne perspective, the discrepancies do not denigrate the culture and philosophical teachings embedded in the origin stories of the Véhoo'o.

The origin of the Véhoo'o is one of the most significant oral traditions of the Cheyenne Nation. Retold through the art of storytelling, the origins of the Véhoo'o survived as parents and grandparents taught children the voilent but poetic history of their system of government. More than entertainment, the origin stories also instilled a sense of belonging and, more important, a sense of ownership of the Council of Forty-Four Chiefs. The oral tradition allowed later generations to maintain the integrity of their system by continuing the legacy and securing legitimization of their nation.

THE ORIGIN OF THE VÉHOO'O

There is no exact date of when the Véhoo'o system began. Bull Thigh stated it was created after the Great Unification.[17] Among the Cheyennes, the time of origin is unimportant as there is an understanding that the Véhoo'o always existed and would always exist. In 1910, White Eagle, a Southern Cheyenne Dog Soldier and member of the Heévâhetaneo'o (Rope People), expressed the longevity and significance of the Véhoo'o from Sweet Medicine's teachings: "He told the people that the chief society should be forever; they shall be different ones every ten years. This is the seventh generation [that has kept this tradition]. This story has been told by [my] ancestors. Try to keep in mind what I have said, and follow the rules. That's the reason why the Cheyennes live on today." This sentiment is shared in the modern era as expressed by Leroy Pine in 2009, a Northern Cheyenne chief and member of the Vóhpoométaneno (White River Band): "The modern government is temporary, and the traditional leadership is permanent, you might say [it will last] forever."[18] The traditional system of governance depended almost entirely on the health of the tribe's oral tradition and survival of the origin stories, the foundation for nationhood. Most important, the Cheyenne people had to remember what life was like without the Véhoo'o: the corruption, cruelty, and social dysfunction.

THE SWEET MEDICINE CHIEF

While the Só'taeo'o were creating and refining the Véhoo'o, the Tsétsêhéstâhese created and institutionalized a warrior society system, which has origins that are traced directly to the prophet Motsé'eóeve. Nobody can say for certain which came first: the original warrior societies or the Véhoo'o. Nonetheless, the two tribes unified their political systems under the principle of hévese'onematsestôtse (brotherhood). Most modern Cheyennes know the origin of the Véhoo'o as part of the Sweet Medicine legacy, which is now the standard of Cheyenne national history. I explore the warrior societies in detail in Part III. The Great Unification, if we were to examine it from the initial perspective of citizens (families), was probably not an easy transition, since uniting members of two peoples of differing cultures, societies, and political systems can be challenging. Although they shared a history and language, the Só'taeo'o are matrilineal and the Tsétsêhéstâhese are patrilineal; the Só'taeo'o possessed the Ésevone (Buffalo Hat) while the Tsétsêhéstâhese held the Maahótse (Medicine Arrows). Both subnations probably viewed the political theories and leadership systems of their neighbors as foreign, and that any change in their existing political organizations could be potentially threatening to future generations. The two subnations, Tsétsêhéstâhese and Só'taeo'o, could have only joined in perpetuity if they sincerely accepted one another as relatives, which is why the ceremonial and ritual aspects of unification were essential. From then on, a reformed political system that functioned as part of the new United Cheyenne Nation ensured truce. Oral traditions, philosophies, spiritual practices, and governing systems had to merge earnestly; this was necessary for effective and long-lasting nation building.

Once the subnations were merged, sacred protectors merged the revisions and additions to old oral traditions as a means to safeguard the legitimacy of the new system for future generations of both tribes. Today the different versions of the origin of the Véhoo'o remain, and I have already reviewed some. The new citizenry of the United Cheyenne Nation, who were both Tsétsêhéstâhese and Só'taeo'o, also had to ensure that the future generations maintained ownership over the unification, which meant that both groups had to be included and allowed to be active participants in the new system. While each culture is recognized in the Cheyenne national history—that is, their original five bands can fit in the national origin story of the Véhoo'o—the new political system had to include a new position that recognized and respected the Tsétsêhéstâhese culture, oral tradition, ceremonial practices, and people. This was done when the leaders created the position of the Sweet Medicine Chief.

While the stories presented earlier highlight an element that the Sweet Medicine versions do not—that a young woman was the principal creator of the Véhoo'o—both oral traditions emphasize that the Véhoo'o was created as a result of either external or domestic conflict. The catalysts for the establishment of a new system of governance were conflict, corruption, and injustice, which are also emphasized in every story about the creation of the Véhoo'o. One of the primary duties of the Véhoo'o is to prevent and resolve violence and dysfunction, whether foreign or domestic. Every origin story highlights that the Cheyenne people desperately needed to improve their way of living. Chaos is memorialized as graphic and gruesome in the stories of tyrants like Havívsts and Nakooss and in the epic of "The Rolling Head." The creation of the Véhoo'o is also memorialized as change, and the resultant new system is valued for its principles of humanity, justice, and fairness.

The Tsétsêhéstaestse prophet, Motsé'eóeve, is credited for bringing the four sacred laws to the Cheyennes: that a Cheyenne must not lie or deceive another or the people; a Cheyenne must not steal or cheat another or the people; a Cheyenne must never marry relatives; and a Cheyenne must not kill another Cheyenne.[19] As Henrietta Mann states: "He also devised their value system, consisting of love, respect, cooperation, generosity, understanding, humility, and maintenance of the Cheyenne cultural way of life.

During the 446 years Sweet Medicine lived with the Cheyennes, they were happy and good."[20] Upon the Great Unification, the heroic Motsé'eóeve was ceremoniously incorporated into the Véhoo'o and the Véhooneome (Chiefs' Lodge). After unification, the Council of Forty-Four Chiefs adapted the fifth position of the Old Man Chiefs to merge with the legacy of the prophet and renamed it the Sweet Medicine Chief or the prophet. An individual who was the epitome of a Cheyenne prophet occupied this position. The adaptation introduced a new political and governing theory that merged with the Great Unification and that also affirmed the spiritual abilities of prophets, who were primarily spiritual leaders and did not necessarily become political leaders. The position of the prophet allowed for prophets to also lead in the highest position of the United Cheyenne Nation.

The Sweet Medicine Chief was also the caretaker of the Chiefs' Bundle, which was handed down successively since the creation of the Véhoo'o. The female Só'taeo'o prophet, Mukije, under the guidance of the supernatural beings, made the Chiefs' Bundle, which contained different medicines and paraphernalia that were used in the creation of the Véhoo'o. All of the bundle's contents were used during the decennial Véhooneome ceremony, when the new chiefs were selected. Upon the Great Unification, new paraphernalia were added from the Tsétsêhéstâhese, including a plant known as "sweet medicine," which came from the prophet of the same name. In 1910, Northern Cheyenne medicine man White Bull or Ice declared: "The reason the medicine of Mattsioiv [Motsé'eóeve] was so powerful was because he had a small piece of medicine which he had obtained from heaven."[21] It was a piece of a plant and it was smoked during the Véhooneome, using the chiefs' pipe, to purify the chiefs so they could remain the sacred leaders who are strong and "healthy in the heart."[22] The plant or root became known as Chiefs' Medicine, and it became central to the decennial Véhooneome when the Véhoo'o swore in new sacred leaders to protect the sacred laws that came from Sweet Medicine's teachings, as well as the teachings articulated from the Só'taeo'o prophet Mukije.[23]

The title of the Sweet Medicine Chief was not one of notoriety, wealth, or status, but it was the highest spiritual rank and filled only by men. The prophet's authority, however, was rarely exerted, since the role of the prophet was primarily ceremonial and spiritual, so whoever held the position had to maintain a high degree of spiritual piety and devotion as well as intellect and wisdom. His actions and pronouncements could and often did affect the future generations of the Cheyenne Nation. His role was elevated during the annual ceremonies, Véhoo'o council meetings, and the annual and decennial Véhooneome ceremonies. During any time other than ceremonies, the prophet lived life as an "Old Man Chief" and was only called upon when the highest opinion was sought in affairs ranging from peacemaking with other nations to ceremonial decisions and decrees.

Not much is known of how the Sweet Medicine Chief was selected, but he was probably selected in private by the four Old Man Chiefs, for his position was also mythical and part of the legacy in oral tradition. The Cheyennes believe that the original prophet Motsé'eóeve lived to be 446 years of age; that he was blessed to live for four lifetimes over the course of four generations of Cheyennes.[24] In some stories, he carried the names of prophets from previous worlds: Netsevôhe'so (Eagle Nest) and Ma'heo'o Ôhnee'êstse (Standing Medicine).[25] This unique oral tradition reveals the endurance of the prophet's character, not the individual. In other words, in every generation of the living-nation, the universe provided a person who was intelligent, spiritual, and wise to fill the role of the prophet, and since this position was maintained across generations, the character endured. The position was maintained until the death of the last prophet, Chief Little Wolf. Frank Waters was identified as the last keeper of the Chiefs' Bundle. Today the bundle is the Arrow Keeper's responsibility.[26]

The principles and responsibilities of the Sweet Medicine Chief were timeless. Given this understanding of sacred leadership, it may appear that the original prophet could have lived for 446 years. Such a position could have only endured if the leaders maintained commitment to the sanctity and secrecy of the selection process as well as the system. Unfortunately, the process and its integrity started to die when the Cheyennes were forced onto reservations.[27] The Cheyennes believe, however, that the character of a prophet can be found among the spirits of all blood Cheyennes; each has the potential to foster and develop this character should they be provided proper instruction and pursue a life of dedication, self-discipline, and love for one's people and nation.

CHAPTER 6

Véhooneome: The Chiefs' Lodge

EVERY GOVERNMENT needs to hold formal meetings where leaders can make official decisions, and every nation needs to protect the sanctity of their decision-making process. For the Cheyennes, decision making was more of a ceremonial affair than a political one. Decisions were made on behalf of the entire nation, not based on the wants and desires of individuals or individual families. There were several formal meetings that the Véhoo'o conducted; each depended on the decision to be made. At the band level, formal meetings of the Véhoo'o included the four band chiefs and any other invited parties. For the most part the band meetings were by invitation only, in which leaders discussed matters pertaining only to their particular band. The band chiefs also met as a judicial body to make decisions on matters pertaining to conflicts that arose within their band. At the highest level, the formal meetings of the Council of Forty-Four were highly ritualized, as these meetings were of the utmost importance since decisions centered on matters pertaining to the entire Cheyenne Nation, like diplomacy, peacemaking, or conflicts with other nations.

THE ANNUAL VÉHOONEOME

The major ceremony of the Véhoo'o was the annual Véhooneome (Chiefs' Lodge), which was a formal council meeting held every year, with a major event occurring every ten years. Although the chiefs may hold a number of ceremonial Véhooneome throughout the year, the first was held before the spring equinox, the following at every change in season. This practice continues today. It was customary that a Véhooneome be held just before the major ceremonies, around the time that the bands start to unite for summer events like communal hunting and before engaging in warfare. At the Véhooneome, sacred leaders erected the traditional, doubled Chiefs' Lodge and held a council meeting to discuss the ceremonial schedule and the movements and potential campsites for each band. They also revisited peace agreements with other nations and evaluated the status of war with enemies. If a warrior society petitioned for war to the Arrow Keeper, the Véhoo'o also had a stake in the decision, so they may have revisited and decided on the petition. Such petitions typically came forth a year in advance.

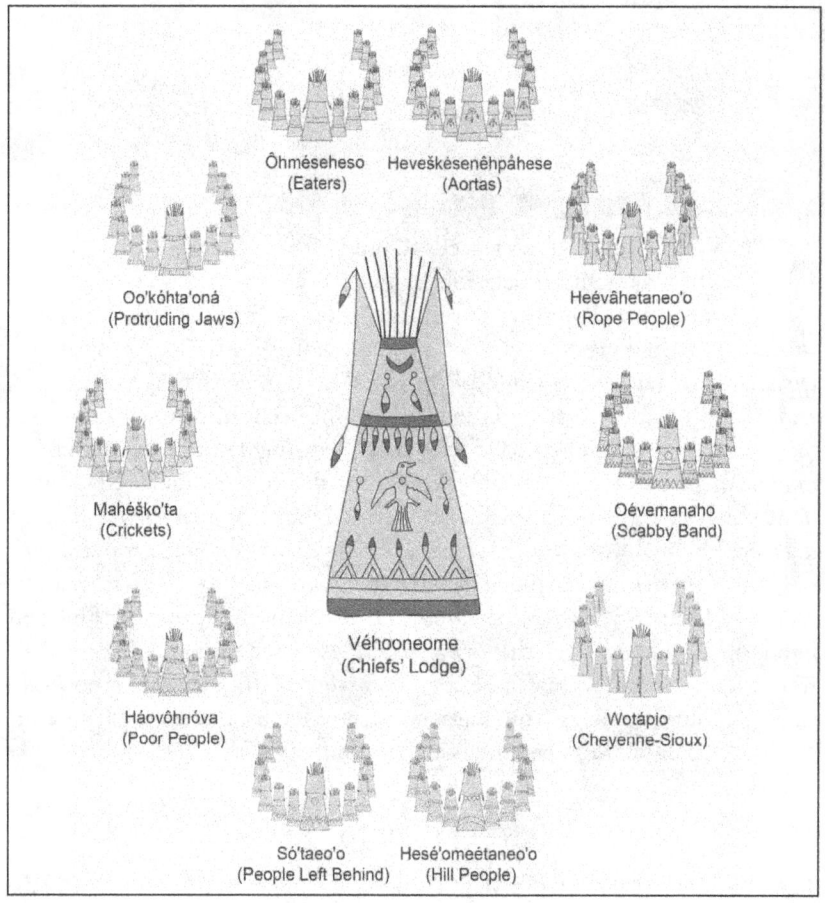

The chiefs' lodge camp circle.

At the annual Véhooneome, all Véhoo'o were to be present, which is why the event typically took place before a major ceremony. During the prime and pinnacle of the nation, the ten bands that were represented in the council were likely camped throughout the Great Plains, making it difficult for leaders to leave on short notice. Band chiefs, or Big Chiefs, were also responsible for the people of their village. Throughout the rest of the year, however, when a number of chiefs held council, they did not need to set up the double lodge. One chief would host a meeting inviting all those who could attend. For example, some general meetings only involved three or four northern bands, while other meetings may have involved only bands that traded at a particular location, like the southern bands that traded at Bent's Fort during a particular time.

Band chiefs typically made decisions concerning their particular bands without the consent of the Principal Chiefs, who were the primary decision makers on matters affecting the entire nation. Principal Chiefs, the "Old Man Chiefs" had to be present if the nation decided to establish a formal peace agreement with another nation or make a decision to approve war petitions against enemy nations. Sometimes band chiefs, speaking on behalf of their specific band, would join with another band or group of bands to make decisions within their locale: like the Southern Cheyenne bands that made peace agreements with the Kiowa and the Northern Cheyenne bands that made peace agreements with the Lakota. The band chief had the responsibility to secure trade relationships with other friendly nations, which is one purpose of the peace agreements. If a few bands established an agreement, then all bands were expected to accept the action once they received word.

The band chiefs also held general Véhooneome meetings to determine the fate of women and children who were captured by enemy tribes. They determined whether or not to accept petitions to rescue them. The fate of orphans and widows was also handled at the band level. Band chiefs were responsible for their care, but it was not necessary to bring their cases to the meetings. At the general meetings, the band chiefs decreed new decisions or temporary laws related to hunting, traveling, and trade. For example, if the Véhoo'o found out that a hunting area was sparse, then they may decree that no one be permitted to enter the land until the next year.

At the general Véhooneome meetings, the band chiefs also held deliberations on recent cases involving any of the sacred laws: murder, incest, lying and cheating, and stealing. As peacemakers, the Véhoo'o were responsible for preventing the proliferation of internal dysfunction, resentment, and hostility. As pipe carriers, the Véhoo'o were the peacemakers of any dispute. The first level of peacemaking occurred on a personal level, on the spot, and on location of the fray. The band chief acted as a mediator, hearing both sides of the dispute. If this did not lead to a prompt solution, then the chief invited the two parties to his lodge where he would host a pipe ceremony. The band chief prepared his pipe and said a prayer for each party to be honest, and then smoked and listened to each of their stories. After each party had its say, he made a decision on the issue, levying a fair ruling based on his sacred responsibilites. Afterward, the chief's family prepared a meal, and they ate together to solidify the peace. If, however, the parties were not satisfied with the decision, then the band chief would hold a formal meeting to call the local band chiefs together. Here the chiefs conducted a pipe ceremony and deliberated on the situation and might have called both parties into the lodge so they could tell their side of the story. From there the band chiefs made a decision. If the matter was still unresolved, the band chiefs brought the case up at the Véhooneome. Although rare, the deliberation on the matter would lead to a decision. If the issue was unresolved and called for more action, and the Véhoo'o could not find a solution, the chiefs would then pass the decision on to the Sweet Medicine Chief, the Arrow Keeper, or the Sacred Hat Keeper. Once one of these authorities made a decision, it was final. There is no record of any internal dispute that reached this level. Most cases were sent back down the system, rather than up—that is, if a matter did not threaten the entire nation, it was considered a matter to be handled at the band level.

One cardinal rule for chiefs is to refrain from personal involvement in disputes, especially if the dispute involved a relative. In a case where a chief's family member was involved, the chief would have to accept the blame and responsibility, even if his relative were innocent, for the sake of keeping the peace. The chief would then offer compensation to the accusing party as part of the relief. The chief might elect to host a meal for both parties, as well as a pipe ceremony if the accusing party was not satisfied. The chief was to accept all responsibility and "absorb" all negativity to bring the dispute to a resolution. If the dispute escalated and the chief could not reach a solution, it was assumed that the accusing party deliberately remained dissatisfied and that family should be shamed. It was against Cheyenne custom to abuse the genorsity of a chief.

Because each band had four chiefs, every family was in some way related to or associated with at least one chief. The bands were small enough for chiefs to easily familiarize themselves with nearly every member of their band. Sometimes band chiefs were known to be a relative of each member, either by blood or by marriage. It was in the best interest of the entire band to maintain solidarity and unity because every family depended on each other for subsistence.

The final task for the band chiefs at general Véhooneome meetings was to map out camp movements and determine the best camp sites for each of the separate bands. Typically, a band traversed and camped at places that they had traditionally for years. A family could move with a different band from time to time, and return to their original band, but it was uncommon for individuals to do so. Bands rarely strayed from their traditional, local

VÉHOONEOME: THE CHIEFS' LODGE

homelands. For example, the Northern Só'taeo'o bands remained along the Cheyenne River, frequently residing around the Black Hills and returning to the Red Rocks of Minnesota. Meanwhile, Southern bands remained near the Arkansas River. Nonetheless, Véhoo'o at the annual Véhooneome planned and discussed their movements with each other. Sometimes a number of chiefs might decide to meet at a particular valley or plain or along a certain river to hold a hunt, perform a ceremony, or prepare for war. There were several locations that were central to the Cheyenne Nation, and most bands frequently united in these areas; most were on or near sacred sites.[1] White Eagle explained the ceremonial task of the Véhoo'o as they directed camp movements: "At the time of moving the chiefs went in [the] center and told what direction to take. They start [moving] first."[2] White Eagle continued: "Everybody shall do what the chiefs wish. They shall obey their rules. All the chiefs had medicine pipes. Whenever the chiefs wanted to stop when on a journey[,] all should stop. Whenever they find some other tribe of Indians, they should capture them and take them for prisoners."[3]

Scalp Cane and his Clan, Most Wearing Blankets, Outside Tipi Framework; Other Tipis, Man with Horse, Wagon, and Children In Travois Basket Behind Them, Christian Barthelmess, 1889. National Anthropological Archives, Smithsonian Museum Support Center, Suitland, Maryland (NAA INV 00385600, OPPS NEG 42022E).

During the annual and general Véhooneome meetings, the rest of the Cheyenne population (families) recalled previous decisions and actions from the Véhoo'o. The past decisions and actions were part of the collective memory of each band and the entire nation. The oral tradition had to be precise and remembered, since there was no written language. Lies were not tolerated. Meanwhile, the sanctity and legitimacy of the system also had to remain a central part of the communal memory. Parents and grandparents recited the Véhoo'o origin stories over the course of several days before and after the annual Véhooneome. Every citizen of appropriate age of the United Cheyenne Nation was versed in the events leading to the creation of the Véhoo'o. The foundation doctrines of governance and nationhood of the Cheyenne Nation are embedded in the oral tradition. Like most Indigenous peoples, citizens of the Cheyenne Nation were responsible for passing down the knowledge of their ancestors orally to younger people. This preserved the unique Cheyenne culture for generations to come. More important, stories allowed for citizens to gain a sense of spiritual belonging and an indigenous identity, which fostered a collective tribal identity and promoted unity. Within origin stories lay the philosophies, doctrines, and values of the Cheyenne cultural way of life, from which sacred leadership principles were taught by storyteller and acquired by listener seamlessly and effortlessly. Simply put, stories held the knowledge and wisdom for effective leadership and governance.

THE DECENNIAL VÉHOONEOME

While the Chiefs' Lodge was held annually and at each quarter, the Big Chiefs' Lodge was a formal seating ceremony for selecting the Véhoo'o and held every ten years. Other than the Chiefs' Lodge, the Cheyennes held at least four, and as many as twelve, other major annual ceremonies or "lodges," and each hosted sacred leaders and dedicated societies. The Véhoo'o maintained influential roles among all lodges, sharing responsibilities with the four different groups of spiritual and sacred leaders in harmony.

The great ceremony of the decennial Véhooneome is the reenactment of the first seating ceremony and the reaffirmation of succeeding seating ceremonies. The rituals and oral traditions of the lodge ensured the perseverance of the entire system, thus strengthening the Cheyenne Nation. The political structure of the Véhoo'o changed significantly at the decennial Véhooneome in that the four Old Man Chiefs became "priestly" for the purposes of facilitating the ceremony.[4] The Sweet Medicine Chief, who also represented the authoritative role of Mukije and Voestaehneva'e, was the head priest as the primary facilitator of the four-day ceremony. Sweet Medicine Chief, as a fifth priestly chief, became the highest advisor on all spiritual matters: he became a "chief among chiefs."[5] The purpose was to "renew" the Véhoo'o, meaning to select new sacred leaders of the nation. Wooden Leg recalled how the entire nation came together for the event: "Every ten years the whole tribe would get together for the special purpose of choosing forty Big Chiefs. These forty then would select four past chiefs, or 'old men' chiefs, to serve as supreme advisors to them and to the tribe."[6]

The seating ceremony was a sacred act of sovereignty; it was a coronation and swearing-in ceremony. "Traditional leaders were not elected," stated Chief Leroy Pine, "they were selected through the customs and the holy ceremonies according to Sweet Medicine Laws."[7] The elaborate seating ceremony evoked oral tradition and the spiritual belief in the Chiefs' Bundle and "connected in all its phases with Sweet Medicine and with the supernaturalism of Cheyenne Cosmology."[8] With the assistance of the four principal ceremonial chiefs, it was truly a reenactment of the original seating ceremony, as the Chiefs' Bundle was emptied of all the Chiefs' Sticks, which were painted red and measured "about eighteen inches long by one-half inch in diameter, pointed at one end so that they may be put into the ground."[9] All current chiefs and candidates had to be present before the Véhoo'o renewed themselves and formally selected the new leaders.

The first four were already "grandfathered in," as they were the principal "Old Man Chiefs" who were the priestly body conducting the ceremony. But if one decided to retire from the position, the four conducted the retirement and initiation ceremonies for the principal position last. The entire ceremony renewed forty chiefs in four sets of ten. All ten bands were represented by four governing chiefs and several retired ex-chiefs. The ceremony required all previous band chiefs, if alive, to be present. The ex-band chiefs were the ceremonial advisors to their band chiefs and the new candidates. New and incumbent chiefs belonged to the same band as their predecessors, who knew which leaders in the band were worthy candidates. As ceremonial advisors, the ex-band chiefs renewed their respective incumbent band chiefs who decided to lead for another term. If an incumbent band chief wished to retire, he then became an ex-band chief and had to choose and vouch for a successor and become his ceremonial advisor for the seating ceremony. Every chief had a predecessor, linking him back to one of the original chiefs of the Cheyenne Nation. The link was spiritual and cultural, but never ancestral unless by circumstance. Before the new chiefs were affirmed, each nominee had to be formally accepted by the Véhoo'o as a worthy candidate—this is done in the ritual portion of the ceremony. The entire four-day ceremony required much planning on the part of incumbent chiefs since they had to ensure that the council accepted their candidate.

The Véhoo'o as a council could decline a nominee; however, this has never occurred in the history of the United Cheyenne Nation.

The Cheyennes did not originally have hereditary chieftainship, but there was no law that prevented it from occurring.[10] Sacred leaders, by their nature, were often reluctant to choose their own kin for fear of public criticism, but there were ways around this, especially if a nominee was an earnest candidate.[11] A retiring chief may not name his son or nephew, but another retiring band chief would sponsor a friend's son for the position, thus averting any public sentiments and preserving integrity in the system.[12] This process occurred to protect a chief from the shame of nepotism, but it is likely that this custom existed to prevent an eventual hereditary monarchy. Rarely would a retiring chief choose his own son, but if his son was a good man and this good man was chosen by the chiefs, then the nomination was accepted.[13] At times, a chief's son may not be elected, even if he was "great."[14] Candidates had the option to decline the nomination if they felt that the decision would not sit well with the people. There are few accounts of when a candidate declined a nomination, but it was customary for candidates to initially refuse, since the burdens were too demanding. One of the only known candidates to decline was Bull Hump, who was asked to serve during the reservation era. He was the son of Morningstar (Dull Knife), an Old Man Chief of the Northern Cheyenne. Before colonization, however, declining such a position was unlikely, as the Cheyennes believe it could lead to misfortune or an early death for the candidate. In the early times, during the height of the nation, it was a man's duty to accept chieftainship or face the shame of cowardice.[15]

Chiefs and their families planned for the four-day ceremony by preparing ceremonial food, gathering gifts, and fashioning paraphernalia for rituals and ceremonial dress. On the first day, the first set of ten band chiefs were seated in a circle inside the double lodge, and their ceremonial advisors sat behind them. The Sweet Medicine Chief sat at the place of honor at the western side of the lodge, with the Chiefs' Bundle and paraphernalia ready for use. Two priestly chiefs sat on each side of the Sweet Medicine Chief as advisors, and the other two priestly chiefs sat on each side of the "door," or entrance, of the lodge to perform the proper rituals and direct the entire ceremony. According to Bull Thigh, the two doormen had the final say in all matters, not the Sweet Medicine chief or his two priestly advisors. Yet the five rarely, if at all, disagreed.[16]

The Arrow Keeper and his priests sat on the south side, while the Sacred Hat Keeper and his priests sat on the north side. Various warrior society leaders and spiritual leaders were invited to sit in the lodge for the ceremony. All spectators were invited to sit outside of the lodge to view the rituals and listen to speeches. The ceremony involved four intervals of ritual. Each interval formally seated ten chiefs, one from each band. Every band was thus represented at each interval. At the start of each interval, each ex-band chief was given the time and opportunity to stand and express why his nominee was a worthy candidate to sit on the Council of Forty-Four Chiefs. No gifts were given at this time. If a returning chief's predecessor was deceased, then another ex-chief from his band may represent and advise the candidate. This scenario was common, and sometimes a single ex-band chief would advise all four candidates at each of the four rounds, while other band representatives assisted.

When each of the ten ex-band chiefs concluded their speeches, they stood with their nominees and escorted them four times around the lodge, then exited the lodge and escorted them around the center of the village, and around the exterior of the Chiefs' Lodge. While the others were making their ceremonial treks, the doormen placed the chief sticks in front of each candidate's seat. As the ex-chiefs and their candidates returned, they returned to their seats. The process was repeated for each of the four intervals. The affirmation of all forty chiefs took place over two whole days: twenty on the first day and twenty on the second day. The purpose of the formal ceremonial process was to publicly acknowledge each candidate so the people saw their leaders bestowed upon them the honor and burden to lead their respective bands and the nation.

Upon conclusion of the formal and public rituals, the Véhooneome became a private ceremonial affair, lasting for more than two days. Some of the practices were lost through colonization and assimilation, while other ritualistic practices were simply not passed on from generation to generation. Nonetheless, on the third day, the candidates had to endure a final set of rituals to establish their position as new chiefs. They smoked from the chiefs' pipe and were instructed by the ex-chiefs on how to lead. The fourth day was reserved for the final two acts of the Véhoo'o: to select the Old Man Chiefs and the Sweet Medicine Chief.[17] This final selection process occurred only if one or more were retiring from any of the five principal positions. The rituals involved in this process are also to remain unpublished. At the conclusion of the Véhooneome, newly seated and ex-chiefs held departure services at their respective band camp circles. The chiefs made speeches, hosted feasts, and held giveaway and naming ceremonies, while warrior and other societies held dances and other rituals. The people came together in celebration; the women gambled and the men played games, like the great hoop and spear game. The selection of new sacred leaders was a celebration, not a competition.

Nakoimens (Bear Wings) with His Wife, Both in Native Dress with Ornaments, One Holding Pipe and Bag, De Lancey W. Gill, June 1908. National Anthropological Archives, Smithsonian Museum Support Center, Suitland, Maryland (NAA INV 06112200, OPPS NEG 00296).

VÉHOO'O AND CHARACTER

The Véhoo'o was a self-perpetuating body who selected among themselves the next leaders. The process of nominating chiefs was a near divine invocation, as candidates were carefully and religiously vetted. Character superseded every other quality when reviewing candidates, and veteran chiefs were meticulous when reviewing the actions and inactions of new candidates in particular. If selected, chiefs served ten-year terms and swore an oath to serve the people with their lives. Retiring chiefs were allowed to choose their own successors, but if a leader "had proved himself a good one, he might be chosen to serve a second term."[18] All forty-four chiefs participated in selecting new leaders; some of the nation's greatest leaders served two or three terms before retiring. Citizens and band members had no say in selecting leaders, but this did not mean that the Véhoo'o did not hold personal interests above the people. The citizenry could not impeach chiefs or remove them, but chiefs could retire on their own accord or be compelled to exile themselves under a code of honor. There is no known case of self-exile before the reservation period.

Upon selection, new chiefs were instructed in the ways of the prophet and reminded to be of "good conduct," practice restraint, and not be easily angered by others. This did not mean a chief had to accept every insult or injury: "It was only when a chief had been four times wronged by the same person that he is said to have been free justifiably to climb off his pedestal of virtue to act."[19] There are no known cases where a chief "climbed off his pedestal" before the reservation period. If a chief was killed or retired without choosing his own successor, the band chiefs appointed a good leader until the Véhoo'o selected a new chief at a special seating ceremony held that same year. During the height of this system of governance the people truly believed in and trusted the sacred leaders, who reciprocated when they held themselves to high standards of integrity and humility.

Chieftainship was a status of dignity, a position with both authority and responsibility.[20] Therefore, chiefs were typically older men who were schooled and experienced in politics, and who usually had good reputations as warriors and as family men. Chiefs embodied the Cheyenne concept of manhood, hetané'hao'o (man power), which is a man's power of procreation. The philosophy behind hetané'hao'o is rooted in traditional notions of the survival and longevity of the Cheyenne people, their way of life, and the living-nation. A man who embodies this power does not simply reproduce, but he understands the sacredness of passing on the "essence of life" and the Cheyenne worldview and identity to his children. Chiefs, as well as other men who endured ceremonial rites and warfare, are believed to have a greater spiritual presence and understanding of the universe—this is hetané'hao'o.

Chiefs had to be fair to maintain internal Cheyenne harmony and justice. The integrity of the entire governing system depended on how well the sacred leaders maintained traditional principles, values, and practices. Such a position required much discipline, but foremost were dedication and love for one's people and nation. There was no room for egotism in this culture. Earning the right to sit at the Council of Chiefs was a serious matter, codified, reinforced, and passed to the next generation in the oral tradition and ceremonial practice.

Ho'neoxhaa'eho'oesêstse (High Backed Wolf) is remembered as one of the greatest chiefs of the Cheyenne Nation.[21] Also known as High Wolf, he was a Sweet Medicine Chief who signed the first treaty between the Cheyenne Nation and the United States in 1825. The last Sweet Medicine Chief, who was selected in secrecy and whose identity was kept anonymous until the reservation era, was the famous Northern Cheyenne chief Little Wolf. Ó'kôhómôxháahketa (Little Wolf) was the headman of the Elk Horn Scraper Society and also a principal chief. The unwritten traditional constitutional laws of the Cheyenne Nation did not necessarily allow a council chief to hold two additional offices, let alone three. Little Wolf was an exception because he was courageous, known for his discipline, physical strength, and skills as a military leader.[22] A rare exception to the unwritten Cheyenne constitution, such as Little Wolf's case, was allowed when the nation was in need of exceptional leadership during cases of instability. Such cases were rare but became common with the increase in white encroachment on Cheyenne lands and the military presence of the Americans. Changes to the governing system were for the benefit of the entire nation, not for a few.

CHAPTER 7

Véhoo'o and Political Organization

THE CHEYENNE language was unwritten before the nineteenth century; therefore, there was no formally written constitution that detailed the duties and responsibilities of sacred leaders and the balance of power. Nevertheless, the absence of a written constitution does not mean that the Cheyennes did not understand and respect the sovereign powers of their government, nor does it mean that the nation was fragile and unpredictable and unworthy of respect by outsiders. In its primacy, the Cheyenne Nation was arranged into ten highly organized and mobile bands. Four Big Chiefs led and represented their respective bands and people, harking back to the old traditions before there were ten bands. The four-chief system provided balance and fairness; there was not one person of authority or a large group of men pushing one agenda. A major challenge for modern political scientists, especially those who study constitutional law and constitutional reform, is that the Véhoo'o were unlike any government known to humankind because it depended on the Cheyennes' own epistemology, experiences, and land to develop its governmental system.

The Véhoo'o were only one component of the system of governance. The entire system involved numerous societies as well as war and ceremonial leaders, yet the institution was extremely efficient. The nation depended on the bison herds that extended over five hundred thousand square miles of what is now known as the Great Plains of North America and therefore adopted a highly organized political system that harmonized with a mobile, hunting lifestyle. The Cheyennes first attained horses in the 1700s, long after the Great Unification. Horses enabled the nation to grow in numbers, which allowed them to break into smaller bands and travel farther beyond their lands. Hoig states, "The tall, lithe warriors of the Cheyennes quickly adapted the animal to effective use in both hunting and warfare, their new mobility offsetting the force of numbers of the larger tribes. The Cheyenne warriors soon came to be among the most feared on the American plains."[1]

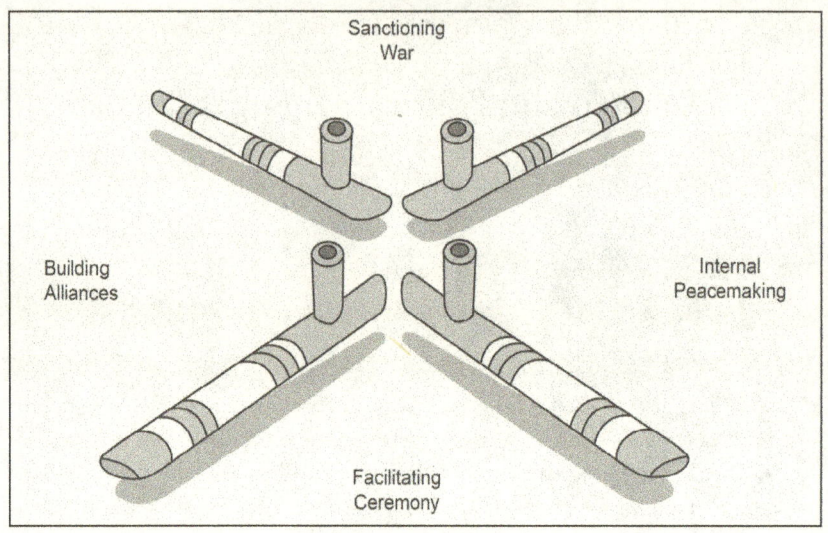

The four sacred responsibilities of the Véhoo'o.

Despite their mobility, the Cheyennes maintained a close relationship with their homelands and sacred sites, as they depended entirely on the lands around the Black Hills. This dependence was reflected in the ceremonial practices, which coincided with the change of seasons and migrations of birds and animals. The Véhoo'o, as the governing body, had four "sacred responsibilities": to organize and conduct ceremonies; to make alliances and secure peace with other nations; to declare and initiate war against other nations; and to rule on internal civil affairs as peacemakers. The Véhoo'o had elaborate diplomatic and peacemaking methods, which centered on spiritual practices, when making alliances and treaties with other Indian nations. The Véhoo'o eventually used these same methods when signing treaties with the United States. Rarely were external political decisions delegated to an authority other than the Véhoo'o. The customary practices changed, however, when the United States imposed its unfair treaty-making practices on the Cheyenne Nation in attempts to condone white trespass and settlement on Cheyenne lands.

The Cheyennes believed that any person could become a sacred leader given the right circumstances and self-discipline. But the Cheyennes also believed that the higher-ranked positions—the Old Man Chiefs and the Sweet Medicine Chief—were divinely created positions reserved for the best and then only bestowed by the divine. In other words, these highly sacred leaders were born, not raised. Those who earned the position of an Old

Man Chief already embodied the character and aura even before they were selected; they were known to the people and other leaders as born chiefs. The Old Man Chiefs were the principal leaders of the Cheyenne Nation, who were first selected as band chiefs. The Old Man Chiefs were elected to govern the entire nation, but these four positions were created after the Cheyenne Nation grew larger than the five original bands. The Tsétsêhéstaestse prophet, Motsé'eóeve, is credited with establishing the four positions of the Old Man Chiefs. He gave specific instructions to the sacred leaders:

> Listen to me carefully, and truthfully follow up my instructions. You chiefs are peacemakers. Though your son might be killed in front of your tepee, you should take a peace pipe and smoke. Then you would be called an honest chief. You chiefs own the land and the people. If your men, your soldier societies, should be scared and retreat, you are not to step back but take a stand to protect your land and your people. Get out and talk to the people. If strangers come, you are the ones to give presents to them and invitations. When you meet someone, or he comes to your tepee asking for anything, give it to him. Never refuse. Go outside your tepee and sing your chief's song, so all the people will know you have done something good.[2]

He instructed further: "You cannot have material things forever, and when you give something away, you won't be at a total loss because Ma'heo'o will reward you in other ways. Feed and talk to the people constantly and tell them of the laws of the nation."[3]

The four principal Old Man Chiefs consistently and diligently worked with their fellow band chiefs to reach compromises and agreements. Decisions were always made through consensus, under the principles of brotherhood, but if the council could not come to consensus in a timely manner, the four Old Man Chiefs, holding higher authority, were called upon to carry out their responsibility of making a final decision. Such occasions were rare, but when they occurred, the other forty leaders became counselors or advisors and each of the Old Man Chiefs shared responsibility in resolving the matter. The forty Big Chiefs, meanwhile, did not lose status after a decision was made; they equally commanded the same respect as their superiors and assumed the same responsibility for the decision, even though their roles were minor.[4] While the decisions of the Old Man Chiefs were paramount, their decrees were not dictatorial, and their decisions "usually received greater consideration than those of other speakers."[5] It was very uncommon for the forty Big Chiefs to defy the orders of the Old

Man Chiefs, but it was equally uncommon for the Old Man Chiefs to act without regard to the concerns of their associates.

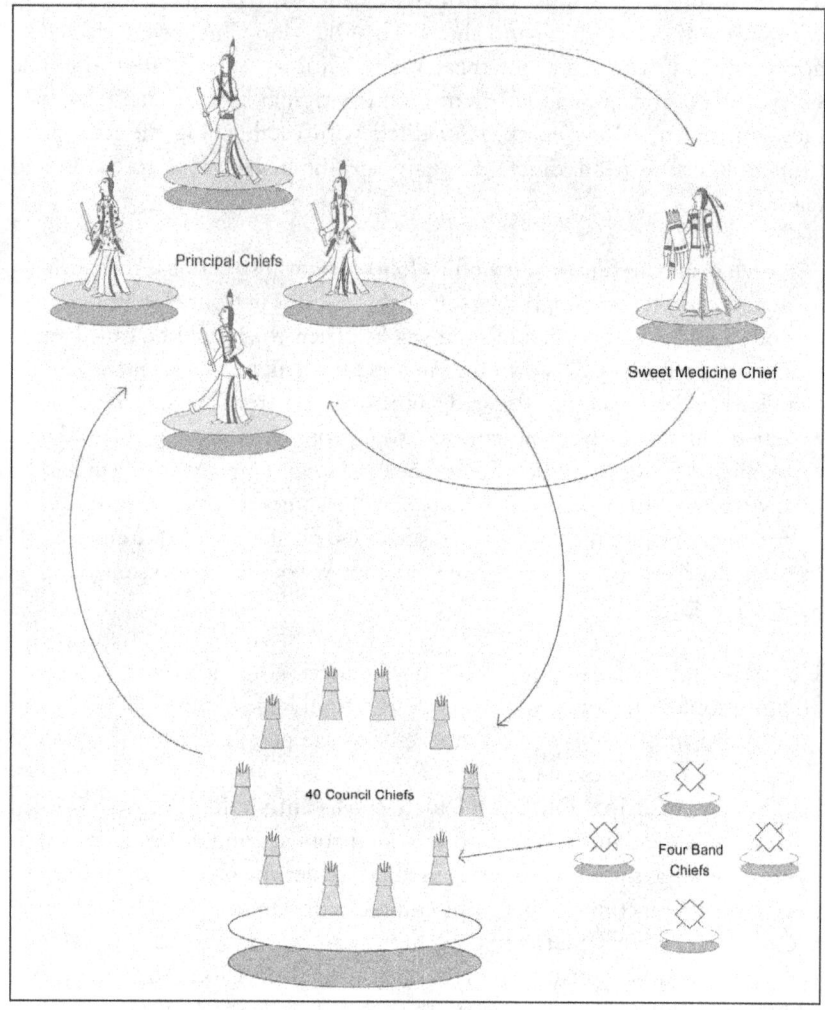

The balance of power and shared responsibility among the Véhoo'o.

In the event that the four Old Man Chiefs were unable to reach a resolution, the Sweet Medicine Chief would make a final decree. The Sweet Medicine Chief's duty was to safeguard the Véhoo'o, and his power was evoked only when both the Big Chiefs and the Old Man Chiefs were unable to reach a prompt conclusion. In the history of the Cheyenne Nation before the twentieth century, decisions made only by the Sweet Medicine Chief were rare and occurred primarily during treaty making with the US government. Ideally, all members of the Véhoo'o sought to make the best decisions, and this required much discussion, deliberation, cooperation, and respectful debate. More often than not, the entire council made political decisions collectively, as the system would fail, disorder would result, and if only one leader made the choices at all times, a band or the nation would fall into dictatorship just as in previous worlds. The sanctity of the system depended entirely on the character of the leaders, which is why only the best men were selected.

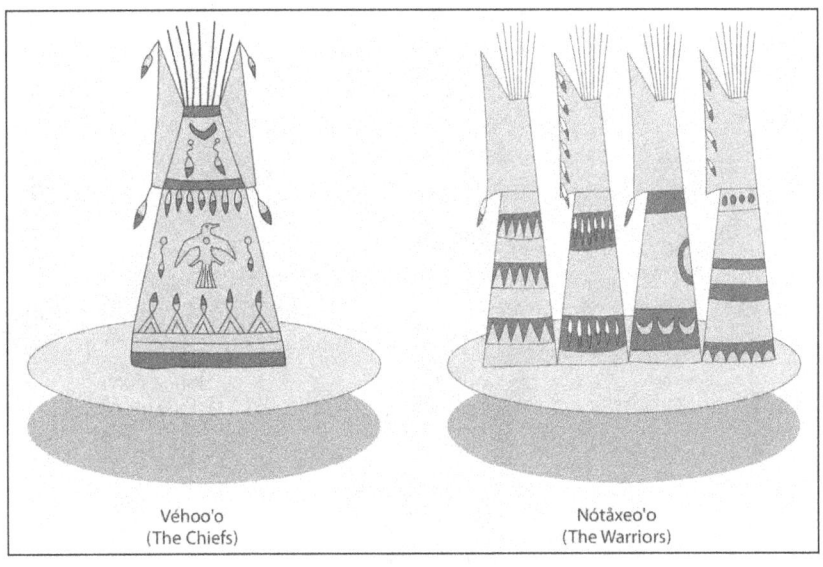

Véhoo'o
(The Chiefs)

Nótâxeo'o
(The Warriors)

The balance of political power and shared authority between the Véhoo'o and the Nótâxeo'o

The Véhoo'o were also the internal peacemakers of the nation, handing down rulings and judgments on either a case-by-case basis or based on precedent as a nonadversarial judiciary. Individual chiefs often gave charity and made personal sacrifices to keep peace among their people. When the ten bands were independently settled throughout the Plains, the Big Chiefs held primary authority. At the band level, the four governing Big Chiefs maintained a balance of power with the band warrior societies, another highly organized system. Both bodies were responsible for the well-being of the band but had clearly defined roles. The Big Chiefs gave orders and managed matters of diplomacy and ceremony, while the warrior societies executed orders, policed the village, and protected the people from outside threat. On the national level, when the ten bands were united for ceremonial purposes, the united Council of Forty-Four Chiefs maintained a balance of power that included two other major entities besides the warrior societies: the Medicine Arrow Keeper and the Sacred Buffalo Hat Keeper.

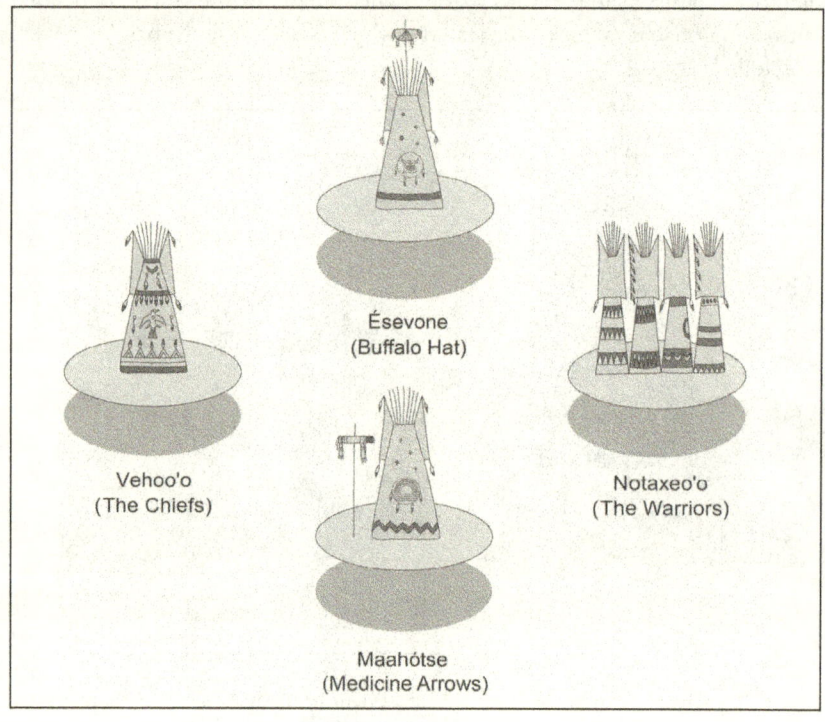

The balance of ceremonial power and shared authority among the four sacred entities.

The balance of power among the four major entities functioned under the Cheyenne principles of balance and brotherhood. This balance between the four entities can be visualized as a scale with four pans, rather than a typical scale, which has two pans. In the political sector, balance shifted responsibility from one entity to another depending on the situation, which could have been to organize a hunt, move camp, hold a ceremony, declare war, or secure peace. Not one of the four entities held supreme power of the entire nation for any prolonged period of time. In fact, each entity held political power only when demanded by the people, directed by nature, compelled by outside threats, or petitioned by one of the other three entities. For example, the people could seek the assistance of the Véhoo'o to resolve internal conflict; the seasons could determine when the Hat Keeper was to hold a Sun Dance ceremony; the Véhoo'o could encourage the Arrow Keeper to "renew" the Medicine Arrows; the Véhoo'o could compel a warrior society to organize a hunt; or the warriors could petition the Véhoo'o to declare war. Each body was driven by cooperation and loyalty, as no entity considered taking power from the other and the leaders merely organized the necessary task at hand.

Traditionally, Só'taa'e men resided with their wives' families, and this custom continued, establishing the Cheyenne Nation as a matrilineal, matrilocal, and matriarchal society. The Cheyenne Nation was, at its core, a nation of families, and the Véhoo'o were, at their core, family men. Traditional camps or bands, under the leadership of chiefs, comprised large, extended families that traced their lineage through their mothers. Véhoo'o paid special attention to the concerns of women, who held positions of authority in women's societies, their households, and over the children. Véhoo'o sometimes had more than one wife, and this allowed for the women of the nation to have much influence in the chiefs' decisions. Although women leaders did not have their own formal institution, they still possessed and exercised sacred leadership in other societies and functions. Women's rights and concerns were conveyed through the chiefs' wives, who then acted as diplomats to achieve results.[6] Chiefs' wives held a high status in the nation, but women were seldom in the forefront. Véhoo'o were aware of the concerns of their citizens and respectful to the families of the nation; never abused power, nor countered public opinion.[7]

PRINCIPLES OF SACRED LEADERSHIP: THE WAY OF THE CHIEFS

Citizens of the Cheyenne Nation would not respect a leader whose reputation did not meet the standards set forth by custom and tradition, which is why only qualified candidates were chosen to join the Véhoo'o. The qualities of sacred leadership and the ideal virtues of chiefs were not part of an on-the-job training program; citizens did not expect leaders to obtain these qualities after appointment. Rather, Véhoo'o were expected to be understanding before they were nominated or even considered for a leadership position, which is why the former band chiefs played a major role as advisors before, during, and at the end of their successor's terms. The ex-chiefs selected only those who exhibited (through speech, action, and service) "the epitome of the Cheyenne ideal personality."[8] This could only be achieved if the culture fostered an ideal personality, which required any potential leader to learn and practice discipline: "The first lesson that the child learned was one of self-control—self-effacement in the presence of its elders. It remembered this all through life."[9] Every child was encouraged to embody the physical, spiritual, mental, and emotional attributes of Cheyenne virtue found in culture heroes of both genders, like Voestaehneva'e and Motsé'eóeve. The virtues of sacred leadership were typically found in the personas of male culture heroes. When a young man heard stories of culture heroes—like Blood Bachelor, Cherry Eater, and Bow-In-Hand—and their extraordinary feats, the ideal virtues of a Cheyenne man were imprinted in his imagination. Such an imprint planted the seed necessary to grow and train good leaders and citizens. By the time a boy matured into a man, the stories he had heard as a child were no longer taken literally, but became part of his sense of being.

Within the stories of prophetic mysticism, phenomenal physical achievements, and supernatural abilities lay a framework that fostered the development of personalities fit for leadership. Parents and elders were the primary teachers of good conduct. Older male relatives advised "grandsons, sons, and nephews and tried constantly to warn them against mistakes and to make life easier for them. A well-brought-up man was likely to advise his grown son occasionally."[10] The sons of chiefs were consistently schooled and instructed on the rules of proper behavior, as expected of Cheyenne cultural customs. Grinnell recalled the experiences of one such chief's child:

> Shell told me that his instruction came chief from his father, who gave much advice to him and to the other boys of the family. He remembered especially the father's warning to his children to be truthful and honest, never to lie. His father was a chief, and almost every night there were many in his lodge, talking about different things, and the children listened to the conversation of their elders, and learned much.[11]

All children were educated and encouraged to uphold standards of morality, since every child had the potential to become a spiritual leader. Children, regardless of blood—some came from other tribes as captives—were brought up to become part of the Cheyenne Nation, physically, spiritually, and mentally. A profound sense of connectedness nurtured a person's identity and loyalty to the living-nation, building and rebuilding a nation of families. When a Cheyenne man became a chief, he was truly honored, for such a position was not designed for any ordinary soul; it was a position for only the finest. As mentioned earlier, nominees of chieftainship often attempted to decline a position because of the heavy demands for strict discipline of spirit and mind. Véhoo'o and the general public demanded that other chiefs show restraint in the presence of another's wrongdoing, and most men knew they were unworthy and too weak of heart to hold themselves to such high standards.

I have identified ten principles of sacred leadership that come directly from the Cheyenne culture. These principles should provide a sense of the culture before colonization. The principles I describe are from years of studying the Cheyenne culture and history, formally and practically, as well as many lengthy discussions with Cheyenne elders and by extracting concepts in both the English and Cheyenne languages. I was also influenced by personal experiences through participating in ceremonies and reflecting upon interactions with my family, friends, relatives, and community members. These ten principles of sacred leadership are the most notable, yet the most difficult to follow, and explain why most nominees for chieftainship were not selected. Bear in mind that these ten principles may be incomplete, as much of our old language has been lost, and these principles should be perceived more as journeys, not destinations.

These principles are for sacred leaders; they are not for everyone and anyone, since not everyone and anyone is fit for sacred leadership. They are not rules to be used to judge others, nor are they a guide to humiliate or shame others. Great leaders apply these principles when making decisions and rely on them in their personal lives. The challenge is to hold oneself to these standards.

1. Ována'xaetanohtôtse (peace)

A sacred leader should practice restraint from outside disturbances and must maintain a high degree of tranquility within and with others. The best leaders have the temperament to face adversity, criticism, and the difficult situations before them without acting unreasonably, unpredictably, or impatiently. Although difficult to practice, the principle of peace was critical to the balance of the entire nation. Before a sacred leader could advocate for peace externally for his nation, he needed an understanding of peace internally, as an individual, in his personal life, and among family members. Without that, his personal problems could become public problems and contribute to turmoil.

Peace was a quality that could be gained through personal discipline, maintaining a healthy individual spirit, and understanding the lessons taught in the oral tradition. "Peace" does not mean that a leader should have a spotless record, but that a good leader has a good relationship with his past experiences, even those that may be considered bad. Most unfit leaders have dysfunctional relationships with their pasts, especially those that may be unfavorable to a leader's cause. Such unfit leaders are uneasy and quick-tempered. Others find that a person who is not at peace is not pleasant to be around because the person alienates others and is vindictive and unfair.

"Peace" also does not mean that the Véhoo'o were passive, weak, or helpless in the face of unfairness, injustice, and belligerence. Patience and peace were qualities that were so closely associated with chiefs that some non-Indian scholars labeled Council chiefs as "peace chiefs."[12] A peaceful and patient presence in a leader was imperative when securing alliances with other Indian nations and, eventually, treaties with whites, so the label of "peace chiefs" is not incorrect. Sacred leaders of the Cheyenne Nation had to exercise restraint to effectively govern and sustain the sacred laws of the people. Stands In Timber discusses these virtues in a time when the destruction of Cheyenne cultural ways of living had already taken its toll, some seventy years after the pinnacle of the Cheyenne Nation. Fortunately, some of the laws and teachings that he discusses have been retained to the present. His advice reveals the qualities of the original Council chiefs:

> I learned the laws from my grandfather. He made me remember them. He told me about fights. A number of times I could have gotten into them, but he used to say there was always someone ready to be jealous and wanting to fight or argue. "Don't give him one word," he would tell me, "even if he should call you bad things. Walk away from him. After a time that man will come back and be one of your best friends." And it is true; I have done it many times.[13]

II. Ševátamehestôtse (compassion)

Compassion, sympathy, mercy, and pity are synonymous in the Cheyenne language. They are all used in prayers to ask for help from the supernatural powers. A sacred leader is compassionate according to custom and spirituality, especially in the most difficult times, for this is when compassion matters most. The Véhoo'o had to practice compassion, also known as "having heart," to all citizens of the nation as instructed by the prophet Motsé'eóeve:

> Now, you who are here have been appointed as chiefs to look after the welfare of all men, women, and children. . . . When the old chiefs wore out, they appointed you to carry on their leadership. We, who are here representing the sacred magicians of old and the sacred arrows and the

sacred sun, earth and animals, have this day advised you and placed every man, woman, and child of the Cheyenne tribe in your care. When it is necessary you will help not only your own tribe, but all other Indians.[14]

Véhoo'o were instructed to help all Indians, but in particular their own people. They often helped widows of fallen warriors by giving them food and other goods, which was done through the chiefs' wife or wives, as custom did not allow for men to converse with another's wife, especially those in mourning. A chief's wife would often help others regardless of whether her husband approved. Her duties were also demanding and required heart.

The most compassionate acts of chiefs were for orphans, as chiefs adopted many and allowed them to live in their households.[15] The child became part of the family with all benefits and responsibilities that were carried into adulthood. Compassion should not be mistaken for weakness: "Yet, though simple, honest, generous, tender-hearted, and often merry and jolly, when occasion demanded [a chief] could be stern, severe, and inflexible of purpose. Such men, once known, commanded general respect and admiration."[16] Council chiefs had to maintain a degree of courage when making decisions, and they had to lead with dignity.

III. *Hoto'åhéstôtse (generosity)*

The Véhoo'o often gave up their own possessions to help others while in a leadership position. Gilbert Whitedirt (Northern Cheyenne) states: "Chiefs are supposed to be nice, kind people. They are supposed to be the poorest ones. Anything that another person liked of his, the chief had to give up."[17] The Cheyenne people valued generosity from each other and especially their chiefs:

> Since so much depended on his example and precept, a chief must be brave in war, generous in disposition, liberal in temper, deliberate in making up his mind, and of good judgment. A good chief gave his whole heart and his whole mind to the work of helping his people, and strove for their welfare with an earnestness and a devotion rarely equaled by other rulers of men. Such thought for his fellows was not without its influence on the man himself; after a time the spirit of good will which animated him became reflected in his countenance, so that as he grew old such a chief often came to have a most benevolent expression.[18]

Véhoo'o often donated any material object—blanket, rifle, horse, or even a lodge—to any Cheyenne person who needed the item more: "The chief was expected to be a paragon of generosity. Whatever was asked for or hinted after he was expected to bestow as a gift."[19] Cheyenne custom dictates that people give gifts without asking for anything in return. The art of trading, however, is another concept and not necessarily a principle for good leadership.

The generosity of the Cheyenne people, especially leaders, was not motivated by the desire to gain personal social status or prestige; it was pure generosity. Generous greetings were always bestowed upon any Cheyenne, since it was custom to always show sincerity among fellow citizens. A welcoming presence was a sign of kindheartedness and generosity, and it was custom for families to feed and be generous to all visitors even if it meant giving them the last of whatever food was left. Traditional Cheyennes trace this custom of generosity to the teachings of Sweet Medicine.[20]

According to Cheyenne belief, people who are not generous are associated with greed and selfishness and are always complaining even when their wishes are granted. Generosity was learned and conditioned into a Cheyenne's personality from childhood. By the time children reached adulthood, they should have disassociated themselves from material objects and abandoned childhood selfishness to truly understand practices of generosity. Unlike non-Indian notions of generosity, which are usually associated with weakness (to give something away is weakness) or superiority (to be "good" or "rich enough to give"), the Cheyenne notion of generosity required training and practice, because it is not easy to be generous.

IV. *Vonanomótåhtsestôtse (forgiveness)*

A sacred leader forgives others and in doing so prevents the proliferation of pain and suffering. A sacred leader takes responsibility for his decisions but sometimes assumes the debt of others for the sake of balance. The Cheyenne concept of forgiveness was much different from that of whites, for the Cheyennes forgiveness could only come from the highest supernatural power, Ma'xema'hēō'e (the Great Medicine).[21] Spiritual leaders, however, could "wipe away" or "wipe off" evil or negative energy from a patient.[22] Véhoo'o were forgiving, but only to the extent allowed by sacred laws. As peacemakers of the nation, the Véhoo'o settled internal disputes and therefore had to be fair and just. They, as sacred leaders, had the responsibility to be firm and forgiving when making rulings on internal disputes. If chiefs could not forgive, why should they expect it from the very people they serve? Forgiveness is a principle that maintained balance and improved the lives of others.

Motsé'eóeve provided instructions to the original Véhoo'o and asked them to maintain their principles even in the most difficult of situations: "You have been appointed on account of your bravery, character, and courage. In the future you will cause no disturbance or help to cause a disturbance among your own people. If another member of the tribe kills your own brother, take your pipe and smoke it to the Great Medicine, and you will prevent disturbance."[23] Leaders who were forgiving were not bitter and did not foster bitterness among people. Without a doubt, anger and indignation are human traits, but a fundamental part of Cheyenne culture is that leaders never used these negative human traits as a basis for their decisions or actions. Véhoo'o held high positions and they were expected to be experienced to handle the toughest of situations. Conversely, if a chief made a mistake he would take full responsibility and do his best to improve the situation. The stoic and forgiving demeanor of Council chiefs could easily be mistaken for ignorance, helplessness, powerlessness, and even stupidity, but the Véhoo'o were quite the opposite; they were even-tempered, liberal, and careful in their actions and reactions.

v. Hetómestôtse (truth)

A sacred leader is honest and will tell the truth if asked, even when the truth is unfavorable to his cause. Truth is a virtue that even the most honest of people have difficulty practicing. Honesty is easily achieved when the majority is truthful; true leaders, however, remain honest especially when lies dominate. All Véhoo'o were the first pipe carriers, meaning they earned the rights to carry and use a ceremonial pipe. Pipe carriers are subject to numerous sacred laws, one of which required them to smoke in prayer; another dictated that they carry their pipes at all times as symbols of a leader's commitment and devotion to the truth. The greatest challenge for sacred leaders is to stand firm in honesty. Véhoo'o were held to such a high standard and often relied on their spirituality to conjure the necessary strength when upholding the truth. Truth was a pillar that determined a person's integrity. A pipe carrier sometimes would have to fight for his rights against those who may accuse him of lying. In such cases a pipe carrier would hold his pipe in hand as he spoke and sometimes say aloud, "Arrows, you hear me; I did (or did not do) this thing."[24] The pipe carrier thus swore his truth on the highest covenant of the nation.

vi. Xanoveostôtse (righteousness)

Sacred leaders must act in accordance with the sacred laws of the Cheyennes and be models of morality. Xanoveostôtse literally means the state of being straight, to be honest, righteous, well respected, proper, "in line."[25] Sacred leaders must be disciplined and have integrity with each action and decision. They must strive to remain free of negativity, shame, and wickedness and not commit any offenses against their own people, as well as against humanity and the natural and supernatural worlds. They represent the integrity of the entire nation to confront and subdue recklessness and belligerence. As peacemakers, they handed down judgments to guilty parties and restored balance and harmony to their respective village or band, and to the entire Cheyenne Nation. How unfair and unjust would the entire system be if those in power were just as guilty or unruly as those prosecuted? The Cheyenne concept of righteousness was reinforced by public opinion in both social and spiritual realms since violators of sacred laws were shunned; their reputations as offenders would last in perpetuity, sometimes long after death. The Council of Chiefs only selected leaders who were righteous; otherwise the entire way of living would be compromised: "They endeavored to choose a man of even temper, liberal and brave; they never selected one who was quick-tempered or stingy. They used to say that a man of mild temper and generous disposition was wise. Regard was had for a man's judgment and discretion, and for the quality of his mind as respects to justice."[26]

VII. *Oto'xovostôtse (knowledge/intelligence)*

A sacred leader cannot make decisions in haste, for the best choices are made only in prayer and through meditation. Sacred leaders must put in much thought and time before making decisions. In the Cheyenne culture, wisdom and knowledge cannot be separated, as one without the other is useless. Poor thinking and the inability to practice a meaningful and careful thought process will lead to poor decision making. The Véhoo'o did not have the privilege of valuing knowledge over wisdom. They were consistently in positions to make tough choices, which could yield either harsh consequences or fair rewards. The Véhoo'o believed that their responsibilities extended for seven generations and therefore they had to be both wise and knowledgeable to make the best decisions or the better of the poorest of choices, since there is not always going to be the "best" choice.

The Véhoo'o had to have the patience and intelligence to contemplate the results of their decisions over the course of time, which is why they had to plan for any unforeseen consequences. As sacred leaders, the Véhoo'o viewed their initial decision as the first action of a series of events. This first action is typically in response to a conflict, imbalance, or need to correct or remedy a problem. For example, if a village has a shortage of food and water, the action of the Véhoo'o is to move camp to land with more water and game to hunt. This first action can be viewed as the first smoke, since the most important decisions are made after a person or leader prays with a pipe before making a decision. This prayer involves meditation and patience, as the person contemplates any foreseeable or unforeseen response. The first smoke is a decision that is sent out to the four directions. The smoke then returns, resulting in one immediate and desired action and three otherwise unpredictable results. Most of the time the second smoke, the one that returns immediately, is the most desired action. For example, if the Véhoo'o moved a camp to find more water and game (first smoke), then the people had more resources to thrive (second smoke). A sacred leader's responsibility was not so simple, however. Sacred leaders have to account for any third or fourth smokes or actions following their decision. If they moved camp to a fertile area, for example, they would have to account for any unforeseen environmental impacts on the area, any conflicts with other nations, and any other consequences that may result from the move. When making decisions, sacred leaders must therefore rely heavily on previous knowledge, experience, traditional teachings, oral traditions, spiritual philosophies, and the knowledge of others.

The best leaders should be able to anticipate for as many as four smokes or resulting consequences of their decisions and plan for them to unfold over the course of four years. This "four smoke planning" and intelligent decision making proved valuable against the invading and unpredictable whites when the Cheyennes secured peace with the 1825 Friendship Treaty and in subsequent years as the Cheyennes successfully defended their homelands through warfare. When whites began to increase in numbers and expand their presence on the Great Plains through settlement and violence, the Cheyenne philosophy of "four smoke planning" remained as sacred leaders accounted for the unpredictable and, at times, unruly whites.

VIII. *Méhósánestôtse (love)*

A true leader loves his people, nation, and way of living above everything else. One of the most famous Northern Cheyenne chiefs was Vóóhéhéve (Morningstar). He is remembered as a leader who was "a goodhearted man who loved his people and his land."[27] Sacred leaders must know what it means to love and be loved to understand the significance of their role. Leaders' love for their people, nation, and way of living is tested while in office, and though leaders may appear to fail or falter from their choices, they should never lose humanity or their soul. A chief pledges his life for his people and would sacrifice his body for the survival of his nation and way of living, not because of patriotism or heroism, but simply because of love. Josephine Glenmore (Northern Cheyenne) described the teachings of a chief:

> At the camps the chief would get up real early, before the morning star. Teeth and Bearsole, he was named. And he would come out early and cry

(announce), he would teach how to live, "Children, love each other, don't be against each other, be good to each other, take care of one another, help each other, don't do things to spite each other. Take care of the old people and orphans who are wandering around, those who are poor, to everyone be good! Children, keep in mind what I have told you. Someday I'll be gone (dead), you will not hear me anymore."[28]

Traditionally, love was taught to all young people, but it was a value that was kept sacred and often reinforced by the highest of spiritual leaders, priests, and the chiefs in formal speeches. As explained by Stands In Timber: "[a]nd the priests, the old Indians, they talk to the people—the chiefs are the ones that do it the most—they walk up on a high hill, just a high knob someplace near the village. He [started] to talk. He never [goes] without saying, 'Be good people. Be good friends. Love one another. You don't have to put your arms around yourselves. In your own feelings, love your friends.'"[29]

IX. *Momotatamahestôtse (humility)*

A sacred leader does not show off, brag, or boast of his deeds or accomplishments. Nobody is in a position to disrespect his fellows. There exists no place, only in imagination, where a person is above others, especially the people he wishes to serve. A leader cannot lose sight of his tasks at hand, nor the goals to improve the lives of his people. A chief is modest for he does not know what challenges are before him. Despite his record and achievements, he can still fail; knowing this is the first step of many to humility.

X. *Ma'heónevetôtse (godliness/sacredness)*

The Cheyenne concept of godliness is not the same as that of whites. Godliness in the Cheyenne sense relates to a person's sacredness or holiness as a human being. A sacred leader has a sacred responsibility to his people. Whether knowingly or not, a leader can fall into one of two categories: a good leader or a bad leader. Both, however, are still respected as humans so long as they do not lose humanity. Most good leaders embody the good qualities of humanity, but great leaders thrive during the most challenging of times. Few words can describe a leader during such situations; godliness is appropriate. Such leaders are spiritually devoted to the ways of people and dedicated to the future generations. Sacred leaders should not strive to attain sacredness, but they should be prepared to make sacrifices to ensure the survival of the current population and those yet to be born. An unknown Cheyenne man describes how sacredness was achieved and taught, from one generation to the next, through daily practices:

Old man, he was my grandfather. No'kévéséhe (One Horn), he was called, the old man. He had one leg. And he used to talk to me. He used to teach me, Grandson, treat him well, welcome a person, everyone whether children, women, men, treat them well, welcome them. This way you will be thought of well, he used to tell me, my grandfather, the old man. You must always help old men or old women. You must be sympathetic. In that way Ma'heo'e will take pity on you. You will live a long time. You will roam a long time here on earth, he used to tell me, my grandfather, that one. And also he used to teach me. He used to make bows. He used to feather the arrows. Look at me, how I'm doing it, grandson! You must always make bows this way or—make arrows, he would tell me, the old man, my grandfather. He would get me up early in the morning. I used to go with him. We sat looking towards the sun, where it appears. He would fill his pipe. Whenever the sun appeared he would light it. He would sit and smoke. He held it up, like he prayed. By the time he finished smoking it had already appeared, the sun.[30]

Ôxho'oehee'ëstse ma'e no'ka éohketšéheše-móhtoehe is a traditional Cheyenne saying that translates to, "when blood is cooked just stir it around in one direction (otherwise it will spoil)." It is an axiom used for leaders who understand that things will not always go as planned and emphasizes that things must continue in one direction; otherwise, more problems will arise. It reiterates Cheyenne principles of sacred leadership, since the probability for an initiative or project to deteriorate or go awry, "through politicization, overly strong egos demanding too much personal control," is more likely to occur than not.[31] Sacred leaders sometimes have to go with the flow, despite knowing that a decision or a course of action is not the best.

CONCLUSION

The key to the success of the chiefs system is that one component, the organization, would not survive without the other, the principles. Without leadership principles, whether sacred or not, selfishness, greed, pompousness, jealousy, and egotism would lead to faulty leadership and compromise the entire system. Safeguards were put in place throughout the organization, either deliberately by its original founders or over years of refinement, to prevent leaders from holding on to power for too long. Theoretically, power is not to be held for a lifetime. Whether political or ceremonial, power and responsibility were to be fairly distributed from one entity to another and shared or transferred from one leader to another. To understand and exercise this form of government, citizens had to have a deep respect for the ways of their ancestors and traditional teachings. The role of the oral tradition was critical since it allowed for change and adaptation where necessary. As the nation expanded, new ideologies could thus synchronize with existing political traditions, especially during external acts of diplomacy and peace-making.

Another critical component of the chiefs system was the significance of ceremonial practices. The original Cheyenne chiefs system demanded a lot from its leaders, but the system also set high expectations for the nation as a whole. The citizenry respected and held ownership over the chiefs system, and it worked only because of the integrity of both the people and its leaders. Before the Cheyenne homelands were threatened by invading non-Indigenous colonizers, the primary purpose for the Véhoo'o was to facilitate spiritual practices, since sovereignty rested in spiritual practices, not in political ones. In other words, the majority of time in the lives of Cheyenne citizens was dedicated to ceremony and living in balance with the supernatural. Although warfare was a component, it was not the primary purpose of organizing. Unfortunately, this would dramatically change. The principles and structure of the Véhoo'o were tested throughout the colonization of the Cheyenne homeland.

Today, the Véhoo'o have returned to their pre-colonization, pre-war duties as facilitators of spiritual practices. The Véhoo'o no longer hold the political power to exert and exercise sovereignty since the formal tribal government is responsible for all major political decisions. Nonetheless, traditional Cheyennes still affirm that sovereignty rests in spiritual practices, not in political ones. The Véhoo'o remain central to the Cheyenne living-nation.

PART III

Nótåxeo'o: The Warriors

One day they heard a great rumbling sound beyond a hill near the camp; and as they looked, they saw an animal come over the hill. As it drew nearer, it was a different animal from what they had thought at first; and then it changed to another animal; and at last it was Motsé'eóeve, playing the wheel-game, and running close to the camp, as if to tempt them to pursue him. The people were all afraid, and said to one another, "Do not trouble him." When he saw that they did not try to take him, he went back the way he had come, and disappeared over the hill; and the rumbling grew fainter as he moved away. They think that he came, intending to have destroyed the people if they had tried to take him.
—Unknown[1]

During his absence there had been a famine in the land. The buffalo had gone into hiding, for they were angry that the people did not know how to live and were behaving badly. When Sweet Medicine arrived at the village, he found a group of tired and listless children, their ribs sticking out, who were playing with little buffalo figures they had made out of mud. Sweet Medicine immediately changed the figures into large chunks of juicy buffalo meat and fat. "Now there's enough for you to eat," he told the young ones, "with plenty left over for your parents and grandparents."
—Unknown[2]

Listen to me carefully; the gods already told me that I would be the one who would reform you in a better way of living, and teach you to govern your people in a good way. You shall have protection—you have no protection the way you are living now. You now live in a bad way. You kill one another. You do things which are bad. The gods do not take pity on you, because you are murderers; that is why you are poor, and hungry, and you starve. All these things shall be no more.
—Motsé'eóeve[3c]

PART III | NÓTÂXEO'O: THE WARRIORS

Son of Jesse Bent, James Mooney, 1861–1921. National Anthropological Archives, Smithsonian Museum Support Center, Suitland, Maryland (NAA INV 06089100, OPPS NEG 88).

THE SECOND governing institution of the traditional Cheyenne political system is composed of several warrior, soldier, or men's societies. The institution is best described as a second leg to a four-branched government. The three others are the Véhoo'o, the Medicine Hat, and the Medicine Arrows. In Part III I explore the Nótâxeo'o (the warriors), their creation, organization, responsibilities, and core principles. The warrior societies were significant to the balance of the entire political and ceremonial structure of the nation. Although their primary purpose was to protect the people from outside threats, organize buffalo hunts, and initiate offensive attacks on enemies, these groups of soldiers were sometimes delegated roles as peacemakers, diplomats, and decision makers. Like the Véhoo'o, the Nótâxeo'o had spiritual and ancient origins and their survival depended on the health of oral traditions and ceremonial practices. Like the origin of the Véhoo'o, the origin of the first four warrior societies is difficult to date. Nonetheless, numerous other Indian nations throughout the Plains adopted strikingly similar warrior societies, which comprised primarily younger men and sometimes women.

Women's societies were also a part of the system, but they functioned as social and ceremonial organizations, rather than military. Today the society system remains with both the Northern and Southern Cheyenne nations, but their roles have significantly diminished because of colonization, assimilation, and modernization. The Nótâxeo'o were part of the larger governing system of the Cheyenne Nation, and each society also consisted of distinct hierarchal organizations that valued the accomplishments of individuals. These organizations fostered loyalty, community, and citizenship. This part reveals how concepts of citizenship were rooted in the responsibilities and duties of each individual citizen, regardless of gender. The organization of the Nótâxeo'o reveals how these responsibilities were institutionalized and sustained through actions. All citizens of the nation were, in some way or another, warriors who protected their way of living and future generations.

According to the oral tradition, Cheyenne life before the establishment of the Nótâxeo'o was dominated by corruption and chaos, just as it was before the establishment of the Véhoo'o. Once created, the Nótâxeo'o became the institutions that created the formal systems of individual development. Members learned to respect and honor an unseen organization that promoted Cheyenne values. The Nótâxeo'o fostered the physical and mental growth of individuals, male and female, encouraging teamwork, loyalty, and discipline. Each society was its own autonomous institution, but each was critical in building the Cheyenne Nation. A better description for the Nótâxeo'o would be men's societies, since these male-dominated groups included members of different professions, such as general members (men and women), warriors (those with status earned in combat), ceremonial leaders (older men and women), and headmen, who were the leaders of each organization. For lack of a better translation, I will refer to these organizations as warrior societies, since this term is the most commonly used in text and in the modern Cheyenne communities.

CHAPTER 8

Before the Nótâxeo'o

BEFORE THE existence of the Nótâxeo'o (warrior societies), the first four bands of the Cheyenne Nation did not have a formal structure that provided protection and enforced law and order. Neither did they have a formal apparatus to provide an avenue for individuals to earn respect, dignity, and rewards for good actions. Every healthy human society needs structures to sustain its way of life, especially for young men and women to find a place and distinguish themselves among their people. Healthy social structures can lead to building healthy nations. Before the Great Unification and before the establishment of the Nótâxeo'o, the first bands of the Tsétsêhéstâhese and the Só'taeo'o were without any social institutions. In the absence of any formal social structure, the first bands easily fell into dysfunction, even though the bands had a single-chief system.

According to Cheyenne national history, the people were often subject to the oppression of groups of men who instigated fights, stole from others, and killed their fellow Cheyennes. These groups of men operated as gangs and were loosely organized. When describing them, storytellers lacked the concept of "gang," since the concept is synonymous with delinquency. "Societies" is a term used to identify groups of men even though these groups were not the guilds of the Nótâxeo'o that were institutionalized by the prophet Sweet Medicine. The underdeveloped "societies" were made up of older men who took advantage of their younger counterparts. There are stories of these men stealing food, taking wives, and sabotaging the lives of their fellow citizens by telling lies and spreading rumors. During the time before the Nótâxeo'o, the Cheyennes suffered and starved, since hunting was unorganized and done carelessly. Parents abandoned their children and some families were broken up because older men stole wives and sometimes killed husbands, leaving children as orphans. In Cheyenne national history, the creation of the Véhoo'o represented a revolution in leadership, but the creation of the Nótâxeo'o represented a revolution in social change and the creation of the Cheyenne concepts of the warrior, the warrior code, and the standards of manhood.

The United Cheyenne history is composed of two major oral traditions that tell of (1) the first warrior societies, and (2) the hard times before the institutionalization of the Nótâxeo'o. A significant body of stories originated from the Só'taeo'o and center on the story of Lime and his brother. The second body of stories originated from the Tsétsêhéstâhese and highlights the culture heroes Cherry Eater, Youngest, and Sweet Medicine. After the Great Unification, the Tsétsêhéstâhese oral tradition synced and converged with that of the Só'taeo'o, but the converged stories tend to highlight the feats of Sweet Medicine. Most of the literature on Cheyenne history, and most traditional storytellers of today, continue to highlight the Sweet Medicine oral tradition over others. Nonetheless, I present oral traditions from both to show how the Cheyenne Nation came to have the great Nótâxeo'o.

Cherry Eater of the Tsétsêhéstâhese

Before the Cheyennes had warrior societies, an old man and his wife were out picking berries when they found a boy living in the sticks at the creek.[1] He had no parents, so the old couple took him home and adopted him. The old couple did not have much food but cut up an old buffalo hide, boiled it, and fed it to the boy. The hide was one of the last prized possessions of the couple because they kept it from a time when the Cheyennes were prosperous and healthy. The boy loved the taste of this animal. He called himself Cherry Eater, and one day his grandfather asked, "Why did you name yourself Cherry Eater?"

The boy responded: "You found me living alone on the creek bank. I was living there a long time, all alone, and I ate nothing but cherries." The grandfather was satisfied, and Cherry Eater asked him to cut long strips from the old buffalo hide and bring green willow branches to the lodge. Cherry Eater made four hoops and strung them with the strips of rawhide, weaving firm nets. He also made four spears. When he completed his implements, he walked out to the center of the village and told his grandfather to roll one of the hoops.

His grandfather rolled a hoop, saying, "This is a yearling buffalo heifer! Shoot her!"

Cherry Eater threw a spear and hit the center of the hoop. Then the hoop turned into a yearling buffalo heifer. The old couple and the boy butchered the animal and shared their meat with their neighbors. The next morning Cherry Eater and his grandfather performed the same ceremony and killed a well-grown heifer. The following morning Cherry Eater and his grandfather performed the ceremony a third time and killed a yearling bull. On the fourth day, Cherry Eater and his grandfather repeated the ceremony and killed a full-grown buffalo bull. The people in the village had food, but Cherry Eater knew this was not enough.

Early the next morning, as the sun rose, Cherry Eater asked his grandparents, "Pull as much fur as you can from your buffalo robes." The grandfather had a buffalo bull robe and the grandmother had a buffalo heifer one. Cherry Eater took the fur in hand and walked through the camp toward a high ridge.

Grandfather announced, "My grandson is going to do something amazing. Everyone follow him and see what he does."

The people could see Cherry Eater on top of the ridge as the sun began to rise and the sky changed colors. He said a prayer and threw the bull fur in the air and the wind carried it throughout the next valley. He said another prayer and threw the heifer fur into the air and the wind carried it in the same direction. He announced to the people, "Come and see what I have done." When the people walked up the ridge and looked into the next valley, they saw a massive herd of buffalo. Every piece of hair turned into an animal; there were an equal number of bulls and heifers. Cherry Eater performed the same ceremony for three mornings, four days total. All of the neighboring valleys were full of buffalo. The grandparents' buffalo robes were bare from hair.

On the fourth day the people organized a hunt, but by this time other men became jealous of the young man. The Cheyennes did not yet develop hunting ceremonies and laws, nor were they organized hunters. Each family went about killing animals at will. Cherry Eater killed a buffalo with his spear and he and his grandparents began to butcher the animal. A man who was not much older than Cherry Eater approached them as they butchered. His name was Medicine Star and he was a member of a family that was known to cause trouble in the village. Medicine Star claimed, "That is my kill. Look at the shape of the wound made by my arrow. You just took out my arrow and claimed this animal yourself."

Cherry Eater knew that Medicine Star was lying, but he did not want to start trouble with Medicine Star and his belligerent family. "All right, Medicine Star," said Cherry Eater. "You can have this heifer if you want it. Come, Grandfather and Grandmother, let us go home. This man has taken the buffalo that I killed." The family walked home and ate a small meal. Cherry Eater was upset and after he ate, he put on his robe, picked up his medicine hoops and spears, and walked out of the lodge. When his grandfather asked where he was going, Cherry Eater responded, "I'm just going to that white butte." The young man never returned to the people.

Cherry Eater walked to "White Butte," where a spring flowed. The young man walked into the spring and never returned. When others asked where the young prophet went, his grandmother told them: "Cherry Eater brought a time of feasting and happiness to our tribe, but he was cheated by Medicine Star. That hurt him, and he went back to his camp under the butte, leaving us to regret his passing and get along as best we can with out him."[2] The Cheyennes no longer starved, but they were still unorganized and the people were vulnerable to persecution.

Cherry Eater's passiveness represents the emotion and frustration that is common when young men mature and face adversity. His discipline represents a response that was fairly uncommon; he secluded himself and withdrew from any conflict. Like the story of Cherry Eater, other early stories include internal conflict, emotion, frustration, and sometimes anger in the hearts of young men. Cherry Eater's story highlights another important purpose of the Nótàxeo'o: to encourage young men to channel their emotions and negative energy. As the Cheyennes grew in population, they eventually progressed to develop the social systems to provide spiritual guidance to the younger generations. The following stories of Lime reveal an underdeveloped Cheyenne Nation, during the time before the Nótàxeo'o. These stories are just as important as those that explain the origin of the Nótàxeo'o.

VÓETSÉNA'E OF THE SÓ'TAEO'O

The epic of Vóetséna'e (White Clay/Lime) is one of emotion because it comprises ideas and concepts that reveal how the people of the early bands, without a formal structure, were dominated by forces of corruption, deception, and manipulation. The stories reveal social and political drama on a level that rivaled Greek history and mythology. The epic of Vóetséna'e reveals how older men could influence young men, especially if the sacred relationship of brotherhood was abused. In this case, Lime's brother uses his younger brother by telling him to commit crimes against the nation. In return, Lime's brother gains short-lived benefits of notoriety and promotion. The young Lime searched for a place or position among his people, an endeavor that is part of all cultures. In the end, Lime achieves his goal, however unconventional. In these pre-Nótàxeo'o stories, the Só'taeo'o identify groups of men as "war-societies" or a single "war-society." These groups of men do not necessarily have any loyalties. The men are easily influenced, operate under a gang mentality, and in the end, reap fitting punishments for their roles as collaborators. The Cheyennes were in need of the Nótàxeo'o, the institution that fostered the growth of young men and instilled traditional values and the warrior ethic.

Crazy Lime, by Harry Black

There being a large camp circle. The hero, Crazy Lime, had a brother who had four wives. The brother was a chief over a band of men. The band of men were afraid of Crazy Lime. Therefore did not like him, so they told their chief that they would agree to make him a bigger chief if he would dispose of his brother Crazy Lime. The chief thus agreed to their request.

Crazy Lime was loved by one of his sisters-in-law (brother's wife). The chief told his brother (Crazy Lime) that he wanted him to go hunting with him and one of his wives. The woman that went along happened to be the lover of Crazy Lime. So they went hunting and the brother killed two deer. The woman sliced the meat and other parts of meat to dry and cure on a rack which they made out of willow poles. The chief gave Crazy Lime a long willow branch with leaves on one end of it, and was told to keep the flies away from the meat by brushing them off with the willow pole. The chief and his wife went home.

Crazy Lime stayed at his post faithfully, walking in circles continuously so that he wore out a path so deep that he only could reach the meat with the pole. "My brother, more ever is made a bigger chief," said he. He used these words from time to time, and continued to drive the flies away even when the meat and bones dried up.

In the meantime the chief was made a bigger chief by his band of men. The lover of Crazy Lime was made a slave to the chief and the band of men. One of her many duties was to sit over the ice in the river to keep it from freezing during the night and to carry water to the chief. She was made to wear earrings made of wolf dung for ear lobes.

When the chief called for a drink of water, she carried it to him with great care and if she happened to spill a drop, the chief wrathfully would say, "Has Crazy Lime returned, that you act so boldly?"

One day the slave stole away from the camp to go to her lover Crazy Lime. Upon nearing the place, she heard him saying, "My brother more ever is made a bigger chief." Still waving the willow pole to drive the flies away from the meat and bones.

"I who love you have come after you to return with me to the camp. Since your absence I was made a slave by the chief and his band of men. I have suffered terribly. I am forced to perform the heaviest and hardest duties and if I happen to do anything awkwardly, the chief scolds me terribly and says, 'has Crazy Lime returned, that you act so boldly?'" said she.

"I will go with you," said he. After helping him out of the path-hole, they immediately started to the camp. On their journey she related her hardships to him. "The wolf dung you see I am wearing, was forced on me to wear," said she.

Upon their arrival in camp, there was a dance going on in a tipi of the camp, wherein sat the chief in the seat of honor. Crazy Lime told the slave to enter the tipi roughly and if the chief wants a drink of water, carry it to him roughly spilling the water purposely. "He will say, 'Has Crazy Lime returned, that you act so bravely and boldly?' Throw the water on his face and say, 'Yes, it is possible that Crazy Lime has returned!' Then detach the wolf dung ear trinkets and toss them to his face. Then I will enter and proclaim myself chief over all people."

So the senior brother was made a slave and [so were] his band of men. Crazy Lime married all of his brother's wives, ruling with relentless power. Thus the length of the legend has ended.[3]

Bull Thigh told the next story of Lime, which is considerably longer and more detailed compared to Black's version. The next two versions of Lime reveal how he was merely a boy when his brother deceived him.

Lime, Part I, by Bull Thigh

First night: The Great Mysterious One placed the red man in this country. A great many generations afterwards there were a great many people camping in a circle. The whole camp was composed of bark of trees and grass. In the center of this camp they made a large hut. There was a man who had two wives. They chose him to be chief. He had a brother about ten years old. The elder brother one day said to him: "My friend, I want you to come here. I'm going to dress you up, paint your face, braid your hair." After he dressed him up he made him a bow and arrows, and he told him: "You must go out and look about the country. If you at any time see any animals, shoot them. If you kill them, hang them on the trees and come home to get dogs and travois to bring them in."

So one day, he climbed on his brother's lodge and looked about. He came down. He went out to hunt. While out he saw a great big rabbit jump out. He shot him as he ran and killed him. He took the rabbit and walked to the timber and hung him on the branches, and came home. He told his brother: "I have done what you told me to do." His sister-in-law got a big dog, a travois, and went out. He went out too. They brought the rabbit home in their travois. He [Lime] loved his younger sister-in-law better than anyone else.

His brother said to him: "My friend, when you want a girl, you must dress up, paint your face, and look about for the girls while they are going to the river." One day he crawled upon his brother's tipi and looked about. He saw a fine girl had gone to the creek. Just as soon as he saw her going to the creek he came right down, got his bow and arrow, and made a charge at her, and shot her three or four times, and killed her. After he had done this, the people called the war-societies to talk it over.

His brother was the chief. After the war-societies were all in, they told him that he must kill his own brother or else get rid of him in some unknown place. The chief said to the war-societies: "Yes, I am going to get rid of him," and he went to his lodge. He told his younger wife to play with Lime while he was going to do something. He said to the younger wife: "Take him near the bank of the river. Tie him tight like a baby; tie some rocks around his cradle and swing him into the river; get another girl to help you." So they did it.

The two returned to the camps and told the chief that they had thrown him into the water. The elder wife was absent. She came home. She inquired: "What has become of Lime?" No one could say a word to her. But the other girl who went with the younger wife told her that they had thrown him in. She stood near the bank. She looked about. While she was looking about she was crying. She saw someone come up from way down below to the top of the water. Lime came to where his sister-in-law was and went home with her.

When she brought him back to the camps, the war-societies came together again, and told the chief that if he killed or got rid of him in some way, he would gain a still higher reputation. So the chief told them: "All right." This time the chief and Lime went to the river and rowed over the deep water to hunt. While they were looking about on the other side of the river, they came to a buffalo. The chief shot him and dressed him. The chief went to the timber, cut a club, and brought it to Lime. He told him to walk around the meat keeping the flies off. "I'm going a little ways to kill another buffalo." So the boy walked around it while his brother went. The brother went back to where he had left the boat and paddled across the river, and went to the camp. He left Lime across the water. When he came back to his lodge, the war-societies were gathered there. He told them he had thrown Lime away. They told him: "It is all right."

Second night: About a year after this, the war-societies began to make complaints against the chief and his wives. The societies used them harshly; tortured them in many ways; and he was deposed from his leadership. He was chief no longer. One day the elder wife said to her husband: "Where did you throw Lime away? Let's get away from this camp and look for Lime." One night they stole a boat and crossed the river. They came over the river. He told his wives to look at where he had left Lime. They saw nothing but a pile of bones. "That's where I left him," said he. After he said that, the younger wife started running for the spot. She came right at the place. She looked down. She saw Lime still walking around with his club still with him. She said to him: "Lime, I'm coming down to see you and hunt you up." Lime did not look up. Then his brother came. "Why friend, brother, I have come." The brother did not look up at him. The elder wife came. "Lime, I've come here; I have come to see you." He said, "Hi!" He jumped up and met them. They sat down and conversed. They told him everything that had been done to them; they showed him how their hands had been burned. Lime said to them: "Let us go back."

When they came to the place where they had left the boat, he put them in a row. He placed the elder wife first, the younger wife second, his brother last. He stood at the head and told them to look at his back. He started into the water and walked on the water as if he was walking on ice and crossed the river. They followed him on the water. When they had crossed it was sundown. He told them they must start running. They ran towards the camp. They arrived at the camp just after dark and went into their grass hut.

Lime got a stick big enough to use. While sitting down fixing the club, two men peeped in and recognized Lime, and walked to their own families to alarm them. The war-societies were in session in the middle of the circle. They sent two more to see if Lime and his brother and his sisters-in-law had come home. The two peeked in, saw Lime, recognized him, and went back to their own families to alarm them to leave camp. Before the societies knew, Lime, his brother and sisters-in-law ran to the lodge where the societies were. They arrived here. The elder wife went in first, the younger wife next; the brother went in; Lime went in. They were caught one by one except Lime: everybody looked at Lime. He stood in the doorway and told the societies to spread a buffalo robe. He told his brother and sisters-in-law to sit down on it. He told the societies to sit down right. He walked to his sisters-in-law. He gave his club to the elder wife, and told the societies to sit with their legs close together. She got up and [hit] every one across the legs. He took the club and gave it to the younger wife and told the societies to sit in a different way. So he told her: "Go hit every one square on their head." She knocked them senseless. After they got their senses, he told them to leave their blankets and go right together and get each one a piece of fire and place it near to where they were. He told them to leave their blankets inside and go out. They went out. They all went to their homes; there were none; everybody was gone except these men. These men started in the same direction where the others went. Lime and his brother and his brother's wives left the camp.[4]

Bull Thigh continues the saga of Lime, which explains how an unknown warrior of equal caliber eventually subdued and restrained him and his actions. The epic battle between the two warriors is the foundation of the warrior ethic.

Lime, Part II, by Bull Thigh

Third night: The people were moving to the Black Hills. They came to the Cheyenne and joined them so they might kill Lime, his brother, and his sisters-in-law. Lime had a club made for himself and painted it red all over. Lime told the three why he had made this club. "Sometime there will be an enemy; the whole tribe of people will come and search for us to kill us; when I am sleeping if you see the enemy coming on the hill, you must ask me to get up and dress for battle. The enemy will cut me in two; when I drop in two, take me to the river. I will be healed as ever."

Early in the morning the enemy came upon the hill. He was sleeping. The younger sister woke him up and told him: "The enemy is at hand." Lime got up, dressed up, and painted his face. When he finished he took his club down. They went out. They walked to near the bank of the river. They stood there. They looked to where the enemy was. The enemy was numerous. Lime called at their leader. "Do your best if you are coming to kill me. Do your first trick." As soon as he finished, their leader waved a stone sword at him and cut him, severing his neck and one shoulder. His head dropped way off. His sisters-in-law took his body to the river and placed his head on. He was healed. He came back and stood up.

The voice of the enemy said: "You can use your club and hit me." As soon as he said this, Lime waved his club at him. He and the enemy all fell dead on the ground. The four looked at them: they were all lying down. While they were looking at them a cloud appeared above and made a large shower over on the dead, and they all rose again.

There was lightning on the heads of all. Lime looked at the North and cried out with a clear voice. As soon as he finished a heavy snow fell, and there was thunder and lightning. The storm of snow and the storm of rain met in the center of the river. They could not see each other. Where Lime was, the snow was a foot deep; on the other side, water poured to the river. Lime heard a voice: "My friend, let us make peace." Lime said, "Yes." The showers and storms ceased on both sides, and all cleared away. Lime and his people walked across the water and met them. That was the first time Lime met the Cheyenne. Then there was peace. They all came to the Black Hills. They promised that hereafter, they would never fight each other again. This is the end.[5]

Tall Bull told a second version of Lime. Although some minor differences are evident, there are not any major inconsistencies, proving the core teachings of the stories and the Cheyenne oral tradition to be healthy. Nonetheless, the epic is well preserved, as it takes place during hoháovonóom (the very ancient time), in the first world, at "the land of stones."

Lime, Part I, by Tall Bull

First night: There was a band of Sutaiu near the Missouri river. A young man was elected from this band to a war-society to look after the people. This young man was very large in appearance. He became an influential man among the people. He was called Lime. He had two wives. One was old, the other younger. The younger one used to play with her husband as if he was a child. She tied him in a cradle. When she did that, she used to throw the rope over the trees so as to swing him. She did not know that Lime was holy.

One day the eldest brother of Lime made a bow and arrow for him. Before that no one ever used bows and arrows. He taught him how to use them. After a bow and arrow had been made for him, Lime went out, looked about to see if he could find something to shoot at. While looking about he found a very large rabbit. He shot at it. It was so big that he couldn't take it home with him. He left the rabbit, came home to get a dog and travois with him to bring the rabbit home.

On the following morning he went out to find something to shoot at. While looking about he found an antelope and shot at him. He was so big that he couldn't carry him home. He came back after a dog and travois, and went out to bring him home. He called two or three war-societies to come and eat the antelope.

On the third morning he went to look out for something to kill. He found one deer and shot at him, and came home to get his dog and travois to bring it home. He called the people to eat at his lodge.

On the fourth day he went out again to find if he could shoot at anything. He saw a moose and shot at him. He killed him and came home, got his dog and travois to bring the moose home. His brother came to his lodge again. His brother dressed him up, painted his face, gave him a buffalo robe. After he had dressed him, he told him to go out along the bank of the creek, to lie there, and to look for the best girl he could get. So he went, and hid himself near the bank.

Second night: There were young girls passing continually in front of the creek. By and by he saw a fine girl. He made a charge at her. He took his knife out and cut her into pieces. His brother told him to do that, but he made a mistake. He was only meant to throw her down and touch her [at knifepoint. He was wrongly convinced to "take" her by force, and ended up killing the girl: both actions are serious crimes.]. There was a war-society that came out of their lodge and complained of him in the presence of his brother. They told him that he had better let his brother go off some place; if he didn't he would kill all the people as he had done one already. His brother asked what he had done. They said: "He has killed the finest girl in the tribe. He tore her to pieces along side of the river." The brother was surprised.

He and his brother conversed together about making a canoe, going into the river and crossing. After they had paddled across the river they left the canoe and walked in an unknown direction. While on the way they saw a buffalo. They came to him. His brother shot and killed him. He cut a large club and gave it to his brother [Lime]. After they dressed the buffalo, he told him [Lime] to walk around keeping off the flies by waving the club, thus he spoke to him. When the elder brother went off he looked for another buffalo. But he went to where he had left the canoe. He went to the tribe again. When he came back, he called all the war-societies to his lodge. He told them that he had taken his brother across the water and left him there to keep away from the tribe. He, the big brother, who returned, was made a big chief. He had two wives.

Third night: One day the war-society came together, decided what punishment to mete out to the chief and two wives. They decided that they would have to be used as servants any time when a society was smoking or anything else. They tortured them for one whole year in every way. They suffered for his brother's act. After one year the youngest wife asked her husband: "Where did you leave your brother?" She asked him to go back with her to where he left his brother so that they might bring his brother back. The three, both the wives and himself, sneaked away one night. They went where they had left the canoe. They got on it and crossed the river. When they crossed they left the canoe there and walked to where he had left his brother.

They came to him at twilight near the morning. The big brother came to where his younger brother had been left. When the elder brother came he found a big pile of bones on the spot where he had told his younger brother to scatter flies off the buffalo. He came right on the spot. He saw his brother still walking around it, under the earth. He listened. He heard a voice. The voice said, "My brother has left me here, and I hope that he is higher than the chief at this time because he has done this to me." The two women and the elder brother saw him still walking. He [Lime] was still waving that club. The elder brother spoke down to him. He [Lime] did not look at them. The eldest wife asked him to look up and have pity on them, that the tribe had tortured them for his sake. He did not look up. The youngest one started to cry when she saw him. She said to him: "Lime, we are in a hard fix. They have almost taken our lives away for your sake."

"Well," he said. He looked up and had pity on her. He walked out. So the four started back to where they left the canoe. They came there. The younger brother told him to look straight at his back. He started to walk on the water. He walked as if on ice. The three followed him. They all walked across. They came back to the tribe. They made a camp on the outskirts of the [main] camp. Their lodge was tall grass. The younger brother said to his sister-in-law: "Go out and cut off a club." They brought it to him. He made a club.

Fourth night: One night when the war-societies came together they asked one of the members to go out and see if the runaways were coming home. So he went out towards the end of the lodges. He saw a fire a distance away from the lodges. He went to it. He peeked in. He saw Lime sitting at the back part of the lodge. He recognized them and went back to where the war-societies were. He made no report. He went to his own lodge; he called his wife and children to get ready to run off from the camp. While the war-societies were waiting for a report, they sent another messenger to find if the runaways were coming home to the same place. He found Lime at the same place. He [the messenger] peeked in. He recognized him [Lime]. He [the messenger] came back and made no report but went to his own lodge, alarmed his own family so they might get away.

Lime said: "They know us now. We will go to the war-societies' place." They came to the lodge. The eldest brother went in first, his two wives next, and Lime the last. Lime carried a club. The leader of one of the societies arose, got his buffalo robe, stretched it in the back of the lodge nearly in the center so they might sit down. They were welcomed. Lime said: "You mustn't sit there." He said to his sisters-in-law: "You sit at the entrance." The whole war-societies became terrified and trembled. Lime said to them: "You sit down the same way." He told the younger wife to get up. He gave her his club to hit the legs of each across the shins with all her might. She hit every one of them. She almost killed them. He called the elder wife to get the club.

He told the men: "Sit down properly." He said to his elder wife: "Now you go ahead and hit each one of them square on the head with all your might." She hit every one. They became senseless. While this was going on, someone peeked in the door. He saw Lime was treating the head of the tribe very severely. He told the people. They became frightened and all ran off that night. The elder brother got up, told the war-societies to get the buffalo robe and spread it. He sat down on it. Lime told the people to fill the pipe and [then] gave it to his brother. He called the last man in the row to take a piece of fire in his own hands as carefully as he could and to place it before his brother. He did so. Lime called on each to do that [until] towards morning. In the morning he turned them loose. When they went to look for their lodges, their families were gone. The four, Lime, his brother, and the latter's two wives crossed the Big River.[6]

Tall Bull continues the epic of Lime, which is an adaptation to Bull Thigh's version. In Bull Thigh's version Lime meets an unnamed foe upon crossing the "Big River," which is assumed to be the Mississippi River. Tall

Bull, on the other hand, identifies the foe of Lime as Sweet Medicine. The "Big River" is in other instances assumed to be the Missouri River. These two factors indicated that Tall Bull's version is exemplary of sacred history convergence; the adaptation likely occurred upon the Great Unification of the Tsétsêhéstâhese and Só'taeo'o. In Tall Bull's account both prophets, who represent their respective subnations, demonstrate physical and spiritual strength, while adhering to the traditional Cheyenne warrior ethic.

Lime, Part II, by Tall Bull

Fifth night: The band that had been frightened away joined the Cheyennes. They told the Cheyenne that they, the Sutaiu, had a leader who never could be killed. The leader of the Cheyenne at the time was Matsiyeiv (Sweet Medicine). Sweet Medicine and Lime wanted to meet each other. The whole band of Cheyenne came to the four [Lime, his brother, and the two wives]. This was near the Mississippi River. There was a little island on the river on which the four lived. Lime had a vision. There was going to be a band of people coming to kill him. So later he told the girls to cut a stick so that he could make a club. He made a club. When he finished it, he put red paint on it. He told his brother and sisters-in-law: "In just about day after tomorrow the enemy will be at hand." He gave them instructions. He said to them: "If Sweet Medicine cuts me in two, you should take my body to the river and put me together. I will become just as ever. He will do that three or four times; you must do what I have told you each time. If I don't happen to get up in time when the enemy appears, you wake me up." At daybreak they woke up Lime. They said: "Lime, get up, the enemy are at hand." So he got up. He dressed up and painted his face in good shape. They went out. They walked a little way to where the stream was. They looked towards the enemy. No one could count how many there were. The great leader stood far ahead of the rest of them. There was a high ridge where the enemy named Sweet Medicine stood far ahead.

He, Sweet Medicine, called out to him: "My friend, today we wish to know each other. I'm going to kill you today. You can do the best you can to cope with me or else you can kill me."

Lime said to him: "Remember today; I'm going to do the same. You must do the best you can to cope with me. I'm surely going to kill you."

Sweet Medicine said: "I'm going to do it now." He raised his sword. It was made of hard rock. He waved it towards Lime. He cut Lime from his neck to his arm. His brother and two sisters took him at once to the river. He was healed. He raised his club and waved it towards Sweet Medicine. He knocked him down. Sweet Medicine told his people to cover him with a robe if Lime should kill him. They covered him with a robe. He was healed. Sweet Medicine raised his sword, waved it towards Lime; he cut him in two. Lime fell. His brother and sisters-in-law took him to the river. He was healed. He hit Sweet Medicine. He knocked him down. They covered him with a robe. Sweet Medicine cut Lime in two just below the juncture of his legs. His brother and sisters-in-law took him to the river. He was healed. He came back. He hit and knocked Sweet Medicine down. They covered him with a robe and he was healed. They moved closer to each other, though still at a distance. Sweet Medicine said to Lime: "My friend, you must have come here to imitate me. I came to save the people hereafter in this world."

Lime said to him: "I guess you have come to imitate me."

Sweet Medicine said: "I know one trick. You shall know it today."

Lime: "I too know one trick. You shall know it today."

Sweet Medicine said: "I know this trick." A big shower came. The thunder was terrific over Lime.

Lime said: "I know this trick too." The storm of snow came together with the shower. There was a big noise between the two. In four successive days of this trick there was a shower of rain and a storm of snow with it. In the morning of the fourth day Sweet Medicine surrendered to Lime. They came together and made peace. There was just the same thing in them. Neither could beat the other.[7]

As oral tradition reveals, this was the first time the Cheyennes "moved the Arrows," which is a full-scale declaration of war according to Tsétsêhéstâhese war custom. However, the reason Sweet Medicine surrendered first is that he did not want to kill his own people with the storm; to do so was a violation of the sacred law prohibiting murder, a strict law of the Tsétsêhéstâhese. Sweet Medicine's surrender was not done out of cowardice, but in accordance with the Tsétsêhéstâhese principle of hévese'onematsestôtse. Lime, for his part, was moved by the love that Sweet Medicine had for his people the Cheyennes, which explains why the Só'taeo'o prophet made peace with the Tsétsêhéstaestse prophet. In the end, both heroes adhere and uphold the sacred teaching of hévese'onematsestôtse. The story is the mechanism that preserves a long-lasting peace, as listeners from either band, Tsétsêhéstâhese and Só'taeo'o, are taught hévese'onematsestôtse. Furthermore, the story emphasizes that the warrior ethic of the Cheyenne Nation originates from both cultures.

THE FIRST WARRIOR SOCIETY OF THE SÓ'TAEO'O

The first warrior society of the Só'taeo'o was made up of four brothers and a sister. The band of brothers, however, is not remembered as being part of the great Nótâxeo'o because the brothers were not a warrior society by the standards that later developed. Nonetheless, the four brothers represent the concepts of brotherhood, which is the foundation of the Nótâxeo'o system. The story is a Só'taeo'o epic. Harry Black tells the story, which highlights the kinship relationships of the Cheyenne people. Sibling relationships are the foundation of the Cheyenne cultural way of life. The principles of kinship are also embedded within each of the warrior societies that make up the Nótâxeo'o. The story "The White Buffalo" reinforces ideal characteristics for brothers, sisters, and grandparents: diligence, loyalty, restraint, and kindness are all traditional Cheyenne values.

The White Buffalo

First Night: There lived four brothers out away from anyone. They lived by hunting and fishing. The youngest one was still of youthful age. He stayed home and hunted birds with his bow and arrows for past time. His arrows were feathered with grasshopper wings. His brothers called him Last Born. He possessed magic power. One day there came a beautiful young maiden to live with them, to be a sister to them, and when the brothers were returning from their hunting, Last Born ran out to meet them, and to tell them that a beautiful young maiden had come to live with them. She shall be my wife said he (the oldest brother). Then Last Born hung his head to the ground, feeling hurt when he heard his eldest brother make this remark and [Last Born] refused to come home.

Then the brothers called to him and said, come let us go and see our sister. So he came for his wish was that the beautiful maiden be their sister. The young maiden made their moccasins and mended their robes for them.

One day the brothers warned her that there would be a powerful witch to entice her away from them. That this witch would appear in different forms and "not to listen to him" and "not to even look up to it to see what he looks like" and "never to go outdoors while we are away on a hunt," said they.

One day a bird with the most beautiful plumage sat on the tipi poles and sang a song, but she did not look up to see what it looked like. She told her brothers, there was a bird that came and sang a song. "It was the witch," said they. "It was good that you did not look up to see what it looked like."

After the brothers had gone away again a little boy entered the tipi, his appearance was very untidy, his hair was all matted, he walked around and around the fire place, pleading to her for something to eat and saying "I am hungry." But she gave him no food and did not even look at him, and he left failing to overpower her. And again her brothers returned from the hunt and she told them about the little boy. "It was the witch," said they. "It was good that you did not look to see what he looked like."

After the brothers had gone to hunt, then the male [witch] tunneled his way underground into the tipi, peeped his head out near her, but she did not look at it and the male [witch] disappeared. So she related to her brothers about the male [witch] on their return. "It was the witch," said they, "it was good that you did not look at him."

After the brothers had gone out hunting again, she stepped outside of the tipi to get some firewood and while getting the wood she snagged her foot with a very sharp thorn. Then when she returned to the tipi she extracted the thorn from her injured foot, placing the thorn by her side. She looked and sitting by her side was the witch and gruffly he ordered her to come along with him. Then she remembered that her brothers had warned her about the witch, but it was too late. When her brothers arrived home from the hunt, she was gone. They knew that the witch had taken her away to be his slave and they mourned for her.

Second night: Last Born decided to go and find her and bring her back to them. He started on the trail taking with him his bow and arrows, and towards nightfall, he came to a very large camp of people [the first camp]. There was a brown wigwam at the edge of the camp circle where in lived an old woman and when Last Born reached the camp, he entered the wigwam and said to the old woman, "Grandmother I am very hungry." The old woman said, "Grandson you are always away all day long and you're home very hungry." She gave him food, not knowing that he was a stranger, but thinking it was her own grandson. [According to Cheyenne custom, an old woman and a child establish a kinship relationship upon meeting regardless of the presence of a blood relationship. The sanctity of the newly founded kinship relationship is determined on how each sustains it. In the story, the grandmothers at each camp sanctify the relationship by feeding the boy as if he were their own grandson. This relationship is important, for Last Born is in need of help from his grandmothers.] While eating, he asked the old woman what she had heard. "My grandson, White Buffalo the most terrible and powerful witch has taken for his slave the sister of the four brothers and is taking her to his own people," said she. And he journeyed on following the trail.

The following day after nightfall, he came to a very large camp of people [the second camp]. There was a brown wigwam at the edge of the camp circle, where in lived an old-old woman, and when Last Born reached the camp he entered the wigwam and said to the old woman, "Grandmother, I am very hungry." Then the old woman said, "Grandson you are away all day long and you come home very hungry." And she gave him food not knowing that he was a stranger but thinking that it was her own grandson. While eating he asked the old woman what she had heard. "Grandson, White Buffalo the most terrible and powerful witch has taken for his slave the sister of the four brothers and is taking her to his own people," said she. Again he started journeying still on the trail.

The following day after nightfall, he came to a very large camp of people [the third camp]. There was a brown wigwam at the edge of the camp circle where in lived an old-old woman and when Last Born reached the camp he entered the wigwam and said to the old woman, "Grandmother, I am very hungry." Then the old woman said, "Grandson you are away all day long and you come home very hungry." And she gave him food not knowing it was [not] her own grandson. While eating he asked the old woman what she had heard. "Grandson, White Buffalo the most terrible and powerful witch has taken for his slave the sister of the four brothers and is taking her to his own people," said she. Again Last Born set out on his journey, still following the trail.

The following day, after nightfall, he came to another large camp of people [the fourth camp]. There was a brown wigwam at the edge of the camp circle where in it lived an old-old woman and when Last Born reached the camp, he entered the wigwam and said to the old woman, "Grandmother, I am very hungry." And the old woman said, "Grandson, you are away all day long and come home very hungry." And she gave him food, not knowing that he was a stranger but thinking that he was her own grandson. While eating he asked her what she had heard. "Grandson, White Buffalo the most terrible and powerful witch has brought home for his slave the sister of the four brothers and his tipi sits near the center of the camp circle," said she.

Then Last Born walked to the tipi to see if he could get to see or talk to his sister. He closed up the "flaps of the draft" and so the slave was told to come out and open the draft-flaps for the smoke from the fireplace could escape. So she came out and Last Born standing behind the tipi told her, "Sister, I have come after you." And she was very anxious to go and stuck a long stick in the ground upright, and putting her robe over it, made it look like her, still standing, trying to regulate the flaps in darkness.

When they reached the outside of the camp circle, Last Born pulled out his bow and arrows and shot one of the arrows towards his home, and the arrow seemed to take them with it. They landed at the third camp circle that Last Born visited when on his pursuit. Again he shot another arrow towards their home and the arrow carried them with it and they landed at the second camp circle that Last Born visited when on his pursuit. Again he shot another arrow and it also carried them with it and they landed at the first camp circle Last Born visited when on his pursuit for his sister. Again he shot another arrow and it also carried them with it and this time they landed home safely.

Third night: Last Born and his brothers built four stone walls around their tipi and in the meantime, White Buffalo missed his slave and rallied on his tribe of men to assist him in getting his slave. While the brothers were watching, they saw a great cloud of dust come over the horizon and they saw a large heard of buffalo coming with White Buffalo in the lead. Then the buffalo herd stopped a little ways from the walls.

White Buffalo told one of his fellow buffalos to go forth and carry a message to the four brothers, demanding that they give up their sister to him. "Or else I shall arise," said he. Last Born was the spokesman for his sister and brothers. "Let White Buffalo arise, I refuse to obey his demand for the return of our sister to him," said he. The messenger then returned with the answer and White Buffalo angered with rage, commanded one of his fighting herd to attack. It tore down the [first] stone wall, many of this herd were injured, by breaking their horns and some died with broken necks and they scattered in all directions.

Then White Buffalo sent another [second] messenger, demanding that they give up their sister to him "or else I shall arise," said he. Last Born being the spokesman for his sister and brothers, "Let White Buffalo arise, I refuse to obey his demand for the return of our sister to him," said he. Then the messenger returned to White Buffalo with Last Born's answer. White Buffalo was very angered and commanded the second fighting herd of buffalos to attack the second stone wall. Then the second herd of buffalos made their attack and tore down the stone wall. Many of this herd were injured by breaking their horns and some died with broken necks and they scattered in all directions.

Then White Buffalo sent another [third] messenger demanding that they give up their sister to him "or else I shall arise," said he. Last Born was the spokesman for his sister and brothers, "Let White Buffalo arise for I will not give up my sister," said he. Then the messenger returned with the answer and White Buffalo being very angry commanded the third herd to attack the third wall and the fighting herd made their attack, and tore down the stone wall, injuring themselves badly and scattered in all directions.

Then White Buffalo with his last and fourth herd was raging in madness and sent again his messenger to the four brothers demanding that they give up their sister to him "or else I shall arise," said he. Last Born was the spokesman for his sister and brothers, "Let White Buffalo arise. I refuse to obey his demand for the return of our sister to him," said he. But the sister being afraid that White Buffalo would kill all of them begged Last Born to just let her go back to White Buffalo. "You alone is afraid of him," said Last Born. Then the messenger returned to White Buffalo with Last Born's answer and White Buffalo, very angry and raging with madness commanded his last and fourth fighting herd of buffalos to attack the remaining stone wall. Then the herd made their attack and tore down the stone wall. Many of this herd were injured by breaking off their horns and some died with broken necks and the rest scattered in all directions.

The sister climbed up the tree and the brothers followed[,] Last Born being the last one to climb. He stayed on the lower limbs where he could watch White Buffalo make his attacks.

Fourth night: White Buffalo commanded the brothers to return to him their sister "or else I shall arise," said he. Last Born said, "arise for I will not give up our sister to you." Then White Buffalo arose and rolled over and over on the ground and rose again and shook the dust off his body and tossing dirt over his back, indicating an act of challenge. He made a running attack. He struck the tree with such a terrific force with his horns that the tree split up to where the sister was sitting. Then the sister begged Last Born to let her go back to White Buffalo. "You alone is afraid of him," said [Last Born]. Upon his second and third attack the tree shook and swayed to and fro. On the fourth attack, Last Born chewed [sic] one end of his arrow and shot White Buffalo in the forehead. As he was making another attack, he dropped to the ground dead and the four brothers and their sister went up to the sky to live. The five group of stars which are known as the four brothers and one sister, can be seen in the sky at nights. Thus the length of the legend has ended.[8]

The first warrior society of the Só'taeo'o created the Pleiades star cluster. They can be seen in the sky next to the White Buffalo constellation, which also happens to be the Taurus constellation of the Greek. A meaningful teaching of the first warrior society is that it promoted an idea that being a warrior was supernatural and truly exceptional, since the first warriors, male and female, earned eternal positions as stars. In the imagination of young, aspiring warriors and society sisters, the pinnacle of warriorism could not have been greater.

THE FIRST WARRIOR SOCIETY OF THE TSÉTSÊHÉSTÂHESE

Storytellers and learners need only the night sky to recall traditional Cheyenne warrior values, which are embedded in the stories of the mano'ëhotóhkeo'o, "star societies." The first warrior society of the Tsétsêhéstâhese was also a lesson in astronomy. Like the four brothers and sister of the Só'taeo'o, seven brothers created the Ursa Major (Big Dipper) star constellation, and their sister became the North Star. Bull Thigh recalled: "There's an old saying. There were seven young men on the earth before the rest. They roamed this country. There was no one else here. They finally disappeared and the saying is they went above and formed the dipper."[9] The story of the creation of the Big Dipper is one of the popular stories of the Cheyennes; it was also featured in the popular film *Dreamkeeper* (2003).[10] The story "Seven Young Men" is similar to "The White Buffalo." Upon the Great Unification, the stories converged as an epic to teach young people the principles of the warrior ethic, emphasizing the use of sacred arrows, thus linking the story to the legacy of the Medicine Arrow Bundle of the Tsétsêhéstâhese. Wolf Chief introduces the story of the first warrior society from a young girl's experience in the story of Otter. The epic of the Seven Young Men immediately follows. The girl is identified as Red Leaf Woman.[11]

Otter

There was a lodge with an old man and an old woman and a young woman. A man watched them named Otter. He wanted the young women as a wife. He made the family a quiver of bow and arrows. He wanted to braid his hair with them as acts of kindness. He made a blanket for the young women and went off with her. They walked off and they stopped. "Shut your eyes," he said to her. Then when she opened them, there was a lodge. They stood at the door. They went in and the old man and old woman sat there. They were the woman's grandparents. The young woman sat on the side of the lodge. The young man took the old man and woman and threw them down a cliff into the water. A[nother] young woman was also trapped there, she told the new girl [Red Leaf Woman] about the bluff and the deep water. "Be careful when he takes you there at night," she said. The young man took the young woman [Red Leaf Woman] out that night. [But] She threw him in the bluff and he fell into the water. From up above the young woman looked down. Then she ran away from that place. She came upon a high hill, where she found a lodge. She walked up to it and met a child playing. There is how she came to meet the seven young men.[12]

There are several versions of the story about the "seven young men." I present a story that combines written accounts, published and unpublished, as well as extant oral traditions.

Seven Young Men

First night: One day, before the Cheyennes had the Medicine Arrows, two orphan brothers decided to leave their village. There was chaos and greed among their people, so they decided to live by themselves. They lived in a conical lodge made of wood, for they had no skins to make a tepee. They were not yet men, but hunted small game and lived well. One morning another young boy came to the camp. He left because he was also an orphan and did not want to live in the main village. The two brothers fed the boy, who was starved and tired, and then they decided that he could stay. The two brothers adopted him, and then there were three. The next day a fourth young boy came to the camp. The three brothers fed their guest what little food they had and adopted him as a brother, and then there were four brothers. On the third day yet another young boy came to the camp, and he was also adopted, making a total of five brothers. On the fourth day, two boys arrived to the camp; one was much younger than the other boys, but the small band of five brothers decided to adopt the two, bringing the total to seven. These seven brothers were once orphans, but they came together and cooperated to make a good living for each other.

Second night: The youngest brother, the last adopted, was simply named Má'kó'se (Youngest) because when he was orphaned he was not yet formally named. He is remembered as a young culture hero.[13] The six older boys went hunting every day while Má'kó'se stayed at home. One day while walking along a pond he saw a beautiful speckled bird standing in the middle. Má'kó'se wanted to kill it and become a true hunter. He shot at it but missed, but the animal did not move. He shot several times until his arrows were depleted. He ran back to camp and retrieved his brothers' arrows and returned to the pond where the bird remained. He depleted all of his brothers' arrows and returned home empty-handed.

His older brothers made more arrows and also made a sacred set. They told him not to take any from the sacred set. The next day, Má'kó'se returned to the pond at the same time of day as before. Once again he saw the bird standing in the middle but could not hit the bird. Once again he depleted his arrows, returned home to retrieve his brothers' arrows, and depleted them. His older brother remade arrows once again. For two more days Má'kó'se repeated his mistakes and could not kill the bird. Finally, on the fourth and final day, he decided to use one of the sacred arrows. He returned to the pond and was able to hit the bird. The arrow stuck into the side of the bird, wounding it, but it flew away. Má'kó'se followed the wounded bird over four mountains. He met an old woman who was living alone in a lodge. "I am hungry, Grandmother," said Má'kó'se, "do you have any food?"

"I have been waiting for you," said the old woman. "Come in and eat." She began to tell Má'kó'se a story about a magical bird that was colored like the sunset, named Hoxtaes. "He lives toward the sunrise but travels over four mountains every day to drink from the clear waters of a pond. One day," said the old woman, "a great hunter shot him with a sacred arrow. Hoxtaes flew away to see his friend named Nhaen hetane (Otter Man), who was a medicine man and knew how to heal wounds."

"I am that great hunter," said Má'kó'se. "That sacred arrow belongs to my brothers and I must retrieve it. Can you tell me where Nhaen hetane lives?" The old woman told the boy where to go and find the lodge of Nhaen hetane. Má'kó'se arrived and watched the medicine man and waited until he left. When he had his chance, the young boy entered the lodge and killed the bird, found the sacred arrow, and departed for home. The older brothers were saddened and believed that Má'kó'se had been killed. But when the young boy returned, he was cheerful and brought happiness to his brothers. Má'kó'se told of his adventure and showed them the colorful bird and the sacred arrow.

The next sections of the story highlight the sacredness of the warrior society culture, emphasizing that the members of a society have the potential to be remembered as heroic into eternity. The story also renames the society upon their departure as "Quillwork Girl and her Seven Star Brothers."[14]

Third night: One day a young woman came to the camp of the Seven Young Men, while the six older brothers were out hunting. Má'kó'se welcomed the young woman, "You are the sister that I have been wanting and you have come to help us." The young woman's name was Mahoemskot and she traveled with a dog and travois. She had a large buckskin bag of clothing for the seven boys: shirts, leggings, moccasins, and gauntlets. She made these items and decorated them with beautiful porcupine quillwork. Each was unique in color and design, but all were works of beauty that none of the Cheyennes had ever seen before. When the six older boys returned, one of the older boys wanted to marry her, but the other boys protested, "You cannot marry her, she is our sister." [According to Cheyenne custom, adopted siblings cannot marry because it is in violation of the incest law.] They all welcomed their new sister and dressed in their new clothes, and from then on she was part of the family.

Mahoemskot cooked for the boys, who only knew how to prepare their meals by roasting it over the fire. She knew a lot about animals, how to prepare hides and how to cook certain parts for different meals and purposes, like making pemmican and dried meat, which they ate for longer hunts. As the boys hunted more animals, the healthier the boys ate. Mahoemskot was also able to create more beautiful clothes and other material wealth. Soon the Seven Young

Men were living in a great tepee that was decorated with beautiful ornaments. No longer were they poor, for they dressed as great warriors, not as orphans.

Fourth night: One day when Mahoemskot and Má'kó'se were home alone, a buffalo visited them. "The chief of the Buffalo Nation wants your sister to live with him," said the buffalo. Má'kó'se told the animal to leave their camp. The next day another buffalo arrived asserting the same demands, and once again Má'kó'se denied the animal. A buffalo returned and was denied on a third day. On the fourth day, the entire Buffalo Nation arrived to the camp with the chief. Some traditional Cheyennes believe that the chief wanted to marry Mahoemskot, but others believe that he wanted to kill the girl for helping the warriors become great hunters and that the buffalo were angry that the humans were going to become prosperous.

The seven brothers were devoted to protecting their sister. "We will die before anything happens to you," one of them proclaimed. The Buffalo Nation charged and destroyed their beautiful lodge, but Mahoemskot and her brothers climbed a tree to avoid the destruction. From the tree the boys shot at the buffalo killing as many as they could. Eventually they depleted all of their arrows. Má'kó'se, however, was able to save the sacred arrows and yelled to his brothers, "I can kill the chief buffalo with these."

One of the eldest brothers protested, "No, Má'kó'se! Shoot the top of the tree." When Má'kó'se shot the highest part of the tree, it began to grow taller and the young people climbed higher. The chief buffalo became angry and started charging and ramming the tree. Má'kó'se kept shooting the treetop and the tree kept growing and the young people kept climbing. Soon they could see that the chief buffalo had killed himself trying to knock the tree down. When Má'kó'se used up all of his arrows, his brothers and sister had reached the land above the clouds.

"What can we do now?" said Mahoemskot. "We are stuck up here in the sky."

"Don't grieve, sister," said Má'kó'se. "I will turn all of us into stars. We will be remembered forever." These seven brothers became the star constellation called "The Seven Young Men," known as the Big Dipper, and Mahoemskot became the North Star, which never moves in the night sky. They are the first warrior society of the Tsétsêhéstâhese, a model for others to follow in principle and in practice.

SWEET MEDICINE OF THE TSÉTSÊHÉSTÂHESE

The best-known Cheyenne epic is that of the Tsétsêhéstaestse prophet Motsé'eóeve (Sweet Medicine), who is credited with establishing the first four warrior societies and the Nótâxeo'o system, among numerous other feats and accomplishments.[15] Motsé'eóeve was also known as Netsevôhe'so (Eagle Nest) and Arrow Boy before he matured into a man.[16] Netsevôhe'so was also the name of an older prophet, and these two personalities became synonymous over time. The legacy of the culture hero Motsé'eóeve provides the most extensive teachings of citizenship and moral character emphasizing the ideal Cheyenne character and values. The teachings of the supernatural feats of heroes encouraged children to believe that they could also do great things, empowering them mentally and spiritually. In one story Motsé'eóeve fed his starving people when he was still a young boy by playing a spear and wheel game, much similar to the feat of Cherry Eater.[17] The story teaches the value of selflessness and service, which is why storytellers kept it throughout the years and adapted it to become part of the legacy of Motsé'eóeve.

In a second story, the young prophet Motsé'eóeve was able to acquire mystical powers of teleportation with the help of a sacred bow and arrows adorned with feathers from an extinct exotic bird. This story was also an adaptation to the feats of Má'kó'se, who was also remembered as a young prophet in his time. A third story tells of how Motsé'eóeve arrived at a ceremonial dance where the great magicians were performing and showing their powers to an audience. While the previous stories were adaptations, the third story is completely original. While at the dance, young Motsé'eóeve was able to sever his own head and then return to life after his grandmother placed a buffalo robe over his body.

The three stories educated children to believe in the power and sacredness of heroes from their nation, and groomed them to become part of the Cheyenne legacy.[18] When a child became an adult, the ideal principles of citizenship and warrior ways became the standard of living. Motsé'eóeve is credited with bringing change to the Cheyennes, who were living under the tyranny and corruption of dictators and their followers. Motsé'eóeve brought change in the form of new laws, ceremonies, and ways of living. In the following pages I present several narratives of the prophet Sweet Medicine. Old She Bear was sixty-eight when he told his story in 1910; his account includes horses, which is a minor flaw in his narrative of a prophet who lived before the arrival of horses.

Sweet Medicine, Part I, by Old She Bear

When the Indians first came to live, they were poor and had nothing to eat. Food was scarce. Matsīyōv gave medicine so they could live long. A woman threw her baby in the river where there were logs, twigs, and brushes.

One old woman who was so old that she had to use a cane went to gather wood. She pulled the twigs out one by one and found the baby still alive, wrapped up. (Interrupted by a prayer). The woman picked up the baby and fixed him up good. She wanted to have him for her benefit, so he could support her. Everyday the baby grew. In ten days, it could walk and it helped the old woman. That boy took care of her two horses. Every morning he would go after them. The Indians asked the old woman where she got that boy. The boy told the old woman that he would take pity on the people. The people did not know where that boy came from. An old man told everybody, "Where does that boy come from?" They still did not know. The woman who threw her baby away didn't show up.[19]

Sweet Medicine, Part I, by Bull Thigh

After the Cheyennes originated at the Black Hills, there was a big camp. On the outskirts was a small grass tipi. In it there was an old woman. She was just about starving. She went to dig, searching for roots to eat. While out doing this, she found a child. She grabbed him and picked him up. The child could barely see. He had a small little robe of a calf hide. She took him home. She got him in her lodge. After the child was warmed up she combed him and washed his face. "Grand child," she said to him, "I am about to starve and the people are about to starve." The boy was seated. He made a quiet little small noise. He looked towards the sky. There was a bunch of prairie birds [that] flew into the lodge right before the old woman. They were all dead. The old woman peeled the wings off and put the feathers into her parfleche. She cooked them for herself and for him.[20]

The abandonment of infant Sweet Medicine remains a mystery, but some storytellers speculate that a virgin girl became pregnant and was shunned by her people.

After being pregnant for four years, some of the men believed that [the girl] and the baby were cursed, so she gave up the baby and disappeared. When the old woman found him, he was found in a raft of driftwood that looked like the nest of a great eagle, which is why they called him Netsevôhe'so (Eagle's Nest). This was Motsé'eóeve (Sweet Medicine). His grandmother raised him, and together the two always camped at the edge of the village to avoid any trouble from others. They were very poor and yet the young Motsé'eóeve remained modest and cheerful. Tyrants and groups of men ruled the band.

One day the chief proclaimed that he wanted a white buffalo hide and offered his daughter's hand in marriage for anyone who brought him a white buffalo robe.[21] The young Motsé'eóeve went hunting one day and happened to kill a calf with a white buffalo. He shot it and killed it. This led to the dispute with the old man. [Traditional Cheyennes assert that Motsé'eóeve did not kill the man and that the story was changed during the assimilation and Christianization of Cheyennes during the reservation era to discredit the prophet.[22]] Nonetheless, the people in the village found out about the incident and accused Sweet Medicine of murder. The group of men who gathered "called themselves soldiers or military," but they were bullies and cruel men who forced the people to follow their orders.[23]

There are numerous versions of the Sweet Medicine epic, but the teachings of the stories emphasize the same core principles. Like the previous stories that tell of the Cheyenne life before the Nótâxeo'o and the Véhoo'o, the smaller and unorganized bands were subject to the rule of tyrants and gangs of men. Before the arrival of the Nótâxeo'o, the small Cheyenne bands were dysfunctional and in need of much reform. This change began when the prophet Sweet Medicine arrived and brought a new way of thinking that would revolutionize the Cheyenne cultural way of living.

CHAPTER 9

The Origins of the Nótâxeo'o

THE SANCTITY of the Nótâxeo'o system depended heavily on the health and knowledge of the Sweet Medicine tradition that reinforced traditional teachings of manhood and citizenship. The integrity of society headmen also sustained the system, which is why the oral tradition was significant to the warrior ethic. The Nótâxeo'o relied deeply on preserving the sanctity of the Cheyenne principles of balance and brotherhood. Although each warrior society maintained autonomy, held its own ceremonies, and had its own origin stories, each group was part of the Unified Cheyenne Nation. The Nótâxeo'o were guilds of men who lived under strict codes of honor and service.

Some traditional Cheyennes believe that Motsé'eóeve created the original societies after the Great Unification, but it is more likely that he created them earlier. Although there are varying accounts of when and which societies were created first, the stories are similar in that they all emphasize traditional laws, ceremonies, and the teachings of the young prophet. The complex system allowed the nation to thrive for hundreds of years in balance, since it was designed so that not one warrior society was above another as each shared authority and responsibility under the principles of sacred sovereignty.

Most stories include the Véhoo'o as an original society, which probably resulted after the Great Unification and is evidence of the convergence of the two oral traditions. While the origin of the Véhoo'o is traced directly to the Só'taeo'o, the origin of the Nótâxeo'o is traced directly to the Tsétsêhéstâhese, long before the Great Unification. The creation of the Nótâxeo'o is also remembered in the Cheyenne national history as an event resulting from the turmoil of Lime just before the unification, further evidence of the sacred history convergence. Bull Thigh recalled the story of "White Clay," who is the same person as Lime in previous stories.[1] Bull Thigh explains how and why the Tsétsêhéstâhese established the Nótâxeo'o in the first place. Bull

PART III | NÓTÁXEO'O: THE WARRIORS

Thigh also provides the Tsétsêhéstâhese version of the origin of the Sun Dance and states that some warrior societies were of Só'taeo'o origin:

> The Sutaiu had only one outfit, no divisions like Cheyennes. Now where Pipestone is, on the Missouri River is where the Sutaio came from. They met the Cheyennes at the Missouri River. The Sutaio didn't have the Sun Dance then. It was at the Black Hills where the Cheyennes and Sutaio got up the dance together. Red Hoofs, Dog Soldiers, Elk Band, Fox Soldiers all came from the Sutaio. White [Clay] was the Sutaio leader. At the time of meeting the Cheyennes White [Clay] had killed a woman and was exiled. After a while he returned to get revenge by killing off Cheyennes. That's why they formed war parties. During the fight they all fell, but rose, and surrendered to each other. They proclaimed peace and went to the Black Hills.²

Yellow Nose drawing of ceremonial figures with full body paint and carrying decorated bow, shield, and pipe, ca. 1889, Yellow Nose, 1848–1910. National Anthropological Archives, Smithsonian Museum Support Center, Suitland, Maryland (NAA INV 08711300, OPPS NEG 57,227-A, OPPS NEG 57,219-A, NAA MS 166032).

THE ORIGINAL NÓTÁXEO'O

Different informants and investigators, each with slight and subtle differences, recorded the epic of the creation of the Nótâxeo'o in numerous publications.³ There is not a single story that supersedes others. Nonetheless, I present one narrative. Nearly every story is set in a time "before the Cheyennes had the Medicine Arrows," when the people were living through a volatile era and were ruled by dictators who were supported by bands of cruel men. I present a lesser-known origin story of the Nótâxeo'o.

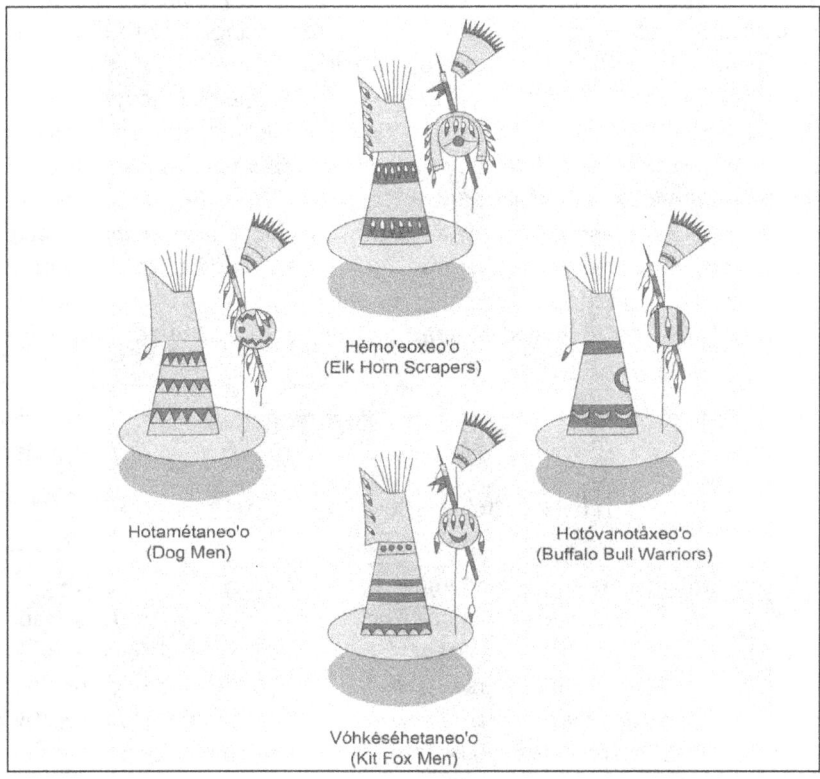

The balance of power and shared responsibility among the four original Nótâxeo'o.

Sweet Medicine, Part I, by Wolf Chief

In due time when the people were starving, a herd of buffalos came galloping towards the clan. In the midst of the buffalos there was a small calf with huge horns on his head. He dropped out of the bunch and went directly towards this buffalo-child. When near them, he was killed at the outskirts of the camp. There was a boy with a little buffalo robe walking to where the buffalo calf had been killed. There were two very old people. They were dressing the calf. The boy sent a man to ask them if they could give up that little buffalo hide to him so he could have it for his robe. The old people would not give up the hide to him. They said it had to be torn up and used in their own tricks. The man came back and reported to the boy that wanted the hide. He asked him what they said about the hide. He said: "They would not give it to you. You are a boy and not respected enough to have the hide." The boy got up angry. He held his bow and arrow and made a motion at the old people who were dressing the calf. At once they were both dead. When they dropped dead, people thought at once that it was this boy who killed them by a trick. The chief of the clan called a war society to come out and kill the boy, but before he was killed, he was inside of the lodge with a bag full of water right close to the fire. The war society surrounded the lodge, and were ready to kill the boy. Just as soon as they made a charge at the lodge, he tipped over the bag into the fire, and a vapor rose from the fire and went out of the smoke hole and disappeared from inside the lodge. The society tore down the lodge, looking for the boy. He had gone away. He was gone many years.[4]

Sweet Medicine, Part I, by White Eagle

When the Indians first started in life, they were crazy. They were living on the prairie. They were very poor. They used flint for knives. They made bows and arrows and wore animal skins for clothing. They used dogs for packing as horses. There were no horses then. The women carried shields on their backs. The women carried lances. They were traveling from place to place. The Indians were living at the Black Hills. They were on the war path with the Assiniboines. The Cheyennes got horses from the Pawnees, they were the first Indians to have horses. They were living in Nebraska.

People didn't know Matsīyōv was living. Once he took up a club and killed a [man]. The different bands gathered. He entered a tipi in the middle where an old woman was living. They surrounded him to kill him. A soup was on the fire. He poured it on the fire. All the smoke went through the hole of the top of the tipi. He went up with the smoke. They looked for him in the tipi, but could not find him. They found him sleeping under a tree. The fellow who found him came back and reported it. After they surrounded him, they saw a coyote running across over the hill. All the Indians tried to find Matsīyōv. They saw him walking towards the brushes. He had turned into a man again. All the Indians surrounded that place. He was out of sight when they walked for him. They saw him coming up with a lance in another direction. He had a whistle in his mouth. He went around zig-zag. He went out of sight.

They didn't notice that once in a while he came back to his own home. While they were camping quite a ways they saw him on a hill sitting down. They all ran after him. They surrounded the place. When he saw them coming he jumped down the bank. They looked for him but could not find him anywhere. They saw a coyote running in another direction. After he had become a coyote a number of times, they could not find him any more. They kept on traveling, looking for him for about four years. They were nearly starved. They walked place to place trying to find something to eat but could find nothing. They found mushrooms and ate them. They cooked hides for days and ate them.[5]

Sweet Medicine, Part I, by White Buffalo

When Sweet Medicine (Matsīyōv) was six [years old], he put a brush on his head. They began dancing. That's the beginning of the Foolish Dance. At eight [years] he introduced a center-pole; this is the introduction of the Willow Dance. This was after the Sutaio and Cheyenne had joined. Matsīyōv was found when all the men had gone on a buffalo hunt. He was with the young men. He killed a bull calf, two years old. He dressed the buffalo, skinned the hide, so he could have it for his robe. An old man came to him and asked him, "I will have that buffalo for my robe."

"No, I'm going to make use of it. I shall use [it] so that my people shall know here after what is going to happen. I'm going to use it for a great [purpose]." But still this old man [asked] him for it four times. Each time he insisted that he could not have [it]. He [Sweet Medicine] cut off the hoof of the buffalo. When the old man went to get the skin, Matsīyōv hit [him] on top of the head. He took the hide home. The old man was missed. Everybody seemed to know Matsīyōv had killed the old man. It was found [true].

All the war societies went to kill him. Every time they tried to catch him he disappeared. He turned into a coyote, a fly: nobody could catch him. The first time they tried, they surrounded the lodge, a coyote ran out. They went, each, to a high bluff; they saw him at the edge of one. They began to surround him. As soon as they were close to him he turned into a deer and got away. Then he was seen again. They surrounded the place again. When they were nearly on the point of killing him, he turned into an owl and flew away. The next time he turned into a blue bird. Then they gave up.

The fifth time he was coming up a hill. He was carrying a cane in his arm. He was walking. He was walking backward and forward. All the people looked to see him. He had a cane with feathers on it. This was for Those With the Lance. The second time he came out he had a bow and arrow with feathers at the ends of the bow, and arrows with stone heads. There were four arrows. The third time he came out he had a stick like a bow but curved at one end, signifying protection for a certain war society (the Contrary Society). The fourth time he had a bow and arrow for the Foxes. The fifth time he had the skin of a buffalo head with horns on and a shield. All the people looked on with surprise. They expected some great event was going to happen. This [was] for [the] Bow Society.

The sixth time he had feathers stuck into his head in all direction and he had a rattle; he was painted all black. That signified the Dog Society. [The] seventh time he came back with a pipe. This was for the Chiefs. He wanted to make peace. Then he disappeared for four years.[6]

In Bull Thigh's version, he identifies Sweet Medicine as "Smallest," the culture hero also known as Má'kó'se, Youngest, and Last Born of the United Cheyenne national history. The below story, however, is of the prophet Sweet Medicine.

Sweet Medicine, Part II, by Bull Thigh

Smallest wanted to get a small buffalo robe. He killed one himself. He skinned it very nicely. While working at it he was transformed to a very ugly person. An old man came to him and told him, "Say I'm going to have that hide." Smallest told him, "I'm going to have my robe for one purpose. I will not let it go." The old man insisted and grabbed Smallest and threw him into the snow. Smallest got up and picked one of the front legs, while the old man was skinning the hide, struck his head and killed him. While he was doing this, everyone looked on.

All the people were alarmed and wanted to kill Smallest. They made a charge at him. When near to him, he went down in a hollow of the hill. Just as he crossed, the people saw him. He turned into a man with a buffalo head; he also had a shield. That was the origin of the Bull Society. He went down a small hill again. They almost overtook him. He changed into a man with feathers on his head; he had a snake in his hand. That's the origin of the Dog Society. They almost overtook him. He went down the hill. When they saw him, he was painted all black, one arm carried the skin of a fox; he had a half-moon on his chest. That's the origin of the Fox Society. They almost caught him. He went just across the hill. He was transformed into another person carrying a lance with one end turned down; in the other hand he carried a snake. That's the origin of the Lances. He was almost caught. He went down the hill just across. He changed into a man with a lance and a big arrow tied on his forehead. That's the origin of the Contrary Society. They nearly overtook him. He went down another hill. When just across he was transformed into a person with a robe of buffalo, carrying a pipe. This is the origin of the Chief Society.

As they almost overtook him, they looked at him, he was raised up from the ground. They almost touched him. They all stopped. He went higher and higher in the air. He disappeared. They could not get him. They went back to their homes. They gave up. After he had disappeared for three days in the air, his wife called two girls and they sang for him. At the edge of a very high bluff, their legs hung down. They were singing the finest songs. They were beautiful to hear. As they sang they called him to come in due time again. While singing for him, they were scared, he appeared just at their backs. And that was the way he came back.[7]

Throughout the history of the Cheyenne Nation, new societies were established and incorporated into the existing warrior society system. "Sweet Medicine's teachings caused or influenced honest men, through visions or dreams, to organize new warrior societies."[8] All of the Nótâxeo'o, old and new, followed the legacy of Motsé'eóeve. Stands In Timber provides in-depth details of the creation of the Crazy Dogs and the Swift Fox, highlighting the roles of Motsé'eóeve and, in later times, the Arrow Keeper, who became the authority in approving or disapproving the creation of new warrior societies.[9] Wolf Chief states that the Bowstrings and Crazy Dogs originated after unification. Other societies were ceremonial and social, such as the Onéhanotâxeo'o (War Dancers), which, according to Wolf Chief, came from the Lakota during the 1800s.[10] They performed the Omaha Dance, which was originally a peace ceremony.[11]

White Buffalo (Northern Cheyenne) described the first reappearance of Sweet Medicine as that of the Hohnóhkao'o (Contraries): "He had a lance and an arrow on his head; he was painted red with white spots all over; green spots on his forehead; a whistle in his mouth; two eagle feathers were tied tight to each leg. This meant the thunder can't strike them hereafter."[12] The Contraries were a sacred society: "The Contraries are afraid of thunder and put up dances to get rid of the thoughts and feelings of being scared. It is a medicine performance."[13] They were part of the Crazy Lodge Ceremony.

The unwritten constitution allowed for new societies to integrate into the existing system of the Nótâxeo'o, not only politically, but also culturally, which is evident in the oral tradition. There are differing accounts of which societies were created first and which were created by Motsé'eóeve, but all accounts affirm the same ideas and teachings. Two societies that were incorporated were the Hotamémâsêhao'o (Crazy Dogs) and the Héma'tanónêheo'o (Bow String Men).

PART III | NÓTÂXEO'O: THE WARRIORS

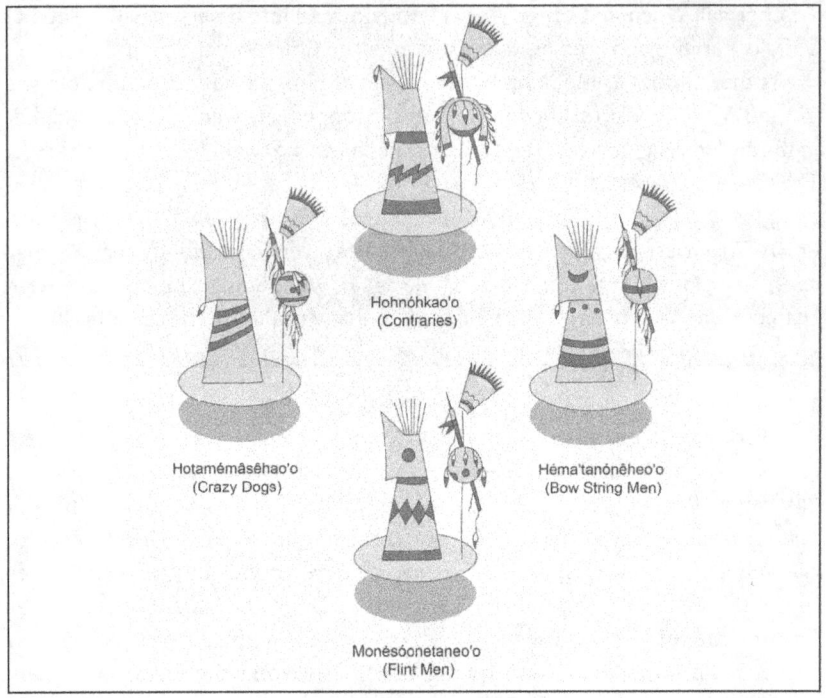

The balance of power and shared responsibility among the four merged Nótâxeo'o.

HOTAMÉMÂSÊHAO'O (CRAZY DOGS)

The Hotamémâsêhao'o have a unique origin story, although sometimes they are incorporated into the Sweet Medicine oral tradition. Old She Bear described the paraphernalia worn by Sweet Medicine in the converged story: he had a "rattle with a lance with many feathers, the lance was covered with rabbit skins."[14] Somers (Southern Cheyenne) told the origin story in 1910, which is fragmented with structural errors. Somers's account may differ from those of other bands, especially the northern bands.

Story of the Great Foolish Dog Society

An Indian was lost amongst the wild beasts of the forests. In due time, before he was found out, he was with the animals on the plains of the country. The people were very much afraid of being lost and never had any idea to where he had been this time. One day many years after, there was a great buffalo hunt by the tribe of Indians in the southern part of this country. Before there was no white man who scared the buffaloes off. While charging the buffalos on the prairie, they saw a human being with the wolves: where the buffalos had been killed in the old places. Soon they saw him. He tried to get away with the beasts. He could have, but the people at once wanted to catch him. Who was it? He was so wild as anybody could not catch him. Still the people would not give up and made up their minds to be sure to get him, "even if it takes a year to get him." So the people went on horseback and followed him up with their ropes, to lasso him and tie him up, if they could catch him. So for the next four days, he was not caught, but he was in the wolves' den with them. When the people came to his den, they saw human footmarks in this den. This was the first time they almost caught him, but the same time he got away with the wolves of that night, by clawing out through some other hole, while they were sleeping that night. Early in the morning there was a great rejoicing of wolves by looking up towards Heaven. By saying that the king of the forest was to be returned to his people, before long, and taught his people what to do here after starting the great foolish dance for the Cheyenne Indians. So in due time he was caught by the band of horsemen on the plains of central parts of this country, and he was taken back to the tribe he departed. He began his time to teach his people how they must hereafter dance as a dog society, which will never die out for them, and to what great deeds that should happen to them, as to make the people rejoice and be brave in time of danger.[15]

HÉMA'TANÓNÊHEO'O (BOW STRING MEN)

In the converged oral tradition, the origin of the Héma'tanónêheo'o (Bow String Men) society often takes the place of the Hotóvanotâxeo'o (Buffalo Bull Warriors), which had lost members and eventually decreased during the time of the horse. According to the adapted origin story, the men chased Motsé'eóeve, who transformed into a wolf to evade prosecution. When they came upon the young Motsé'eóeve, like the men before, one man took this style of dress and songs back to the people, thus creating a new society. The Bow String Men warriors dressed a certain way, as Petter described: "The members were painted red and carried a kind of bow spear similar to the two special ones carried by the Hemoeoxessô [Headed-Lances], only painted red instead of yellow. This society seems to have gathered the more earnest, thoughtful men of the tribe who had a deep sense for their handiwork of the Creator in the nature."[16]

The society origin story of the Héma'tanónêheo'o is quite different and took place after Motsé'eóeve established the four original societies.

A prophet named Mestaa'êhetane (Owl Man) was lost in a cold winter storm of freezing rain.[17] He kept warm with a buffalo robe and was able to find shelter. His horse froze to death but he continued toward the west, following the directions of a spirit guide. As he walked, he heard people drumming and singing in a distance. He followed the music to a creek where a large teepee stood. His clothes were frozen stiff and he was exhausted nearly dying. He managed to enter a large lodge where he passed out immediately. He awoke alone but could hear people outside of the lodge talking.

Mestaa'êhetane could easily understand the speech and expected his own people to be outside. When he opened the door he saw wolves talking and quickly closed the door. The wolves were trying to determine whether to eat him or not. The animals spotted him when he peeked out, so they entered into the lodge. Mestaa'êhetane spoke plainly: "I heard you wanted to eat me. If you wish to do so, please allow me to return to health before you do so." Once the animals knew that he could speak their language, they changed into humans.

Mestaa'êhetane was amazed as each one became human before his eyes. The wolves became men and women whose bodies were painted yellow and their limbs red. They all wore thick, fine wolf furs that had been cut as capes so the heads draped in front upon their chests and the tails hung down their backs. The head chief of these wolf people talked to Mestaa'êhetane and told him how to conduct ceremonies. The chief also told Mestaa'êhetane how to harness the power of wolves, to work together in hunting and in battle. That night the wolf people had a feast and celebration in honor of Mestaa'êhetane. For the next four days the animals held ceremonies and danced using spears, animal pelts, and red pipes. The next day four wolf-men took Mestaa'êhetane to the Cheyenne village, but before they reached their destination, the four men changed back into wolves and ran away.

Mestaa'êhetane came back to his people and told of how he survived the winter storm. He erected a lodge and conducted the same ceremony that he witnessed among the wolf people. He selected new members to join a new warrior guild and this is how the Héma'tanónêheo'o (Bow String Men) came into existence; they are also known as Ho'nehenótâxeo'o, Wolf Soldiers.

THE ORIGINS OF THE NÓTÂXEO'O

The Ho'nehenótâxeo'o ceremony was incorporated into the Cheyenne cycle of rituals as the Wolf Pup or Wolf Ceremony, but it was eventually merged into the Medicine Lodge and Crazy Dance, disappearing completely as a separate practice.[18] The Wolf Soldiers also held social dances with the Elks, as they were closely associated groups.

Convergence across band histories led to the differing origin stories of the Nótâxeo'o, and this led to inconsistencies as to which societies were the first. One certainty is that there were four and others followed. Sweet Medicine's role in establishing the original warrior guilds is paramount, but the establishment of the Crazy Dogs and Bow Strings also proves that the Cheyenne system of governance was highly adaptable, as long as the adaptations fit within the existing traditions and culture. In subsequent years, other societies were added to Sweet Medicine's system. Most warrior societies continue to function in the Northern Cheyenne and Southern Cheyenne reservations today.

PART III | NÓTÂXEO'O: THE WARRIORS

Cheyenne and Arapaho Social Dance, 1903. National Anthropological Archives, Smithsonian Museum Support Center, Suitland, Maryland. George Amos Dorsey, Willis G. Tilton, collector (OPPS NEG T9769).

CHAPTER 10

Traditions and Customs of the Nótáxeo'o

Each warrior society developed its own body of oral traditions, customs, and unwritten constitutions that detailed its governing structure. As organizations, these warrior guilds also functioned as clubs where members could conduct social dances, weddings, and feasts as a united, independent organization. The Nótáxeo'o were easily incorporated into the unwritten constitution of the United Cheyenne Nation after the Great Unification. Upon unification, the Véhoo'o were also written into the origin story as a fifth original warrior society, which may explain some inconsistencies in written accounts.

As oral tradition reveals, four men pursued Sweet Medicine and they were the toughest men and the leaders of the group. The grandmother invited them in and as soon as they sat down, Sweet Medicine kicked the boiling water into the fire pit, and the men quickly stumbled out of the lodge as the hot steam filled the inside. From outside they watched the steam exit through the smoke hole and one noticed a golden eagle plume floating out. It fluttered farther away and they watched it in wonder. It continued onto a treeless hillside where Motsé'eóeve was standing, and he caught the plume with one hand and placed it in his hair. This began the chase.

As each man saw Sweet Medicine, they returned to their village, until Motsé'eóeve vanished and the final man gave up. The men returned to their village with the memories of his amazing feats, and these strongest and most pompous men changed their way of thinking and each founded the first warrior guilds of the Cheyenne Nation. While Motsé'eóeve was away, each man organized younger men of the nation to initiate a new era among the people. Men changed their ways and held ceremonies and dances to formally honor and praise individuals who accomplished feats of manhood. They also honored and acknowledged women for embodying Cheyenne virtues of womanhood. The origin story reveals two lessons for two generations of men: the older should not be greedy and jealous of younger men, and the younger should control their tempers. Both teachings reaffirm Cheyenne virtues of good conduct and honorable citizenship. The origin of the Nótâxeo'o reveals not only the material culture of each group, but also elements to their war customs, ceremonial practices, and their emblem or representative animals.[1]

SOCIETY DANCES AND CEREMONIES

Each of the warrior societies customarily conducted their own ceremonies, had different songs, and practiced their own "ways of dancing."[2] Society autonomy promoted unity by dress and dance style, with members wearing their finest society attire and colors.[3] Individual members, who were proven brave and successful in battle, distinguished themselves by wearing war bonnets with long trails of eagle feathers that were decorated in diverse manners; some wore buckskin shirts decorated with eagle feathers and human hair. Each warrior society had "four sacred and four war songs, besides many other songs."[4] War dances were of particular significance as each club showcased their beauty, shared stories, honored older members, and gave generously. Each dance was an exhibition of traditional Cheyenne values and was always done in the large camp circles, but sometimes in smaller gatherings. At large dances, there could have been as many as a thousand warriors and nearly one hundred men who held leadership positions as society chiefs or Council chiefs.[5] Each society developed its own dances, but each continued to honor the founders of the societies—the men who pursued Sweet Medicine—as well as the prophet himself.[6] They did this by replicating the same weapons, regalia, songs, and dances found in the origin story of the Nótâxeo'o. Wolf Chief, Wrapped Hair, Coyote, White Buffalo, and Petter provided the following descriptions of the societies and their regalia.

HOTAMÉTANEO'O (THE DOG MEN) DANCES

On the first chase of the origin story, Motsé'eóeve changed into a dog and then later reappeared dressed as a Dog Soldier: "Painted black. All kinds of feathers on his head; feathers on his breast; feathers on his back dragging on the ground."[7] The first man said, "I like the way he looks, I think I will take his style of dress and learn his songs." This man was the founding member of the Hotamétaneo'o, the Dog Men.[8] Their regalia, weapons, paraphernalia, and songs were representative of Sweet Medicine. Petter described them:

The society or organization used to be the controlling power of the tribe and had by far the largest number of members. Four of its bravest men wear peculiar pieces of skin streamers, two of which are about 1 foot wide and 7–8 feet long, hanging from the left shoulder and trailing behind them. They are adorned with quillwork and eagle feathers. These pieces are worn by the two most daring of the four braves. They have also their leggings fixed up with human hair. The other two streamers are narrower. These four braves are expected to protect their comrades. After their deaths others succeed them. All the Dogmen wear a war bonnet, but different from the common kind. Each member has also a peculiar rattle resembling a snake, painted red and having dew-claws of deer tied to its whole length. For dancing a belt is worn which is made of four skunk skins, the heads being left whole, two in front and two behind. They dance in forward stooping position.[9]

Wolf Chief (Northern Cheyenne) witnessed the dances of the Hotamétaneo'o:

They have a feather headgear. They used red paint on their bodies and two special ones use black paint during dances. They had a box of bear claws to form a rattle. When they were to dance, they dress that way. The dance must commence before an old man gets up and dances and tells of his scouting trips, how many scalps he's taken, etc. The dance then can commence. When the dance is to finish, this same fellow will get up, make another speech, and then the dance is over. They only dance in the daytime so everybody can see them. This is not a medicine or sacred performance. They only dance when they are happy, over a victory or something. They sit in a circle but dance mixed up. The two black-painted ones represent black horses when they dance. Four officers in this dance; the two representing the black horses are supposed to keep order in the dance. No women are allowed in the dance except if members ask their wives to come in and sing. This is the only society that won't let women dance.[10]

Wrapped Hair (Só'taeo'o), who was seventy-four years old at the time he recounted the events, also witnessed the traditional dance customs of the Hotamétaneo'o.

They had a headdress of bird feathers with a row of eagle tail feathers in a row in the center. They had a rattle box made up of buffalo horn matter found above their feet, tied on a stick, wrapped in buckskin and beaded in different places. They had a tanned hide 7 feet long, 6 inches or so wide, with a slit, beaded in different places. It passed over the head and under the arm. Women are not allowed to join. They dance in the daytime, going around the camp circle. They are supposed to stop four times in circle. They were given presents while they danced. They moved in single file.[11]

The Dog Men danced with half of the Elk Soldiers, since they were close and associated together. This eventually led to a split in the Elk Society and the creation of a new Elk Society. The split was not done out of resentment, but as part of the adaptive nature of Cheyenne institutions.

VÓHKÈSÉHETANEO'O (KIT FOX MEN) DANCES

On the second chase in the story, Motsé'eóeve changed into a fox and then later reappeared dressed as a Kit Fox Soldier: "Painted black down his knees, from there down red; from elbows through hands red. He had a lance with a bowstring."[12] This was the dress for the Foxes. In the story, the second man said, "I like the way he looks. I will imitate his dress and learn his songs." This man was the founding member of the Vóhkèséhetaneo'o, the Kit Fox Men. Petter described this society:

> This society has four maidens as honorary members. These girls are to have a good name, be chaste, modest and from good families. They are called sisters by the men and are not married to any one of them. The emblem is an elk antler fashioned like a snake. Two of the bravest members carry each a spear in the form of a shepherd's crook, whose one end is provided with a spearhead. Otter skins are wrapped around it. The other men have straight spears and each carries a rattle made out of a stick of wood to which dewclaws of deer are fastened. In dancing they jump up and down.[13]

Wolf Chief witnessed their traditional dance, which did not take place until they put up a tent or dance lodge:

> They have to put up a tent when they want to dance. After the male members are in, they call in four women. They paint all over the body in different colors. They have no headdress. They dance by a drum and have a big rattle-box in their hand as they dance. It can't commence until an old man gets up and makes a speech. They also use a bow and arrow, a long spear with different kinds of bird feathers. If a dog enters, they all string up their bows and shoot at it. They give presents away to any of the visitors they might select. When they are through dancing the old man gets up, makes a speech, and the dance breaks up.

The four women are supposed to be unmarried; supposed to be decent girls and belong to a popular family; applies to Elk Society. There [are] supposed to be six headmen, two sit on each side of the door, the others are seated inside. When they give presents they give to those that are thought to be in need. At a certain time these four girls dance alone. At this time they will gather a meal for these girls.[14]

Coyote (Northern Cheyenne) described his participation in a Kit Fox Society Dance:

One day when all the Cheyennes were camped in circle, this is usually the case when something out of ordinary is to take place—ceremony, or social dances and other functions. At this particular camp, it was the purpose of the Fox Clan to overhaul and repair the spears. This was the first opportunity I had since joining the clan, I was more than anxious to be there.

I heard the announcer crying out in loud voice, calling all the members to one certain tipi; upon this invitation, I and my chum, who was also a member, went together. We were kindly received. After lunch, the leaders announced that there would be four days of dancing and feasting. In this clan there [were] four workers or door men. Four leaders or headmen. May also be called judges. The workers receive orders from headmen. These workers', may, in turn select helpers or assistants. It was at [this] time that the workers business was to see about getting a tipi to be used by them. They borrow everything they use such as cooking vessels and dishes. The tipi is erected in the center of the camp. After the tipi is up, there is no further need of calling the members, but must come at their own accord. The inside of the tipi is made smooth by taking out all the grass. This is done before it can be used for dancing purposes.

Where all is ready, the headmen are notified of the fact. They enter the tipi and occupy their places. They then give further orders to the workers to fetch food, one person will call for coffee, another one sugar, etc. All things necessary to prepare the food brought by the workers, they then proceed to prepare the food. The tipi and poles, food, utensils, are borrowed from the people in the camp. Everything is to be returned in good shape, except the food of course. One man sings four songs using a rattle gourd. These are sacred songs. There are four men with hand drums. These are used in the dance. I noticed a number of spears on the backside of the inside of the tipi. These had been prepared and were to be dedicated by some warrior who had won valor in battle before the owner could use the spear in the dance. The singers using hand drums then proceed to sing, only one man would get up and dance. This done, he would tell his war incident, either about other tribes or white soldiers.

At the end of the fourth day, we could not conclude the dance because we had no fresh buffalo heart bladder and other parts of the buffalo that were used at the conclusion of the Fox Clan dance. During the four days, we would circle the camp, any one sick would sit out in our path. Stop and circle around the sick person. The leader gives herbs and gestures. There are four maidens in this clan. They are called sisters and they call us brothers.[15]

HÉMO'EOXEO'O (ELK HORN SCRAPERS) DANCES

On the third chase in the Sweet Medicine epic, Motsé'eóeve changed into an elk and later reappeared dressed as an Elk Soldier: with a "Lance with one end curved down. Feathers on each end of the lance."[16] The third man said, "I like this look, so therefore it must be mine." He became the founding member of the Hémo'eoxeo'o, Elk Horn Scrapers. Wolf Chief explained their traditional dance customs:

> These dancers dress up in beaded costumes, fancy regalia. They have to put up a dance [lodge] to dance. They have drums. They have a couple of sticks with notches to rattle as they dance. The tent is put up only in [the] middle of [the] camp circle. Four women alone are allowed to dance with [them]. The dance starts by an old man [who] makes a speech. The dance commences. At near quitting time all dancers run a race outside and back in. Then the same old man will make a speech and the dance breaks up.
>
> The headmen pick four unmarried girls to be members of the society. These girls are not supposed to marry for a certain length of time. As soon as they marry, they fell out of the society.[17]

Wrapped Hair also described the traditional dance customs of the Hémo'eoxeo'o:

> The Elks had no regular headdress. During the dance, they used whatever they had for a headdress. Not a sacred dance. While dancing the onlookers would give them presents and at times they would give presents. The tent was pitched in the center of camp. They danced inside the tent. They had straightened piece of elk horn with notches, used with another piece of elk horn to make a sort of noise. Dancers also used [them]. Four women can join the society. They can't dance while the members dance in the tent.[18]

The Elk Society was also called the Hemoeoxessô (Headed-Lances) or Hoomenotxeo (Coyote-Warriors), which resulted when the society grew in numbers and eventually split. Petter described another dance of this society:

> This organization considers the coyote pelt sacred. They have a rattle made out of a gourd loosely filled with stones and painted red. The Keeper of this rattle is the leader in singing and dancing. Four maidens are also admitted to this society. Two of the bravest warriors carry a spear in the form of a bow, bent inward at the center and provided with a string. One end forms the spearhead. The other members have common spears. The men of this band are painted yellow except the lower part of arms and legs. In dancing they jump up and down, ever faster according to the accompanying music. The coyote hide is their emblem.[19]

HOTÓVANOTÅXEO'O (BUFFALO BULL WARRIORS) DANCES

On the fourth chase, Motsé'eóeve changed into a buffalo and later reappeared dressed as a Buffalo Bull Warrior: "Painted white on some parts of the body, with a shield with marks on it, a buffalo head headdress, with horns."[20] The fourth man said, "Now that is how a warrior should look. I am going to imitate his dress." This man became the founding member of the Hotóvanotåxeo'o, Buffalo Bull Warriors, which is also known as the Red Hoof Society. Petter described the society:

> This organization also selected four maidens as honorary members. Each man carried a circular red painted shield cut out from a buffalo hide in such a way as to include the tail with its hairs. As head dress they wore the horns of a buffalo with some of the skin attached to them. Each carried a spear. Shield, horns and spear were painted red. They danced partly running, partly halting with bodies bent forward and jumping up and down uttering sounds in imitation of the buffalo.[21]

Wolf Chief explained their traditional dance customs:

> This was the first society formed after the Cheyenne and Só'taeo'o came together. They wore a shield as part of [their] custom. They had a headdress with two buffalo horns on it. They painted the body all over in different colors. They had a dance of their own and allowed but four women to participate. It is not a sacred ceremony, mostly a dance.[22]

Wrapped Hair also described the traditional dance customs of the Hotóvanotâxeo'o:

> The Red Hoof use headdresses of buffalo head, with horns on it, with a shield painted red. They painted themselves red all over. It is not a sacred dance; more for a good time. They only danced when there was a big camp circle. They danced in the daytime so the people could see them. Women [were] excluded. During the dance it was custom for travelers to give presents to them and the dancers at various times gave presents.[23]

VÉHONE NÓTÂXEO'O (CHIEF SOLDIERS)

After the Great Unification, the Véhoo'o were included in the origin of the Nótâxeo'o. After each chase in the Sweet Medicine epic, four warriors returned home after seeing Motsé'eóeve. After all returned, a single man continued the pursuit; he was the strongest and best runner. On the fifth chase, the last man pursued Motsé'eóeve the farthest and chased him into an area of big granite rocks, located in the Black Hills. The last man believed that he cornered Motsé'eóeve and yelled out, "The others have left, but I have you now." Not long after, an eagle flew out from the rocks and the man followed it past the summit of a mountain—Bear Butte. From the top of the mountain, he could see Motsé'eóeve across a small valley. Here he stood singing the chiefs' song and was draped with a white buffalo robe.

He wore in his hair one golden eagle plume that stood upright and one golden eagle tail feather that stuck out to the side; both were black and white, center-tail feathers. In one hand Motsé'eóeve held a peace pipe and in the other he held a bundle of red-painted sticks, the Chiefs' Bundle.[24] His body was painted white, his leggings were black, and his moccasins were decorated with white porcupine quillwork. The man looked upon Motsé'eóeve and said, "I am the last one and have walked the farthest. This style of dress must be mine." This man was the founding member of the Véhone Nótâxeo'o, the Chief Soldiers. This was the Véhoo'o, the Council of Forty-Four Chiefs, but they were also known as a warrior society. Wrapped Hair described the traditional dance customs of the Véhone Nótâxeo'o: "The Chiefs were usually with the Red Hoof Society, as they had nearly the same songs. They had no regular costume, but danced in their best regalia. They are recognized by the tribe as headmen-officers of the tribe."[25]

The Véhoo'o and the Nótâxeo'o worked together in harmony, serving the interests of the people. As mentioned before, not much is known of which came first, but oral and written traditions reveal that the unification of the

Tsétsêhéstâhese and Só'taeo'o also brought adaptations to origin stories. One account of the origin of the Véhoo'o, as told by the traditional Cheyenne storyteller Tangle Hair, bridges both philosophies as the storyteller asserts that the Véhoo'o originated from the four warrior societies:

> The man who had brought the buffalo said, "Now you must make chiefs." He took four sticks and stuck them in the ground, one at the door, one at the back, and one on each side, so that there was a stick toward each of the four cardinal points. Between each pair of these first sticks, ten others were set in the ground, making in all forty-four. The people were called in, and from the four bands of soldiers forty-four chiefs were chosen. Then he said to the people "Now, the smartest men among you must look about over the earth and examine the plants and herbs that grow, and you will find medicine with which to doctor the sick, and you can cure them. Now you have buffalo, and you must kill them to eat, and to make robes for your beds, and clothing. From their hides you can make everything that you need to wear. When you go out to hunt, you will find many other animals, deer, elk, and smaller creatures, and you can use their skins also to make clothing."[26]

Although there is not much detail that could identify "the man who brought the buffalo," both the Tsétsêhéstaestse prophet Motsé'eóeve and the Só'taeo'o prophet Tomôsévêséhe (Erect Horns) could fit this role. On one hand, Motsé'eóeve performed a miracle when he brought buffalo to the starving Tsétsêhéstâhese during an ancient time.[27] On the other hand, "the man who brought the buffalo" could also refer to the prophet Tomôsévêséhe, who is known for bringing herds of buffalo to the Só'taeo'o when they were starving.[28] Like before, the Tsétsêhéstâhese and Só'taeo'o converged their oral traditions for the sake of long-lasting security and cultural survival.

LEADERSHIP AND THE NÓTÂXEO'O

The Nótâxeo'o each comprised numerous warriors, warrior women, society sisters, and war chiefs who were all part of the internal societal structure. Because of their inclusiveness and multiple roles, the Nótâxeo'o were not exclusively "warrior" societies, even though the values and philosophies were warrior in nature. Bull Thigh explained the basic membership standards of the Nótâxeo'o:

> The age of society members was immaterial; they had children as well as the old. There must be a few old people to carry on the songs. Anyone can

PART III | NÓTÂXEO'O: THE WARRIORS

sing that wants. The number of drums were not fixed. A man after joining a society, if he doesn't like it, can drop out and join another. Only the best men were taken in at first, when the societies were organized. But subsequently anyone could join. If the society found out that he was not fit, the society would tell him he must leave. At the joining of a society, the initiate would get up and give a present to some one and say he was going to join the society. This was usually done at a dance so all would know about it. There was no regulation about a brother replacing dead brothers in a society. But the society of the dead would give presents to the surviving brother to show friendship.[29]

The balance of power and shared responsibility among Nótâxévêhoo'o (Warrior Society Chiefs).

All members were to be paragons of citizenship, upholding respectable character and discipline. Not one leader was selected as the headman, but veteran society members elected several leaders based on stature and deeds in war. Each society had a different set of unwritten by-laws and rules of conduct, from which the entire society was directed. Wooden Leg (Northern Cheyenne) described the basic society leadership organization with a total of ten society chiefs: one leading head chief, or "war chief," and nine subordinate chiefs, or "little chiefs."[30] Hoebel, however, details a different organization at the individual warrior society level:

> Each club has four officers or leaders. The two head chiefs, who are the ritual leaders, sit at the back of the lodge when the club is meeting. The other two sit on either side of the door and serve as messengers—one might even say "ambassadors"—to the Council of Forty-Four and the other military societies whenever a big issue is being discussed within the camp. These two are the bravest men in the society.[31]

White Eagle described a different system, including how the Council of Forty-Four Chiefs were selected from the societies: "Each society has 8 chosen chiefs. They put up a lodge in the center of camp when 8 chiefs wanted new members. The people of the newly initiated gave the outfit presents, horses, etc. Every 10 years the old chiefs retired, others chosen from war societies."[32] The organization of each society differed depending on that particular society's customs, laws, and tradition. Like the organization of the Véhoo'o, society leaders shared responsibilities and authority so not one headman made decisions at all times. Nevertheless, the head leaders of a society commanded their members, warriors and civilians, in military fashion.

One commonality for all societies was that ten leaders or headmen had to be represented at the major ceremonial events and when the entire nation met. The organization of the Nótâxeo'o is complex when compared to non-Indian notions of leadership, especially when whites first encountered the Cheyennes expecting only one leader to speak for all. The Nótâxeo'o was the military force of the nation, and the responsibilities of the nótâxevêhoo'o (society chiefs or headmen) were even more demanding, as leaders were required to be forceful in carrying out orders. But like the Véhoo'o, the society leaders valued and shared power, authority, and responsibility, especially with other ceremonial and political institutions.

Society headmen were typically between the ages of twenty-five and thirty-five, more experienced than the average warrior, but younger than the average Council chief. A society headman held a position of status: "The chief of a soldier band occupied a position of great responsibility, which some men felt to be too serious a burden to assume."[33] If he was a good leader, a society chief could potentially be selected to sit on the grand Council of Forty-Four Chiefs. A potential headman improved his reputation through military accomplishments, administrative and organizational skills on a policing level, in ceremony and spiritual practices, or his ability to accomplish assignments. Each society chose leaders carefully by observing for long periods of time "which is the best man in character" and which men are "brave" and have proven themselves "by doing great things in battle."[34] Non-Indians sometimes referred to society headmen as "war chiefs" because they were in the forefront of any military engagement. Their daring actions did not mean that war chiefs were always seeking war, but that the society headmen were prepared to fight even if they were not the best diplomats of the Cheyenne Nation.

Unlike other Plains Indian nations, whose leaders were identified by the popular eagle-feather war bonnet, Cheyenne custom did not require even the highest-ranking leaders to bear the feathered crown. The war bonnet was based in spirituality and individual honor, and most worthy warriors did not wear the headpiece because of modesty. This does not mean that all war chiefs were not "war bonnet men."[35] Modesty, in dress and demeanor, was an important attribute of Cheyenne concepts of leadership but not necessarily in citizenship, and a person who dressed like a "chief" was not necessarily always a chief of the entire nation. Leaders were not defined by their possessions, they were defined by their actions, and the best leaders were often the poorest in the band or nation, even if they could possess a lot.[36]

Each society, acting as an individual unit, voted and elected their headmen at seating ceremonies, typically held at major events like the Medicine Lodge. Modesty sometimes prevented a worthy candidate, who was a seasoned warrior, from accepting the honor, but this declination did not forfeit his society membership. The status of a society headman was understood as a person whose primary responsibility was sacrifice in war:

> The position was understood to be one of such danger that death was always to be expected—a soldier chief was chosen to be killed. Only a man at all times ready to face death could be selected for this office. The soldier chief possessed a high sense of the dignity of his position, and if he thought he was not treated with the consideration due him, he was ready to demand his rights. His position was always respected, partly because people generally feared to quarrel with him.[37]

Headmen were dedicated to the art of war and, in plain terms, were selected to die. Until his retirement or promotion, a headman "would give away most or all of his possessions, and might give up buffalo hunting and social activities to devote himself entirely to war medicines, prayer, and fasting."[38] Headmen accepted a deep understanding of death because they had to have

TRADITIONS AND CUSTOMS OF THE NÓTÂXEO'O

no fear of it. The Medicine Lodge (Sun Dance) and the Arrow Worship Ceremony facilitated a maturing warrior's development as he meditated and contemplated his death. This allowed potential leaders to spiritually mature by accepting and embracing their inevitable demise. Wolf Chief explained the importance of death and the societies: "If a man was shot or wounded in battle, his society will have to help him. If he was killed, they bury him."[39] In the end, the headmen were responsible for the funerary and burial rituals of their fallen.

The balance of power and shared responsibility among the eight United Nótâxeo'o.

Headmen did not seek status in the same manner as modern politicians, employees, or businessmen who seek promotion for a greater salary or prestige. Instead, warriors were elected to leadership positions because their society members trusted them and were certain that they would be the best person to follow in battle. A society headman did not have to apply for his position, nor did he have to argue why he was a better candidate than his society brothers. Within the Cheyenne warrior society code, leadership skills were measured by, among other things, a person's deeds and actions. Character was judged on emotional and moral discipline before, during, and after these actions. Herein lay important characteristics of "warrior citizenship."

CITIZENSHIP AND THE NÓTÅXEO'O

Warrior citizens dedicated their lives to all Cheyenne people at all times and adhered to four core ideologies of the life-nation: cooperation, responsibility, loyalty, and service. The balance of the nation rested in the sanctity of these four core concepts, since citizens who wanted to belong had to remain responsible and loyal while providing service. Individual rights and privileges were secondary to those of the society, third to those of the band, and fourth to those of the living-nation. In fact, according to Cheyenne custom, individualism was honored only when warriors accomplished brave acts in battle and captured property from enemies in the heat of battle or in its aftermath, and such individualism rarely went beyond the realm of battle. The Véhoo'o demanded unity and expected the best behavior from warriors, while fostering an environment of healthy competition. Warriors were expected to engage and participate in rivalries to compete for honor as explained by Wooden Leg, when there were only three societies during his younger days:

> The effort at all times was to carry out well whatever governmental tasks was placed upon the warriors, either on the hunts, at the camps, during a journey, in the time of battle or under any conditions where they were vested with authority. The three societies competed against each other for efficiency in governmental action as well as in all other affairs appertaining to respectable manhood. There was competition also within each society, every ambitious member trying to outdo his fellows in all worthy activities.[40]

Wooden Leg discusses concepts of the Cheyenne world that transcends mere individual status; he describes the warriors' desire to serve to the best of their ability, which sustained a healthy nation. Competition promoted efficiency, but it did not dominate, since warrior societies shared power and shared the success of a healthy nation. Not one warrior society was placed above another. Men were supposed to know this sociopolitical structure and were expected to consistently participate to their fullest and sincerest ability under the principle of brotherhood.

During the precontact era of the Cheyenne Nation, the people lived an ideal lifestyle, guided by their spiritual teachings and ceremonial practices. If they failed to participate, warriors could have lost respect from their relatives and other citizens. Inactive warriors would be shunned as noncitizens, unworthy of the rights, privileges, and benefits provided by the Cheyenne Nation. They would become without families and therefore alien or outcasts. There are accounts buried in the oral tradition of individuals and families who did achieve the outcast label. All of the people, not just warriors, were expected to live by the customs and cultural norms demanded by warrior citizenship. Be it ceremonial, military, communal, familial, or political, every citizen contributed in one way or another, or else they lost out.

NÓTÂXÉ'E

When people, men or women, joined a society, they became part of a nation that was built upon and sustained itself by sharing power. Young men and women could join a society, but since one of the primary functions of these groups was war, few women joined as warriors; most joined as sisters. Most leaders in the original government of the Cheyennes were men, but women were active participants in the nation and, more important, were respected as caregivers, mothers, teachers, and the backbone of the people. In almost every warrior society, four young women were selected to represent the group and serve as social and ceremonial ambassadors of womanhood.[41] Warrior societies often honored young women, typically the daughters of society chiefs, for exemplifying the beauty of ideal Cheyenne womanhood.[42] Wooden Leg described the role of these women:

> Four unmarried and virtuous young women were chosen as honorary members of each warrior society. If one of these entered into marriage or became unchaste she lost her membership and some other young woman was chosen in her place. The young women took no active part in the proceedings. They were allowed merely to sit inside the lodge of assemblage, there quietly looking on.[43]

Girls in these positions have been referred to as nótâxé'e: warrior women, society sisters, soldier girls, or female soldiers.[44] The nótâxé'e were especially important during the ceremonies and dances, as explained by Wolf Chief: "Four women belong to each lodge and used as singers. The societies had a custom of letting their sisters dance with them. These [women] were the only ones who were permitted this."[45]

Nótâxé'e were afforded the formal opportunity to become "warrior women" when they went into battle with their respective society and earned honors as the men warriors. One of the most popular nótâxé'e was Buffalo Calf Road Woman, who rescued her brother, Chief Comes In Sight, at the Battle of Rosebud on June 17, 1876.[46] Another was Kate Bighead, who was present at the Washita Massacre and the Battle of the Little Bighorn. Warrior women also took part in the most sacred ceremony that honored procreation, the Medicine Lodge. The ceremonial position of women in the lodge may have held no political power, but it was still an important aspect of the warrior society system: "Usually a good-looking girl was chosen, who devoted herself to the position in much the same spirit that a nun gives herself up to her vocation."[47]

Nótâxé'e were revered and honored by the entire village, as all men and women respected the feminine spirit and the woman's power of procreation. Nótâxé'e were chosen if they were from good families and exhibited the epitome of Cheyenne womanhood. They maintained their status until they married worthy suitors. Some societies prevented their nótâxé'e from marriage unless the society collectively agreed, as was the "law" of the Dog Men.[48] Once married, the woman lost her status but retained her reputation and respect. A man could never marry his own society sister; such an act was considered incest and a violation of sacred law.[49] A man could marry the sister of one of his society brothers; she then became a general member of the society through the marriage. When a soldier girl was married, she symbolically sought the approval of the entire warrior society at the wedding ceremony. Once the society condoned and blessed the marriage, all of the society families planned and organized an elaborate wedding ceremony.[50] The Cheyennes strongly believe that one of the duties of a male warrior was to honor and respect his fellow tribeswomen, which is why the nótâxé'e were so important. The male-centered society organization could have become imbalanced if no homage was paid to Cheyenne women. One virtue of Cheyenne men is to be family oriented, and this meant that young men had to learn respect for women at an early age, through adulthood. Such honoring and safeguards also prevented sexual violence against other citizens as well as captives from other nations, who were potential adoptees into the nation.

WOMEN'S SOCIETIES

Women also organized into social societies, such as the Moneneheo'o (Selected Ones), which was a beading and quilling guild.[51] Another society was the "Tipi Decorators," who held formal ceremonies to decorate the lodges of worthy families.[52] These women's societies were composed of experts in the craft of bead and quillwork, and young women aspired to join the societies following the teachings and oral traditions of Mahoemskot. Women from the societies knew and taught the traditional meanings of colors and designs and how to create exquisite works of art. The Moneneheo'o determined the material wealth of the nation, as they gifted or awarded their prized possessions to only the finest of citizens and leaders. They made the elegant war shirts, leggings, pipe bags, cradleboards, dresses, and other garments of beauty. Most of the society members earned their membership by exhibiting good behavior and talent in their crafts. As regulators of material wealth, the Moneneheo'o were a society with status.

Wife and Four Daughters of Man on a Cloud with Ornaments, near Wood Frame Building, 1892, James Mooney, 1861–1921. National Anthropological Archives, Smithsonian Museum Support Center, Suitland, Maryland (NAA INV 06110000, OPPS NEG 282 B).

Another women's society was the Mámaa'e Nótãxé'évoo'e (Women's War Bonnet Society), which included several young women who were exemplars of womanhood, chastity, service, compassion, and dignity. An old custom allowed for women to wear war bonnets because they fought alongside the men.[53] These war bonnet women thus institutionalized a society that honored the role of women in war. The guild adopted its own ceremony that included the Hemámaa'evôhomó'hestôtse (War Bonnet Dance), in which young women, typically daughters of warriors and chiefs who possessed a war bonnet, ceremonially blessed the sacred hats. Under the tutelage of older "sponsor" women, these young women represented the balance between the two genders and the significance of women in the Cheyenne worldview, even among warrior men. Traditionally, women could not handle eagle feathers or pipes, for their natural feminine supremacy could compromise a man's acquired spiritual powers. The Mámaa'e Nótãxé'évoo'e, however, were allowed to possess feathers, and young men often asked them to make an eagle-feathered crown. When the Cheyennes were placed on reservations, the Mámaa'e Nótãxé'évoo'e became part of other dance societies.

THE NÓTÃXEO'O AND COMBAT

While the Véhoo'o were matrilineal in nature, the Nótãxeo'o were patriarchal and patrilineal and honored the male identity. The Nótãxeo'o were of Tsétsêhéstâhese origin and fostered the development of manhood. The Nótãxeo'o held governmental authority like political parties and organized like squadrons of the National Guard, "fundamentally alike in their internal organization and activities," but had major differences in their customs, ceremonies, and organization.[54] Most scholars immediately identify the Cheyenne warrior societies as first and foremost "military societies," whose primary purpose was war and whose secondary functions were internal policing.[55] But since the Cheyenne Nation was not in a state of perpetual war, the societies were not in perpetual states of aggression, and individual Cheyennes did not join a group because of a thirst for war and aggression. The term "military societies" does not accurately define the Nótãxeo'o, and although the term "warrior societies" is more appropriate, the idea of a "warrior" must be examined from the Cheyenne perspective.

The Nótãxeo'o did function in war, since they were the military units that were the main defense against outside threats of aggression. With the increase in violence on the Plains, which resulted from the colonization of Indian lands to the east, the Nótãxeo'o quickly met the challenges to protect against invasion and act as aggressors as each Indian nation fought to keep their ways of living. The Nótâxeo'o thus developed a sophisticated warrior culture, which I examine in detail in chapter 8. As part of their traditions, as described by White Eagle, each society had medicine bundles and covenants: "Each war society has a certain protector. In war, the war society used their protectors. They dismounted and danced in the thick of the fight."[56]

The war leaders and the Council chiefs did not determine responsibilities of an individual warrior in battle. Instead, warrior responsibilities were understood as duties given by the supernatural powers of the earth and Ma'xema'hēō'e (Great Medicine), which is why warriors were trained psychologically, physically, and spiritually. Discipline, loyalty, courage, and ambition were important values and each warrior was to master these values to become a successful warrior.[57] From boyhood, would-be warriors were "trained to be daring and fearless," but they first had to learn the feats of previous warriors in stories of culture heroes.[58] Once a boy matured into a man, he was already conditioned to serve his people by conducting the most sacred of acts.

Warrior societies were always seeking new recruits to attain the "warrior status," and there was always a new generation of young men who were ready and willing to contribute to the society, to the band, and to the Cheyenne Nation. When a young man matured, around thirteen to sixteen years of age, he was recruited to formally join a warrior society and thus gain status as a warrior.[59] Manhood was identified by the physical growth of a young man: primarily his height and the change in his voice. Although a rarity, there were instances when young men would never initiate into a warrior society and never earn a warrior reputation. In such cases, a young man may instead pursue spirituality as a profession and eventually become a priest or spiritual leader, joining a ceremonial society instead.

The eldest son of a family gained status among his peers by joining his father's society and, through the exhibition of warfare, hunting, and policing, he could eventually become a society leader, but leadership was not hereditary.[60] In the traditional environment, a young man learned the duties and responsibilities of being an adult from the best teachers and, more important, to be a "warrior citizen," which was done without going into battle. Although the majority of young men joined their father's society, should a society headman have two sons, the younger was encouraged to join a different society to avoid a saturation of members from one family. There were no strict laws that prevented a young man from joining a group of his male relatives, but they were encouraged to join different societies to ensure balance and integrity in the system. Such generational relationships in the warrior society structures allowed for kinship to remain an important aspect in the traditional Cheyenne government, as relatives would often be in the same warrior society, but families could not dominate one.[61] Should one family dominate a society, the entire system could be compromised. It would become plagued with family feuds and no longer would the warriors be organized for the benefit of the nation; each group would become a mini-kingdom and fall back into the chaos that the Cheyennes left behind.

The Nótâxeo'o employed safeguards to protect the sanctity of the Cheyenne Nation. If one tyrant-family wanted to gain control and power, it would need to overrun several warrior societies as well as the Council of Forty-Four Chiefs. Family units rarely had political aspirations like those of European cultures, where wealthy families could gain control of the political atmosphere. But this safeguard did not prohibit family units from being represented. In fact, the Cheyenne kinship system was the foundation of the Nótâxeo'o and was reinforced by society members and leaders through ceremony and custom. Kinship relationships became very important when a warrior died, because his widow and children had to rely on blood relatives and sometimes on their ceremonial societies. Orphans were sometimes overlooked by warrior societies during recruitment, since they had no male relative to vouch for them. They had to work extra hard to prove their loyalty and service, as emphasized in the stories of Sweet Medicine, Last Born, Cherry Eater, and other orphans who became great leaders.

The ideal age for a Cheyenne boy to become a warrior, as opposed to a general member, of a society was around age fifteen, but the telltale sign for a young man to become a warrior would be found in his athletic abilities, his daring in hunting, and his desire to engage in the art of war. The Nótâxeo'o system fit in with the natural male aggressive and competitive tendencies, which usually arise after puberty. Becoming a warrior was no small matter for a potential candidate, especially for his family. The young man underwent an initiation ceremony and exchanged gifts between his family and a headman of the selected society. The mother would ceremonially be withdrawn from her motherly duties, as her son would be under the "ownership" of the entire warrior society or society chief. The boy would then become part of a unit acting on behalf of the society before acting on behalf of his parents.

A warrior was obliged to execute all governmental orders, especially for warfare. Until a warrior was unable to fight or until he was killed in battle, his warrior status depended on his success in warfare. The "young, prime years" of a man were the time for sacrifice, as described by Stands In Timber: "When you give your body to the enemy on behalf of your people by going among them, and being killed, your name will not be forgotten in future generations."[62] Most warriors retired around the age of thirty-five or forty, or when their sons were old enough to take their place in representing the family.[63] By age forty-five to fifty, a man was expected to be completely retired and determined to exclusively care for his family.[64] Upon retirement, a warrior's status within a society was not diminished even if he was not a headman. Retired warriors could still function in positions of respect as counselors, ceremonial leaders, or military organizers. Wooden Leg described the roles of young and old warriors:

> If a warrior's father or some other older person put himself unnecessarily forward in a battle he was likely to be criticized for his needless risk, and also the young warriors felt aggrieved at his taking from them whatever of honors might be gained in the combat. In general, the young men were supposed to be more valuable as fighters and less valuable as wise counselors, while the older men were estimated in the opposite way. It was considered not right for an important older man to place himself as a target for the missiles of the enemy, if he could avoid such exposure.[65]

A warrior could change societies later in life, but his society brothers did not usually accept this and it caused much animosity, especially if he was a good warrior. Loyalty was a virtue and society brothers felt betrayed at the loss of a fellow member. After the loss, no animosity or bitterness was carried into the future. Unlike the chiefs, whose loyalty was to the entire nation, warriors had to be loyal to their societies first. During the early reservation years, when the societies could no longer function as military units, a man could join two societies, but they had to be closely associated with one another. Old She Bear was originally a Dog Soldier, but also joined the Bow String Warriors, which were societies that often held dances and ceremonies together.[66]

CHAPTER 11

Nótåxeo'o and Political Organization

THE ROLES of the Nótåxeo'o shifted from the band level to the national level when all or the majority of the bands of the entire Cheyenne Nation worked to accomplish a unified goal. As a political body, the Nótåxeo'o functioned as its own branch since it was responsible for specific tasks, which only the societies could execute. Balance and shared authority were necessary for the Cheyenne system of governance to function effectively. While the Nótåxeo'o had autonomy on matters exclusive to war and society, for matters concerning the entire nation the Nótåxeo'o were subject to the orders of the Véhoo'o. In the end the Véhoo'o were the highest authority of Cheyenne national sovereignty.

The responsibilities delegated from the Véhoo'o to the Nótåxeo'o were, at times, matters of life and death, which is why headmen had to be conscious that their actions could affect the entire Cheyenne Nation for generations. Warrior society leaders also had to follow the codes of sacred leadership and balance. The most crucial component to successful governance required cooperation and balance between the Véhoo'o and the Nótåxeo'o as described by Wooden Leg:

> The warrior chiefs had original authority only in their societies, each in his own special organization. By alternation, though, the tribal chiefs delegated governmental power to the warrior chiefs. That is, one group or another of the warrior chiefs and their followers were called upon to serve as active subordinate officials to carry out the orders promulgated by the big chiefs. Such warrior society group, when on this duty, was like the white man's sheriffs and policemen, soldiers.[1]

In essence the Nótåxeo'o executed the decisions of the Véhoo'o, and since every young man and some women, aged fourteen to thirty-five, were expected to be in a warrior society, it can be assumed that every man took part, in one way or another, in exerting the inherent sovereignty of the Cheyenne Nation.[2] Whether as primary decision makers, as enforcers of laws, or as executers of directives from Véhoo'o, all men and women took part in moving the nation forward. The system truly made an autonomous living-nation.

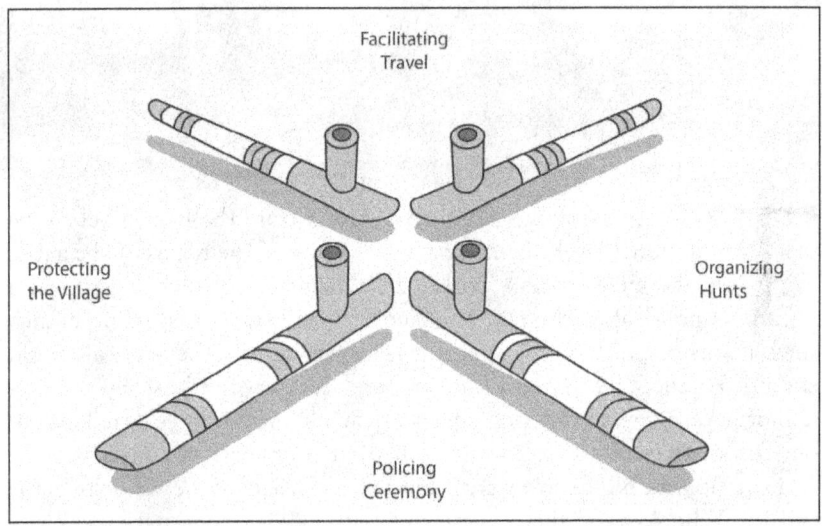

The four sacred responsibilities of the Nótâxeo'o.

To avert corruption, not one society was assigned to wield power for long periods of time; each of the four rotated in its assigned responsibility. This was done to prevent centralization, which led to abuse of power and is remembered in the Cheyenne national history as lawlessness. The Véhoo'o summoned warrior headmen on all military matters, especially those requiring urgent action, such as when society chiefs decided to wage war against another Indian nation or against invading whites. Declaring war was considered a sacred act among three other responsibilities of the Véhoo'o. The four "sacred tasks" of the warrior societies that were the most important to national autonomy were (1) providing military protection for the village; (2) facilitating camp moves; (3) organizing hunts; and (4) organizing and policing annual ceremonies. Tall Bull elaborated: "Not all were assigned to attack at once. Protection of the camp was the most important duty, and one of the warrior societies would remain in camp to guard it against enemy attack. Hunting and caring for the horse herds was the second most important duty and was carried out by another of the warrior societies."³

The original society leaders established new laws and customs related to hunting, which can be traced to the story of Motsé'eóeve and the incident with the old man. Like all young men, Sweet Medicine liked to hunt, but his actions led to the dispute. The Nótâxeo'o regulated and facilitated hunting as a community event, organized and executed with respect and for the benefit of all. Tribal citizens adhered to this tribal law after the Great Unification and after they acquired horses. Large hunts were done ceremoniously and could not be done without the approval of the Véhoo'o. Wolf Chief explained the punishments for the crime of poaching:

> The societies had charge of regulations about hunting. If a man made trouble in camp, the societies would destroy his camp, kill horses, at times whip the offender. A man's own society would not touch him. After awhile the punishing society, if they thought the man had property, by his punishment might [compel him to] give [them] presents: a couple of horses and clothes and sort of apologize [to the society].⁴

The Nótâxeo'o shifted duties from being a national guard, to military escorts, to providers, to ceremonial practitioners. During these times, young warriors endeavored to exhibit exceptional behavior through the warrior etiquette. Wooden Leg describes these tasks: "In the camp circles, in the tribal movings from place to place, in the great tribal hunts, in the times of Great Medicine or other general ceremonial dances—in fact, at all times of our lives some or other warrior society was authorized or commanded by the tribal chiefs to take charge of the government."⁵ The cooperation and balance of power between the Nótâxeo'o and the Véhoo'o, when one "takes charge of the government," should not be confused with political unrest or instability.⁶ Instead it is evidence of a delicate balance between two highly organized institutions, its foundations built on the Cheyenne principle of brotherhood. The idea of a "takeover" in Western culture usually conjures images of revolution or coup d'état, but among the Cheyenne, power was sacred and had to be shared.

The temporary shifts in governance of original Cheyenne national government, in which the warrior societies would take charge, were understood as part of the system. Both the Véhoo'o and the Nótâxeo'o could change roles to accomplish a task in a unified and disciplined manner. If the Véhoo'o could not make a decision on a matter, they may "turn" the decision over to the Nótâxeo'o, or vice versa.⁷ Such instances were uncommon, but were part of the system. By nature of the system, warrior societies became competitive to be the best above others, earning honors and gaining notoriety for being selected to fulfill orders or complete tasks. Despite the fierce competition, the system was structured so no society sought to undermine the entire political organization of the Cheyenne Nation. Wooden Leg describes:

> Ordinarily there was a shift of the delegated authority by regular rotation, but such change in regular order was not always the case. The conclave of big chiefs decided which society should have it. A society might be appointed to act for one day, two days, three days, any stated length of time, or they might be appointed to serve during the continuation of some certain event. At any time their appointment might be revoked by the big chiefs and another society named in their stead.[8]

Although the societies competed with one another, not one held a desire to undermine or annihilate other societies for political gain. The societies kept each other in check. When delegated power, a warrior society and its members were the authority figures, but only for that assigned event or for a short period of time. Policing was not a full-time position of power for a certain group of men. At any moment, the role of an individual warrior could easily be changed from the discipliner to the disciplined. This police system prevented warriors from abusing their powers while protecting all citizens equally. Such organization on such a grand scale required discipline and commitment from each society as well as from each individual society member. The integrity of the entire governing structure could not be compromised by an individual's egotism or selfishness, or a leader's thirst for more power and control. The system worked for the benefit and welfare of the entire Cheyenne Nation, but at times the Nótâxeo'o did overstep their boundaries. Before doing so, they would likely oblige or pledge a higher-ranking ceremonial man to petition on their behalf. In extreme cases, a society may force its actions upon even the highest priest, the Arrow Keeper. This was done in 1836 when White Thunder was forced to renew the Medicine Arrows.[9]

Warrior societal interventions over the Véhoo'o and even the keepers of the sacred covenants did not become a major problem until the wars with the United States and until the eventual destruction of the Cheyenne government beginning in the late 1800s. Although imbalance occurred before, it never led to a complete breakdown of the Cheyenne Nation. After imbalance, the Cheyenne national government regained stability and continued to protect future generations of Cheyennes.

The traditional government of the Cheyenne Nation was unlike Western governments where dictatorship, social class systems, and power managing dominated sovereign states. Western civilization's history of revolution, dictatorship, slavery, and social class division is completely opposite to the traditional Cheyenne government. Simply put, the ways of the Western world were foreign. Nevertheless, it was only a matter of time until the Cheyenne Nation would begin to engage in diplomacy and eventually war with the invading whites. The two worlds differed in philosophy, leadership, and values, as well as in governance. Conflict was unavoidable.

PRINCIPLES OF CITIZENSHIP: THE WAY OF THE WARRIOR

Other than physical demands, the Cheyenne "way of the warrior" centered on the spiritual development of each citizen. There were four ways in which people could improve their spiritual essence: naturally through enduring the changes of each phase of life, by hunting buffalo, by engaging in warfare, and the highest, through ceremonial practices. Younger Cheyenne men had to prove to themselves, before proving to others, that they could gain an understanding of the pure essence of life by overcoming the fear of death, thus establishing a spiritual relationship with Ma'xema'hēō'e, the Great Medicine.

Women were blessed with the ability to create life, and naturally endure four sacred phases of life: (1) birth to womanhood (indicated by puberty); (2) womanhood to motherhood; (3) motherhood to grandmotherhood (indicated by menopause); and finally, (4) grandmotherhood to death. In each phase a woman gains spiritual knowledge and wisdom and endures mental, emotional, and physical changes, but she must also endure spiritual changes to make sense of it all. These spiritual changes are acknowledged through ceremonial practices, which bring her closer to the Great Medicine.

Men, for their part, only endure three phases of life: (1) birth to manhood (indicated by puberty); (2) manhood to fatherhood; and (3) fatherhood to death. Men endure physical, mental, emotional, and spiritual change and must gain wisdom by engaging in appropriate ceremonies and through the guidance of spiritual leaders. Men, however, are not blessed with birthing children and do not endure the same physical, mental, and emotional challenges as women when they endure pregnancy and menopause. Men, therefore, must endure at least one more spiritual change as they mature as humans, which is why most ceremonies require young men to undergo physical and mental hardship through sacrifice and endurance. Their spiritual and emotional growth follows.

In ceremonies like the Medicine Lodge (Sun Dance) or the Arrow Lodge, young men were able to gain spiritual enlightenment in controlled environments. Some of the primary goals of such ceremonies were to encourage practitioners to accept their mortality and submit to the forces of the spiritual world. Both men and women could participate in such ceremonies, but custom required that men participate in some form of sacrifice. The ceremonial fast, commonly known as the vision quest, was another means of attaining spiritual trainings.

> Sometimes an Indian would go out to some lonesome place and fast there a certain number of days. Young men would go to the top of a hill or mountain (to be left unmolested) and stay there, abstaining from food or water, or from both, until a vision would appear to them and determine their future. None could become an Indian doctor unless a special apparition would have given him this right. Not a few young men fasted for several days, without having any vision, but the ordeal had been gone thru and they were satisfied. The "shapes" appearing to them were usually the spiritual progenitors and controllers of the present animals. At other times a man would have a lodge pitched apart and do his fasting there. Then either in connection with the Sundance or at other times, single individuals would have a day of fasting and "penance," from sunup until sunset, either in lying or standing posture (also hanging from a pole) and facing the sun constantly.[10]

Aside from ceremonies, there were few opportunities where a person could endure spiritual change. Sometimes during the heat of a buffalo hunt, young men experienced (felt or saw) glimpses of the Great Medicine. Hunting buffalo was always a dangerous practice, as hunters would often meet their demise in the rush of the hunt after falling under the hooves of thousands of the sacred animals. Warfare, because of the chance of death, also proved to be a time for a person to gain spiritual enlightenment. The heat of battle required the most tactic, wit, and physical ability, and therefore became the best way for young men to gain spiritual enlightenment during the "time of the buffalo" and the "time of the horse." Warfare, to the Cheyennes, was a part of life, as a "fighting spirit" was encouraged, even though fighting itself was not necessarily accepted among youth.[11] Death was not to be feared, as boys were trained to be daring and courageous.

To be a warrior, a person intentionally exposed him or herself to death. A near-death experience was a spiritual death of the shallow self. The person is then reborn and, under the right circumstances, he or she can overcome the fear of death. The rebirth spurs a spiritual awakening in the person, who thus gains a sense of the essence of life. If this rebirth is done at an early age, after puberty, it gave potential sacred leaders a head start in becoming headmen, Council chiefs, or ceremonial leaders. Part of the warrior tradition was to allow for young men to experience and develop the physical demands of leading in war. Later in life, these warriors developed their leadership skills in diplomacy and peacemaking. The buffalo hunt, ceremony, and war were a spiritual initiation to life and Ma'xema'heō'e. War was a sure method for a young man to expose himself to death. The Cheyenne had a war custom that was a vow of death, which is not a vow of suicide, but one's dedication to sacrifice and selflessness in battle. A candidate required the guidance from a sponsor, one who also made a vow of death but survived. The custom made the Cheyennes into some of the bravest warriors on the Plains, but other nations say that the Cheyennes "were not brave, just crazy."[12]

The spiritual development of young adults reinforced unity, loyalty, and a dedication to one's family, society, band, and nation, which transcended mere allegiance and membership. Citizenship, as understood through the Cheyenne cultural way of life, requires much sacrifice centered on the relationships between humans, the earth, and the spiritual forces. The Cheyenne world could only be sustained if the people were healthy, and the Cheyenne Nation could only survive if its citizens were disciplined and cultured.

In the following pages I reveal ten principles of "warrior citizenship." These principles emphasize action, which means that citizens had to not only know these through teachings in the oral tradition and ceremonies, but they also had to practice and commit to do these acts on a daily basis. Several elders and traditional people taught me these principles throughout my life, but I also found warrior citizenship hidden in records and published accounts of the Cheyennes. One of my teachers, Alva Stands In Timber, asked me every time I saw her: "Tell me something good that you have done for your people today." She explained to me once that her grandparents always asked her and her siblings this question, and I believe this request reveals the core of a person's warrior citizenship and loyalty to the living-nation.

1. He'eévestôtse (womanhood)

While historically women held no political positions of power, today it is very common for women to sit in high positions of political power in the modern tribal government. Women are viewed as the backbone of the entire Cheyenne Nation; they are the only ones who can bear children and therefore allow the nation to live into the unknown future. Daughters were especially important and held a lot of responsibility over the younger children, siblings, and cousins.[13] Women are the mothers of the nation and respected

PART III | NÓTÂXEO'O: THE WARRIORS

Two Women (Incl. Pauline Warren) and a Child; Woman, Pauline Warren, in Native Dress; Two with Ornaments; Tipis Nearby, 1893, James Mooney, 1861–1921. National Anthropological Archives, Smithsonian Museum Support Center, Suitland, Maryland (NAA INV 06077700, OPPS NEG 12a).

as sisters of Mother Earth, and therefore the daughters of the Universe. Young women were encouraged to refine their talents by sewing, beading, and creating exquisite works of art, no different from their ability to create the beauty of life. They were not to be diverted, but to keep looking ahead, never looking back in time, always moving toward something good and beautiful.[14] Women are the primary caregivers and have the burdens of teaching their children the values of humanity and the essence of life. Elaine Strange Owl (Northern Cheyenne) discusses key teachings of womanhood:

> When a woman has a daughter, she talks to her and reminds her even while young, how to work, how to sew, how to bead, how to read, and how to be a woman. She is taught when she is ten years old, how to work as a woman, how to listen, and how to learn something. She is also taught how one is respected as a young lady and how to accompany a young man. She is taught how to be respected and how there is purity; that one's body is not to be played with, to keep clean, so she will not have an illegitimate pregnancy. "Kåse'ééhe, nėstsevé'nėheséve! Hene ėsåanėhesóháne! Ėsåapėhéva'éháne!" (Young woman, don't do that! That is not to be! It is not good!)[15]

Womanhood among the Cheyennes means that women are sacred by nature and must respect themselves but must also be respected and honored by their male counterparts, families, and communities through ceremonial practices. Women's ceremonies must be practiced at each change in their life to ensure that they remain healthy in mind, body, and spirit.

Womanhood is intertwined with motherhood and therefore women should be the best mothers they can be to their children. Their roles as mothers never end even as their children mature into adults. They will also become grandmothers, at which stage in life they will become mothers of the Cheyenne Nation and continue as part of the legacy of the life-nation and as part of the land. The land represented the body of a woman since the earth was considered a female; the nation also represented a woman since the living-nation was also female. In the Cheyenne culture, womanhood means sisterhood and this means that all Cheyenne women are united and spiritually bound as sisters of one nation. Young women were groomed to represent their families with honor and dignity.

II. *Hetanévestôtse (manhood)*

Male citizens must protect all past, present, and future generations of women and children of the nation from harm, foreign and domestic, at all costs. Since most warriors are men (some were women), all men are held to a high standard, as military and political leadership is not perceived as a privilege; it is an obligation. A Cheyenne man has to be a good son, brother, husband, father, and uncle. A man should always be present for his family, especially his children and his wife. He learns these values through example in the household as a child, and his mother and aunts are his primary teachers, as explained by Elaine Strange Owl:

> Young men are [all] warned: "Ó'tôsêvotse'oestse! Ó'tôsétánôtse! Héne'enováhétánôtse!" (Keep on working! Strive! Be educated!) No matter what, start to learn how you are going to live now! You are going to make a home, keep learning more. And when you start to accompany a young lady: "Néstsevé'eévèhavèsévo'éého! Pėhéve'tovoo'o! Néstsevé'tanéhevo'éého!" (Don't treat her badly! Be good to her! Don't embarrass her!) Don't do anything wrong, it isn't good. You won't be respected when you do wrong and be regarded badly. Young men need to start working early so he knows how to work. One does not hold back in convincing him, one keeps on persuading him, one keeps talking to him and doesn't give up on him so he will know.[16]

A boy's older male relatives fostered his development at puberty, into manhood, through initiation ceremonies. In Cheyenne culture there was little desire for a man to become "perfect," since all humans are bound to make mistakes. A man was trained to endure pain, suffering, and the unknown, unpredictable challenges of life. Manhood was not an accomplishment; instead, it was perceived as a call of duty that all men were to accept. Stands In Timber discussed the significance of manhood in maintaining balance:

> The Cheyennes were not supposed to marry too young, or to anyone related to them; they have forgotten that today. They were not to take anything by force, from another person, or use it without permission, or to say bad things about others, especially the leaders or chiefs. They were to take pride in their bodies and the way they appeared, to keep clean and stay healthy. They were not to talk to their mothers-in-law or fathers-in-law, and that one rule saved a lot of trouble. I have noticed, since that custom is not used so much anymore, that the daughter-in-law and mother-in-law start quarreling many times over little things.[17]

Both young men and women were held to high standards of conduct, but the behavior of men was especially subject to public scrutiny; especially, if a man were to become a leader and represent his family and people. Men were bound by sacred laws of chivalry and were in endless training to become elders of the nation. The following eight principles developed from these first two.

III. *Hestsêstahe (to have compassion)*

Although the warrior culture fosters a form of controlled aggression for young men, they must also master the art of compassion by consistently exhibiting compassion to their fellow citizens, to other humans, to beings of nature, and to the supernatural powers. First and foremost, both male and female citizens must have compassion for themselves. Compassion was traditionally exhibited through two means: by invitation and voluntarily. When a citizen warrior, man or woman, is summoned to serve, he or she must never decline the request. Doing so is considered disrespectful. Invitations to demonstrate compassion, however, were rare, since most acts of compassion were voluntary and expected in the moment. Other adult citizens, especially immediate family members, typically asked for compassion and were thus the best judges of a person's compassionate acts. A warrior citizen who is without compassion is without family, without friends, and without a nation.

IV. *Hetsevahe (to be fearless of physical harm)*

When young men and women mature into adults, they endure physical changes in puberty. Traditionally, the Cheyennes held puberty ceremonies for both young men and women. Through these ceremonies, older family members administered numerous activities to initiate their younger relatives into adulthood. Young people endured challenges that tested their physical, mental, and spiritual strength. Young men, for example, would endure an "old man's" sweat lodge ceremony, in which older male relatives taught the proper conduct of manhood. In some cases the young man would be taken out into the woods and left alone, without food or water, for a day or two. Here the young man must overcome his fear of animals, the elements of nature, and the spiritual world. Young men would not endure the more structured and lengthy fasting ceremony, popularly known as the vision quest, until after their initiation into manhood.

Young women, after their first menses cycle, would endure a ceremony in a lodge where they were taught about the responsibilities of motherhood and childrearing. The old Só'taeo'o tradition required a young woman to sit in the lodge of the Ésevone. Female family members and medicine women were available to teach them of the significance of enduring physical pain for the sake of procreation. For four days, she is bound from practicing a number of seemingly trivial activities and must not touch anything belonging to a man that may compromise the medicine that he had earned related to that object. She is purified with numerous herbs and welcomed into the world as a new person, a woman.[18]

Both the male and female initiation ceremonies were designed to instill mental and physical strength for all citizens of the nation. After such ceremonies, young adults could pursue higher ceremonials to refine, reinforce, and improve mental and physical development. Citizens must be fearless of physical harm to protect themselves and, more important, their children from harm.

v. *Héestaáhá (to be courageous mentally and spiritually)*

Courage is valued at nearly every stage of Cheyenne life, but it is especially fostered in young male warriors who wish to be physically courageous in their efforts to achieve status. Mental and spiritual courage, however, are values that require more patience and practice. Mental courage cannot be achieved without the development of the mind. Traditionally, the Cheyenne people had no formal educational institutions or schools. They had a culture that encouraged the development of intellect through conversation, listening, and sharing of knowledge and wisdom. The mental development of citizens was just as important as physical development. The family unit was responsible for fostering intellectual growth, especially in bridging the gap between grandparents and grandchildren. Learning was a daily activity and achievement was judged by the quality of a citizen. If a person lived a balanced life, then he or she made wise decisions. To have mental courage means that a citizen has mastered decision making to a high degree and is unafraid to make the tough choices. Mental courage is intelligent, graceful poise in the face of potential hardship. Spiritual courage is the solace and confidence after a citizen makes a decision. Spiritual courage is developed in ceremonies. While physical courage is limited by the physical health of a citizen, there are no limits to mental and spiritual courage, as all citizens can refine and develop their minds and spirits well into old age.

vi. *Ó'tôsétano (to be diligent in action)*

To truly be a citizen means that one must dedicate his or her life to serve the people, which does not mean that citizenship is equivalent to a life of servitude. Instead, it means that a citizen must always remember to act in the best interests of those Cheyennes not yet born. According to Cheyenne custom, a person's diligence is a measure of his or her spiritual discipline and temperament. A diligent person is mindful of his or her actions and how they will impact those around them, even after long periods of time.

To be diligent in action requires much devotion and belief in the unseen and unspoken powers that a citizen holds toward his people, homeland, and living-nation. A citizen will naturally develop a strong sense of devotion if he or she is raised in the proper setting and in an environment that values service as its own reward. A citizen must honor work, the process of completing a task, as much as finishing the work. The effort, time, and energy are more valuable than merely reaping the benefits.

VII. *Tâhpe'êstáha (to be kind and courteous)*

The most noteworthy citizens are those who hold themselves to high ethical and cultural standards. They are kind and courteous to their fellow citizens, and even show respect to their enemies. A citizen should be pleasant to be around and exhibit a warrior etiquette that honors life and all living things. Historically, any tribal member could become part of another family unit through marriage or adoption. This meant that every citizen had the potential to become a family member and any family could possibly join another. How careless would citizens be if they treated other people and families with disdain, disrespect, and dishonor and come to find that one of their close kin marries into the same family? The same can be said for captives of an enemy nation. At any moment a captive could become a citizen's sister or brother, so they were treated with the same kindness and courtesy while in captivity and after adoption. Acts of kindness from one citizen to another were believed to reciprocate to other citizens throughout the nation, thus sustaining balance, unity, and spiritual health. Children were taught at an early age to ignore arrogant people and to remain silent among disrespectful egotists. Before the introduction of alcohol and the vices of white culture, Cheyenne citizens rarely engaged in angry quarrels, family feuds, and intratribal conflict. In the event that some citizens lost their composure and forgot their principles and traditional ways, none other than the Véhoo'o employed conflict resolution and peacemaking strategies.

VIII. *Xanovahe (to be honest and righteous)*

Honesty is a fundamental virtue in the Cheyenne culture. Citizens are taught at an early age, by experienced parents and grandparents, the significance and benefits of honesty and righteousness. Nearly every story in the Cheyenne oral tradition emphasizes the importance of honesty in character and the necessity to uphold righteousness in the world. In order to continue the living-nation, Cheyenne citizens must practice the ceremonial ways and live honest and righteous lives. Should the pitfalls of lies and injustice creep into one sector of their way of life and dominate, then the entire way of living will be compromised. An individual must practice the art of honesty and continually learn and revisit the meaning of righteousness. These are not ideas of individualism and selfishness; instead, they require much commitment and selflessness.

IX. *Momáxahe (to be humble)*

A citizen must learn to be humble for even the smallest and simplest of accomplishments and success. This is not to say that Cheyenne families do not celebrate joy and humor. On the contrary, humbleness generates more authentic expressions of happiness and elation. Children learn best from parents how to react and maintain humbleness, when they witness restraint and discipline in the first person. If parents do not exhibit humbleness at all times, their children will see and come to mimic immodest and conceited behavior. Should a child mature into adulthood to believe that this behavior is the cultural norm, then he will become vain and do things for self-gratification and not for the good of the living-nation. To be humble is to realize that there are greater things in life than self-image. Humbleness is a principle that should be refined as young citizens mature into adulthood, leadership, and parenthood.

x. *Méohtåhé'heōneve (to be loving)*

As citizens, individual Cheyenne adults encompass a spiritual bond that connects every person to a much larger body of the living-nation. This bond is sustained through the love that one has for his or her nation, which is the love that one has for the Cheyenne homeland, oral tradition, spiritual practices, and ways of living. Elaine Strange Owl explained "one'seómeméhotåhtsestôtse" (true love) to be when a married man and woman discuss everything together, even if they have anxiety or bad feelings.[19] They had to talk things out, without arguing and fighting, to help one another. Children learn to love from their parents, grandparents, and other relatives, close and distant. Strange Owl elaborates:

> Right away they start to want to know how to talk, children. You can't think of anything else, but that the child is taught and that he is loved. They understand even as babies until they grow up. They are also taught how to play and how to work. Right away as they are helped and taught, they understand that they are loved. The child learns to love as a man and a woman love when he is loved.[20]

If a child does not learn what love is, then he or she will mature into an adult who cannot build and hold on to any relationships: romantic, familial, or social. Cheyenne families are united not by blind loyalty and kinship, but by spiritual bonds fostered and nurtured by each person's love for their parents, siblings, and relatives.

CONCLUSION

Warrior citizenship of the traditional Cheyenne cultural way of life demanded responsibility from individuals; whether as military protection or as family members, every citizen was a warrior in his or her own right and duty. Responsibilities for fellow citizens, one's family, and, most important, one's self were the highest of priorities for those born into and adopted into the nation. Traditional Cheyennes often ridiculed or criticized a person's family if that person was acting out of the ordinary or going against principles of citizenship. If a young man was unpleasant to be around, pompous, or consistently lied, then older women of the community would warn their children and grandchildren not to associate with him or his family members. Cheyenne boys were often told not to play with kids who lied because those kids could lie about events and blame them for the troubles they themselves had created. Children were also taught to avoid those who liked to brag and to not brag about themselves, because people who boasted or showed off were asking for trouble, unworthy of what they had, or in need of something they would not earn. Parents, they were taught, had to be models of good citizenship by enduring the challenges of being righteous and telling the truth, but also revealing the true meaning of humility, spiritual strength, and righteousness. If a young woman was lazy, gossiped, or was unloving to her family members, then older women would warn other young men and women to avoid this person and her family. Such warnings were not in spite or in hate of other families, but to protect the immediate family members from the burdens of hardship, potential pain, and suffering that such people and families may impose.

Elder Cheyennes understood the powers of the supernatural, the delicate balance of energy, and the importance of protecting their own from outside and immediate dangers, both little and big. Citizenship is not a right, it is a privilege, and citizens must remember these principles, for they will be tested from time to time. To truly be a citizen is to accept the life afforded by the living-nation, devote oneself to the Cheyenne cultural way of living, and learn to sacrifice and submit to the unseen forces of the living-nation. It is a lifetime goal.

PART IV

Colonizing and Decolonizing the Tsėhéstáno

A spider was walking along a river valley. It sure was a beautiful sight as the summer was in full bloom. He came to a patch of plum trees and the first was ripe and looked very tempting and good to eat. To one tree he went and standing under it, tried to reach for the fruit. But the fruit was beyond his reach. He then got a stick and tried to knock the fruit down. The fruit would not fall. He then raised his hands up towards the fruit on the tree. "You pretty round plums, pretty ripe plums come down," he sang. And the fruit fell. The spider ate and ate the fallen plums. Near the top of the tree hung a very large plum. The spider said again: "You that biggest plum come down to me," he sang. The big plum came down upon him and knocked him unconscious, and when he was about conscious, he reached for the plum and laid there eating it all up. Then he began to feel as though he would explode. He started for his home and came to a low place on the ground. He squatted down and his stomach just poured out until he had to swim out of his dung nearly exhausted. Thus the length of the legend is ended.
—Mack Haag (Southern Cheyenne)[1]

CHAPTER 12

Vé'hó'e: The Trickster

LONG BEFORE the arrival of whites, the Cheyenne people had developed a rich oral tradition to teach proper conduct and reinforce acceptable behavior. These behavioral teachings, which were part of the Tsėhéseamanėō'o, applied to all citizens and certainly all leaders. Other than origin stories, trickster stories were a body of stories that were fundamental to the Cheyenne cultural way of life. Cheyenne trickster stories revealed how some humans can and will use deceit and manipulation to acquire short-term gains. Vé'hó'e (Spider) is the Cheyenne trickster, and his stories are humorous and entertaining, but also serve as teaching tools.[1] The Cheyenne trickster stories are also cryptic and emotional because they reveal the dark side of humanity. This is done to warn and remind Cheyennes that some people are selfish, ruthless, and without regard for the traditional teachings and principles of the Tsėhéseamanėō'o. Vé'hó'e is unlike any other character found in European cultures and like nothing found in Christian belief.[2] The central purpose of the Vé'hó'e tradition is to remind the Cheyennes of human nature and the human thought process.

Vé'hó'e stories can be quite disturbing for young people, especially when he succeeds in his crafty and manipulative plans, but the stories serve a sacred purpose: to mentally and spiritually prepare young people for adulthood. Although there is no single origin story of Vé'hó'e, the story below is likely the one that best introduces the trickster to Cheyenne reality.

The Powerful Boy and Spider

There was a very large camp near a creek. The chief of this camp of people had two beautiful daughters, one much older than the other. The oldest daughter had grown into young womanhood and had many admirers. One day a young man from a distant country was to arrive to the camp seeking her for his bride.

A spider hunting along the nearby creek met this young man and knowing of his expected arrival at the camp was jealous of him, for he wished for the young maiden for his wife. The spider shot an arrow with his bow up a very tall tree and it hung up near the top.

Upon meeting the young man the spider said, "Climb for my arrow," said he. The young man being all dressed in his best costume replied, "You climb for it yourself." Then the spider kept on begging him to climb for the arrow until he finally consented. Then the young man pulled off his clothes and climbed up naked, and when he neared the top the spider called, "Stick up there," said he. And the young man stuck to the tree and could not get loose to come down. The spider then pulled off his clothing and took the young man's costume and dressed himself in it and painted his face so that the people would not recognize him. He then left the young man and walked away. The young man finally became loose and turned into a very small child, living in the tall grasses along the creek.[3]

The young man's ability to transform himself into a "very small child" allowed him to escape from the trap. Unfortunately, this feat also left him powerless to change himself back to a young man, since he also lost his knowledge and power to do so. Throughout the epic of the Powerful Boy and Spider, this young boy endures numerous challenges but proves that he was indeed very powerful, especially as listeners learn how he essentially reteaches himself to be the powerful young man he was before Vé'hó'e deceived and cheated him. In the oral tradition, the two main characters, Powerful Boy and Spider, cross paths on several later occasions and each time, Vé'hó'e attempts to deceive the people and manipulate situations to best serve him. In the end, Vé'hó'e is banished, and we can assume that he then begins his own trials and tribulations. Thus begins the adventures of Vé'hó'e.

There are two major categories of Vé'hó'e stories; the first are those before the arrival of whites and the second are those after the arrival of whites. All of the stories have several commonalities. One major theme is that Vé'hó'e is respected as a member of the community and has his own family. We can assume that the Cheyennes believed that every family had a person who embodied the characteristics of Vé'hó'e or, from a Western perspective, was the "black sheep" of the family. In nearly every story Vé'hó'e is a jealous and selfish person who finds himself the victim of his own doings, especially in his attempts to sabotage others or in his efforts to cheat his way to fame and glory. Although Vé'hó'e freely and frequently violates customs and traditions of the Tsêhéseamanēō'o (the Cheyenne cultural way of living), he does not violate any of the sacred laws of the Tsêhéstanove, the

Cheyenne spiritual way of living. In the end, Vé'hó'e is not completely written off as an evil person that should be permanently banished, since that punishment is reserved only for proven murderers. Vé'hó'e is a forgivable fool.

Vé'hó'e stories from before the arrival of whites tend to focus on hygiene, etiquette, social practices, and personal choices, especially those made in private. Vé'hó'e primarily interacts with plants and animals. In these stories Vé'hó'e is a dupe and reminds us that everyone has inappropriate thoughts or makes poor decisions from time to time. The lessons highlight that only a fool will continually make the same wrong decisions, expecting different results. These stories were primarily told to children, but their teachings were to be carried into adulthood. These stories reinforce that any Cheyenne person who behaved as Vé'hó'e did would face humiliation and shame, even if these actions were done in private.

Vé'hó'e is significant to the cultural sovereignty of the Cheyenne Nation because the teachings from his sacred stories helped sustain an entire way of living.[4] They tell the Cheyennes how to live in harmony with one another and with nature, when alone or in public. Vé'hó'e uncovers the delicate balance and the interconnectedness of all living beings on Earth. In other stories, Vé'hó'e deliberately abuses his knowledge and power at the expense of other living beings, as in the story below.

Wihio, by Belle Highwalking

I am going to tell a story about [Vé'hó'e]. As he walked along, the prairie dogs stood up looking at him. "[Vé'hó'e], where are you going?" they asked him. "What are you packing on your head?"

"These are my songs," he said. "I'm going to sing for someone."

"Could we dance for you?"

He said, "Yes but these are hard songs. Everyone has to close their eyes because whoever opens them will get pink eye."

"We will dance for you."

He put them in a row with the fat ones close to him. Among them was a bird. I don't know what kind of bird. The small prairie dogs were placed beside the bird.

[Vé'hó'e] said, "Let me go make a drum stick." He got a heavy stick and started to sing to them and pounded on something. After they started to dance, he said, "Whoever opens their eyes will get pink eye." After they began dancing hard, he knocked all the fat ones on the head.

The bird, who was dancing with them, thought something was funny because he couldn't feel the ones dancing near him. He opened his eyes and saw that he was the only one left. He shouted, "Run for your lives! He has killed most of us!" He ran to the creek and, since that time, that kind of bird has pink eye from time to time.

[Vé'hó'e] made a fire and, while he sang, he dressed the prairie dogs and cooked them. As he was sitting there waiting for the prairie dogs to cook, the trees began to squeak and rub. He said, "Don't scold one another. Don't fight. Oh, you just don't listen." He crawled up the tree and got his hand stuck between two trees. The trees must have been rubbing in the wind. While the man was up there, a coyote came smelling around. [Vé'hó'e] told him, "I suppose you had to come around. I suppose you want my food. Just eat that one." And then he told him just to eat the next one only, and they kept this up until all the prairie dogs were eaten. [Vé'hó'e] had the livers and hearts buried in the coals and he told the coyote not to eat those too. So the coyote dug in the coals and got them out and in the pouch in which they were cooking, he put ashes. Then he went away.

[Vé'hó'e's] hand came loose and he climbed down. He grabbed the pouch out of the coals and bit into it but found nothing but ashes. He cried and cried. "Ha, there you go, you funny thing. I'll catch you somewhere."

[Vé'hó'e] followed the trail of the coyote and found him sleeping off his feast. [Vé'hó'e] thought of many things he could do to the coyote. "I could hit him on his head but I might only bruise him. Or I could boil him. Or I could throw him in a fire." So he built a fire and picked up the coyote whose neck was hanging limp. He threw him in the fire but the coyote jumped right over it and ran away from him.[5]

Before the arrival of whites, Vé'hó'e's trickster actions typically led him to come face to face with personal shame and embarrassment. It was assumed that if any Cheyenne person behaved as did Vé'hó'e, then they would also face personal shame and embarrassment. Sometimes, however, Vé'hó'e would do something that warranted public shame and embarrassment. In some stories he endured public shame and embarrassment, like the story that follows.

The Spider and the Rat

There was a large camp circle. In the camp was a big chief. He had a daughter became of marriageable age. Her father the chief wanted to choose her husband for her from the young men in the camp. So he the chief instructed the crier of the camp to announce that there would be a dance for all the young men in nude. And that the chief was going to select from the dancers one young man who would have the smallest penis. So the crier announced that the dance would take place in the afternoon and that all the young men should dance in nude and that the chief would choose from the dancers the young man with the smallest penis.

In the camp was a spider, he too admired and wished for the chief's daughter as a wife. Walking towards the river he hunted for a pack rat pile and laid down close by it pretending to sleep. And the rats would run over across his chest. And he would try to grab for them but they would escape from him every time. One would escape he would say, "The creature runs swiftly," said he. Finally he caught one and holding it in his hand began to pray to the rat. "For the sakes of your mother and father and all your beloved relatives, have pity on me and loan me your penis, for this afternoon and I will leave mine with you, until I return your penis to you," said he. The rat agreed to fulfill his wish. So the spider returned to the camp where the dance had already begun. He immediately joined the dance yelling and shouting and dancing mostly in sight of the chief.

When the singing and drumming had ceased for a short interval, the spider heard a cry from the rat saying, "Spi-der, Spi-der! These boys are shooting your penis with arrows."

The spider then yelled and shouted saying the dancers should shout in merriment. The dance then started with more and bigger noise.

When the singing and drumming had ceased for a short interval, the spider heard again the cry from the rat. This time a little closer, "Spi-der! Spi-der! These boys are shooting your penis with arrows."

The spider then yelled and shouted saying, "The dancers should shout in merriment," said he.

The dance then started again with more and bigger noise, when again the singing and drumming ceased. The spider heard the cry from the rat still closer, "Spi-der! Spi-der! These boys are shooting your penis with arrows."

The spider then yelled and shouted saying the dancers should shout with merriment. . . . The dance then started again with more and bigger noise and the chief came forward from his seat to select his son-in-law. When right near the tipi they all heard the cry from the rat saying, "Spi-der! Spi-der! These boys are shooting your penis with arrows."

Right then and there the dancers and singers ran out with the chief following them and found the rat dragging the spider's penis, pierced by arrows, which were inflicted by the boys. The spider picked up the rat with his penis and ran towards the woods out of sight. Where upon he scolded the rat and called him all kinds of inferior names. Thus the length of the legend is ended.[6]

This Vé'hó'e story reveals humor in traditional Cheyenne band life. At its core, the story highlights vulgarities to reinforce proper conduct when courting, and it is particularly important to adolescent males.[7] The Cheyennes need Vé'hó'e, for he is the epitome of improper behavior. The Cheyennes have pity for him, but do not inflict any more pain or suffering than what he has caused for himself.

Despite all of his shortcomings Vé'hó'e is not perceived as a villain or an enemy. He possesses all the attributes of a sane person, but continually fails to make the right choices. He is a sacred figure only in that he manages to resurrect or regenerate himself for each story. The stories are short but meaningful accounts of his poor decision making. Vé'hó'e is not a leader, and in the traditional Cheyenne belief system, a person who embodied his character would never rise to a leadership position. He is crafty; Vé'hó'e is a fool, a narcissist, and representative of all that is wrong with people who have overinflated egos. However, the people who interact with Vé'hó'e do not devalue him, nor do they ridicule, bully, or enslave him. No person judges or mistreats Vé'hó'e, nor is he corrected for his shortcomings and poor choices. The beings of nature—plants and animals—however, always appear in stories as the judge and executioner of Vé'hó'e. In the end, nature restores balance to the imbalances created by Vé'hó'e, as in the story presented next.

The Spider and the Coyote

A spider and his large family of children camped out on a prairie. The spider hunted and hunted for game, but always returned home empty-handed at the close of the day. His wife and children were at the point of starvation for need of food.

The spider while out hunting killed a large buffalo near the banks of a deep stream of water. A large shady tree stood near the edge of the bank with some of its branches extending out above the water. The spider after killing the buffalo carried the meat under the shade of the tree. Then he [went] home to tell his wife and children to help him to bring the meat to their tipi.

During his absence a coyote came along and found the pile of buffalo meat under the large shady tree on the banks of a deep stream of water. The coyote seeing no one nearby carried the meat up the tree and hung it on the branches extending out above the water. Then the spider returned with his wife and children to the spot where he had left the meat and the meat was not there. They hunted and searched for the meat and could find no trace of it. Then the spider looked over the bank into the water and there he saw the pile of meat at the bottom of the water. And being so hungry he leaped into the water and dived for the meat. And again and again he dived searching for the meat in the water, but could not find the meat. He thought by staying under the water longer he could find it.

He then told his wife and children to tie a large stone to his neck. "My children, when my coals appear on top of the water yell with merriment," said he. So he dived again and stayed under the water until his coals appeared on the surface of the water and the children yelled with merriment. He finally floated to the top all but drowned. His wife and children dragged him to the bank. His face to the skin [were] in a dying condition. When he was sufficiently revived he saw the coyote and the meat on the branches of the tree up above him.

He begged the coyote to throw down a small piece of meat for his children. "Have the children to stand in a group so they can catch the meat," where upon the coyote tossed a large piece of meat killing them all. And [then the coyote threw] another large piece down upon the wife [and] killed her too. And [then the coyote threw another and] killed the spider. Thus the length of the legend is ended.[8]

In later stories, after the arrival of whites, the plots of the stories change. They include Cheyenne spiritual leaders who try to help and teach the trickster, but because Ve'ho'e is a true trickster by nature, he does not change and inevitably endures hardship. The stories are typically titled, "The Old Man and the Spider," or "The Indian Man and the Spider." As history shows, the Cheyenne trickster tradition became very useful and meaningful when whites arrived to Cheyenne country.

THE WHITE TRIBE

The histories of the Tsėhéstáno and the United States of America have very similar stories. They both built their nations after triumphing over tyranny. The Tsėhéstáno united ten bands, while the United States unified thirteen colonies. The building of the Tsėhéstáno comprises numerous origin stories, heroic and tragic alike. Accordingly, the history of the building of the United States of America also includes stories of heroes. But before the United States was born, the Cheyennes had already encountered white men. The northern bands of Cheyennes first encountered white men from the northeast in the late 1700s.[9] These were the French traders who initially introduced rifles and cloth, and trade centered on beaver pelts and tobacco. For the most part, the French traders were of no real threat to the Cheyenne Nation, probably because they were not settling Cheyenne lands in hordes. The Cheyennes perceived these white men as aliens but who belonged to an unknown "white tribe."[10] They were viewed as trade and commerce allies. While the Cheyenne Nation began to make peace and unify with the Indian nations like Arapaho and Lakota on the Great Plains, to the east the "white tribe" began rebuilding itself.

On July 4, 1776, the United States declared independence from the British Empire and was truly a "fledging nation" compared to the Tsėhéstáno and other American Indian nations.[11] America's victory in the Revolutionary War led the fledging nation to the experiment of nation building, with a primary task to unify the recently liberated independent colonies under one sovereign. While each state held on to its own power, rights, and sovereignty, each state was also reluctant to give up such power for the sake of creating the federal union we now call the United States.[12] In early June of 1776, just before the declaration, the Continental Congress appointed a committee to construct a blueprint to unify the colonies into a confederation. On November 15, 1777, the Congress adopted the Articles of Confederation as the first constitution of the White Tribe, but ratification did not occur until all thirteen states agreed to the articles on March 1, 1781. A founding principle of the articles was "friendship," and the colonies and their leaders were to rely on this principle to establish a unified nation. Given the history of British centralized power, the Americans were hesitant to give up any authority, even to supposed "friends."[13] The White Tribe was doomed to fail under the articles, as corruption, instability, and the general lack of executive and judicial powers crumbled under state sovereignty. Before George Washington, the White Tribe had eight presidents under the Articles of Confederation. This was not the government that we now know.

After the Constitutional Convention in 1787, the leaders of the White Tribe were able to develop a new government based on the democratic principles of the Six Nations of the Iroquois Confederacy.[14] The newly founded United States of America then began treatying with Indian nations to acquire more Indian land. Initially the Americans did not want to settle on Cheyenne and other Indigenous nations' lands in the Great Plains, but as the white population grew, so did their need to expand. After the Louisiana Purchase was brokered between the US and French governments, the White Tribe began to invade. In a modest form of colonization in 1803, the Lewis and Clark Expedition was sent out to lay claim to the newly purchased land.[15] In the middle of this land was the United Cheyenne Nation and their allies.

The Lewis and Clark Expedition, or "Corps of Discovery," proclaimed political and economic jurisdiction on behalf of the United States. The Corps was to also note the flora and fauna, including the Indians, identifying the "friendly" Indians from the "hostile." Among the trade items the Corps brought were medals. These peace medals were not to secure peace, but to secure safe passage through hostile Indian territories. When a delegation of Cheyenne chiefs met the Corps in August of 1806, they were unimpressed. The chiefs refused the gifts from the whites because they had knowledge that the whites had a strange medicine. Mainstream historians translate the refusal of the gifts as a response to the "fear" or a "pagan superstition" that the Cheyennes felt toward foreign objects, such as peace medals.[16] However, the refusal of these gifts occurred because the Véhoo'o perceived these items as "tainted" with a "murderer's stench": the sacred leaders were keenly aware, sensing the energy of items that came from the whites.[17]

To the south, southern bands of Cheyennes were modestly trading with the Mexicans and Spanish for items such as dried meat, buffalo robes, and animal products.[18] An act of colonization came to the Cheyennes when the Mexicans tried to settle the lands of the southern bands of Cheyennes in the 1840s, when the Arkansas River was the US-Mexico border. Their colony failed. Bent (Southern Cheyenne) described the Mexican colonists as unambitious to settle in Indian lands, for they lived "in deadly fear of the Indians, so the little settlement soon broke up."[19] Most white men of the east shared the same views of the Indians that the Mexicans held, but when gold was discovered in California, hordes of white men flooded across the Great Plains. The prophet Sweet Medicine warned of these white men:

> They will be looking for a certain stone. They will wear what I have spoken of, but it will be of all colors, pretty. Perhaps they will not listen to what you say to them, but you will listen to what they say to you. They will be people who do not get tired, but who will keep pushing forward, going, going all the time. They will keep coming, coming. They will try always to give you things, but do not take them. At last I think that you will take the things that they offer you, and this will bring sickness to you. These people do not follow the way of our great-grandfather. They follow another way. They will travel everywhere, looking for this stone which our great-grandfather put on the earth in many places.[20]

COLONIZING THE TSÉHÉSTÁNO

American Indians today must have a general understanding of colonization in order to have an understanding of decolonization; unfortunately, they are closely related. Furthermore, today's American Indians must understand how their ancestors, who were victims of colonization, perceived it and how they preserved it in the oral tradition. For the Cheyennes, colonization was simply invasion, violence, and assimilation. The Cheyenne people understood colonization as a destructive force from alien peoples from the east, as foretold in the cryptic Sweet Medicine prophecy, which has been published in numerous places. White Eagle's (Southern Cheyenne) unpublished account from 1910 also includes instructions on how to survive colonization:

> "There shall come from the place the sun rises from men who shall destroy all the buffalo and take the land from the Indians. The cow and calf shall take the buffalo's place. They shall be all over the place. The white men shall come thick as bugs. They shall be all over the land. You shall give up your fighting." He, Mattsĭ'ō'iv, was telling the people everything what was going to be: the railroads and people. He told the people that the chief societies should be forever, they shall be different ones every 10 years. This is the 7th generation; change of societies. This story has been told by his ancestors. Try to keep in mind what I have said, and follow the rules. That's the reason the Cheyennes live so today.[21]

In 1963, Hoffman (Southern Cheyenne) shared the Sweet Medicine prophecy, which became synonymous with colonization and emphasized what the colonizer, the white man, will do: "He'll destroy for you everything that you used to depend on. He'll destroy everything."[22] In 1977, Elaine Strange Owl (Northern Cheyenne) also recalled the prophecy: "A person will come to you, he will be wrapped up, he said. With this word he referred to clothing which we wear now. This person who will come to you will distract you from your way of life, he will do away with your way of life, he said."[23] The Cheyennes believed that anything from the white man was a product of colonization and therefore not to be trusted.

THE FRIENDSHIP TREATY

In 1825, the leaders of the Cheyenne Nation signed the "Friendship Treaty" with the United States. Given that this was the first of several treaties between the Tsėhéstáno and the White Tribe, and that it was based on the white people's principle of "friendship," it was doomed to fail: if whites could not be friends among themselves, how did they expect to achieve friendship with others? This so-called Friendship Treaty affirmed three goals: (1) to affirm that the Cheyenne Nation was recognized under the authority of the United States within its territory and "supremacy"; (2) to regulate trade and intercourse between the two; and (3) to enter into the "friendship" of the United States, "under their protection and to extend to them, from time to time, such benefits and acts of kindness as may be convenient, and seem just and proper to the President of the United States."[24]

VÉ'HÓ'E: THE TRICKSTER

During this time the Tsėhéstáno was one autonomous nation, and not yet divided into the Northern and Southern Cheyenne. Upon the signing and ratification of this first treaty with the US government, the Cheyenne Nation's sovereignty was formally recognized, just as other Indian nations were when they signed treaties with the White Tribe. General Henry Atkinson was responsible for negotiating this treaty, as well as other treaties on the Plains at the time, but he did not realize that the Véhoo'o who signed the 1825 treaty were representing only one of the ten bands of the entire Tsėhéstáno.[25] This band was a southern band under the leadership of Council Chiefs High Backed Wolf, Little Moon, Buffalo Head, and One Who Talks Against Others. Nevertheless, the treaty was ratified and applied to all bands of the Tsėhéstáno.

The first full-scale American effort of colonization, beyond trade relations, began in the late 1840s in the same era and is remembered among the Cheyennes as when the white Americans cut through their country to mine gold in California and Oregon. The gold rush of 1849 affirmed the Sweet Medicine prophecy and led to the mass extinction of the sacred buffalo and the introduction of exotic diseases like cholera. The southern bands suffered the most from starvation and sickness. The Cheyennes no longer associated the white men with trade, but rather with sickness and death.[26] The white men and their vices, culture, and material came to represent the destructive forces of colonialism articulated in the Sweet Medicine prophecy. But the Cheyennes continued to engage in peacemaking, following the Cheyenne principles of brotherhood and peace, not white man's "friendship."

After the Cheyennes interacted with numerous white men, they viewed white culture as odd and in some cases contradictory and hypocritical. It did not take long for the Cheyennes to name individuals of the white race as Vé'hó'e, the trickster. Most of the whites that the Cheyennes encountered and interacted with behaved as Vé'hó'e. These encounters and interactions became so common that the Cheyennes no longer believed that these white men belonged to a White Tribe; instead they were a nation of vé'hó'e, tricksters. The behaviors of the white man fit those of this character well, and the name vé'hó'e became synonymous with all whites. Eventually the meaning of vé'hó'e completely changed to simply mean "white man." This change is evident in the trickster stories. After the arrival of the whites, the trickster stories began to have a new meaning with a new face of a new character: vé'hó'e the white man.[27] Most involve an Indian man who teaches "white man" a power or trick. The Indian man advises "white man" to never use the power or do the trick more than four times. Does white man obey? Below are examples of trickster stories set in a time after the arrival of whites. The stories and their meanings need no further interpretation.

White Man and the Buffalo, by Handing Crow (1910)

In due time there were seven buffalos sitting besides a white man came upon the hill crying. The oldest she buffalo asked him, "What are you crying for?"

"Yes," he says. "I am crying, I wish to become a buffalo." The oldest bull asked him which one of those seven shall be yourself. He looked over the seven. He picked a scabby bull to be himself. Scabby Bull got up and stood beside him and told him to run with him. When he ran with him, he himself became a scabby bull. He was with the buffalo. He ate grasses and played [with] them. He ate all he could. When he looked about the country he saw Indians. He scared the buffalo off. He did this until they were played out. When they all sat down, they were surrounded by Indians and they made a charge at them, and ran away. The White Man Bull was overtaken by a young band of Indians. They shot him with [their] bow and arrows. He tried to make them stop by shouting, "I am White Man, I'm not a buffalo!" And that's the last of it.[28]

White Man and the Wooden Horse, by Medicine Top (1910)

There was a man charming the buffalo at a distance. At the same time a white man came up crying, saying, "I wish my brother would give me that trick."

He replied, "Brother, I have got pretty hard ways. When I do this trick, I do it once, twice, or thrice. I cannot do it four times."

White Man said, "I can do that once in a long while." He was crying for that trick.

"Well," the man said to him, "come on, jump on this horse," showing him a wooden horse. He jumped on the wooden horse. The man told him to shut his eyes. Then he whipped the wooden horse, and it went as swift as any bird. He was right in the middle of the buffalos with bow in hand. He shot and killed one.

"Oh yes! I can do that once in a long while." As soon as he killed one he went home, thinking he would come back with his wife to dress it afterwards. While on the way home, he saw another bunch of buffalos. He thought he could charge and kill another. In this trick he killed another buffalo. He left him and went on. Thinking he would come back with his wife [to] dress [it] later. And so the third time he saw another bunch in the bottom of a riverbed. So he made a charge at them, thinking it would be the third one he would kill. He killed one.

He was greatly rejoiced. He expected his wife and children to come after the [meat]. The fourth time he went on a kill he could see his tipi and the smoke coming out. He looked around and saw another bunch of buffalo. He charged at them and killed one. The fourth time the horse stumbled and broke his neck and the man also [broke his neck]. So the man was lost from the camp. The woman wondered where he had gone. One day when she felt sorry, she went down the creek. She saw in the distance something like crows flying about. She went over there. She found her husband had broken his neck and his horse. She was surprised that he had a horse. So she buried him right beside his horse. And that's the last telling.[29]

White Man and the Sweet Potatoes, by Handing Crow (1910)

There was a man digging wild sweet potatoes and ate them raw. There was another man [White Man] who came up crying to him and asked him, "I wish I could eat what you ate."

The man said, "Brother, you can eat all you want." So the man ate all his belly could carry. The sweet potato said, "You mustn't eat me too much, something might happen." While he was eating them, gas formed in his belly. It almost reached to his mouth, but went the other way. He exploded. He never quit but ate again, and made a[nother] big explosion. It threw him high in the air. When he came down he was scared, and quit eating and ran home. Before he got home he hollered, "Old woman, put all your children into the travois, something very bad is going to happen." So the old woman put all the children in the travois by the time the man got there. He crawled under the travois and exploded again. He drove the children high in the air and killed them all. And that's the end.[30]

White Man Calls Feathers, by Ruben Black Horse (1931)

There was a big flat, an Indian was walking alone and he stopped on the prairie. After he stopped he hollered out, "Red feathers and white feathers." After he called them out, red and white feathers began to fall from the sky. He walked on a little distance and repeated, "Red feathers and white feathers."

They fell again. He did this 3 times. After the 3rd time, a white man came in sight crying. This white man while crying said, "I wish my brother would give me his power." And the white man met the Indian and the Indian said, "All right, whatever I give you, you must repeat this 4 times." This white man walked away and he stopped after he got off a little way and started repeating what the Indian told him. And he repeated the same words the Indian had used: "Red feathers and white feathers." And the feathers began to fall. He walked and repeated the same thing. The white man said, "I've repeated it twice now." Though he had said it only once. He walked off and repeated it again. It was his third time, though, the white man said it was his second. He walked and repeated the same. And the white man said it was his 3rd time, though it was his 4th time. And he walked off and repeated it again. Instead of the feathers falling, all kinds of bones fell from above and hurt him so badly that he started to cry. Of course that ended him. He died for overdoing the power given to him.[31]

White Man Loses His Eyes, by Ruben Black Horse (1931)

There was a man going up a creek and as he walked along he came to a high bank. There were tall trees and bushes. This Indian said, "My eyes are hanging on the brush," and both were hanging. And he said, "Come back in my sockets," and they came. He walked away from this spot and came to a similar place, and he repeated what he said. He said this 4 times. And after he said it the 4th time, a white man came upon him. The white man was crying: "Brother, I wish you would give me your power," and the white man was told to repeat it 4 times. And the white man walked off and repeated the words and his eyes were hanging in the tree. And he said, "My eyes come back to my sockets," and they did. This man repeated it 4 times. The 5th time he repeated, "My eyes come back to my sockets." But they did not come back. And his eyes hung until they dried up. And he started to cry, got down on his hands and knees, crawling around. While crawling around a number of mice were rolling around him, and he caught one. And he said to the mouse, "Partner give me your eyes." And the mouse said his eyes were too small for him. "Partner, give me one of your eyes." So the mouse did. After the mouse gave his eye, Whiteman put it in his socket. You could barely see the mouse's eye; it was so far in the socket. The white man could [see] through the eye given him. Walking around he saw some buffalos. He walked up crying to a buffalo, "Partner, my eyes are hanging in the brush all dried up. Give me your eyes." The buffalo gave up one eye. So the white man had one big eye and one little one.[32]

The new definition for the Cheyenne trickster Vé'hó'e changed the meaning of trickster stories from mere stories of entertainment to warnings against potential disaster. For nearly a century after the signing of the Friendship Treaty, the Cheyennes and their nation would continue to face numerous challenges from their white "friends" to the east.

Conclusion: Decolonizing "The Rez"

MUCH OF HOW the Cheyenne people lived over the course of nearly a thousand years cannot be easily documented in a single book, and what remains of our traditional ways should be protected and remain undisclosed to outsiders, as these ways continue to persist as central parts of the Cheyenne culture. As I reflect upon a conclusion of this book, I must reassert its purpose: to provide a narrative of the history of the Tsėhéstáno, from a Cheyenne perspective, and to provide a foundation for much-needed change in Indian country, in particular, within the Northern and Southern Cheyenne Nations. I provided a detailed description of the Cheyenne national identity and way of life, highlighting principles, teachings, concepts, ideas, customs, and laws that survived the tests of time, the violence of white invasion, and the assimilation policies of the United States government. The path to resurgence and autonomy must begin with a single step, and I believe that this book is a move in a positive direction.

In reexamining the theoretical framework for this study, I must highlight four key concepts: indigenousness, sovereignty, colonization, and decolonization. These concepts provide a framework to decolonize history, but they can also be a process of decolonization. If American Indians can re-create their histories from their perspectives, then they can begin to reestablish what they believed was "indigenous," as well as their definition of "sovereignty," and what was "colonized": taken from them and their nations through colonization. They can also re-envision "decolonization," any effort to retrieve what was taken.

Indigenousness, the first concept, is embedded within the precolonial, precontact world of Indigenous people and their way of living. If the people want to regain their Indigenous identities, they must thoroughly and earnestly recover who their ancestors truly were: how they thought, lived, and perceived the world, and what guided them in their attitudes and decision making.

I was careful not to reinforce a perception of the Cheyenne past that presents a false reality in revealing the Cheyenne worldview of Cheyenne history. The old worlds of the Tsėhéstáno were by no means utopias, but they were uncolonized worlds and without the influences of Western culture and colonial ways of thinking, which have continued to wreak havoc on Native peoples and nations. The *precolonized time* or worlds without a doubt are the best resources to decolonize and reclaim indigenousness: that is, what it means to be Cheyenne.[1] The old worlds are preserved in our languages and oral histories, which are now written guides to decolonization.

Decolonizing history, through a concerted effort to regain what was lost, is also a means to regain sovereignty, the second concept. Throughout the colonizing process, the US crippled and destroyed Indian nations by diminishing and undermining their sovereignty. Decolonizing history then is a path to regaining, redefining, and reestablishing sovereignty to set practical and realistic goals and resolve long-standing problems. In American Indian communities today, however, decolonization can be challenging, since traditional concepts of sovereignty are relatively unknown and sometimes nonexistent: a result of the destructive and enduring effects of colonialism.

Sometimes sovereignty is known through the colonial lens, which centers on the powers and paternalistic authority of the Bureau of Indian Affairs (BIA), the dependency of Indian nation governments on the federal government, and ineffective governance and leadership practices. American Indians can decolonize their current perceptions of sovereignty by regaining and reinstating traditional concepts of sovereignty. A decolonized perspective of sovereignty undermines the perceived authority of the BIA and the culture of dependency that breeds paternalism. A decolonized perception of sovereignty will inevitably lead to the liberation of American Indians from the powers of domination and oppression. A decolonized perception of sovereignty is spiritually based.

Ma'xenéheto'stôtse, the Cheyenne concept of sovereignty or "high authority," rested in responsibility: the people's responsibility to uphold the spiritual teachings bestowed by the covenant ceremonies; the people's responsibilities to one another as citizens of a nation; and the people's responsibilities to other Indian nations that shared the Great Plains as their homeland. In terms of government-to-government relations between the United States and Indian nations, the Cheyenne concept of brotherhood, hévese'onematsestôtse, is better fitting, is much more appealing, and establishes a relationship that is not based on paternalism or dominance. The fundamental question of sovereignty is: can the United States, the White Tribe, ever view Indian nations as brothers? Another important challenge would be if Indian nations could foresee a brotherly relationship with the United States, rather than a fatherly one. Sovereignty, like indigenousness,

CONCLUSION: DECOLONIZING "THE REZ"

is a concept that disrupts, destroys, and suppresses the foundations for colonization, but only if exercised and exerted effectively.

Colonization, the third concept, is defined as the taking and settling of land once belonging to Indigenous people, through deceit, force, violence, and oppression. White scholars, whether they know it or not, have written about the territorial colonization of Native America in military and American Indian history, highlighting Indian wars, warriors, chiefs, and the bloody battles between Indigenous peoples and US forces. The Plains Indian wars have been particularly of great interest, but rarely framed through a system of dominance. Sartre explained: "Colonialism denies human rights to human beings whom it has subdued by violence, and keeps them by force in a state of misery and ignorance that Marx would rightly call a subhuman condition. Racism is ingrained in actions, institutions, and in the nature of the colonialist methods of production and exchange."[2] Colonization is mental, spiritual, and psychological oppression as much as it is territorial. Sartre continues:

> Colonialism creates the patriotism of the colonized. Kept at the level of a beast by an oppressive system, the natives are given no rights, not even the right to live. Their condition worsens daily. And when a people has no choice but how it will die; when a people has received from its oppressors only the gift of despair, what does it have to lose?[3]

Nothing best affirms this form of colonialism than the assimilation policies of the US government that were forced upon Indian people before the last so-called battle at Wounded Knee in 1890. America has yet to acknowledge its history of colonization of Native America following Memmi's theory: "The most serious blow suffered by the colonized is being removed from history and from the community. Colonization usurps any free role in either war or peace, every decision contributing to his destiny and that of the world, and all cultural and social responsibility."[4] To decolonize history, it is imperative that American Indian people gain an understanding of what colonization is, how their lands and peoples were colonized, and what was lost in the colonization process. For me to do this for the Cheyennes and other Great Plains Indian nations, I would have to write an entirely new book.

Decolonization, the fourth concept, is an effort to move Indian people forward, beyond the gutter of the reservation system of dependence and paternalism. Decolonization is a move toward a new way of living that reaffirms our original instructions to uphold our sacred covenants. Today the path of decolonization should be imagined as a realistic goal, a destination to something different than what exists today in most Indian communities: a move away from the cycles of pain and suffering. Reservations are a product of colonization, which do not promote the Indigenous way of thinking or living and privileges assimilation over Indigenous ways. To decolonize means to reclaim indigenousness.

Outside of the academy, American Indian people are generally unaware of the principles and goals of decolonization, even though they likely pursue decolonization in their everyday lives and do not even know it. Decolonization occurs on different spectrums, ranging from the reclaiming of an Indian name to the reclaiming of lands. At the basic level, decolonization is understood as "the old ways" and includes speaking Native languages, eating Indigenous foods, and attending cultural events, dances, games, and performances. The basic level of decolonization encompasses a people's culture, but unfortunately does not adequately represent a people's true Indigenous identity. Non-Indians, non-tribal members, or noncitizens can easily replicate cultural elements at this basic level and they often do. This level of decolonization cannot lead to mental and spiritual liberation, nor can it resolve the persisting social problems in Indian country, but it most definitely is a starting point.

Decolonization at its highest level centers on the reclamation and protection of land (i.e., treaty lands and reservation lands), but more important, decolonization is reclamation of identity (i.e., concepts of leadership, citizenship, sovereignty, and spirituality). Decolonization is not a literal return to the "old ways," but it privileges the "old ways" above the colonial ones. Decolonization is not a step back, nor is it a process of regression to literally live "the old ways." Instead, decolonization is a move toward health, balance, and harmony, relying on the teachings and philosophy of our "old ways" to guide us. It is best to decolonize with guidance and with a common goal, and both are embedded in "the old ways." Decolonization cannot be imagined, nor achieved, if people do not know what was lost and if they do not know what they truly want. How can American Indians pursue and achieve decolonization?

A PATH TO DECOLONIZATION

Today most Indian people do not have positive views of their tribal leaders and their tribal governments. The roots of these governments are also the roots of colonialism. They were not built out of the hard work and diligence of the Indian people, but out of the minds of white politicians from an era that promoted assimilation. They were not built out of the traditional principles of brotherhood, love, and responsibility, but out of the

CONCLUSION: DECOLONIZING "THE REZ"

colonial concepts of power and authority. Decolonization for American Indian nations means that the people must come together with sincerity and diligence to dismantle the colonial systems. They must plan and rebuild a new system that best serves their people and protects their homelands.

Throughout the years, citizens of Indian nations have expressed their discontent toward their governments, which has increased resentment and cynicism. For Indian people, the challenges before them have existed for years and today there are few people who can provide reasonable and realistic solutions to long-standing problems of corruption, mismanagement, and a general lack of leadership and direction on Indian reservations. I believe that citizens and leaders can find answers to pressing issues if they relearn and reestablish traditional concepts of leadership, citizenship, and sovereignty. There are still a lot of people who believe in the philosophies of the Tsêhéseamanēō'o (the Cheyenne cultural way of life), but our leaders do not consider the traditional way as a resource for solving modern problems. At best, the Cheyenne culture is imitated as a solution, without understanding, thought, and planning. For example, the Cheyennes cannot simply reinstate the traditional government based on the ten bands and the chief system. The system took nearly one thousand years to develop, and to simply reinstate it would create more dysfunction because the Cheyenne people are not mentally, spiritually, and psychologically healed from the ravages of colonization. A people must be decolonized to decolonize their nation.

The Cheyennes must remember that when their ancestors lived under ten bands and the chief system, they were uninfluenced by the vices and culture of the vé'hó'e. Their ancestors were not oppressed and colonized when they thrived under the sophisticated system of government. They were Indigenous and had profound knowledge of the United Cheyenne national history, the Cheyenne culture. They lived a completely different lifestyle than the lives modern Cheyennes live today. In order to remedy the enduring legacy of colonialism, the Cheyennes must initiate a decolonization process to better gauge and solve the root problems they face today. Decolonization depends completely on how many people and leaders believe in it, how many are willing to sincerely give it a chance to fail or succeed, and how many people will dedicate their lives to see it through. The process must begin by understanding the true meaning of colonization.

The colonization of the Tsêhéstáno extended beyond their territory. The colonial system, through US policy, marginalized and violently oppressed all facets of the Cheyenne culture. Colonization is not merely the taking and settling of Indigenous land, nor was it the systematic destruction of cultures, languages, and philosophies. Colonization was exactly what the old Cheyenne storytellers said it would be: a complete destruction of Indigenous ways. Realistically speaking and given the current situation in Indian communities, it would be quite difficult for proponents of decolonization to argue that the colonization process and its result are the most destructive forces to the Tsėhéstáno and future generations of the Cheyenne people because the majority of problems can be traced to individual and immediate concerns like the poor decisions of leaders or poverty. Yet almost every social, mental, and spiritual problem can be traced to a form of direct or indirect colonization, and most are incapable of seeing it. Colonialism has created a culture where ignorance is bliss, naivety is prized, and arrogance is rewarded.

Probably the most damaging form of colonization has been the Indian peoples' negative perception of themselves as Indians. The majority of modern American Indians see the world through the lens of the colonizer. Through this lens the Indian and the Indigenous are unfortunate and lawless "savages": redskins, brutes, pagans, lost souls, and heathens without any values. Through this lens the Indian is dumb, illiterate, uncultured, hopeless, a burden, and unworthy of the fruits of civilization, let alone respect or basic human rights. The colonizer does not give him a chance because through this lens, disappointment and embarrassment precede the Indian. The colonizer does not think the Indian will succeed and out of pity the colonizer saves the poor Indian from his own failure. Luther Standing Bear (Lakota) described the colonial perception of Indians:

> White men seem to have difficulty in realizing that people who live differently from themselves still might be traveling the upward and progressive road of life. After nearly four hundred years living upon this continent, it is still popular conception, on the part of the Caucasian mind, to regard the native American as a savage, meaning he is low in thought and feeling, and cruel in acts; that he is a heathen, meaning that he is incapable, therefore void, of high philosophical thought concerning life and life's relations. For this "savage" the white man has little brotherly love and little understanding. From the Indian the white man stands off and aloof, scarcely deigning to speak or to touch his hand in human fellowship. To the white man many things done by the Indian are inexplicable, though he continues to write much of the visible and exterior life with explanations that are more often than not erroneous. The inner life of the Indian, is of course, a closed book to the white man.[5]

A colonized Indian person's shameful perception of the American Indian, through the colonial lens, is no different from his shameful perception of his

CONCLUSION: DECOLONIZING "THE REZ"

own people and nation. To decolonize the perception of the individual is to decolonize the perception of the nation. As Indians begin to decolonize, they must unlearn what it means to be colonized, by relearning what it means to be Indian and Indigenous. The Cheyennes are currently losing an endless fight to remain Indigenous as the outside, unseen pressures of colonialism and assimilation continue to devour their individual and national identities. Today the task of learning and relearning the Cheyenne worldview is as challenging as it is to preserve and honor it. Once, however, Cheyenne people begin to learn and relearn their true identity, the urgent need to protect this identity will become paramount.

Today the Northern Cheyenne people reside on the Northern Cheyenne Indian Reservation in Montana and the Southern Cheyenne reside in Oklahoma. The communities continue to face social ills resulting from the years of assimilation and abandonment. They live in a culture of "petty tyrants" created by the bureaucracy of modern tribal governments: "each one, being socially oppressed by one more powerful than he, always finds a less powerful one on whom to lean, and becomes a tyrant in his turn."[6] Alcohol and drug abuse continue to plague the Cheyennes, and health disparities like diabetes, depression, and despair continue to make reservation life difficult. The people suffer from poverty, high crime, and social unrest amidst a toxic and sometimes emotionally painful political climate. There are numerous social, political, and spiritual problems and the people do not know where or how to begin resolving these issues and collective pains when immediate concerns, like buying food and paying bills, are more pressing. The ceremonial practices, language, and philosophies have survived, yet some spiritual ways are fragmented, in shambles, and continually threatened by the death of elders, the influences of white culture, and the environmental threats to the land. The Cheyennes need new leaders and new types of leaders to initiate long-term changes that will bring the Cheyennes out of despair. These new leaders must find wisdom in the old ways, knowledge in the new ways, and the balance between the two.

The Cheyennes of today are products of two worlds. First is the Tsėhéstáno, which is the living-nation with its great legacy: a national history, a wealth of sacred knowledge, and deep and extraordinary spiritual philosophical principles. The second is the "rez," which is a lifeless and stale concept bound by the shackles of colonization and assimilation; riddled, ravaged, and scarred with unhealed violence, pain, and anguish. It is a place of contradiction that represents lawlessness and negativity. It has all the characteristics of a prison where its citizens believe they have no freedom and where dependency and paternalism work hand-in-hand to maintain a system that has not worked and will never work for the Cheyenne people. The "rez" is the predictable consequence of colonization and not the reward of civilization. The "rez" is known throughout the colonized world in other contexts, as Fanon explains:

> The town belonging to the colonized people, or at least the native town, the Negro village, the medina, the reservation, is a place of ill fame, peopled by men of evil repute. They are born there, it matters little where or how; they die there, it matters not where, nor how. It is a world without spaciousness; men live there on top of each other, and their huts are built one on top of the other. The native town is a hungry town, starved of bread, of meat, of shoes, of coal, of light. The native town is a crouching village, a town on its knees, a town wallowing in the mire.[7]

If American Indians were to decolonize the concept of the "rez" and reclaim an Indigenous concept, then they will abandon the construct "rez" and see the true identity of their nation. It is a living-nation, the Tsėhéstáno, the sacred being that was born from a sacred female being of the universe. It survived through numerous changes and adversity by adapting and building and rebuilding itself under spiritual and traditional beliefs. It survived the devastation and destruction of colonization, yet it has been abused, abandoned, and left unhealed. Its people, the Cheyennes, the sacred people, represent the pain of the damaged nation, and it is up to them to heal it. After all, the sacred living-nation cared for ancestors throughout the ages so they could live and thrive today. It is time for us to care about it.

The question before American Indian and Indigenous peoples today is: How do we decolonize? Decolonization should be perceived as a journey and not necessarily a destination, but destinations of decolonization should be articulated as national goals. For example, if the Northern Cheyenne Nation endeavored to reduce the rates of child and domestic abuse, then decolonization would become a destination when the goal is met. Decolonization can then be perceived first as a journey, then a destination, and finally as a way of living, since the new decolonized culture has to sustain itself to make the destination a reality. Here I outline ways the Cheyennes can decolonize as individuals, families, bands, communities, and a united nation:

1. *Reintroduce the Oral Traditions*

The oral tradition embodies the necessary teachings to rebuild a nation because stories were the foundation of nation building from the moment it was born. The stories re-create worlds and teachings that reinforce healthy citizenship and leadership practices. They also provide an intellectual framework and worldview so citizens can address problems in practical and culturally appropriate means. Ideally the oral tradition should be told in the Cheyenne language, but the language is not thriving as it once did. Even if parents do not speak the language, they can read or orally transmit to their children the beautiful stories and legends, which convey traditional Cheyenne values and principles of leadership, citizenship, spirituality, and sovereignty. While the Cheyenne language is a key to the Cheyenne culture, the oral tradition is the foundation for all sacred teachings.

II. *Effectively Revive the Cheyenne Language*

Language is a key to the Cheyenne culture and the oral tradition. The Cheyenne language alone cannot bring the Cheyenne people to decolonize, because most language preservation programs rely on linguistic studies by Christians, especially Catholics who used language to proselytize.

I have personally witnessed the failure of our Cheyenne language programs, but found that those who had a strong sense of identity and knowledge of the ceremonial practices and oral tradition were more likely to succeed in relearning the Cheyenne language than those who perceived learning the Cheyenne language as a task, chore, or part of schooling. Once a strong identity is established, language learners are inspired and dedicated to learn and relearn the Cheyenne language, making it fun and easy, rather than burdensome and uninteresting. Schools located within Cheyenne boundaries and with significantly high enrollments of Cheyennes should privilege and prioritize the oral tradition above other narratives, especially the mainstream, colonial narratives in American history and literature. Many of these schools already have language programs, so integrating the oral traditions would not be difficult.

III. *Reintroduce and Reinvigorate the Concept of Héstanovestôtse, Living-Nation*

If Cheyennes can regain an understanding that they are part of a living-nation, and that their minds, bodies, and spirits contribute to the health of this living-nation, then they have regained a sense of what it means to truly be a citizen of the Cheyenne Nation. The shallow concept of "tribal membership" has done nothing to promote unity; instead, it has been attacked as a divisive and colonial form of Cheyenne identity. To belong to the Cheyenne Nation is more than just being enrolled. It requires dedication and loyalty to the living-nation.

IV. *Reintroduce and Reinvigorate Band Identities*

The Cheyennes traditionally belonged to two sovereign entities. The first was the Cheyenne Nation, and the second was their respective band. At present, both the Northern and Southern Cheyenne Nations named their communities using the band system. If Cheyennes began to identify with these communities using their traditional names and following the traditional concepts of citizenship, then they come closer to understanding what it means to be part of a traditional Cheyenne community.

v. Reintroduce and Reinforce the Concept of Hévese'onematsestôtse, Brotherhood

This concept is the foundation of traditional Cheyenne governance, but also of the Cheyenne cultural and spiritual identity. Cheyennes cannot sustain themselves if they continually perceive one another using colonial concepts of paternalism or friendship. They must begin to see one another as siblings, brothers and sisters.

vi. Reintroduce and Value Traditional Principles of Citizenship

Cheyenne parents and families can reinforce traditional concepts of identity by holding each other accountable to cultural and traditional laws. This is a challenge because most families do not know cultural and traditional laws, but this does not mean they cannot be reintroduced with the present generations. Principles of citizenship can also be taught and reinforced in schools, colleges, and tribal organizations and government programs; they can be written into codes of conduct and rules of order. Cheyenne parents and adults should always be training the next generation of Cheyennes to honor and live by the Cheyenne way of life in a more proactive way than previous generations. They must act with urgency and earnestly to ensure the survival of the ways of our ancestors. The Nótâxeo'o, for example, continue to sustain a ceremonial presence, but they could also reenvision and expand their roles by participating as non-profit, community organizations. They can adapt to establish a stronger presence in the community and among the people, while maintaining their traditional responsibilities. The arrival of the new warrior is long overdue.

vii. Reintroduce and Value Traditional Principles of Leadership

Cheyenne leaders, elected and nongovernmental, should be rewarded for their dedication and commitment to the communities they serve. Principles of leadership can be included in oaths of office and other areas as guiding principles, core values, missions, and goals. Every Cheyenne organization should acknowledge, affirm, and promote traditional principles of leadership, like truth and compassion, and this can be done realistically without rejecting existing ones. The goal should be to hold leaders to higher standards, like the Cheyennes from ages ago. Once a culture is established to where the majority of citizens know and practice traditional principles of leadership, then it will be easier to raise the standards of leadership in government. Today's Cheyenne citizens can do that now, but there are colonial-rooted challenges that remain. One is that American Indian people suffer from a defeatist attitude and therefore feel disempowered and are unwilling to hold leaders to higher standards unless out of anger and resentment. Another colonial-rooted challenge is that assimilation has created a passive culture of compliance and fear. These colonial-rooted cultures and assimilation-based attitudes need to end. The people need to re-establish a new culture of leadership: one that values unity, civility, honor, and integrity.

VIII. *Regain Traditional Lands and Reestablish Relationships to Them*

Achieving either one of these two goals concerning land—regaining the land and restablishing a relationship with the land—would be an act of decolonization, but to achieve both would be true decolonization. History tells us that the colonizer emphatically wants the land of the Indigenous peoples; meanwhile, the Indigenous people wanted nothing other than the material items of the colonizer. The colonizer violently took the land and then created a culture of want for material things, which in the end were useless compared to the lost land. Colonization severed the Cheyenne people from their traditional lands, physically and spiritually. A false reality created by the colonizer reinforced the idea that the reservation boundaries are the limits of the Cheyenne physical and spiritual presence.

Today the traditional homelands of the Cheyennes are owned by non-Indians and littered with cities, towns, farms, and ranches. The present owners of these lands, however, have shown appreciation to Indians, something that the older white culture did not necessarily desire. Americans are searching for identity and meaning, and justice for Indian people should be part of this search. The Cheyennes are without a doubt a major part of the history and culture of settled treaty lands, and from my experience I have noticed that most people who live on traditional Cheyenne homelands have a general appreciation for Cheyenne history and culture. The Cheyenne people must establish strong relationships with the willing to regain access to homelands, sacred places, and other areas of cultural and historical significance. This means that traditional and elected leaders must reach out and demonstrate a genuine need to reestablish a physical relationship to lands to hold ceremonies, gather plants and other items from nature, and enjoy the beautiful lands and waterways that were once ours.

PART IV | COLONIZING AND DECOLONIZING THE TSÈHÉSTÁNO

Today Indian nations can acquire traditional lands through purchase and, in rare cases, through diplomacy.[8] In some instances, as with select lands around Bear Butte State Park, the Northern and Southern Cheyenne Tribes have purchased lands. But given the financial situations of both nations, as well as allied nations, the purchasing of lands is difficult and expensive, but the trend should continue. Individual Cheyenne citizens and their families can and should reestablish physical and spiritual relationships to homelands by traveling to and visiting places to hold ceremonies, gather plants, and even camp. Some Cheyenne families continue to do so at certain places. But the ultimate goal should be to establish a permanent Indian presence in places and lands that were traditionally ours.

STINK BAT REMEMBERED

At the beginning of this book I told the story of Stink Bat and asked several questions that served as the guiding topics of study. Stink Bat was just an ordinary young man, yet everything he had done during his short time on Earth is revered as heroic. The truth is that any young Cheyenne man of his time would have done the exact same thing. He embodied all that the Cheyenne people had lost. It is unfortunate that today's Cheyennes are conditioned to believe that only one or two leaders of the Cheyenne Nation were ever born, and that they are remembered exclusively for their interactions with the invading white culture. The truth is that there were numerous leaders but only a few have won the respect to be remembered in the history of the American West. Cheyenne leaders like Roman Nose, Black Kettle, Dull Knife (Morningstar), and Little Wolf have come to represent the Indians as noble warriors, paragons of a righteous cause to remain Indian. How easy do people praise the strength of Dull Knife and Little Wolf, as they brought three hundred members of their nation from the despair of the reservation life in 1878, while forgetting that they were doing what was merely demanded from all leaders for hundreds of years?

Other Indian leaders, warriors, and chiefs like Sitting Bull, Crazy Horse, and Chief Joseph remain as icons in the history of America, but they were products of their culture and the living-nations from which the culture was built. The personalities of the old Indian leaders should not overshadow these cultures from which they were raised. How easy is it to think of the great warrior leader Crazy Horse, while ignoring the pain and suffering that so many of his Oglala people endured when the United States was removing them from their traditional homelands? Once the Cheyennes begin to examine how these leaders were raised and begin to understand the cultures that created such leaders, they will find that their personalities,

CONCLUSION: DECOLONIZING "THE REZ"

ranks, and statuses were of little significance to the teachings embedded in ceremonies, oral traditions, and spiritual beliefs. If these personalities did not exist, another leader, from the same culture, era, and nation, would have risen to fight for the same beliefs and ways of living. These ways are worth saving.

If we wish to judge the old world of the Cheyennes by today's standards, we should do so by examining the modern world of the Cheyenne people, not of the privileged mainstream white people who are the benefactors of colonization. If we do this we will find that, comparatively speaking, the old world of the Cheyennes is much closer to a utopia than can be imagined, especially when considering the dramatic loss of land, culture, language, and spiritual ways; the high rates of suicide, homicide, and violence against women and children; the poverty, drug and alcohol abuse, and poor health care; and the political, social, and cultural dominance of an alien people. Today our people are not enjoying the fruits of colonization, only the wrath of conquest. Returning to the old ways is always in the back of the minds of traditional Cheyenne people, but not in a literal sense. There is no going back, but this should never be the goal in the first place.

The decolonization process need not be lamented, nor criticized for failure if it has not even been imagined, let alone begun. If the Cheyennes decide to decolonize, individually and as a Cheyenne Nation, they must do so with grace and under the principles of the teachings that each person so dearly wants to reintroduce. We do not need to fight with our own people, nor do we need to storm a failed tribal government, justice system, or college. We first need to heal ourselves and ensure that we are adhering to the teachings of the "old ones." We need to first acknowledge that the unseen and omnipresent living-nation exists, and we need to acknowledge that it has survived the tests of time, colonization, and sometimes the dysfunction of the very people who are the caretakers of the living-nation. Once we make these affirmations, we then can begin to heal through a conscious and united effort to reawaken the sacred teachings that are within us, in our blood and bones. We must abandon the shame, guilt, and insecurities that have kept our spirits from feeling and expressing the very emotions and feelings that make us humans: that make us Indigenous.

Once the Cheyennes individually reach personal decolonized selves and have a sense of what it means to be Cheyenne, we can reunite and reinvent ourselves, our communities, and our nation into images that we can respect, love, and honor. When we adhere to the principles of the Cheyenne culture, we subconsciously allow others around us—our friends, family, and most important, our children—to do the same. We then strengthen and heal the living-nation that is the Tséhéstáno and thus begin to heal one another.

PART IV | COLONIZING AND DECOLONIZING THE TSÈHÉSTÁNO

Through our daily lives, work, and interactions with others, we will start to make decisions that are in line with sacred principles and responsibilities. We may need to make deliberate choices to change on this journey, but a reawakened Tsėhéstáno will reciprocate by providing for us, just as before, no different from how it had provided for our ancestors centuries ago.

In sharing the complexity of the Cheyenne culture, I never intended to provide a sentimental narrative. Instead my goal was quite the opposite. Authoring this book has been inspirational and enlightening for me. I hope you, in reading, have also felt the same.

Notes

PREFACE

1. John H. Moore, *The Cheyenne Nation: A Social and Demographic History* (Norman: University of Oklahoma Press, 1987), 2.
2. Vine Deloria, Jr., *Custer Died for Your Sins: An Indian Manifesto* (Norman: University of Oklahoma Press, 1969), 10.
3. The purpose of this book is not to highlight my challenges as an Indian scholar, nor is it to identify those who have been unsupportive or apathetic in my pursuit of revising history.

INTRODUCTION

1. John Stands In Timber and Margot Liberty, *Cheyenne Memories* (New Haven, CT: Yale University Press, 1967), 12.
2. Bill Tallbull (Wolf Feathers), "We are the Ancestors of those yet to be Born: Northern Cheyenne History of the Battle of 100-In-The-Hands (the Fetterman Battle)," *Fort Phil Kearny/Bozeman Trail Association,* last modified March 22, 2004, http://www.philkearny.vcn.com/fpk-tallbull.htm.
3. Sandy Grande, *Red Pedagogy: Native American Social and Political Thought* (Lanham, MD: Rowman & Littlefield, 2004); Margaret Kovach, *Indigenous Methodologies: Characteristics, Conversations, and Contexts* (Toronto: University of Toronto Press, 2009); Devon A. Mihesuah, *Natives and Academics: Researching and Writing About American Indians* (Lincoln: University of Nebraska Press, 1998); Mihesuah, *Indigenizing the Academy: Transforming Scholarship and Empowering Communities* (Lincoln: University of Nebraska Press, 2004); Linda Tuhiwai Smith, *Decolonizing Methodologies: Research and Indigenous Peoples,* 2nd ed. (New York: Zed Books, 2012); Shawn Wilson, *Research Is Ceremony: Indigenous Research Methods* (Black Point, NS: Fernwood, 2009).
4. Taiaiake Alfred, *Peace, Power, Righteousness: An Indigenous Manifesto,* 2nd ed. (New York: Oxford University Press, 2009); Alfred, *Wasáse: Indigenous Pathways of Action and Freedom* (Toronto: University of Toronto Press, 2005).
5. Inspired by Graham Smith, "Kaupapa Maori Theory: Theorizing Indigenous Transformation of Education & Schooling," paper presented at the International Education Research/AARE-NZARE Joint Conference Auckland, New Zealand, December 2003, http://www.aare.edu.au/03pap/pih03342.pdf; Graham Smith, "Theorizing, Transforming & Reclaiming 'Our Indigenous Selves,'" paper presented at the American Anthropology Association Conference, November 19, 2006; and Smith, *Decolonizing Methodologies,* 39–41.

6. Smith, *Decolonizing Methodologies*, 29–30.

7. John Collier, *Indians of the Americas: A Long Hope* (New York: New American Library, 1975), 137.

8. Moore, *Cheyenne Nation*, 24.

9. George B. Grinnell, "Some Early Cheyenne Tales," *Journal of American Folklore* 20, no. 78 (1907): 173.

10. John Stands In Timber and Margot Liberty, *A Cheyenne Voice: The Complete John Stands In Timber Interviews* (Norman: University of Oklahoma Press, 2013), 253.

11. Ibid., 310.

12. Ibid., 280.

13. Ibid., 280–81, 415.

14. Ibid., 281.

15. Alfred, *Wasáse*, 79.

16. James Riding In, "Editor's Commentary: An American Indian Studies Paradigm Statement," *Wicazo Sa Review* 26, no. 2 (Fall 2011): 5–12.

17. Rodolphe Petter, *English-Cheyenne Dictionary* (Kettle Falls, WA, 1913–1915).

18. Susan A. Miller, "Native America Writes Back: The Origin of the Indigenous Paradigm in Historiography." *Wicazo Sa Review* 23, no. 2 (2008): 9–28. Also see Susan A. Miller and James Riding In, "The Indigenous Paradigm in American Indian Historiography," in *Native Historians Write Back: Decolonizing American Indian History*, ed. Susan A. Miller and James Riding In, 9–24 (Lubbock: Texas Tech University Press, 2011).

19. Richard W. Randolph, *Sweet Medicine and Other Stories of the Cheyenne Indians* (Caldwell, ID: The Caxton Printers, 1937), 8.

PART I

1. Wayne Leman, ed., *Náévóo'ôhtséme/We Are Going Back Home: Cheyenne History and Stories told by James Shoulderblade and Others*, Algonquian and Iroquoian Linguistics, Memoir 4 (Winnipeg, Manitoba: Algonquian and Iroquoian Linguistics, 1987),11.

2. Grace J. Penney, *Tales of the Cheyennes* (Cambridge, MA: The Riverside Press, 1953), 35.

3. Williams discusses the "language of Indian savagery" in depth; see *Like a Loaded Weapon: The Rehnquist Court, Indian Rights, and the Legal History of Racism in America* (Minneapolis: University of Minnesota Press, 2005), 33–39; *Savage Anxieties: The Invention of Western Civilization* (New York: Palgrave and Macmillan, 2012), 219–36.

4. Richard W. Randolph, *Sweet Medicine and Other Stories of the Cheyenne Indians* (Caldwell, ID: The Caxton Printers, 1937), 8.

5. Penney, *Tales of the Cheyennes*, vii.

6. Ibid., viii–ix.

7. John Stands In Timber and Margot Liberty, *A Cheyenne Voice: The Complete*

NOTES

John Stands In Timber Interviews (Norman: University of Oklahoma Press, 2013), 189.

8. Manuscript 2134, National Anthropological Archives, Smithsonian Institution, Washington, DC (hereafter cited as NAA MS 2134), i, 2–3.

9. Rodolphe Petter, *English-Cheyenne Dictionary* (Kettle Falls, WA, 1913–1915), 1055.

10. Stands In Timber and Liberty, *A Cheyenne Voice*, 340.

11. George E. Hyde, *Life of George Bent: Written from His Letters*, ed. Savoie Lottinville (Norman: University of Oklahoma Press, 1968), 4.

12. For a brief description of Cheyenne storytelling see George B. Grinnell, *By Cheyenne Campfires* (Lincoln: University of Nebraska Press, 1962), xix–xxiv; Penney, *Tales of the Cheyennes*, vii–x.

13. NAA MS 2704, a.2

14. Petter, *English-Cheyenne Dictionary*, 422-3; Henry Tall Bull and Tom Weist, *Cheyenne Legends of Creation* (Billings, MT: Montana Council on Indian Education, 1972).

CHAPTER 1

1. Vine Deloria, Jr., *Evolution, Creationism, and Other Modern Myths: A Critical Inquiry* (Golden, CO: Fulcrum Publishing, 2002), 167.

2. Irvin Morris, *From the Glittering World: A Navajo Story* (Norman: University of Oklahoma Press, 2000); Ethelou Yazzie, ed., *Navajo History* (Rough Rock, AZ: Navajo Curriculum Center, 1982); Thomas Banyaca, "Essence of Hopi Prophecy" (unpublished manuscript), 1994, http://tierra-y-vida.blogspot.com/2007/12/hopi-declaration-of-peace-essence-of.html; Edmund Nequatewa, *Truth of a Hopi* (Radford, VA: Wilder Publications, 2007); George Manuel, *The Fourth World: An Indian Reality* (New York: Free Press, 1974).

3. "Sacred geography," which is the combination of history and geography, is discussed by Deloria, in *God Is Red: A Native View of Religion* (Golden, CO: Fulcrum Publishing, 1992), 122. Leo Killsback, "Indigenous Perceptions of Time: Decolonizing Theory, World History, and the Fates of Human Societies," *American Indian Culture and Research Journal* 37, no. 1 (Winter 2013): 119–47.

4. Moore, *Cheyenne Nation*, 276.

5. George B. Grinnell, *The Cheyenne Indians* (Lincoln: University of Nebraska Press, 1972), 1: 4–5; Grinnell, "Some Early Cheyenne Tales," *Journal of American Folklore* 20, no. 78 (1907): 170; Petter, *English-Cheyenne Dictionary*, 806.

6. John H. Segar, *Early Days Among the Cheyenne and Arapahoe Indians* (Norman: University of Oklahoma Press, 1979), 33; John Stands In Timber and Margot Liberty, *Cheyenne Memories* (New Haven, CT: Yale University Press, 1967), 13–16.

7. Petter, *English-Cheyenne Dictionary*, 229.

8. Grinnell, *Cheyenne Indians*, 1:16; NAA MS 2822, f1, c, 17.

9. As recalled by William Somers (Southern Cheyenne) in 1910, NAA MS 2822, f2, g, 1–5.

10. NAA MS 2822, f2, g, 1–5.

11. Grinnell, *By Cheyenne Campfires*, 182–93. A similar, fragmented story

appears in A. L. Kroeber, "Cheyenne Tales," *The Journal of American Folklore* 13, no. 50 (1900): 186.

12. Red Star is also known as Fallen Star and Star Drops. Randolph, *Sweet Medicine*, 23–30.

13. In this era, stars were of particular interest to the Cheyenne. In one creation story, the first woman "saw a fallen star and went to where it fell," thus finding the first red earth paint; see NAA MS 2704, a, 5.

14. Petter, *English-Cheyenne Dictionary*, 622; Stands In Timber and Liberty, *A Cheyenne Voice*, 190.

15. Petter, *English-Cheyenne Dictionary*, 165–66.

16. Segar, *Early Days Among the Cheyenne*, 133–34.

17. Stands In Timber and Liberty, *A Cheyenne Voice*, 190–91.

18. Petter, *English-Cheyenne Dictionary*, 229.

19. The story of Eagle Nest and Fallen Star were merged, apparently, in the story of Grinnell's informant, which states that the culture hero was taken in by a meadowlark, instead of being born in an eagle's nest; see Grinnell, *Cheyenne Campfires*, 184. Also see Randolph, *Sweet Medicine*, 26. Randolph identifies the prophet as Star Drops.

20. Petter, *English-Cheyenne Dictionary*, 229.

21. Wayne Leman, ed., *Cheyenne Texts: An Introduction to Cheyenne Literature*, Occasional Publication in Anthropology, Linguistic Series, No. 6 (Greeley: Museum of Anthropology, University of Northern Colorado, 1980), 1.

22. Leman, *Náévóo'óhtséme*, 1–4; Leman, *A Reference Grammar of the Cheyenne Language* (Busby, MT: Cheyenne Translation Project, 1991), 202–23; Hyde and Lottinville, *Life of George Bent*, 13–14.

23. According to Grasshopper (Northern Cheyenne), NAA MS 2822, f1, c, 17.

24. American Horse (Northern Cheyenne), NAA MS 2822, f1, c, 11.

25. Hyde and Lotttinville, *Life of George Bent*, 13.

26. NAA MS 2822, f1, c, 1.

27. Truman Michelson's Northern Cheyenne informant named "White Bull" is not the same as the medicine man who is also known as Ice or White Bull. To prevent any confusion, I replace the name of the young man named White Bull with White Buffalo, and retain the name for the famous medicine man as Ice. NAA MS 2811, f4, 1. A similar account is in Grinnell, "Some Early Cheyenne Tales," 185.

28. According to White Buffalo and Somers, NAA MS 2811, f1, g, 2. Also see American Horse, NAA MS 2822, f1, c, 11.

29. NAA MS 3218, 1–2.

30. Randolph, *Sweet Medicine*, 48–50; Grinnell, *Cheyenne Campfires*, 185–86.

31. Randolph, *Sweet Medicine*, 29–30; Grinnell, *Cheyenne Campfires*, 186–87.

32. Randolph, *Sweet Medicine*, 31–35; Grinnell, *Cheyenne Campfires*, 190–92; Kroeber, "Cheyenne Tales," 184; Henry Tall Bull and Tom Weist, *Mista!* (Billings, MT: Montana Council on Indian Education, 1971).

33. NAA MS 2704, f, 1–2; NAA MS 2828-f1, f1, d, 1–7.

34. Grinnell, *Cheyenne Campfires*, 192–93.

35. NAA MS 3218, 1–2.

36. Stands In Timber and Liberty, *A Cheyenne Voice*, 332.

37. Peter J. Powell, "Ox'zem: Box Elder and His Sacred Wheel Lance," *Montana: The Magazine of Western History* 20, no. 2 (Spring 1970), 30–41. Grinnell mentions this lance in three war stories in *Cheyenne Campfires*, 6, 15, and 28. Also see Karl H. Schlesier, *The Wolves of Heaven* (Norman: University of Oklahoma Press, 1987), 15–17.

38. The exact location of this event is not known, but what is known is that the Cheyennes traveled from East to West.

39. George A. Dorsey, *The Cheyenne: Sundance,* Anthropological Series 9, no. 1 (Chicago: Field Columbian Museum, 1905), 37–38.

40. Penney, *Tales of the Cheyennes*, 37; Grinnell, *Cheyenne Campfires*, 206–7.

41. Randolph, *Sweet Medicine*, 39. Randolph names the prophet as Star Drops or Fallen Star, which is evidence that the story of the prophet Bow-In-Hand and Fallen Star/Star Drops was adapted to fit across families and bands.

42. Randolph, *Sweet Medicine*, 39–41; Penney, *Tales of the Cheyennes*, 44–51; Grinnell, *Cheyenne Campfires*, 210–11.

43. Randolph, *Sweet Medicine*, 37–38; Penney, *Tales of the Cheyennes*, 36–43; Grinnell, *Cheyenne Campfires*, 207–9.

44. Grinnell, *Cheyenne Campfires*, 209–10.

45. Randolph, *Sweet Medicine*, 51–59.

46. Ibid., 59–63.

47. Leman, *Cheyenne Texts*, 314–17.

48. Grinnell, *Cheyenne Campfires*, 200–205.

49. NAA MS 2704, 2.

50. NAA MS 2796, f2, i, 1–7. I attempted to capture content from both translations since they differ.

51. Stands In Timber and Liberty, *A Cheyenne Voice*, 190.

52. Dorsey, *Cheyenne Sundance*, 38–39.

53. Randolph, *Sweet Medicine*, 189–92.

54. Stands In Timber and Liberty, *Cheyenne Memories*, 19–24; Grinnell, *Cheyenne*, 252–54; Kroeber, "Cheyenne Tales," 162.

55. NAA MS 2811, f4, 1.

56. NAA MS 2704, a, 3.

57. James Mooney, "The Cheyenne Indians," *American Anthropological Association*, Memoirs, I, pt 6 (1905) (repr., Whitefish, MT: Kessinger Publishing, 2009), 368.

58. Bent believed the Moiseyu to be Sioux. Hyde and Lotttinville, *Life of George Bent*, 13.

59. Wolf Chief states that the "Moisiu comes from Sioux," NAA MS 2822, f1, c, 1. American Horse also confirmed: "Moisiu: they seem to have come from Sioux," ibid., 12.

60. Stands In Timber and Liberty, *A Cheyenne Voice*, 73.

61. Ibid.

62. The English term "sacred laws" is found in Richard Erdoes and Alfonso Ortiz, eds., *American Indian Myths and Legends* (New York: Pantheon Books, 1984), 204. The term is also found in Greek mythology; see Williams, *Savage Anxieties*, 16–17. The Cheyenne term "ma'heóneho'emanestôtse" (sacred laws) is part of a

body of sacred language frequently used among traditional Cheyenne practitioners of ceremonies. This language has deteriorated over the years.

63. Henrietta Mann, *Cheyenne-Arapaho Education, 1871–1982* (Niwot, CO: University Press of Colorado, 1997), 2; Eugene Fisher, "Cheyenne Indian lore Related by Holy Bird and Yellow Nose, Tribal Historians," Conference Between Grant A. Solberg and Members of the Cheyenne Indian Tribe, September 28, 1939 (unpublished manuscript). Both Mann and Fisher, former Northern Cheyenne Tribal President, affirm these four sacred laws, but they have interpreted them slightly differently. I provide a clearer interpretation here.

CHAPTER 2

1. Stands In Timber also asserts that this was a teaching of Sweet Medicine: "Do not camp too long in one place. Keep moving and keep yourselves healthy" (Stands In Timber and Liberty, *A Cheyenne Voice*, 343).

2. Standing Bear, *Land of the Spotted Eagle*, new ed. (Lincoln: University of Nebraska Press, 1960), 120.

3. Moore, *Cheyenne Nation*, 177–204.

4. George Bird Grinnell, "Early Cheyenne Villages," *American Anthropologist*, New Series, vol. 20, no. 4 (1918): 359–80; E. Adamson Hoebel, *The Cheyennes: Indians of the Great Plains*, 2nd ed. (New York: Harcourt Brace, 1988), 37.

5. NAA MS 3218, 70.

6. NAA MS 3336, 5.

7. Randolph, *Sweet Medicine*, 8–10.

8. Grinnell, *Cheyenne Indians*, 1:321–25.

9. James Mooney, "The Cherokee Ball Play," *The American Anthropologist*, Old Series, vol. 3, no. 2 (1890): 105–32.

10. Robert Odawi Porter, *Sovereignty, Colonialism and the Indigenous Nations: A Reader* (Durham, NC: Carolina Academic Press, 2005), 655.

11. Randolph, *Sweet Medicine*, 117–26.

12. Bureau of American Ethnology, Smithsonian Institution, *Annual Report of the Bureau of American Ethnology to the Secretary of the Smithsonian Institution, 1895*, vol. 24 (Washington, DC: Government Printing Office, 1902–1903), 442–43, 442–43; Petter, *English-Cheyenne Dictionary*, 827.

13. Stands In Timber and Liberty, *A Cheyenne Voice*, 73.

14. Grinnell, "Some Early Cheyenne Tales," 179–81; Kroeber, "Cheyenne Tales," 163; Erdoes and Ortiz, *American Indian Myths and Legends*, 26–29. In Kroeber's story the two wore headdresses.

15. Moore suggests the two Cheyenne bands were completely autonomous from one another and they united to make the first Cheyenne camp circle. According to Moore's thesis, "the story of the two young men in fact represents the amalgamation of a predominantly farming group, the Aortas, with a predominantly hunting group, the Eaters." Moore assumes that the two bands were completely different peoples, divided by lifestyle and language. I contend otherwise. See Moore, *Cheyenne Nation*, 100–102.

16. NAA MS 2796, f1-e-07 to 08.

17. NAA MS 2704, 7–8; NAA MS 2822, f1, a, 17–20.

18. I cannot claim to know why the Cheyennes quit using clay pots, but I presume it was because of trade. Wrapped Hair states that the Cheyennes "ceased making them about 10 years before fight at Dry Creek." NAA MS 2684-a, 44.

19. Grinnell, "Some Early Cheyenne Tales," 179–94; Grinnell, *Cheyenne Campfires*, 256–63. Grinnell also describes this event as the origin of the Buffalo Hat.

20. Although White Buffalo does not name the two young men, Grinnell provides five similar stories about "The Buffalo and the Corn," each story featuring different named men, but the same teacher as Mā-tā-mā' (Old Woman). See Grinnell, "Some Early Cheyenne Tales," 179–94; Grinnell, *Cheyenne Campfires*, 256–63; Dorsey, *Cheyenne Sundance*, 39–41; Leman, *Cheyenne Texts*, 2–3.

21. NAA MS 2704, a, 7–8; NAA MS 2822, f1, a, 17–20.

22. Stands In Timber and Liberty, *A Cheyenne Voice*, 254.

23. Stands In Timber and Liberty, *A Cheyenne Voice*, 41; Grinnell, "Some Early Cheyenne Tales," 185.

24. Grinnell spells it Nī-ŏm-a-hé-tăn-iu in "Some Early Cheyenne Tales" (169). Stands In Timber spells it Ni-oh-ma-até-anin-ya and translates it to mean "Prairie People" in *Cheyenne Memories* (15).

25. NAA MS 2822, f1, a, 13; NAA MS 2704, a, 5; Moore, *Cheyenne Nation*, 93–96.

26. NAA MS 2822, f1, c, 2–4.

27. According to Bull Thigh, NAA MS 2828-f1, b, 1; Grasshopper, NAA MS 2822, f1, c, 19; American Horse, NAA MS 2822, f1, c, 21; Old She Bear, NAA MS 2822 f1, i, 3; and Grinnell, "Some Early Cheyenne Tales," 185, 189, 191.

28. NAA MS 2811, f4, 1.

29. According to Wolf Chief, NAA MS 2822, f1, c, 1.

30. NAA MS 2828, f2, a, 1. I omitted the statement: "The Sutaiu were at the Black Hills before the Cheyennes" because it is contradictory to his other statements and the narratives of others. Bull Thigh states: "Cheyennes originated at foot of Black Hills, Sutaiu from Red Rock in Minnesota." NAA MS 2828, f1, a, 2.

31. Wolf Chief, NAA MS 2822, f1, b, 3.

32. NAA MS 2828, f2, a, 1–2.

33. Bull Thigh, NAA MS 2828, f1, a, 2.

34. Stands In Timber and Liberty, *A Cheyenne Voice*, 92–93.

35. NAA MS 2684-a, 1.

36. Ibid., 17.

37. NAA MS 2704, d, 7–8; Grinnell, "Some Early Cheyenne Tales," 189.

38. Bull Thigh, NAA MS 2828, f1, a, 2–3.

39. NAA MS 2822, f1, f, 1.

40. NAA MS 2822, f1, g, 2, for Ice; f1, c, 17, for Grasshopper.

41. Wolf Chief, NAA MS 2822, f1, b, 3.

42. NAA MS 2828, f1, 2. Bull Thigh stated that the meetings also took place at Red Rock and the Black Hills, which are different locations from his other accounts, which state the meetings took place on the Missouri River.

43. NAA MS 2811, f4, 1.

44. Ibid.

45. NAA MS 2684-a, 13.
46. NAA MS 2684-a, 28.
47. Michelson recorded: "The Sutaio met the Cheyennes 1st because then the Sioux and other Indians were not out so far west then. Sutaio and Cheyenne had to fight against each other. At the time of meeting the Cheyenne planted corn on Missouri River but is uncertain whether Sutaio did or not. NAA MS 2684-a, 4.
48. NAA MS 2684-a, 14–15.
49. NAA MS 2811, f4, 2–3.
50. Tom Weist, *A History of the Cheyenne People* (Billings, MT: Council for Indian Education, 1977), 24.
51. Wolf Chief, NAA MS 2684-a, 1.
52. Mooney, *Cheyenne Indians*, 368–70; Stands In Timber and Liberty, *Cheyenne Memories*, 73; Grinnell, *Cheyenne Indians*, 2: 339–45; Stands In Timber and Liberty, *A Cheyenne Voice*, 254–56.
53. Coyote, NAA MS 3218, 9.
54. Bull Thigh, NAA MS 2684-a, 17.
55. White Buffalo, NAA MS 2811, f4, 2.
56. Stands In Timber and Liberty, *A Cheyenne Voice*, 216.
57. Ibid., 6, 192.
58. Bull Thigh, NAA MS 2828, f1, a, 2.

CHAPTER 3

1. Tom J. Holm, Diane Pearson, and Ben Chavis, "Peoplehood: A Model for the Extension of Sovereignty in American Indian Studies," *Wicazo Sa Review* 18, no. 1 (Spring 2003): 7–24.
2. Deloria, *God Is Red*, 101–2.
3. Vine Deloria, Jr., *Red Earth, White Lies: Native Americans and the Myth of Scientific Fact* (Golden, CO: Fulcrum Publishing, 1997) 23–24.
4. Deloria, *God Is Red*, 251.
5. Grinnell, *Cheyenne Indians*, 2: 112–17.
6. Petter, *English-Cheyenne Dictionary*, 775.
7. Grinnell, *Cheyenne Indians*, 2: 337–39.
8. Ibid., 2: 104.
9. Petter, *English-Cheyenne Dictionary*, 422.
10. Erdoes and Ortiz, *American Indian Myths and Legends*, 484–85; Kroeber, "Cheyenne Tales," 164.
11. Stands In Timber and Liberty, *A Cheyenne Voice*, 15.
12. Petter, *English-Cheyenne Dictionary*, 74.
13. Ibid., 1008–9.
14. *Lakota Winter Counts: An Online Exhibit*, National Anthropological Archives, Smithsonian National Museum of Natural History, http://wintercounts.si.edu/index.html; Candace S. Green and Russell Thornton, eds., *The Years the Stars Fell: Lakota Winter Counts at the Smithsonian* (Lincoln: University of Nebraska Press, 2007).
15. Petter, *English-Cheyenne Dictionary*, 74.

NOTES

16. Ibid., 254.
17. Leman, *Náévóo'ôhtséme*, 207.
18. Petter, *English-Cheyenne Dictionary*, 330.
19. Ibid., 271.
20. Grinnell, *Cheyenne Campfires*, 277–78; Grinnell, *Cheyenne Indians*, 2: 379–81
21. Leman, *Cheyenne Texts*, 4–5.
22. Stands In Timber and Liberty, *Cheyenne Memories*, 40.
23. Stands In Timber and Liberty, *A Cheyenne Voice*, 97–98.
24. NAA MS 2811, f1, 13–14.
25. Leman, *Cheyenne Language*, 196–97.
26. Stands In Timber and Liberty, *A Cheyenne Voice*, 97–98.
27. Erdoes and Ortiz, *American Indian Myths and Legends*, 204–5.
28. Thomas B. Marquis, *The Cheyennes of Montana* (Algonac, MI: Reference Publications, 1978), 207.
29. US Senate, Subcommittee of the Committee on Indian Affairs, 71st Cong., 2nd Sess. (1930), *Survey of Conditions of the Indians in the United* States, Part 23, 12844, 12848. Cited in Marquis, *Cheyennes of Montana*, 207n1.
30. Petter, *English-Cheyenne Dictionary*, 867.
31. *The Chiefs' Prophecy: Survival of the Northern Cheyenne Nation*, DVD, directed by Leo Killsback, 2009, Tucson, AZ: Arizona Public Media.
32. Vision statement, Cheyenne Nation website, 2008.
33. NAA MS 3336, 4.
34. Petter, *English-Cheyenne Dictionary*, 517.
35. Stands In Timber and Liberty, *A Cheyenne Voice*, 38.
36. Most scholars of the Cheyenne Indians usually translate Ma'heo'e to mean something similar or equal to "Creator," "Great Spirit," "All Father," or simply "God." See Powell, *Sweet Medicine*, 864; John H. Moore, *The Cheyenne* (Malden, MA: Blackwell Publishers, 1996), 20; Schlesier, *Wolves of Heaven*, 5. Other scholars have linguistically mistranslated and thus misinterpreted the greatest of the Cheyenne holy spirit being, *Heammaveho* ("whiteman sitting above": the name given to Jesus Christ) thus missing the meaning and significance of Ma'heo'e. Hoebel, *The Cheyennes*, 88–89; Grinnell, *Cheyenne Indians*, 2: 88.
37. "Great Medicine" is a translation that I have found to make more sense and this was the translation used by some scholars of Cheyenne Indians; see Dorsey, *Cheyenne Sundance*, 1–2; Marquis, *Wooden Leg: A Warrior Who Fought Custer* (Lincoln: University of Nebraska Press, 1962), 123–54. The term "Great Medicine" is similar to the Lakota term Wakan Tanka, which translates to "Great Mystery."
38. Petter, *English-Cheyenne Dictionary*, 424.
39. Ibid., 200–201.
40. Grinnell, *Cheyenne Indians*, 2: 93–94.
41. NAA MS 3336.
42. Mann, *Cheyenne-Arapaho Education*, 13.
43. NAA MS 2684-a, 4.
44. Grinnell, *Cheyenne Indians*, 2:193.
45. Stands In Timber and Liberty, *A Cheyenne Voice*, 285.
46. NAA MS 3343, 8.

NOTES

PART II

1. The ethnographers who recorded the story from which this excerpt comes, did so in 1967 in Lame Deer, Montana, from "members of the Strange Owl family." See Erdoes and Ortiz, *American Indian Myths and Legends*, 203.
2. Stands In Timber and Liberty, *Cheyenne Memories*, 44.
3. Hoebel, *Cheyenne Indians*, 47.
4. Stands In Timber and Liberty, *A Cheyenne Voice*, 60.
5. *The Chiefs' Prophecy*.
6. John H. Moore, "Cheyenne Political History, 1820–1894," *Ethnohistory* 21, no. 4 (Autumn 1974): 334; Hoebel, *Cheyenne Indians*, 43.
7. Deloria and Lytle, *American Indians, American Justice* (Austin: University of Texas Press, 1983), 85–87.

CHAPTER 4

1. Petter, "Hevis'onemazistoz," *English-Cheyenne Dictionary*, 190.
2. Leman, *Náévóo'ôhtséme*, 349–61.
3. NAA MS 2704, i, 1–5.
4. NAA MS 2134, d, 1–9.
5. Leman, *Náévóo'ôhtséme*, 360–61.
6. Yazzie, *Navajo History*.
7. NAA MS 2796, f1-e, 7.
8. Randolph, *Sweet Medicine*, 87–99; Kroeber, "Cheyenne Tales," 177–79.
9. NAA MS 2798.
10. Randolph, *Sweet Medicine*, 195.
11. Ibid., 87.
12. Ibid., 195.
13. Ibid., 99.
14. Randolph, "Heron's Revenge," in *Sweet Medicine*, 65–86.
15. Randolph, *Sweet Medicine*, 69.
16. Ibid., 78.
17. Ibid., 85.
18. Stands In Timber and Liberty, *A Cheyenne Voice*, 101.

CHAPTER 5

1. NAA MS 2811, f4.
2. NAA MS 3218.
3. Laura Rockroads, quoted in Leman, *Náévóo'ôhtséme*, 251.
4. NAA MS 2822, f1-n, 1–4.
5. NAA MS 2822, f1-f, 1–8.
6. Laura Rockroads, quoted in Leman, *Náévóo'ôhtséme*, 251–63; Albert Hoffman, quoted in Leman, *Cheyenne Texts*, 53–55; Bull Thigh, "Smallest and the girl," NAA MS 2704; Somers, NAA MS 2822. Also see Henry Tall Bull and Tom Weist, *The Rolling Head* (Billings, MT: Montana Council on Indian Education, 1971).

NOTES

7. NAA MS 2822, f1-n, 4–8.

8. Laura Rockroads, quoted in Leman, *Náévóo'ôhtséme*, 251–63; Albert Hoffman, quoted in Leman, *Cheyenne Texts*, 53–55; Bull Thigh, "Smallest and the girl," NAA MS 2704; Somers, NAA MS 2822.

9. NAA MS 2822, f1-f, 8.

10. Karl N. Llewellyn and E. Adamson Hoebel, *The Cheyenne Way: Conflict and Case Law in Primitive Jurisprudence* (Norman: University of Oklahoma Press, 1941), 69–73; Hoebel, *Cheyenne Indians*, 45–49.

11. Grinnell, *Cheyenne Indians*, 1: 347–48; Mooney, "The Cheyenne Indians," 371.

12. Grinnell, *Cheyenne Indians*, 347–48. The stories were told to Grinnell by the Cheyenne spiritual leader Tangle Hair.

13. Mooney, "The Cheyenne Indians," 371.

14. Ibid.

15. Petter, *English-Cheyenne Dictionary*, 230–31.

16. Paul Wallace, *White Roots of Peace: The Iroquois Book of Life* (Sante Fe, NM: Clear Light Publishers, 1994); Jerry Fields and Barbara Mann, "A Sign in the Sky: Dating the League of the Haudenosaunee," *American Indian Culture and Research Journal* 21, no. 2 (1997): 105–63; Chief Oren Lyons, "Indian Self-Government in the Haudenosaunee Constitution," *Nordic Journal of International Law* 55 (1986): 117–21; Lyons, "Sovereignty and Sacred Land: Bardie C. Wolfe, Jr. Keynote Address," *Thomas Law Review* 13 (2000–2001): 19–28; Lyons, "Law, Principle, and Reality," *New York University Review of Law and Social Change* 20, no. 2 (1993): 209–15.

17. NAA MS 2684-a.

18. *The Chiefs' Prophecy*.

19. Mann, *Cheyenne-Arapaho Education*, 2; Fisher, "Cheyenne Indian Lore."

20. Mann, *Cheyenne-Arapaho Education*, 2.

21. NAA MS 2704, a, 9.

22. Stands In Timber and Liberty, *A Cheyenne Voice*, 99–101.

23. Ibid., 305.

24. Powell, *Sweet Medicine*, 859; Erdoes and Ortiz, *American Indian Myths and Legends*, 204; Penney, *Tales of the Cheyennes*, 33.

25. Grinnell, *Cheyenne Indians*, 2: 339; Petter, *English-Cheyenne Dictionary*, 867.

26. Stands In Timber and Liberty, *A Cheyenne Voice*, 109.

27. Stands In Timber and Liberty, *Cheyenne Memories*, 48–50; Stands In Timber and Liberty, *A Cheyenne Voice*, 109.

CHAPTER 6

1. Grinnell, "Early Cheyenne Villages."

2. NAA MS 2822, f1-f, 2.

3. NAA MS 2811, f3, 8-9.

4. Harold Driver, *Indians of North America*, 2nd ed. (Chicago: University of Chicago Press, 1975), 300-301.

5. Powell, *Sweet Medicine*, 93.

6. Marquis, *Wooden Leg*, 56.

7. *The Chiefs' Prophecy.*
8. Llewellyn and Hoebel, *Cheyenne Way*, 74.
9. Dorsey, *Cheyenne Sundance*, 13; Stands In Timber and Liberty, *A Cheyenne Voice*, 101.
10. Marquis, *Wooden Leg*, 56.
11. Stan Hoig, *The Peace Chiefs of the Cheyennes* (Norman: University of Oklahoma Press, 1980), 11.
12. Stands In Timber and Liberty, *Cheyenne Memories*, 49.
13. Grinnell, *Cheyenne Indians*, 1: 340.
14. Stands In Timber and Liberty, *A Cheyenne Voice*, 107.
15. Ibid., 343.
16. NAA MS 2684-a.
17. Dorsey, *Cheyenne Sundance*, 12–15. Dorsey's account of the seating ceremony from 1903 is missing the northern bands, but it is still one of the most complete descriptions of the Chiefs' Ceremony.
18. Grinnell, *Cheyenne Indians*, 1: 340.
19. Llewellyn and Hoebel, *Cheyenne Way*, 78.
20. Ibid., 89.
21. Stands In Timber and Liberty, *A Cheyenne Voice*, 361.
22. Leo Killsback, "The Legacy of Little Wolf: Rewriting and Righting Our Leaders Back into History," *Wicazo Sa Review* 26, no. 1 (2011): 85–111.

CHAPTER 7

1. Hoig, *Peace Chiefs*, 15.
2. Stands In Timber and Liberty, *Cheyenne Memories*, 44.
3. Stands In Timber and Liberty, *A Cheyenne Voice*, 102–3, 305.
4. Grinnell, *Cheyenne Indians*, 1: 340.
5. Ibid., 337.
6. Llewellyn and Hoebel, *Cheyenne Way*, 78.
7. Grinnell, *Cheyenne Indians*, 1: 336.
8. Hoebel, *Cheyennes*, 43.
9. Grinnell, *Cheyenne Indians*, 1: 108.
10. Ibid., 120.
11. Ibid.
12. Hoig, *Peace Chiefs*, 8–9.
13. Ibid.
14. Dorsey, *Cheyenne Sundance*, 14.
15. Grinnell, *Cheyenne Indians*, I, 336.
16. Ibid., 337.
17. *The Chiefs' Prophecy.*
18. Grinnell, *Cheyenne Indians*, 1: 336–37.
19. Llewellyn and Hoebel, *The Cheyenne Way*, 79.
20. Stands In Timber and Liberty, *A Cheyenne Voice*, 33, 103.
21. The term Ma'xema'hēō'e is not used as much among contemporary Cheyenne

NOTES

speakers. Leman, et al., *Cheyenne Dictionary*, 136; Petter, *English-Cheyenne Dictionary*, 516–17.
22. Petter, *English-Cheyenne Dictionary*, 596–97.
23. Dorsey, *Cheyenne Sundance*, 14.
24. Grinnell, *Cheyenne Indians*, 2: 33.
25. Literally means "being straight" with the Cheyenne culture. Leman, et al., *Cheyenne Dictionary*, 318; Petter, *English-Cheyenne Dictionary*, 917.
26. Grinnell, *Cheyenne Indians*, I, 341.
27. Stands In Timber and Liberty, *A Cheyenne Voice*, 278.
28. Leman, *Náévóo'ôhtséme*, 206.
29. Stands In Timber and Liberty, *A Cheyenne Voice*, 32.
30. Leman, *Náévóo'ôhtséme*, 220–1.
31. Leman, et al., *Cheyenne Dictionary*, 152.

PART III

1. Grinnell, "Some Early Cheyenne Tales, II," 275.
2. Told by a Northern Cheyenne informant in Lame Deer, Montana in 1967, recorded in Erdoes and Ortiz, *American Indian Myths and Legends*, 203.
3. Stands In Timber and Liberty, *A Cheyenne Voice*, 37.

CHAPTER 8

1. Randolph, "Cherry Eater's Magic Hoops," in *Sweet Medicine*, 117–26.
2. Ibid., 125–26.
3. NAA MS 2134, c, 1–5.
4. NAA MS 2704, b, 1–5.
5. Ibid., b, 5–6.
6. NAA MS 2704, d, 1–7.
7. NAA MS 2704, d, 7.
8. NAA MS 2134, f, 1–19.
9. NAA MS 2684-a, 35.
10. Kroeber, "Cheyenne Tales," 182–83; Erdoes and Ortiz, *American Indian Myths and Legends*, 205–9.
11. Penney, *Tales of the Cheyennes*, 52–63.
12. NAA MS 2790-c.
13. The story is recorded in Randolph, *Sweet Medicine*, 154–58; Grinnell, *By Cheyenne Campfires*, 216–20; and Stands In Timber and Liberty, *Cheyenne Memories*, 30–33. Stands In Timber identifies the hunter as Sweet Medicine, but the arrow belonging to "Seven Young Men." Leman, *Cheyenne Texts*, 304–13.
14. Erdoes and Ortiz, *American Indian Myths and Legends*, 205–9; Grinnell, *By Cheyenne Campfires*, 220–31; Randolph, *Sweet Medicine*, 158–64; Penney, *Tales of the Cheyennes*, 52–62; Stands in Timber and Liberty, *A Cheyenne Voice*, 57–59.
15. Grinnell, *Cheyenne Indians*, 2: 337-81; Erdoes and Ortiz, *American Indian Myths and Legends*, 199–205.
16. Petter, *English-Cheyenne Dictionary*, 867; Erdoes and Ortiz, *American Indian*

Myths and Legends, 29–33; Henry Tall Bull and Tom Weist, *Cheyenne Warriors: Stories of the Northern Cheyenne* (Billings, MT: Montana Council on Indian Education, 1983).

17. Stands In Timber and Liberty, *Cheyenne Memories*, 28–30; Stands In Timber and Liberty, *A Cheyenne Voice*, 7–8, 10–12; Grinnell, "Some Early Cheyenne Tales II," 271–73.

18. The three stories were also remembered as "miracles" in the Christian sense, probably because traditional Cheyenne storytellers during the assimilation era wanted to equate the prophet Motsé'eóeve to a Christian saint.

19. NAA MS 2811 f1, 1–2.
20. NAA MS 2799, f1, 1–2.
21. Randolph, *Sweet Medicine*, 179–83.
22. Stands In Timber and Liberty, *A Cheyenne Voice*, 22, 24; Erdoes and Ortiz, *American Indian Myths and Legends*, 202.
23. Stands In Timber and Liberty, *A Cheyenne Voice*, 22.

CHAPTER 9

1. Bull Thigh actually identified the person as White Dirt. The person whom Bull Thigh is discussing is also the person identified as Lime in previous stories. The correct translation for Vóetséna'e (Lime) is literally "white clay," which is the white powder that is used as ceremonial paint.

2. NAA MS 2684-a, 14–17.

3. Published accounts of the creation of the warrior societies are found in Grinnell, *Cheyenne Indians*, 2: 353-59; Dorsey, *Cheyenne Sundance*, 15–29; Stands In Timber and Liberty, *Cheyenne Memories*, 33–35; Petter, *English-Cheyenne Dictionary*, 777–79. Stands In Timber and Liberty, *A Cheyenne Voice*, 38–40, 42–45, 87, 89, 91, 309–11; and Erdoes and Ortiz, *American Indian Myths and Legends*, 29–33. Stories told today differ slightly from family to family, and among the different communities in both the Northern and Southern Cheyenne tribes. My account is not meant to devalue or diminish the living oral tradition of our peoples, but I've made an effort to provide a complete account with much honor and respect.

4. NAA MS 2822, f1-c, 4–6.
5. NAA MS 2811, f3, 1–4.
6. Ibid., f4, 3–8.
7. NAA MS 2799, f1, 16–21.
8. Stands In Timber and Liberty, *A Cheyenne Voice*, 87.
9. Ibid., 34–40, 91, 309–10.
10. NAA MS 2684-a, 2.
11. Stands In Timber and Liberty, *A Cheyenne Voice*, 387–88, 460.
12. NAA MS 2822, f1 h, 1.
13. NAA MS 2684-a, 49.
14. NAA MS 2822, f1-i, 3.
15. NAA MS 2822, f2-b 1-3.
16. Petter, *English-Cheyenne Dictionary*, 778.
17. Dorsey, *Cheyenne Sundance*, 26–29; Grinnell, *Cheyenne Indians*, 2: 72–78.

18. The details of this ceremony have long vanished. See Stands In Timber and Liberty, *Cheyenne Memories*, 102.

CHAPTER 10

1. For details on society customs, see Grinnell, *Cheyenne Indians*, 2:48–72.
2. NAA MS 2811, f1-h, 2.
3. Grinnell, "Some Early Cheyenne Tales II," 301–303.
4. Petter, *English-Cheyenne Dictionary*, 778.
5. Wooden Leg only mentioned three societies (Elk warriors, Crazy Dog warriors, and Fox warriors), counting seventy-four who could have claimed to be society chiefs or Council chiefs. See Marquis, *Wooden Leg*, 56.
6. Stands In Timber and Liberty, *A Cheyenne Voice*, 42–45.
7. NAA MS 2822, f1-h, 2.
8. Stands In Timber and Liberty, *A Cheyenne Voice*, 87.
9. Petter, *English-Cheyenne Dictionary*, 777. Descriptions are also from Wolf Chief (NAA MS 2684-a, 17–18) and Coyote (NAA MS 2684-a, 28).
10. NAA MS 2684-a, 17–18.
11. NAA MS 2684-a, 28.
12. NAA MS 2822, f1-h, 1.
13. Petter, *English-Cheyenne Dictionary*, 777–78.
14. NAA MS 2684-a, 29.
15. NAA MS 3218, 99–103.
16. NAA MS 2822, f1-h, 1.
17. NAA MS 2684-a, 19.
18. Ibid., 29.
19. Petter, *English-Cheyenne Dictionary*, 778.
20. NAA MS 2822, f1-h, 1.
21. Petter, *English-Cheyenne Dictionary*, 778.
22. NAA MS 2684-a, 17.
23. Ibid., 28.
24. NAA MS 2822, f1-d, 2.
25. NAA MS 2684-a, 30.
26. Grinnell, *Cheyenne Indians*, 1: 345.
27. Stands In Timber and Liberty, *Cheyenne Memories*, 28–30.
28. Dorsey, *Cheyenne Sundance*, 39–41.
29. 2684-a, 21.
30. Marquis, *Wooden Leg*, 56.
31. Hoebel, *Cheyennes*, 41.
32. NAA MS 2822, f1-1, 2.
33. Grinnell, *Cheyenne Indians*, 2: 51.
34. Stands In Timber and Liberty, *A Cheyenne Voice*, 91.
35. Marquis, *Wooden Leg*, 85–86.
36. *The Chiefs' Prophecy*.
37. Grinnell, *Cheyenne Indians*, 2: 51.
38. Moore, *Cheyenne*, 129–30.

39. NAA MS 2684-a, 3.
40. Marquis, *Wooden Leg*, 63–64.
41. Hoebel, *Cheyennes*, 41.
42. Dorsey, *Cheyenne Sundance*, 16.
43. Marquis, *Wooden Leg*, 58.
44. Stands In Timber and Liberty, *Cheyenne Memories*, 68; Stands In Timber and Liberty, *A Cheyenne Voice*, 45.
45. NAA MS 2684-a, 2.
46. This battle is known to the Cheyenne as "where the girl saved her brother." Buffalo Calf Road Woman saved her brother, Chief Comes in Sight, who was pinned down by US fire. See Stands In Timber and Liberty, *Cheyenne Memories*, 181.
47. Grinnell, *Cheyenne Indians*, 2:50.
48. Stands In Timber and Liberty, *A Cheyenne Voice*, 89.
49. NAA MS 2684-a, 3.
50. Stands In Timber and Liberty, *Cheyenne Memories*, 68.
51. Petter, *English-Cheyenne Dictionary*, 97.
52. Truman Michelson, "The Narrative of a Southern Cheyenne Woman," Publication 3140, *Smithsonian Miscellaneous Collections* 87, no. 5 (March 21, 1932): 8–9.
53. Mooney, *Cheyenne Indians*, 415; Warren E. Schwartz, *The Last Contrary: The Story of Wesley Whiteman (Black Bear)* (Sioux Falls, SD: The Center for Western Studies, 1991), 81; Thomas E. Mails, *Fools Crow* (Garden City, NY: Bison Books, 1990), 61. See a photo of a war bonnet woman in John Wooden Legs, *A Northern Cheyenne Album: Photographs by Thomas B. Marquis*, ed. Margot Liberty (Norman: University of Oklahoma Press, 2007), 170. For another photo of a member of this women's society, see Thomas B. Marquis and Ronald H. Limbaugh, eds., *Cheyenne and Sioux: The Reminiscences of Four Indians and a White Soldier* (Stockton, CA: Pacific Center for Western Historical Studies, 1973), insert XII, "Big Crow and wife, 1927."
54. Hoebel, *Cheyennes*, 40.
55. Grinnell, *Cheyenne Indians*, 2: 48; Hoebel, *Cheyennes*, 40; Moore, *Cheyenne*, 126.
56. NAA MA 2822, 1-f, 3.
57. Grinnell, *Cheyenne Indians*, 2: 48.
58. Hoig, *Peace Chiefs*, 9.
59. Ibid.
60. Moore, "Cheyenne Political History," 337.
61. Hoebel, *Cheyennes*, 40.
62. Stands In Timber and Liberty, *A Cheyenne Voice*, 91.
63. Marquis, *Wooden Leg*, 118.
64. Stands In Timber and Liberty, *A Cheyenne Voice*, 327.
65. Marquis, *Wooden Leg*, 118–19.
66. NAA MS 2811.

CHAPTER 11

1. Marquis, *Wooden Leg*, 57.
2. Moore, *Cheyenne Nation*, 106.
3. Bill Tallbull (Wolf Feathers), "We are the Ancestors of those yet to be Born: Northern Cheyenne History of the Battle of 100-In-The-Hands (the Fetterman Battle)," *Fort Phil Kearny/Bozeman Trail Association*, last modified March 22, 2004, http://www.philkearny.vcn.com/fpk-tallbull.htm.
4. NAA MS 2684-a, 6.
5. Marquis, *Wooden Leg*, 59–60.
6. Moore asserts that a major "problem" for the Cheyenne Nation was the instability in the government structure. This problem, however, was not common until the time of the buffalo, when more white cultural influences began to show presence on the Plains (i.e., guns, alcohol, manufactured goods). During these times the warrior societies would overrun the Council of Forty-Four Chiefs or their decision. See Moore, "Cheyenne Political History," 330–34.
7. Stands In Timber and Liberty, *A Cheyenne Voice*, 176.
8. Marquis, *Wooden Leg*, 60.
9. Grinnell, *Cheyenne Indians*, 2: 49: "Sometimes one or more of these societies, acting unitedly, might force the tribe to adopt some certain course of action that it was not generally desired to take, or might even oblige some priest or important man to perform an act that he felt to be wrong or to threaten harm to the tribe. Such a case occurred about 1836, when one of the soldier bands forced White Thunder, the keeper of the medicine arrows, to renew them at a time when the spirits were unfavorable."
10. Petter, *English-Cheyenne Dictionary*, 467.
11. George B. Grinnell, *The Fighting Cheyennes* (Lincoln: University of Nebraska Press, 1955), 10: "The fighting spirit was encouraged. In no way could a young man gain so much credit as by the exhibition of courage. Boys and youths were trained to feel that the most important thing in life was to be brave; that death was not a thing to be avoided; that, in fact, it was better for a man to be killed while in his full vigor rather than to wait until his prime was past, his powers were failing, and he could no longer achieve those feats which to all seemed so desirable."
12. Stands In Timber and Liberty, *A Cheyenne Voice*, 381–82, 440–42.
13. Wilma Mankiller, *Every Day Is a Good Day: Reflections of Contemporary Indigenous Women*, Memorial Ed. (Golden, CO: Fulcrum Publishing, 2011), 160.
14. This "Straight Teaching" is explained by Elaine Strange Owl in Leman, *Náévóo'ôhtséme*, 216–17.
15. The direct translated terminology was adapted from original text, which was recorded in Cheyenne, by author to provide a much more precise narrative in English. Leman, *Cheyenne Texts*, 83.
16. Leman, *Cheyenne Texts*, 84–85.
17. Stands In Timber and Liberty, *Cheyenne Memories*, 45.
18. George B. Grinnell, "Cheyenne Woman Customs," *American Anthropologist*, New Series, vol. 4, no. 1 (1902): 13–16.
19. Leman, *Cheyenne Texts*, 80.
20. Ibid., 82.

NOTES

PART IV

1. NAA MS 3220, c, 1–2.

CHAPTER 12

1. Lawrence W. Gross, "The Comic Vision of Anishinaabe Culture and Religion," *American Indian Quarterly* 26 no. 3 (Summer 2002): 436–59.
2. Vine Deloria, "The Trickster and the Messiah," in *Spirit and Reason: The Vine Deloria, Jr., Reader* (Golden: Fulcrum Publishing, 1999).
3. NAA MS 3342, c, 1–34.
4. Lawrence W. Gross, "Cultural Sovereignty and Native American Hermeneutics in the Interpretation of the Scared Stories of the Anishinaabe," *Wicazo Sa Review* (Fall 2003): 127–34.
5. Katherine M. Weist, *Belle Highwalking: The Narrative of a Northern Cheyenne Woman* (Billings, MT: Montana Council for Indian Education, 1979), 45–46.
6. NAA MS 3220, e, 1–5.
7. Franchot Ballinger, "Coyote, He/She Was Going There: Sex and Gender in Native American Trickster Stories," *Studies in American Indian Literatures* 12, no. 4 (Winter 2000): 15–42.
8. NAA MS 2134, Southern Cheyenne legends, June 1932, Mack Haag.
9. Grinnell, *Cheyenne Indians*, 1: 34.
10. Hyde, *Life of George Bent*, 108–9.
11. Killsback, "The Legacy of Little Wolf," 96.
12. Frank Pommersheim, *Broken Landscape: Indians, Indian Tribes, and the Constitution* (New York: Oxford University Press, 2009), 27.
13. Ibid., 29.
14. US Senate, *Concurrent Resolution to acknowledge the contribution of the Iroquois Confederacy of Nations to the development of the United States Constitution and to reaffirm the continuing government-to-government relationship between Indian tribes and the United States established in the Constitution,* October 4, 1988 (Calendar Day, October 18), 1988, 100th Cong., 2nd sess., 1988, H. Con. Res. 331.
15. For a discussion on the American Indian perspective on the Lewis and Clark Expedition, see Elizabeth Cook-Lynn and James Riding In, "Editors' Commentary," *Wicazo Sa Review* 19, no. 1, American Indian Encounters with Lewis and Clark (Spring 2004): 5–10..
16. Hoig, *Peace Chiefs*, 17; Grinnell, *Cheyenne Indians*, 1:39; Weist, *History of the Cheyenne People*, 27.
17. Llewellyn and Hoebel, *Cheyenne Way*, 85–86.
18. Ibid., 36.
19. Hyde, *Life of George Bent*, 85.
20. Grinnell, *Cheyenne Indians*, 2:379–80.
21. NAA MS 2811, f3, 11–3.
22. Leman, *Náévóo'ôhtséme*, 6.
23. Ibid., 12.
24. Charles J. Kappler, ed., "Treaty with the Cheyenne Tribe, 1825, July 6, 1825. 7 Stat., 255. Proclamation, Feb. 6, 1826," *Indian Affairs: Laws and Treaties*, vol. 2

(Washington, DC: Government Printing Office, 1904), http://digital.library.okstate.edu/kappler/Vol2/treaties/che0232.htm.

25. Weist, *History of the Cheyenne People*, 39.

26. Hyde, *Life of George Bent* 96.

27. In defense of the image of the "white man," George Bird Grinnell offered his own interpretation of why the Cheyennes viewed white men as the trickster, stating: "Often he [the trickster] seems to possess intelligence greater than that of most Indians, as the etymology of his name might seem to suggest." *By Cheyenne Campfires*, 281. Grinnell is himself a vé'hó'e. In his compilation of traditional Cheyenne stories, *By Cheyenne Campfires,* he deliberately changes the titles of all of the trickster stories to protect the image of the "white man."

28. NAA MS 2822, f1, k, 1–2.

29. NAA MS 2822, f1, j, 1–3.

30. NAA MS 2822, f1, l, 1–2.

31. NAA MS 3219, f2, 1–3.

32. NAA MS 3219, f2, 3–7.

CONCLUSION

1. Linda Tuhiwai Smith, *Decolonizing Methodologies: Research and Indigenous Peoples,* 2nd ed. (New York: Zed Books, 2012), 25.

2. Albert Memmi, *The Colonizer and the Colonized* (Boston: Beacon Press, 1991), xxiv.

3. Ibid., xxviii–xxix.

4. Ibid., 91.

5. Standing Bear, *Land of the Spotted Eagle,* preface.

6. Memmi, *The Colonizer and the Colonized,* 17.

7. Frantz Fanon, *The Wretched of the Earth* (New York: Grove Press, 1963), 39.

8. Charles Wilkinson highlights the Taos Pueblo, the Passamaquoddy and Penobscot, and Alaska Natives in Wilkinson, *Blood Struggle: The Rise of Modern Indian Nations* (New York: W.W. Norton, 2005), 206–40.

Bibliography

Alfred, Taiaiake. *Peace, Power, Righteousness: An Indigenous Manifesto*, 2nd ed. New York: Oxford University Press, 2009.
———. *Wasáse: Indigenous Pathways of Action and Freedom*. Toronto: University of Toronto Press, 2005.
Ballinger, Franchot. "Coyote, He/She Was Going There: Sex and Gender in Native American Trickster Stories." *Studies in American Indian Literatures* 12, no. 4 (Winter 2000): 15–42.
Banyaca, Thomas. "Essence of Hopi Prophecy" (unpublished manuscript). 1994. http://tierra-y-vida.blogspot.com/2007/12/hopi-declaration-of-peace-essence-of.html.
Bass, Althea, *The Arapaho Way: A Memoir of Indian Boyhood*. New York: Clarkson N. Pottter, 1966.
Bear Chum, Wallace. "Northern Cheyenne Vision Page." *Northern Cheyenne Tribe: Official Site of the Tsististas and So'taa'eo'e People*. 2008.
Berthrong, Donald J. *The Cheyenne and Arapaho Ordeal: Reservation and Agency Life in the Indian Territory, 1875–1907*. Norman: University of Oklahoma Press, 1976.
———. *The Southern Cheyennes*. Norman: University of Oklahoma Press, 1986.
Bonnerjea, Biren. "Reminiscences of a Cheyenne Indian." *Journal de la Société des Américanistes* 27, no. 1 (1935): 129–43.
Brown, Joseph E., ed. *The Sacred Pipe: Black Elk's Account of the Seven Rites of the Oglala Sioux*. Norman: University of Oklahoma Press, 1989.
Bureau of American Ethnology, Smithsonian Institution. *Annual Report of the Bureau of American Ethnology to the Secretary of the Smithsonian Institution, 1895*, vol. 24. Washington, DC: Government Printing Office, 1902–1903, 442–43. http://archive.org/stream/annualreportofbu24smit/annualreportofbu24smit_djvu.txt.
Calloway, Colin G. *First Peoples: A Documentary Survey of American Indian History*, 5th ed. New York: Bedford/St. Marin's, 2016.
Chamberlain, M. E. *Decolonization*, 2nd ed. Malden, MA: Blackwell Publishing, 1999.
The Chiefs' Prophecy: Survival of the Northern Cheyenne Nation, DVD. Directed by Leo Killsback. 2009, Tucson, AZ: Arizona Public Media.
Coffey, Wallace, and Rebecca Tsosie. "Rethinking the Tribal Sovereignty Doctrine: Cultural Sovereignty and the Collective Future of the Indian Nations." *Stanford Law and Policy Review* 12, no. 2 (2001): 191–221.
Collier, John. *Indians of the Americas: A Long Hope*. New York: New American Library, 1975.

Cook-Lynn, Elizabeth, and James Riding In. "Editors' Commentary." *Wicazo Sa Review* 19, no. 1, American Indian Encounters with Lewis and Clark (Spring 2004): 5–10.
Crow Dog, Mary, and Richard Erdoes. *Lakota Woman.* New York: HarperPerennial, 1991.
Deloria, Vine, Jr. *Custer Died for Your Sins: An Indian Manifesto.* Norman: University of Oklahoma Press, 1969.
———. *Evolution, Creationism, and Other Modern Myths: A Critical Inquiry.* Golden, CO: Fulcrum Publishing, 2002.
———. *God Is Red: A Native View of Religion.* Golden, CO: Fulcrum Publishing, 1992.
———. *Red Earth, White Lies: Native Americans and the Myth of Scientific Fact.* Golden, CO: Fulcrum Publishing, 1997.
———. "A Redefinition of Indian Affairs." In *Image and Event: America Now*, edited by David Bicknell and Richard Brengle, 303–15. New York: Appleton-Century-Crotfts, 1971.
———. *Spirit & Reason: The Vine Deloria, Jr., Reader.* Ed. by Barbara Deloria, Kristen Foehner, and Sam Scinta. Golden, CO: Fulcrum Publishing, 1999.
Deloria, Vine, Jr., and Clifford Lytle. *American Indians, American Justice.* Austin: University of Texas Press, 1983.
Deloria, Vine, Jr., and Clifford M. Lytle. *The Nations Within: The Past and Future of American Indian Sovereignty.* Austin: University of Texas Press, 1984
DeMallie, Raymond J., ed. *The Sixth Grandfather: Black Elk's Teachings Given to John G. Neihardt.* Lincoln: University of Nebraska Press, 1985.
Diné Bi Beenahaz'áanii (1 N.N.C. §§ 201-206), http://www.navajocourts.org/dine.htm.
Driver, Harold. *Indians of North America*, 2nd ed. Chicago: University of Chicago Press, 1975.
Dorsey, George A. *The Arapaho Sundance: The Ceremony of the Offerings Lodge.* Field Columbian Museum Publication 75, Anthropological Series Vol. IV. June 1903.
———. *The Cheyenne: Sundance.* Anthropological Series 9, no. 1. Chicago: Field Columbian Museum, 1905.
Echo-Hawk, Walter R. *In the Courts of the Conqueror: The 10 Worst Indian Law Cases Ever Decided.* Golden, CO: Fulcrum Publishing, 2010.
Echo-Hawk, Walter R., and James Anaya. *In the Light of Justice: The Rise of Human Rights in Native America and the UN Declaration on the Rights of Indigenous People.* Golden, CO: Fulcrum Publishing, 2013.
Erdoes, Richard, and Alfonso Ortiz, eds. *American Indian Myths and Legends.* New York: Pantheon Books, 1984.
Fanon, Frantz. *The Wretched of the Earth.* New York: Grove Press, 1963.
Fields, Jerry, and Barbara Mann. "A Sign in the Sky: Dating the League of the Haudenosaunee." *American Indian Culture and Research Journal* 21, no. 2 (1997): 105–63.
Fisher, Eugene, interpreter. "Cheyenne Indian Lore Related by Holy Bird and Yellow Nose, Tribal Historians." Conference Between Grant A. Solberg and

Members of the Cheyenne Indian Tribe, September 28, 1939. Unpublished manuscript.
Getches, David, Charles Wilkinson, Robert Williams, and Matthew Fletcher. *Federal Indian Law: Cases and Materials*, 6th ed. St. Paul: West Academic Publishing, 2011.
Grande, Sandy. *Red Pedagogy: Native American Social and Political Thought*. Lanham, MD: Rowman & Littlefield, 2004.
Green, Candace S., and Russell Thornton, eds. *The Years the Stars Fell: Lakota Winter Counts at the Smithsonian*. Lincoln: University of Nebraska Press, 2007.
Green, Jerome A. *Battles and Skirmishes of the Great Sioux War, 1876–1877*. Norman: University of Oklahoma Press, 1996.
———. *Lakota and Cheyenne: Indian Views of the Great Sioux War, 1876–1877*. Norman: University of Oklahoma Press, 2000.
———. *Morning Star Dawn: The Powder River Expedition and the Northern Cheyennes, 1876*. Norman: University of Oklahoma Press, 2003.
———. *Washita: The U.S. Army and the Southern Cheyennes, 1867–1869*. Norman: University of Oklahoma Press, 2008.
Grinnell, George B. *By Cheyenne Campfires*. Lincoln: University of Nebraska Press, 1971.
———. *The Cheyenne Indians*, 2 vols. Lincoln: University of Nebraska Press, 1972.
———. "Cheyenne Woman Customs." *American Anthropologist*, New Series, vol. 4, no. 1 (1902): 13–16.
———. "Early Cheyenne Villages." *American Anthropologist*, New Series, vol. 20, no. 4 (1918): 359–80.
———. *The Fighting Cheyennes*. Lincoln: University of Nebraska Press, 1955.
———. "The Great Mysteries of the Cheyenne." *American Anthropologist*, New Series, vol. 12, no. 4 (1910): 542–75.
———. "Some Early Cheyenne Tales." *Journal of American Folklore* 20, no. 78 (1907): 169–194.
———. "Some Early Cheyenne Tales, II." *Journal of American Folklore* 21, no. 82 (1908): 269–320.
Gross, Lawrence W. "The Comic Vision of Anishinaabe Culture and Religion." *American Indian Quarterly* 26, no. 3 (Summer 2002): 436–59.
———. "Cultural Sovereignty and Native American Hermeneutics in the Interpretation of the Scared Stories of the Anishinaabe." *Wicazo Sa Review* (Fall 2003): 127–34.
Harry, Debra. "Biocolonialism and Indigenous Knowledge in United Nations Discourse." *Griffith Law Review* 20 (2011): 702–28.
———. "Indigenous Peoples and Gene Disputes." *Chicago-Kent Law Review* 84 (2009–2010): 147–96.
Hedren, Paul. *Fort Laramie and the Great Sioux War*. Norman: University of Oklahoma Press, 1998.
———. *The Great Sioux War, 1876–77*. Lincoln: University of Nebraska Press, 1991.
Hilger, Sister M. Inez. "Notes on Cheyenne Child Life." *American Anthropologist* 48, no. 1 (1946): 60–69.

Hoebel, E. Adamson. *The Cheyennes: Indians of the Great Plains*, 2nd ed. New York: Harcourt Brace, 1988.
———. *The Law of Primitive Man: A Study in Comparative Legal Dynamics*. Cambridge: Harvard University Press, 1961.
Hoig, Stan. *The Battle of the Washita: The Sheridan-Custer Indian Campaign of 1867–69*. New York: Bison Books, 1979.
———. *The Peace Chiefs of the Cheyennes*. Norman: University of Oklahoma Press, 1980.
———. *Perilous Pursuit: The U.S. Cavalry and the Northern Cheyennes*. Boulder: University Press of Colorado, 2002.
———. *The Sand Creek Massacre*. Norman: University of Oklahoma Press, 1974.
Holm, Tom J., Diane Pearson, and Ben Chavis. "Peoplehood: A Model for the Extension of Sovereignty in American Indian Studies." *Wicazo Sa Review* 18, no. 1 (Spring 2003): 7–24.
Hyde, George E. *Life of George Bent: Written from His Letters*. Edited by Savoie Lottinville. Norman: University of Oklahoma Press, 1968.
———. *The Pawnee Indians*. Norman: University of Oklahoma Press, 1974.
———. *Red Cloud's Folk: A History of the Oglala Sioux Indians*. Norman: University of Oklahoma Press, 1987.
———. *Spotted Tail's Folk: A History of the Brulé Sioux*. Norman: University of Oklahoma Press, 1974.
Jablow, Joseph. *The Cheyenne in Plains Indian Trade Relations, 1795–1840*. Lincoln: University of Nebraska Press, 1994.
Kappler, Charles J., ed. "Treaty with the Cheyenne Tribe, 1825, July 6, 1825. 7 Stat., 255. Proclamation, Feb. 6, 1826." *Indian Affairs: Laws and Treaties*, vol. 2. Washington, DC: Government Printing Office, 1904. http://digital.library.okstate.edu/kappler/Vol2/treaties/che0232.htm.
Killsback, L. Jace. "Culture Changes, Tradition Remains." *The Cheyenne Way: Health News & Information from the Northern Cheyenne Tribal Board of Health* (August 2015): 2–3.
Killsback, Leo. "Indigenous Perceptions of Time: Decolonizing Theory, World History, and the Fates of Human Societies." *American Indian Culture and Research Journal* 37, no. 1 (Winter 2013): 119–47.
———. "The Legacy of Little Wolf: Rewriting and Righting Our Leaders Back into History." *Wicazo Sa Review* 26, no. 1 (2011): 85–111.
Kroeber, A. L. "Cheyenne Tales." *The Journal of American Folklore* 13, no. 50 (1900): 161–90.
Kovach, Margaret. *Indigenous Methodologies: Characteristics, Conversations, and Contexts*. Toronto: University of Toronto Press, 2009.
Lakota Winter Counts: An Online Exhibit. National Anthropological Archives, Smithsonian National Museum of Natural History, http://wintercounts.si.edu/index.html.
Lame Deer, John (Fire) and Richard Erdoes. *Lame Deer Seeker of Visions: The Life of a Sioux Medicine Man*. New York: Simon & Schuster, 1972.
Leman, Wayne, ed. *Cheyenne Texts: An Introduction to Cheyenne Literature*.

Occasional Publication in Anthropology, Linguistic Series, No. 6 (Greeley: Museum of Anthropology, University of Northern Colorado, 1980).

———. *Náévóo'ôhtséme/We Are Going Back Home: Cheyenne History and Stories told by James Shoulderblade and Others*. Algonquian and Iroquoian Linguistics, Memoir 4. Winnipeg, Manitoba: Algonquian and Iroquoian Linguistics, 1987.

———. *A Reference Grammar of the Cheyenne Language*. Busby, MT: Cheyenne Translation Project, 1991.

Leman, Wayne, et al. *Cheyenne Dictionary*. Lame Deer, MT: Chief Dull Knife College, 2004–2006.

Lewis, Meriwether, William Clark, et al. "1st of October Monday 1804" entry, "Part 5: Missouri River Miscellany, undated, winter 1804–5" entry, "Friday 22nd August 1806" entry. In *The Journals of the Lewis and Clark Expedition*, edited by Gary Moulton. Lincoln: University of Nebraska Press, 2005. http://lewisandclarkjournals.unl.edu/index.html.

Llewellyn, Karl N., and E. Adamson Hoebel. *The Cheyenne Way: Conflict and Case Law in Primitive Jurisprudence*. Norman: University of Oklahoma Press, 1941.

Lyons, Chief Oren. "Indian Self-Government in the Haudenosaunee Constitution." *Nordic Journal of International Law* 55 (1986): 117–21.

Lyons, Oren. "Law, Principle, and Reality." *New York University Review of Law and Social Change* 20, no. 2 (1993): 209–15.

———. "Sovereignty and Sacred Land: Bardie C. Wolfe, Jr. Keynote Address." *Thomas Law Review* 13 (2000–2001): 19–28.

Mails, Thomas E. *Fools Crow*. Garden City, NY: Bison Books, 1990.

Mankiller, Wilma. *Every Day Is a Good Day: Reflections of Contemporary Indigenous Women*, Memorial Ed. Golden, CO: Fulcrum Publishing, 2011.

Mann, Henrietta. *Cheyenne-Arapaho Education, 1871–1982*. Niwot, CO: University Press of Colorado, 1997.

Manuel, George. *The Fourth World: An Indian Reality*. New York: Free Press, 1974.

Marquis, Thomas B. *The Cheyennes of Montana*. Algonac, MI: Reference Publications, 1978.

———. *Keep the Last Bullet for Yourself: The True Story of Custer's Last Stand*. Algonac, MI: Reference Publications, 1976.

———. *Wooden Leg: A Warrior Who Fought Custer*. Lincoln: University of Nebraska Press, 1962.

Marquis, Thomas B., and Ronald H. Limbaugh, eds. *Cheyenne and Sioux: The Reminiscences of Four Indians and a White Soldier*. Stockton, CA: Pacific Center for Western Historical Studies, 1973.

Michelson, Truman. "The Narrative of a Southern Cheyenne Woman." Publication 3140, *Smithsonian Miscellaneous Collections* 87(5): 1–13.

Mihesuah, Devon A., ed. *Indigenizing the Academy: Transforming Scholarship and Empowering Communities*. Lincoln: University of Nebraska Press, 2004.

———, ed. *Natives and Academics: Researching and Writing About American Indians*. Lincoln: University of Nebraska Press, 1998.

Miller, Susan A., and James Riding In, eds. *Native Historians Write Back: Decolonizing American Indian History*. Lubbock: Texas Tech University Press, 2011.

Mooney, James. "The Aboriginal Population of America North of Mexico." *Smithsonian Miscellaneous Collections* 80(7).

———. "The Cherokee Ball Play." *The American Anthropologist*, Old Series, vol. 3, no. 2 (1890): 105–32.

———. "The Cheyenne Indians." *American Anthropological Association*, Memoirs, I, pt 6 (1905); repr., Whitefish, MT: Kessinger Publishing, 2009.

———. *In Sun's Likeness and Power: Cheyenne Accounts of Shield and Tipi Heraldry*. Transcribed and edited by Father Peter J. Powell. Lincoln: University of Nebraska Press, 2013.

Moore, John H. *The Cheyenne*. Malden, MA: Blackwell Publishers, 1996.

———. "Cheyenne Names and Cosmology." *American Ethnologist* 11, no. 2 (1984): 291–312.

———. *The Cheyenne Nation: A Social and Demographic History*. Norman: University of Oklahoma Press, 1987.

———. "Cheyenne Political History, 1820–1894." *Ethnohistory* 21, no. 4 (Autumn 1974): 329–59.

———. "The Developmental Cycle of Cheyenne Polygyny." *American Indian Quarterly* 15, no. 3, Special Issue: American Indian Family History (1991): 311–28.

———. "Evolution and Historical Reductionism." *Plains Anthropologist* 26, no. 94, pt. 1 (1981): 261–69.

———. "Native Americans, Scientists, and the HGDP." *Cultural Survival Quarterly* 20, no. 2 (1996): 60.

———. "The Reproductive Success of Cheyenne War Chiefs: A Contrary Case to Chagnon's Yanomamo." *Current Anthropology* 31, no. 3 (June 1990): 322–30.

———. "Review: The Wolves of Heaven: Cheyenne Shamanism, Ceremonies, and Prehistoric Origins." *American Anthropologist*, New Series, vol. 90, no. 2 (1988): 450.

Morris, Irvin. *From the Glittering World: A Navajo Story*. Norman: University of Oklahoma Press, 2000.

Neihardt, John G. *Black Elk Speaks: Being the Life Story of a Holy Man of the Oglala Nation*. Lincoln: University of Nebraska Press, 1961.

Nequatewa, Edmund. *Truth of a Hopi*. Radford, VA: Wilder Publications, 2007.

Penney, Grace J. *Tales of the Cheyennes*. Cambridge, MA: The Riverside Press, 1953.

Petter, Rodolphe. *English-Cheyenne Dictionary*. Kettle Falls, WA, 1913–1915.

Pommersheim, Frank. *Braid of Feathers: American Indian Law and Contemporary Tribal Life*. Los Angeles: University of California Press, 1995.

———. *Broken Landscape: Indians, Indian Tribes, and the Constitution*. New York: Oxford University Press, 2009.

Porter, Robert B. "The Meaning of Indigenous Nation Sovereignty." *Arizona State Law Journal* 34, no. 75 (2002): 75–112.

———. "Two Kinds of Indians, Two Kinds of Indian Nation Sovereignty: A Surreply to Professor LaVelle." *Kansas Journal of Law and Public Policy* 11, no. 3 (2001–2002): 629–56.

Porter, Robert Odawi. *Sovereignty, Colonialism and the Indigenous Nations: A Reader.* Durham: Carolina Academic Press, 2005.

Powell, Peter J. "Ox'zem: Box Elder and His Sacred Wheel Lance." *Montana: The Magazine of Western History* 20, no. 2 (Spring 1970): 30–41.

———. *People of the Sacred Mountain: A History of the Northern Cheyenne Chiefs and Warrior Societies, 1830–1879, With an Epilogue, 1969–1974.* 2 vols. San Francisco: Harper & Row, 1981.

———. *Sweet Medicine: The Continuing Role of the Sacred Arrows, the Sun Dance, and the Sacred Buffalo Hat in Northern Cheyenne History.* Norman: University of Oklahoma Press, 1969.

Randolph, Richard W. *Sweet Medicine and Other Stories of the Cheyenne Indians.* Caldwell, ID: The Caxton Printers, 1937.

Riding In, James. "Editor's Commentary: An American Indian Studies Paradigm Statement." *Wicazo Sa Review* 26, no. 2 (Fall 2011): 5–12.

Schlesier, Karl H. *The Wolves of Heaven.* Norman: University of Oklahoma Press, 1987.

Schrems, Suzanne H. "The Northern Cheyennes and the Fight for Cultural Sovereignty: The Notes of Father Aloysius Van Der Velden, S.J." *Montana: The Magazine of Western History* 45, no. 2 (Spring 1995): 27.

Schwartz, Warren E. *The Last Contrary: The Story of Wesley Whiteman (Black Bear).* Sioux Falls, SD: The Center for Western Studies, 1991.

Segar, John H. *Early Days Among the Cheyenne and Arapahoe Indians.* Norman: University of Oklahoma Press, 1979.

Smith, Graham. "Kaupapa Maori Theory: Theorizing Indigenous Transformation of Education & Schooling." Paper presented at the International Education Research/AARE-NZARE Joint Conference Auckland, New Zealand, December 2003. http://www.aare.edu.au/03pap/pih03342.pdf.

———. "Theorizing, Transforming & Reclaiming 'Our Indigenous Selves.'" Paper presented at the American Anthropology Association Conference, November 19, 2006.

Smith, Linda Tuhiwai. *Decolonizing Methodologies: Research and Indigenous Peoples,* 2nd ed. New York: Zed Books, 2012.

Standing Bear, Luther. *Land of the Spotted Eagle,* new ed. Lincoln: University of Nebraska Press, 1960.

———. *My People the Sioux,* new ed. Lincoln: University of Nebraska Press, 1975.

Stands In Timber, John, and Margot Liberty. *Cheyenne Memories.* New Haven, CT: Yale University Press, 1967.

———. *A Cheyenne Voice: The Complete John Stands In Timber Interviews.* Norman: University of Oklahoma Press, 2013.

Straus, Anne S. "Northern Cheyenne Ethnopsychology." *Ethos* 5, no. 3 (1977): 326–57.

Sutter, Virginia. *Tell Me, Grandmother: Traditions, Stories, and Cultures of the Arapaho People.* Boulder: University of Colorado Press, 2004.

Tall Bull, Henry, and Tom Weist. *Cheyenne Legends of Creation.* Billings, MT: Montana Council on Indian Education, 1972.

———. *Cheyenne Warriors: Stories of the Northern Cheyenne.* Billings, MT: Montana Council on Indian Education, 1983.

———. *Mista!* Billings, MT: Montana Council on Indian Education, 1971.
———. *The Rolling Head*. Billings, MT: Montana Council on Indian Education, 1971.
———. *Winter Hunt*. Billings, MT: Montana Council on Indian Education, 1971.
Tallbull, Bill (Wolf Feathers). "We are the Ancestors of those yet to be Born: Northern Cheyenne History of the Battle of 100-In-The-Hands (the Fetterman Battle)." *Fort Phil Kearny/Bozeman Trail Association*. Last modified March 22, 2004, http://www.philkearny.vcn.com/fpk-tallbull.htm.
Taylor, Graham D. *The New Deal and American Indian Tribalism: The Administration of the Indian Reorganization Act, 1934–45*. Lincoln: University of Nebraska Press, 1980.
Tsosie, Rebecca. "Introduction: Symposium on Cultural Sovereignty." *Arizona State Law Journal* 34, no. 1 (2002): 1–14.
———. "Sacred Obligations: Intercultural Justice and the Discourse of Treaty Rights." *UCLA Law Review* 47, no. 6 (1999–2000): 1615–1672.
Wallace, Paul. *White Roots of Peace: The Iroquois Book of Life*. Sante Fe, NM: Clear Light Publishers, 1994.
Weist, Katherine M. *Belle Highwalking: The Narrative of a Northern Cheyenne Woman*. Billings, MT: Montana Council for Indian Education, 1979.
Weist, Tom. *A History of the Cheyenne People*. Billings, MT: Council for Indian Education, 1977.
Wilkins, David E. *American Indian Politics and the American Political System*, 3rd ed. Oxford: Rowman & Littlefield, 2011.
———. *American Indian Sovereignty and the U.S. Supreme Court: The Masking of Justice*. Austin: University of Texas Press, 1997.
Wilkinson, Charles. *Blood Struggle: The Rise of Modern Indian Nations*. New York: W.W. Norton, 2005.
Williams, Robert A. *The American Indian in Western Legal Thought: The Discourses of Conquest*. New York: Oxford University Press, 1990.
———. *Like a Loaded Weapon: The Rehnquist Court, Indian Rights, and the Legal History of Racism in America*. Minneapolis: University of Minnesota Press, 2005.
———. *Savage Anxieties: The Invention of Western Civilization*. New York: Palgrave and Macmillan, 2012.
Williams, Robert A., Jr. *Linking Arms Together: American Indian Treaty Visions of Law and Peace, 1600–1800*. New York: Routledge, 1999.
Wilson, Shawn. *Research Is Ceremony: Indigenous Research Methods*. Black Point, NS: Fernwood Publishing Co, 2009.
Wooden Legs, John. *A Northern Cheyenne Album: Photographs by Thomas B. Marquis*. Edited by Margot Liberty. Norman: University of Oklahoma Press, 2007.
Yazzie, Ethelou, ed. *Navajo History*. Rough Rock, AZ: Navajo Curriculum Center, 1982.

BIBLIOGRAPHY

NATIONAL ANTHROPOLOGICAL ARCHIVES, SMITHSONIAN INSTITUTION, WASHINGTON, DC

NAA MS 2134.
NAA MS 2684-a.
NAA MS 2704.
NAA MS 2790.
NAA MS 2796.
NAA MS 2798.
NAA MS 2799.
NAA MS 2811.
NAA MS 2822.
NAA MS 2828, folder 1.
NAA MS 2828, folder 2.
NAA MS 3188-b.
NAA MS 3218.
NAA MS 3219.
NAA MS 3220.
NAA MS 3336.
NAA MS 3338.
NAA MS 3342.
NAA MS 3343.
NAA MS 3355.

Index

Page numbers in *italics* represent figures and photographs.

adoption, xxx, 42, 164, 196, 215, 217
alcoholism, xxviii, 56, 243, 249
Alfred, Taiaiake, xxxv
All Father. *See* Ma'heo'e
alliance, xv, 34, 44, 46, 122, 130
American Horse
    Moisiu, 255n59
Angry White Buffalo. *See* Momáta'évoestahe
Aortas. *See* Heveškéseněhpáhese
Arapaho, 24, 29, 46, *180*, 228
Arkansas River, 113, 229
Arrow Ceremony. *See* Arrow Lodge
Arrow Keeper, 108, 110, 112, 116, 127, 175, 206
Arrow Lodge, 26, 207
Arrow Worship Ceremony, 193
Articles of Confederation, 228
assimilation
    annihilation of Indian identity and culture, xxx, 58, 229, 247
    Christianity, xxxiii–xxxiv, 168, 264n18
    loss of Véhooneome practices, 117
    US government's policies, xxviii, 237, 239–40, 243
    ways of living lost, xxvii, xxxviii, 141
    See also colonization
Assiniboine. *See* Hóheehe
Atkinson, Henry, 231
aura. *See* Máhta'sóoma
badger as hōva of power, 52
Badger (Southern Cheyenne)
    Michelson's informant, xxxi
    Só'taeo'o's way of life, 39
balance, philosophy of, xvi, 75, 77
bands. *See* manáhéno
Battle of Rosebud, 195
Battle of the Little Bighorn, 195
Bear Butte, 188, 248
bears, pet, 95
Bearsole (chief), 135
beaver as hōva of power, 52
Bent, Daisy, 99
Bent, George (Southern Cheyenne)
    children of, 99

Mexican colonists, 229
    Moiseyu, 255n58
Bent, Jesse (son of), *140*
Bent, Mary, 99
Bent's Fort (Colorado), 111
BIA. *See* US Bureau of Indian Affairs
Big Chiefs. *See* Véhoo'o
Big Dipper. *See* Ursa Major
Big White Crow. *See* Okohke Ôhvo'omaestse
Bighead, Kate, 195
bison. *See* buffalo
Black Crane, Mrs. (Southern Cheyenne)
    Michelson's informant, xxxii
Black, Harry, (Southern Cheyenne)
    Crazy Lime story, 147–48
    Hestáhkeho (Twins), Version II story, 80–81
    Michelson's informant, xxxi
    The White Buffalo story, 157–61
Black Hills
    Cheyenne arrival, 24, 38, 41–42, 151, 167, 188
    gold, 54, 55
    Great Flood, 23
    Great Unification meeting, 43, 170, 257n42
    homeland, 19, 37, 113, 172
    Só'taeo'o arrival, 40, 41, 267n30
Black Horse, Ruben (Southern Cheyenne)
    Michelson's informant, xxxi–xxxii
    White Man Calls Feathers, 233–34
    White Man Loses His Eyes, 234–35
Black Kettle, 248
Black Lodge Band, 37
Black Wolf
    The Rolling Head, Part III story, 95–96, 97
Blood Bachelor. *See* Cherry Eater; Mai-tŭm'
blood quantum, xli, 58
boarding schools, 56
Born for Water (Navajo Hero Twin), 82
Bow-Fast-to-his-Body. *See* Bow-In-Hand story
Bow-In-Hand story, 19–20, 128, 255n41
Bow Society, 174
Bowstrings. *See* Héma'tanónêheo'o
breath. *See* ómótóme
brotherhood. *See* hévese'onematsestôtse
buddy relationships. *See* brotherhood

INDEX

buffalo, 13, 18, 20, 23–25, 54, 55, 94, 139, 208–9, 230, 231. *See also* fourth world
The Buffalo and the Corn story, 33, 257n20
Buffalo Bull Warriors. *See* Hotóvanotâxeo'o
Buffalo Calf Road Woman, 195, 266n46
Buffalo Hat. *See* Ésevone
Buffalo Head, 231
Buffalo people. *See* Só'taeo'o
Bull Hump, 116
Bull Looks Back, 95
Bull Society, 174
Bull Thigh (Southern Cheyenne Dog Soldier and Keeper of the Sacred Arrows)
   creation of the Big Dipper, 161–62
   creation of Véhoo'o, 105
   Great Unification, 40, 257n42
   Hestáhkeho (Twins), Version I story, 78–80
   Lime, Part I story, 148–50
   Lime, Part II story, 151–52, 154
   Méstae, the Big Ghost, 16–17
   Michelson's informant, xxxi
   Nótâxeo'o membership standards, 189–90
   seating ceremony, 116
   Só'taeo'o arrival to Black Hills, 41–42, 257n30
   Sweet Medicine, Part I story, 167
   Sweet Medicine, Part II story, 174–75
   White Clay story, 169–70, 264n1
Bureau of Indian Affairs. *See* US Bureau of Indian Affairs
Burning Thighs band, 39
California gold rush, 229, 231
camp
   band, 27–28, 256n1
   chiefs' lodge — circle, 110
   circle, 256n15
   family — location, 28
   medicine wheel — formation, 97
   movements/sites, 112–13, 126
cannibalism, 93, 94, 95
captives, fate of, 111, 113, 196
Catholicism, xxxiv, 245
cedar, blessing of, 4
ceremonial practices, 3, 8, 9, 14, 53, 56, 62, 122. *See also specific ceremony*
Cherry Eater, 30, 36, 82, 128, 166, 200. *See also* Mai-tŭm'; Má'kó'se
Cherry Eater of the Tsétsêhéstâhese story, 144–46
Cheyenne Memories (Stands In Timber and Liberty), xxxiii
Cheyenne Nation. *See* Tséhéstáno
The Cheyenne Nation (Moore), xxxi
Cheyenne River, 16, 19, 33, 37, 41, 43, 89, 113
Cheyenne River Sioux Indian Reservation, 41

A Cheyenne Voice (Stands In Timber and Liberty), xxxiii
chief/chieftainship, concept of, 74, 119. *See also* Véhoo'o
Chief Joseph, 248
Chief Soldiers. *See* Véhonenótâxeo'o
Chiefs' Bundle, 96, 103, 107, 108, 115, 116, 188
Chiefs' Lodge. *See* Véhooneome
Chiefs' Prophecy, 57. *See also* decolonization
Chiefs' Society, xl, 57, 73, 89, 104, 182. *See also* Véhoo'o
Chiefs' Sticks, 115
childhood. *See* ka'eškónevestôtse
Christianity, xxxiii–xxxv, 168, 245, 264n18
citizenship, 29, 141, 169, 182, 190, 192, 207–17, 248
Clark, William, 59, 228
clay pots, 33, 257n18
colonization
   impact on Véhoo'o, 138
   increase in violence, 198
   Indian peoples' negative perception of themselves, 242
   key principle of Indian history, xxxvi, xxxix, 237–39
   loss of Véhooneome practices, 117
   Motsé'eóeve's legacy, 166
   perception of history, 9
   reservation as product of —, 240
   Vé'hó'e: the trickster, 221–35
   ways of living lost, xxvii–xxviii, 53, 58
   See also decolonization
Comes In Sight (chief), 195, 266n46
community ceremonies. *See* ceremonial practices
compassion. *See* ševátamehestôtse
compassion, to have. *See* hestsêstahe
Continental Congress, 228
Contraries. *See* Hohnóhkao'o
Corn Dance, 14
corn farming, 14–15, 18, 24, 37, 39, 258n47
Corn Kernel. *See* Mâháeme
Corps of Discovery. *See* Lewis and Clark Expedition
cosmology. *See* star knowledge
Council of Forty-Four Chiefs. *See* Véhoo'o
courageous, to be mentally and spiritually. *See* héestaáhá
courteous, to be. *See* tâhpe'êstáha
courtship. *See* marriage
Coyote (Northern Cheyenne)
   band membership, 29
   farming days, 15, 18
   Michelson's informant, xxxi
   societies and regalia, 182
   Vóhkêséhetaneo'o, 185–86

INDEX

Coyote-Warriors. *See* Hoomenotxeo
Crazy Dance, 179
Crazy Dogs. *See* Hotamémâsêhao'o
Crazy Horse, 248
Crazy Lime story (Harry Black), 147–48
Crazy Lodge Ceremony, 175
The Creation of the Universe story (Left Hand Bull), 5–6
the Creator. *See* Ma'heo'e
Cree. *See* Vóhkoohétaneo'o
Crickets. *See* Mahéško'ta
crime rates, 243
crow meat, 94
Dakota
　band circle, 39
　Lake Oahe, 42
dances, xxx, 182. *See also specific dance*
death, 192–93, 207–9, 231, 267n11
decolonization
　defined, xxvii–xxviii
　holistic approach, 69
　key principle of Indian history, xxxix, 237, 239–40
　path to —, 240–50
　the reservation, 237–50
　return to healthy/balanced way of living, 57
　See also colonization
depression, 56, 243
Desert People. *See* Só'taeo'o
disease, brought by white men, 54, 56, 91, 231
Dog Men. *See* Hotamétaneo'o
Dog Society/Soldiers. *See* Hotamétaneo'o
dog, time of the. *See* third world
Dorsey, George, xxx, xxxi, 180, 262n17
Double Eyes. *See* Ôhnešêstse'exanehe
Double Teeth Bull. *See* Momáta'évoestahe
Dreamkeeper (movie), 162
dress style. *See* regalia
drug abuse, xxviii, 243, 249
Dull Knife. *See* Vóóhéhéve
Duster, Albert (Southern Cheyenne)
　Michelson's informant, xxxi
Eagle Nest. *See* Netsévôhé'so
Eagles of Busby (White River Band basketball team), 37
Earth. *See* Éškemane; Ho'e
ehōstonevoeoxz (telling clouds), 53
Elk Band, 96, 170, 179, 184, 186, 265n5
Elk Horn Scraper Society. *See* Hémo'eoxeo'o
Elk River
　The Rolling Head story (recorded version), 95
embarrassment. *See* shame/embarrassment
Erect Horns. *See* Tomôsévêséhe

Ésevone (Buffalo Hat), 39, 40, 43, 45, 46, 105, 126, 213, 257n19
Éškemane (Earth/grandmother), 58–59, 75, 98
Fallen Star. *See* Hotohketana'ôtse
family, 9, 28. *See also* kinship system
Fanon, Frantz, 244
farming, 9. *See also* corn farming
fasting ceremonies, xxxv, 63, 213
fatherhood. *See* héhe'estovestôtse
fifth world, 26, 53
First Great Flood, 14
first world ("time of the horse"), 10–12
Fisher, Conrad (Northern Cheyenne), 73
Fisher, Eugene, 256n63
fishing, 18
Flathead (Cheyenne informant), 52–53
Foolish Dance, 173, 177
forgiveness. *See* vonanomótâhtsestôtse
Fort Berthold Indian Reservation (North Dakota), 41
Fort Peck Indian Reservation (Montana), 41
four, sacred number, xxxix, 94
four smoke planning, 135
fourth world, 19–26, 27, 54
Fox Society, 174
Fox Soldiers, 170, 265n5
French traders, 227–28
friendship principle in Articles of Confederation, 228
Friendship Treaty, 136, 232–33, 237
frost. *See* Hooema'hahe
Frost, Jim (wife and children), 66
generosity. *See* hoto'âhéstôtse
Glenmore, Josephine (Northern Cheyenne) méhósánestôtse, 135
God. *See* Ma'heo'e
godliness. *See* ma'heónevetôtse
gold rush, 54, 55, 229, 231
Grasshopper (Southern Cheyenne)
　Black Hills homeland, 41
Great Cheyenne and Sioux War, 55
Great Flood, 23, 27, 38, 39
Great Medicine. *See* Ma'xema'hēō'e
Great-Mysterious. *See* Ma'xema'hēō'e; Wanka Tanka
Great Race, 23–24, 52
Great River. *See* Mississippi River
Great Spirit. *See* Ma'heo'e
Great Spiritual Power. *See* Ma'heo'e
Great Unification. *See* unification
Green Corn Dance, 15
Grinnell, George, xxx, xxxi, 33, 63, 100, 128, 254n19, 255n37, 257nn19, 20, 24, 261n12, 269n27
Haag, Mack (Southern Cheyenne)
　customary laws of storytelling, 4

| 283 |

INDEX

Michelson's informant/interpreter, xxxii
parable of the insatiable spider, 219
sickness, 62
Hairy Hand (Southern Cheyenne)
Michelson's informant, xxxi
Halley's Comet, 54
Handing Crow (Southern Cheyenne)
Michelson's informant, xxxi
White Man and the Buffalo, 232
White Man and the Sweet Potatoes, 233
Haudenosaunee Confederacy, 30, 104
Havevs (Many Horns), 83–86, 88
Havívsts story (Wolf Chief), 83–86, 106
Headed-Lances. See Hemoeoxessô
health care, 243, 249
Heammaveho (whiteman sitting above; Jesus Christ), 259n36
he'eévestôtse (womanhood), 207, 209–11
héestaáhá (to be courageous mentally and spiritually), 214
Heévâhetaneo'o (Rope People), 37, 97, 105
héhe'estovestôtse (fatherhood), 64–65, 207
Hemámaa'evôhomó'hestôtse (War Bonnet Dance), 198
Héma'tanóneheo'o (Bow String Men), 175, 176, 177–79, 193, 201
Hémo'eoxeo'o (Elk Horn Scrapers), 120, 171, 193, 186–87
Hemoeoxessô (Headed-Lances), 177, 187
Heova'chetohke'e (Yellow Star Woman), 12
Heovésta'e'e (Yellow Top-to-Head Woman), 40
Heron story. See Hovesenehev story
heške'estovestôtse (motherhood), 65–67, 207, 211, 213
Hesta'hēso (Cheyenne sacred twin), 82
Hesta'hēso (Little Afterbirth) story, 78, 82
Hestâhkeho (Twins), Version I story (Bull Thigh), 78–80
Hestâhkeho (Twins), Version II story (Harry Black), 80–81
Héstanéheo'o (humankind), 61
héstanovestôtse (living nation)
Cheyenne national history, 10
described, 7–10
fifth and sixth worlds, 26
first world, 10–12
fourth world, 19–26
reintroduce, 245
second world, 12–14
The Star Husband story, 11–12
third world, 14–18
hestsêstahe (to have compassion), 213
hetané'hao'o (man power), xxxv, 119–20
hetanévestôtse (manhood), 211–13
hetómestôtse (truth), 133

hetsevahe (to be fearless of physical harm), 213–14
hévese'onematsestôtse (brotherhood), 77–88, 105, 156, 238, 246
Heveškésenêhpâhese (Aortas), 35–36, 37, 38, 42–43, 44, 46, 56, 75, 97, 110, 256n15
high authority. See ma'xenéheto'stôtse
High Backed Wolf. See Ho'neoxhaa'eho'oesêstse
High Walker, Mrs. (Southern Cheyenne)
Michelson's informant, xxxii
High Wolf. See Ho'neoxhaa'eho'oesêstse
Highwalking, Belle
Wihio story, 223–24
Ho'e (Earth), 6, 7, 11–12, 211. See also Ma'etohke'e
Hoebel, E. Adamson, 95, 191
Ho'ehêvésénóó'e. See Hō-ĭv'-nĭ-ĕsts; Tomôsévê-séhe
Hoffman, Albert (Southern Cheyenne)
Sweet Medicine prophecy, 230
Hohâatamaahestôtse (power), 60–61
Hóheehe (Assiniboine), 18, 24, 37, 100–104, 172
Hohnóhkao'o (Contraries), 175, 176, 193
Hoig, Stan, 121
Hō-ĭv'-nĭ-ĕsts (Standing on the Ground), 40, 45
homicide. See murder
Ho'nehenótâxeo'o (Wolf Soldiers), 178–79
Ho'neoxhaa'eho'oesêstse (High Backed Wolf; High Wolf), 120, 231
honest, to be. See xanovahe
Hooema'hahe (Winter Man or Frost), 19–20
Hoomenotxeo (Coyote-Warriors), 187
hoop and spear games, 30–35, 37, 45, 75, 94, 117, 144, 166
Hopi, 8
horse, 26, 29, 53–54, 57, 121, 172. See also fifth world
Hotamémâsêhao'o (Crazy Dogs), 175–76, 176, 179, 193, 265n5
Hotamétaneo'o (Dog Men), 75, 170, 171, 174, 182–84, 196, 201
hoto'âhéstôtse (generosity), 131–32
Hotohketana'ôtse (Fallen Star), 12, 15–17, 254nn12, 19, 255n41
Hotóhkôhma'aestse (Red Star, Star Drops), 12, 254nn12, 19
Hotóvanotâxeo'o (Buffalo Bull Warriors), 171, 177, 187–88
Hovesenehev (Heron) story, 86–88
Hoxtaes, 163–64
humanity, sacred laws of, 25–26, 54, 55–56, 257n62, 256n63
humankind. See Héstanéheo'o
humble, to be. See momáxahe

| 284 |

INDEX

humility. *See* momotatamahestôtse
humor, xxxvi, 216, 221, 226
hunt, communal and ceremonial, 94, 109, 121, 126, 127, 141, 204–5, 209. *See also* buffalo
Hyde, George, xxx
Ice. *See* White Bull
incest, 25, 30, 106, 111, 164, 196
Indian, modern ideas of, 58
Indian agents, 56
The Indian Man and the Spider, 227
Indian Reorganization Act, xxx
indigenous, key principle of Indian history, xxxix, 237–40
Indigenous Peoples. *See* Xamaevo'ėstaneo'o
indigenous theorizing, xxix–xxxv
initiation ceremonies, 115, 200, 212–14
intelligence. *See* oto'xovostôtse
Iron Shirt (Southern Cheyenne) Michelson's informant, xxxi
Iroquois Confederacy, 228, 268n14
It Goes In. *See* Máháeme
Jesus Christ, xxxiii, 259n36
Joseph (chief). *See* Chief Joseph
ka'ėškónevestôtse (childhood), 67–68
Killsback, Damion, 77
Killsback, Dion, 77
Killsback, Hattie, xxxvi, 77
kind, to be. *See* tâhpe'ėstáha
kinship system, 9, 29, 58, 73, 157, 158, 200
Kiowa, 111
Kit Fox Men. *See* Vóhkėséhetaneo'o
knowledge. *See* oto'xovostôtse
Krober, Alfred, 83
Lake Oahe, 41, 42
Lakota, 5, 14, 28, 34, 39, 42, 46, 59, 111, 175, 228
Lakota Sioux, 24. *See also* Sioux
Lances, 174
lands, regaining traditional, 247–48
language, xxxviii, 38, 243, 249, 256n62
Last Born. *See* Má'kó'se
leadership principles, 73–75, 108, 114, 116, 120, 127–38, 191–93, 203, 207, 246–47
Left Hand Bull
  The Creation of the Universe story, 5–6
Leman, Wayne, xxxiv
Leonid meteor shower, 52
Lewis, Meriwether, 59
Lewis and Clark Expedition, 59, 230–31, 268n15
Liberty, Margot
  Cheyenne Memories, xxxiii
  A Cheyenne Voice, xxxiii
  interviews, xxxiv
life, necessities of, 7
life-nation. *See* héstanovestôtse

life of the people. *See* héstanovestôtse
Lime. *See* Vóetséna'e
Lime story
  Part I (Bull Thigh), 148–50
  Part I (Tall Bull), 152–54
  Part II (Bull Thigh), 151–52
  Part II (Tall Bull), 155–56
lions, pet, 95
Little Afterbirth story. *See* Hesta'hēso
Little Bear. *See* Nakooss
Little Calf. *See* Mo'keheso
Little Calf story, 20–21
Little Moon, 231
Little Wolf. *See* Ó'kôhómôxháahketa
Little Wolf Band, 90
living nation. *See* héstanovestôtse
lodge. *See specific ceremony*
Lone Wolf, 103
Louisiana Purchase, 228
love. *See* méhósánestôtse
loving, to be. *See* méohtâhé'heōneve
lying, 95, 111, 114, 133
Maahótse (Medicine Arrows), 25–26, 45, 46, 105, 126, 127, 141, 162, 171, 206
Ma'ėhoomahe (Red Painted Robe), 101
Ma'etohke'e (Red Star Woman), 12
The Magic Arrows story, 83
Máháeme (Corn Kernel), 34, 35
Maheo. *See* Ma'heo'e
Ma'heo'e (Sacred Medicine), 55, 59, 137, 259n36
Ma'hēō'e. *See* Ma'heo'e
"ma'heóného'emanestôtse" (sacred laws), 255n62, 256n63
ma'heóného'xeváheo'o (prophets), 51–54
ma'heónevetôtse (godliness/sacredness), 136–37
Ma'hëö'o. *See* Ma'heo'e
Ma'heo'o Ôhnee'ėstse (Standing Medicine), 18, 32, 108
Mahėško'ta (Crickets), 37, 38, 44, 97
Mahoemskot, 164–65, 196
Mahōtsts (Red Buck). *See* Mo'keheso
Mahpe (water), 11–12. *See also* Heova'ehetohke'e
Mâhta'sóoma (spirit/soul/aura), 61–62, 64
Mai-tŭm' (Red, red, red, red), 34, 35, 36, 82. *See also* Cherry Eater
Má'kó'se (Last Born; Youngest), 22–23, 163–65, 166, 174. *See also* Cherry Eater; Motsé'eóeve
Mámaa'e Nótáxé'évoo'e (Women's War Bonnet Society), 198
Man on a Cloud, 197
manâhéno (bands)
  balance of power, 124–26
  band camps, 28

INDEX

described, 27–30
division into, 25
first five bands of United Cheyenne
  Nation, 44
Great Unification, 40–42
Heveškėsenêhpȧhese (Aortas), 35–36
histories, 9
hoop and spear games, 30–35
leaders' role, 89–91, 109–12, 114
marriage, 30
Ohmésêhese (Eaters), 36–38, 75
original bands of Tsétsêhéstȧhese, 38, 98, 256n15
reintroduce/reinvigorate, 245–46
Só'taeo'o, 38–40
Só'taeo'o and Heveškėsenêhpȧhese, 42–43
Só'taeo'o and Ohmésêhese, 43–45
Só'taeo'o and Tsétsêhéstȧhese, 45–47
Ten bands of the United Cheyenne Nation, 46
tribe versus —, 28
twenty bands of the United Cheyenne Nation, 56
Véhoo'o based on, 74
manhood. *See* hetanévestôtse
Mann, Henrietta (Southern Cheyenne), 62, 106, 256n63
mano'ėhotóhkeo'o (star societies), 163
Many Horns. *See* Havevs
Ma'ȯhōnaiiva (Red Rocks), 39, 45, 113
marriage
  courtship, 39
  intertribal, 14, 24, 30, 45, 47, 215
  polygamy, 67, 127, 147
  prohibition, xxx
Marx, Karl, 239
Mā-tā-mā' (Old Woman), 257n20
Mā-tā-mā' Hėh'k-ā-ĭt (Old Woman's Water), 33, 37
Matsiyeiv. *See* Motsé'eóeve
Matsīyōv. *See* Motsé'eóeve
Mattsī'ō'iv. *See* Motsé'eóeve
Ma'xema'hēō'e (Great Medicine; Great-Mysterious)
  answer to chaos caused by buffalo, 23
  balance with, 75
  Bow-in-Hand story, 19–20
  The Creation of the Universe story, 5–6
  described, 59–60, 259n37
  gift of corn, 15
  humanoid as child of, 7, 35
  Lime, Part I story, 148–50
  powers given to Nótȧxeo'o, 199–200, 209
  sacred laws of nature, 24
  vonanomótȧhtsestôtse, 132, 262n21
  warriors' relationship, 207

ma'xenėheto'stôtse (high authority), 238
Medicine Arrow Bundle, 162
Medicine Arrow Keeper, 126
Medicine Arrows. *See* Maahótse
medicine bundles/covenants, 199
Medicine Hat, 141
Medicine Lodge, 24, 179, 192, 193, 196, 207.
  See also Sun Dance
Medicine Lodge (chief), 39
medicine men, xxx, 51
Medicine Star, 145–46
Medicine Top (Southern Cheyenne)
  Michelson's informant, xxxi
  White Man and the Wooden Horse, 232–33
medicine wheel formation, 95, 97
Méhne (giant water serpent), 15
méhósánestôtse (love), 135–36
Memmi, Albert, 239
méohtȧhé'heōneve (to be loving), 216–17
Méstaa'e (giant owl), 15
Mestaa'ėhetane (Owl Man), 178
Méstae, the Big Ghost story (Bull Thigh), 16–17
Mexican traders, 229
Michelson, Truman, xxx, xxxi, xxxii, 78, 254n27, 258n47
military alliance. *See* alliance
Miller, Susan, xxxix
Mississippi River, 11, 14, 36, 38–39, 155
Missouri River, 18, 33, 37, 40, 41, 42, 152, 155, 170, 257n42, 258n47
mobility. *See* horses
Moiseyu (relatives of the Lakota), 14, 24, 255n58
Moisiu, 255n59
Mo'keheso (Little Calf, Red Buck), 20–21, 22, 23, 83–85, 86
Moksaess. *See* Mo'keheso
Momáta'évoestahe (Angry White Buffalo, Double Teeth Bull), 22–23
momáxahe (to be humble), 216
momotatamahestôtse (humility), 136
Moneneheo'o (Selected Ones), 196–97
Monster Slayer (Navajo Hero Twin), 82
Mooney, James, xxx, xxxi, xxxv, 66, 100, 103, 140, 197, 210
Moore, John H., xxxi, 256n15, 267n6
Morning Star People, 90
Morning Stars of Lame Deer (Black Lodge Band) basketball team, 37
Morningstar. *See* Vóóhéhéve
móstamámȯhevéstanovėhevóhe. *See* unification, Só'taeo'o with Tsétsêhéstȧhese
motherhood. *See* heške'estovestôtse

INDEX

Motsé'eóeve (Sweet Medicine; Sweet Root Standing)
   dressed as Dog Soldier, 182
   Elk soldiers' dress, 96, 186
   embodiment of ideal personality, 128
   hoto'áhéstôtse, 132
   hunter in Seven Young Men story, 263n13
   importance of women, 65
   legacy, 37
   Medicine Arrows, 45
   Nótáxeo'o origins, 105, 143, 144, 155–56, 165, 166–68, 169–76, 179, 181, 188–89, 205, 264n18
   popular prophet, 54–57, 170
   position of Old Man Chiefs, 123
   sacred laws, 25–26, 106, 115
   ševátamehestôtse, 130
   teachings of manhood and citizenship, 169, 175
   teleportation powers, 168
   tradition, xxxiii–xxxiv
   Véhoo'o origin as part of — legacy, 89, 91, 97, 100, 105–8
   "virgin birth," xxxiii
   warning about white men, 229–31
   See also Netsévôhé'so
move the arrows. *See* war
Mukije (Short Woman), 95, 97–98, 107, 114
murder, 25, 43, 111–12, 156, 168, 223, 229, 249
mustang. *See* horse
Nakoimens (Bear Wings), 118
Nakooss (Little Bear), 86–88, 106
naming, 47, 62
nation building, móstamámôhevéstanovéhevóhe as foundation, 40
National Anthropological Archives, xxxi
national identity category of stories, 3
National Museum of Natural History, xxxi
nationhood, critical elements of, 8
Native, modern ideas of, 58
"Native America Writes Back: The Origin of the Indigenous Paradigm in Historiography" (Miller), xxxix
nature, sacred laws, 24, 25, 26, 27, 55, 59, 63, 255n62, 256n63
Navajo, 8, 82
Né'ohma'ehétaneo'o (Prairie People; Sand Hill People), 35, 45, 257n24
nepotism, 116
Netsévôhé'so (Eagle Nest), 14, 108, 166, 167, 254n19
Nhaen hetane (Otter Man), 39, 164
Ni-oh-ma-até-anin-ya (Prairie People), 257n24
Nĩ-ŏm-a-hé-tăn-iu, 257n24
No Colds band, 39

No'kévéséhe (One Horn), 137
North Star, 52, 161, 165
Northern Cheyenne and Friendship Treaty, 230–31
Northern Cheyenne Indian Reservation (Montana), 243
Nótâxé'e (warrior women), 195–96. *See also* women
Nótâxeo'o (warrior societies)
   balance of power, 125, 126, 127, 141, 171, 176, 190, 203–16, 267n6
   before the —, 143–68
   body of authority, 74
   brotherhood as foundation of system, 157
   camp moves, 113, 126, 205
   Cherry Eater/Sweet Medicine of the Tsétsêhéstâhese, 144, 165–66
   codes of honor and service, 169, 194, 206
   combat, 198–201
   concept of, 143
   cooperation with Véhoo'o, 74
   described, 141–42
   execute Véhoo'o's decisions, 203–4
   first warrior society of the Só'taeo'o, 157–61
   first warrior society of the Tsétsêhéstâhese, 161–65
   honoring womanhood, 195–96, 207–9
   leadership, 191–95
   medicine bundles/covenants, 199
   military force, 191, 198, 201, 205
   modern, 246
   organizing hunts, 113, 127, 207
   origins, 89, 105, 169–79
   petition for war, 110
   police force, 126, 203, 206
   political organization, 203–17
   principles of citizenship, 193, 207–17, 267n11
   recruitment, 199–200
   retirement, 201
   sacred responsibilities, 125, 199–200, 203, 204, 213
   seating ceremony, 192
   society dances and ceremonies, 181–87
   society headmen, 192–93
   standards of citizenship/manhood, 144, 169, 192
   traditions and customs, 181–201
   Vóetséna'e of the Só'taeo'o, 146–56
   warrior citizenship, 193–95
   warrior culture, 199
   warrior status, 199–200
oestóonôtse (sacrifices), 59, 63–64, 66, 125, 136
Oglala, 248
Ohmésêhese/Ôhméseheso (eaters people/

INDEX

Eaters), 35, 36–38, 43–45, 56, 90, 97, 110, 256n15
Ôhméseheso Band, 42
Ôhnešêstse'exanehe (Double Eyes), 16, 17
Okohke Ôhvo'omaestse (Big White Crow), 20
O'kôhómôxháahketa (Southern Cheyenne; Little Wolf)
    as Cheyenne leader, 248
    Old Man Chief, 108
    Sweet Medicine Chief, 120
The Old Man and the Spider, 227
Old Man Chiefs, 90–91, 98, 107–8, 111, 114–17, 122–24
Old She Bear (Eater Band)
    Bow String Warriors, 201
    Dog Soldier, 201
    Hotamémâsêhao'o, 176
    Sweet Medicine, Part I story, 166–67
    Sweet Medicine's prophecy, 54–55
Old Woman. *See* Mā-tā-mā'
Old Woman's Water. *See* Mā-tā-mā' Hěh'k-ā-īt
Oldest (Cheyenne sacred twin), 82
Omaha Dance, 175
ómótóme (breath), 61
One Horn. *See* No'kévéséhe
One Who Talks Against Others, 231
Oneha (Cheyenne), xl, 85
Onéhanotåxeo'o (War Dancers), 175
Ó'oxêtséme (flint-headed spear), 18, 32, 255n37
oral tradition
    bands united through national history, 9, 47, 82
    beliefs kept alive in memories, 4
    educational system, 3
    governance and nationhood foundation doctrines, 114, 189
    heroic feats and tragic losses, xli
    major oral traditions of United Cheyenne history, 144
    means for organizing and explaining change, 8
    preservation of American Indian history, 3
    qualities of, xxx–xxxix
    reintroduce, 244–45
    transmission of national qualities, 8, 120
    See also storytelling
Oregon, discovery of gold, 231
orphans, 65, 111, 131, 200
ó'tósétano (to be diligent in action), 214–15
oto'xovostôtse (knowledge/intelligence), 134–35
Otter Man. *See* Nhaen hetane
Otter story (Wolf Chief), 162
ována'xaetanohtôtse (peace), 129–30
ovanhestôstse (prophecy), 49–50, 55
Owl Man. *See* Mestaa'êhetane

Ówū'qeo, 103–4
paint, 25, 33–34, 39, 92, 170, 177, 183, 187–88, 254n13, 264n1
paternalism, xxviii, 238, 239, 243, 246
Pawnees, 37, 67, 172
peace. *See* ována'xaetanohtôtse
peace medal, 59, 228–29
peacemaking, 40, 46–47, 90, 108, 109, 111, 122, 209, 231. *See also* ována'xaetanohtôtse
Pearl. *See* Voestaa'e
Petter, Rodolphe
    dictionary, xxxiv, xxxix
    Héma'tanónêheo'o, 177
    Hémo'eoxeo'o, 187
    Hotamétaneo'o (The Dog Men) dances, 182–83
    Hotóvanotåxeo'o, 187
    scholar of Cheyenne studies, xxx
    star prophets, 52
    Véhoo'o origin, 104
    Vóhkéséhetaneo'o, 184–85
philosophical category of stories, 3
physical harm, to be fearless of. *See* hetsevahe
Pine, Leroy (Northern Cheyenne)
    leadership selection, 115
    system of government, 105
pipe, 35–36, 39–40, 45, 107, 113, 117
pipe carriers, 111, 133–34 (*see also* Véhoo'o)
pipesmoking, 4, 11–12, 125
pipestone, 39
Pipestone, Minnesota, 41, 170
Pleiades star cluster, 161
poaching, punishment for, 205
police force. *See* Nótåxeo'o
political infighting, xxviii
political organization. *See* Véhoo'o, political structure
polygamy. *See* marriage
poverty, 242, 243, 249
Powell, Peter, xxxv
power. *See* Hoháatamaahestôtse
The Powerful Boy and Spider story, 221–22
Prairie People. *See* Né'ohma'ehétaneo'o
Principal Chiefs. *See* Old Man Chiefs
prophecy. *See* ovanhestôstse
prophets. *See* ma'heónéhóo'xeváheo'o
Quillwork Girl and her Seven Star Brothers story, 164–65
rabbit people. *See* Vóhkoohétaneo'o
Randolph, Richard, xl, 4, 85, 254n19, 255n41
Red Buck. *See* Cherry Eater; Mo'keheso
Red Hair. *See* Cherry Eater
Red Hoofs. *See* Hotóvanotåxeo'o
Red Leaf Woman, 162
Red Paint. *See* Mai-tŭm'

INDEX

Red Paint (Heveškėsenėhpåhese head chief), 43, 89
Red Painted Robe. *See* Ma'ėhoomahe
Red Rocks. *See* Ma'ōhōnaiiva
Red Rocks (Minnesota), 39, 45, 113, 257nn30, 42
Red Star. *See* Hotóhkôhma'aestse
Red, red, red, red. *See* Cherry Eater; Mai-tŭm'
Ree country, 41
regalia, 182, 186, 188
reservation, xxviii, 56–57, 75, 108, 201, 239–41, 243–48
Return of the Chiefs. *See* Chiefs' Prophecy
return to greatness. *See* Chiefs' Prophecy
Revolutionary War, 228
rez, 243–44. *See also* reservation
righteous, to be. *See* xanovahe
righteousness. *See* xanoveostôtse
rites of passage, xxx
Rockroads, Laura (Northern Cheyenne), 53, 91
The Rolling Head story
    Part I (Wolf Chief), 91–92, 106
    Part II (Wolf Chief), 93–94, 106
    Part III (Black Wolf), 95–96, 106
    recorded versions, 95, 97, 106
Roman Nose, 248
Rope People. *See* Heévâhetaneo'o
Rowland, William, xxxii
"rules of civilizing," xxx
Sacred Buffalo Hat. *See* Ésevone
Sacred Buffalo Hat Keeper, 126
Sacred Corn Covenant, 40
sacred geography, critical element of nationhood, 8, 253n3
Sacred Hat. *See* Ésevone
Sacred Hat Keeper, 112, 116, 127
sacred historical convergence theory (SHCT), xxxii–xxxiii, xxxvii
sacred history, critical element of nationhood, 3, 8, 9, 13, 49, 91, 169
sacred language, 256n62
sacred laws, 8–9, 91, 106, 111–12, 133, 255n62, 256n63. *See also* humanity; nature
sacred leadership. *See* Véhoo'o
Sacred Medicine. *See* Ma'heo'e
sacred protector, xxxv, xxxvii, 103, 106
sacred scholar, xxxv–xxxvii, xl
sacred twins stories, 77–82
sacredness. *See* ma'heónevetôtse
sacrifices. *See* oestóonôtse
Sand Hill People. *See* Né'ohma'ehétaneo'o
Santee band, 39
Sartre, Jean-Paul, 239
Scalp Cane, *113*
scalping, 17–18
seating ceremony, 95, 114–15, 119, 192, 262n17

second world, 12–14
secular category of stories, 3
The Selected Ones. *See* Moneneheo'o
ševátamehestôtse (compassion), 130–31
Seven Young Men story, 162–65, 263n13
shame/embarrassment, 224, 242
SHCT. *See* sacred historical convergence theory
Shell (chief's child), 128
Short Woman. *See* Mukije
siblinghood. *See* hévese'onematsestôtse
Sioux, 29, 41, 55, 255nn58, 59, 258n47
sisterhood, foundation of Cheyenne governance, 77
Sitting Bull, 248
Six Nations of the Iroquois Confederacy, 228, 268n14
sixth world, 26
Smallest. *See* Motsé'eóeve
Smith, Linda, xxix
Smithsonian Institution, xxxi
Social Dance, *180*
societies, use of term, 143
Somers, William (Southern Cheyenne)
    cannibalism, 95
    Havívsts story, 83–85
    informant, xxxii
    The Rolling Head story, 92–93
    The Star Husband story, 11–12
    Story of the Great Foolish Dog Society, 176–77
    Tsétsėhéstâhese twins story, 82
Só'taeo'o (Buffalo People; Desert People)
    Heveškėsenėhpåhese and —, 42–43
    manåhéno, 38–40
    naming children, 47
    Ohmésêhese and —, 43–45
    Tsétsėhéstâhese and —, 45–47
    See also Nótåxeo'o; Tsėhéstáno; unification
soul. *See* Måhta'sóoma
Southern Cheyenne and Friendship Treaty, 135, 230–31
Southern Cheyenne Indian Reservation (Oklahoma), 243
sovereignty
    hoop and spear game as foundation, 95
    key principle of Indian history, xxxix, 237–38
    ma'xenėheto'stôtse, 238
    móstamámôhevėstanovėhevóhe as foundation, 40
    Tsėhéseamanėō'o embedded in —, 49
Spanish traders, 229
The Spider and the Coyote story, 226–27
The Spider and the Rat story, 224–25
spirit. *See* Måhta'sóoma (spirit/soul/aura)

| 289 |

INDEX

Standing Bear
  band system, 28
  colonial perception of Indians, 242
Standing Elk, Eugene (Southern Cheyenne)
  Michelson's informant, xxxi
Standing Medicine. See Ma'heo'o Ôhnee'ěstse
Standing on the Ground. See Hō-īv'-nī-ěsts
Standing Rock Sioux Indian Reservation, 41
Standing Rocks (Sioux), 41
Stands In Timber, Alva, 209
Stands In Timber, John
  challenge of authority, xxxiv
  Cheyenne Memories, xxxiii
  A Cheyenne Voice, xxxiii
  creation of Crazy Dogs and Swift Fox, 175
  hunter in Seven Young Men story, 263n13
  Lakota peace alliance, 34
  manáhéno, 27
  méhósánestôtse, 134
  moving camp, 256n1
  Ni-oh-ma-até-anin-ya, 257n24
  Nótâxeo'o recruitment, 200
  ována'xaetanohtôtse, 130–31
  significance of manhood, 212
Star Drops. See Hotóhkôhma'aestse
The Star Husband story (William Somers), 11–12
"star knowledge," 12, 52–53, 161, 165, 254n13
star prophets, 52
star societies. See mano'ěhotóhkeo'o
Stink Bat, xxxvii, xli, 74, 248
Story of the Great Foolish Dog Society (William Somers), 176–77
Story of the Holy Head of Eaters (Wolf Chief), 36–37
storytelling, xxxii, xxxvi, xxxviii, 3–5, 104, 264n18. See also oral tradition; *specific stories*
Straight Horns. See Tomôsévêséhe
Strange Owl, Elaine (Northern Cheyenne)
  méohtâhé'heōneve, 216
  Sweet Medicine prophecy, 230
  teachings of manhood, 212
  teachings of womanhood, 211, 267n14
Strange Owl, Rachel
  sacred laws of humanity and nature, 55–56
suicide, 209, 249
Sun Dance ceremony, xxxv, 24, 39, 40, 44, 59, 63, 127, 170, 193. See also Medicine Lodge
Sutaiu. See Só'taeo'o
sweat lodge ceremony, 61, 63, 213
Sweet Medicine. See Motsé'eóeve
Sweet Medicine
  Part I story (Bull Thigh), 167–68
  Part I story (Old She Bear), 166–67
  Part I story (White Buffalo), 173–74
  Part I story (White Eagle), 172–73
  Part I story (Wolf Chief), 171–72
  Part II story (Bull Thigh), 174–75
Sweet Medicine Chief, 106–8, 112, 114, 116–17, 120, 122, 124, 125–26
sweet medicine plant, 107
Sweet Root Standing. See Motsé'eóeve
Swift Fox, 175
Swift Head, 23
tâhpe'ěstáha (to be kind and courteous), 215
Tall Bull (Southern Cheyenne)
  Lime, Part I story, 151–54
  Lime, Part II story, 154–56
  Michelson's informant, xxxi
  Nótâxeo'o responsibilities, 204
Tangle Hair
  Grinnell's informant, 100, 261n12
  Véhone Nótâxeo'o, 189
Taurus constellation, 161
Teeth (chief), 135
telling clouds. See ehōstonevoeoxz
third world ("time of the dog"), 14–18, 26, 32
Those With the Lance, 173
time, perceptions of, 4–5, 13
Tipi Decorators, 196
tobacco, 25, 35, 39, 227
Tomôsévêséhe (Erect or Straight Horns), 45, 189
Tongue River Indian Reservation, xxxiv
trade relations, 111, 227–28, 229, 231
tribe/tribal/tribalism, 7, 28, 58, 114, 245
trickster stories, 221–35
truth. See hetómestôtse
Tséhéseamanēō'o (cultural way of life)
  behavioral teachings, 221, 241
  described, 49
  ma'heónéhóo'xeváheo'o (prophets), 51–54
  Motsé'eóeve, 54–57
  ovanhestôtse (prophecy), 49–50
  principles, 58–68
  sovereignty embedded in —, 49
  Vé'hó'e's violation of customs/traditions, 222
Tséhéstáno (Cheyenne Nation)
  adaptations from other nations, xxxii–xxxiii
  before the Nótâxeo'o, 143–68
  colonization, 221–35
  decolonizing "the rez," 237–50
  degradation of way of life, xxx
  héstanovestôtse (living nation), 7–26
  hévese'onematsestôtse (brotherhood), 77–88
  indigenous, xxxix
  living conditions, xxviii
  manáhéno (bands), 27–47

INDEX

migration, 8
modern, 243–44, 249
nation of families, xxx
national history, 10
Nótåxeo'o origins, 169–79
Nótåxeo'o political organization, 203–17
Nótåxeo'o traditions and customs, 181–201
political organization, 121–38
population, 25, 27, 29, 30, 37, 42
preservation of culture, xxxvii
territorial expansion, 27–28
Tsëhéseamanēō'o (cultural way of life), 49–69
Tsëhéstanove (spiritual way of living), 222–23
Véhooneome, 109–20
Véhoo'o origin, 89–108
war with Hóheehe, 18
war with US military, xxx
warlike culture, xxx, 199
worldview, xxx–xxxi, 8, 237–38, 243
Tsëhéstanove (spiritual way of living), 224–25
Tsétsëhéståhese
    naming children, 47
    original bands, 38
    unification with Só'taeo'o. See unification
    See also Nótåxeo'o; Tsëhéstáno; unification
Two Moons Band, 90
umbilical cord, 62
unification
    sacred historical convergence theory, xxxii
    Só'taeo'o with Tsétsëhéståhese (Great Unification), xxxiii, 40–42, 45–47, 82, 83, 89–91, 97–98, 100, 105–7, 121, 143, 155–56, 162, 169, 181, 188, 257n42
United Cheyenne Nation. See Tsëhéstáno
universe, Earth as child of, 6, 211
Ursa Major (Big Dipper), 161–62, 165
US Bureau of Indian Affairs (BIA), 57, 238
    Court of Indian Offenses, xxx
US Constitution, 268n14
US military, xxx
Vé'hó'e, 221–35, 269n27
Véhone Nótåxeo'o (Chief Soldiers), 73, 188–89
Véhooneome (Chiefs' Lodge), 103, 104
    annual —, 111–14, 116
    ceremony, 106–7
    decennial, 114–17
    Véhoo'o and character, 119–20
Véhoo'o (Council of Forty-Four Chiefs)
    balance of ceremonial power/shared responsibility, 124
    balance of political power/shared authority, 121, 125, 126, 141, 191, 205–6, 267n6
    based on band system, 74
    camp movements, 109, 112, 113, 126, 134–35
    character, 119–20, 127–28
    Cheyenne national origin version, 100–105
    colonization and —, 138
    cooperation with warrior societies, 75
    creation, 83–88, 103
    decisions on war petitions, 111, 127, 204
    described, 73–75
    hévese'onematsestôtse (brotherhood), 77–88
    medicine wheel camp formation, 97, 98
    Motsé'eóeve legacy, 105–8
    origin, 89–108, 112, 169
    peacemakers, 109, 111, 122–23, 125, 127 (see also peacemaking)
    political structure, 114–17, 121–38
    Powell's initiation into, xxxv
    process of nominating chiefs, 110–20
    sacred leadership/responsibilities, 73–75, 109–12, 114, 122, 123, 127–37, 203, 208
    seating ceremony, 94, 114–15, 119, 262n17
    selection of Old Man Chiefs and Sweet Medicine Chief, 114–17
Só'taeo'o origin version, 89–99
Véhooneome, 109–20
violence, xxviii, xxx, 104, 135, 198, 229, 239, 243
    domestic, 249
    sexual, 196
Voestaa'e (Pearl; White Buffalo Calf Woman), 84, 101
Voestaehneva'e (White Buffalo Woman; Vosta), 40, 86–88, 100–103, 114, 128
Vóetséna'e (White Clay or Lime), 39, 40, 146, 147–56, 169–70, 264n1
Vóhkéséhetaneo'o (Kit Fox Men), 171, 184–86, 193
Vóhkoohétaneo'o (Cree or rabbit people)
    Cheyenne allies, 14, 24
    Cheyenne enemies, 37
    tobacco, 35
Vóhpoométaneno (White River Band) 37, 40, 105
vonanomótåhtsestôtse (forgiveness), 132–33
Vóóhéhéve (Dull Knife; Morningstar), 116, 135, 248
Vosta. See Voestaehneva'e
Wanka Tanka (Great Mystery), 59
war ("move the arrows")
    bonnet, 183, 198
    ceremonies, 182
    Cheyenne's warlike culture, xxx, 199

INDEX

combat, 198–201
declaring, 156. *See also* Véhoo'o, decisions on war petitions
parties, 170
time of spiritual enlightenment, 207–9, 267n11
with United States, 206
See also women, warrior women
War Bonnet Dance. *See* Hemámaa'evôhomó'hestôtse
War Dancers. *See* Onéhanotâxeo'o
war shirt, 5, 197
Warren, Pauline, 210
warrior, concept of. *See* Nótâxeo'o
warrior code. *See* Nótâxeo'o
warrior societies. *See* Nótâxeo'o
warrior status. *See* Nótâxeo'o
Washington, George, 228
Washita Massacre, 195
water. *See* Mahpe
Waters, Frank (Chiefs' Bundle keeper), 108
wedding ceremony, 196
Wheel Ceremony, 32, 33, 37
wheel games. *See* hoop and spear games
White Buffalo (Northern Cheyenne)
  buffalo revolutionized cultural way of life, 24
  Double Teeth Bull story, 22–23
  gift of corn from Ma'xema'hēō'e, 14–15, 257n20
  Heveškėsenêhpåhese, 35
  Michelson's informant, xxxi, 254n27
  reappearance of Sweet Medicine, 175
  societies and regalia, 182
  Sutaiu and Heveškėsenêhpåhese, 43
  Sweet Medicine, Part I story, 173–74
  Two Young Men story, 32–33
White Buffalo Calf Woman. *See* Voestaa'e
White Buffalo constellation, 161
The White Buffalo story (Harry Black), 157–61
White Buffalo Tail (head chief of Só'taeo'o), 43, 89
White Buffalo Woman. *See* Voestachneva'e
White Bull/Ice (Northern Cheyenne)
  arrival of Só'taeo'o, 38
  Black Hill homeland, 41
  Michelson's informant, xxxi, 254n27
  Motsé'eóeve's powerful medicine, 107
White Clay. *See* Vóetséna'e
White Clay story (Bull Thigh), 169–70
White Dirt, 264n1
White Eagle (Southern Cheyenne)
  Black Hills homeland, 41
  camp movements, 113
  Michelson's informant, xxxi
  Nótâxeo'o leadership, 191

Nótâxeo'o medicine bundles/covenants, 199
surviving colonization, 230
Sweet Medicine, Part I story, 172–73
Sweet Medicine's teachings and Véhoo'o, 105
White Man and the Buffalo story (Handing Crow), 232
White Man and the Sweet Potatoes story (Handing Crow), 233
White Man and the Wooden Horse story (Medicine Top), 232–33
White Man Calls Feathers story (Ruben Black Horse), 233–34
White Man Loses His Eyes story (Ruben Black Horse), 234–35
White Medicine (Southern Cheyenne)
  Michelson's informant, xxxi
  White River Band. *See* Vóhpoométaneno
White Thunder
  renew Medicine Arrows, 206, 267n9
Whitedirt, Gilbert (Northern Cheyenne)
  hoto'âhéstôtse, 131
whiteman sitting above. *See* Heammaveho
whites
  blamed for imbalances in nature, 53–54
  cultural influences, 267n6
  Indians viewed as "savages," xxxiii
  invasion, 74
  land settlement, 37, 120, 122
  perspective of Cheyenne society, xxx
  Sweet Medicine's prophecy, 54–57
  time of the white man (*see* sixth world)
  treaties with, 130, 135
  trickster stories, 221–29
  war, violence and destructive assaults, 26, 91, 206–7, 229–30
  white tribe, 227–29
  See also colonization
Wihio story (Belle Highwalking), 223–24
Willow Dance, 173
Winter Man. *See* Hooema'hahe
Wise Buffalo (Ôhméseheso leader), 43
Wolf Ceremony, 179
Wolf Chief (Northern Cheyenne)
  Bowstrings and Crazy Dogs origination, 175
  Havívsts story, 83–85
  Hémo'eoxeo'o, 186
  Hotamétaneo'o dances, 182–84
  Hotóvanotâxeo'o, 187–88
  importance of death, 193
  Michelson's informant, xxxi
  Moisiu, 255n59
  Nótâxé'e, 195
  Nótâxeo'o leadership, 191

Óhméscheso Band, 42, 43–44
Otter story, 162
punishment for poaching, 205
The Rolling Head, Part I story, 91–92
The Rolling Head, Part II story, 93–94
societies and regalia, 182
Story of the Holy Head of Eaters, 36–37
Sweet Medicine, Part I story, 171–72
Vóhkėséhetaneo'o, 184–85
Wolf Pup Ceremony, 179
Wolf Soldiers. *See* Ho'nehenótâxeo'o
womanhood. *See* he'eévestôtse
women
    captives, 196
    concerns of, 128
    dances and —, 184, 185–86, 187–89, 195
    importance of, 65, 181, 195–96, 209–11
    violence against, 249
    virtue, 211, 213
    warrior —, 195, 200
    See also he'eévestôtse
women's societies, xl, 127, 141, 196–98
Women's War Bonnet Society. *See* Mámaa'e Nótâxé'évoo'e
Wooden Leg (Northern Cheyenne)
    balance of power between Véhoo'o and Nótâxeo'o, 203, 205–6
    Cheyenne womanhood, 195
    decennial Véhooneome, 115
    Nótâxeo'o citizenhip, 194–95
    Nótâxeo'o leadership, 191
    roles of young and old warriors, 201
    society dances and ceremonies, 265n5
Wōtsitsí ōwō'a (Blood Bachelor). *See* Mai-tŭm'
Wounded Knee, battle at, 239
Wrapped Hair (Northern Cheyenne)
    clay pots, 257n18
    customs for children, 62
    Great Unification, 41
    Hémo'eoxeo'o, 186
    Hotamétaneo'o, 182, 183
    Hotóvanotâxeo'o, 188
    Véhone Nótâxeo'o, 188
Xamaevo'êstaneo'o (Indigenous Peoples), xxvii–xxviii, xxxix. *See also specific peoples*
xanovahe (to be honest and righteous), 215–16
xanoveostôtse (righteousness), 133–34
Yellow Eagle, Mrs. (Southern Cheyenne)
    Hesta'hēso (Little Afterbirth) story, 78, 81–82
Yellow Nose, 170
Yellow Star Woman. *See* Heova'ehetohke'e
Yellowstone River, 41, 42, 89
Yellow Top-to-Head Woman. *See* Heovèsta'e'e
Youngest. *See* Cherry Eater; Má'kó'se

www.ingramcontent.com/pod-product-compliance
Lightning Source LLC
Chambersburg PA
CBHW021948280725
30246CB00023B/208